PENGUIN REFERENCE BOOKS

THE PENGUIN DICTIONARY OF ARCHAEOLOGY

DR WARWICK BRAY is Lecturer in American Archaeology at London University. He received his MA and Ph.D from St John's College, Cambridge, and has taken part in excavations in Britain, Italy and the Colombian Andes, and spent a year in archaeological research in Sardinia. He has written *Everyday Life of the Aztecs* (1968).

DAVID TRUMP is Staff Tutor in Archaeology at the Cambridge University Board of Extra-mural Studies. He studied at Pembroke College, Cambridge, where he received a BA, MA and Ph.D. He worked at Pembroke College on a Research Fellowship, and was Curator of Archaeology at the National Museum of Malta for five years. He has worked on excavations in many countries. His previous books, *Central and Southern Italy before Rome* and *Skorba: The Prehistory of Malta*, were published in 1966.

THE PENGUIN DICTIONARY OF

ARCHAEOLOGY

WARWICK BRAY · DAVID TRUMP

DRAWINGS BY JUDITH NEWCOMER

PENGUIN BOOKS

Penguin Books Ltd, Harmondsworth, Middlesex, England
Penguin Books, 625 Madison Avenue, New York, New York 10022, U.S.A.
Penguin Books Australia Ltd, Ringwood, Victoria, Australia
Penguin Books Canada Ltd, 2801 John Street, Markham, Ontario, Canada L3R 1B4
Penguin Books (N.Z.) Ltd, 182–190 Wairau Road, Auckland 10, New Zealand

—

First published by Allen Lane The Penguin Press 1970
Published in Penguin Books 1972
Reprinted 1973, 1975, 1977, 1978

—

—

Made and printed in Great Britain
by Hazell Watson & Viney Ltd,
Aylesbury, Bucks
Set in Monotype Bembo

CONTENTS

FOREWORD

THE biggest difficulty in compiling a work of this sort lies in deciding what to put in and what to leave out. We have made no attempt to cover classical, medieval or industrial archaeology, partly because these are closer in content to classics, history or local history, but mainly because their inclusion would have meant either an over-sized volume or else cutting down on the number and length of the other entries.

In writing this dictionary we have had in mind particularly the many people who have been made aware of archaeology (through television, the press or evening classes, through chance finds or visits to ancient monuments) but who have found difficulty in taking their interest further. The necessary technical terms are intimidating, and many archaeological books assume that the reader already knows more than he in fact does. This will in part explain such inconsistencies of policy as the inclusion of entries on Roman and Dark Age Britain, which are so often the first point of contact with the subject. We hope this dictionary will help many people forward from chance acquaintance to real familiarity with a most enthralling and rewarding study.

At the same time, we hope our efforts will prove of value to serious students, particularly when they are dealing with aspects beyond their immediate specializations. Here again space is the difficulty. In a subject so full of unsolved problems it has been impossible to do anything like justice to every theory or interpretation. We have had to offer those that seem to us the most reasonable and to dismiss the rest, often without even a mention. Dating, in particular, is frequently a matter for controversy. Every archaeological statement should be prefaced by the phrase 'In the light of present evidence', and we trust that our readers will supply for themselves the 'ifs', 'buts' and 'probablys' which would have so overweighted the text.

We cannot, unfortunately, claim that all the material in the following pages falls within our own special fields, and in consequence we have to thank a great many colleagues for advising us on the selection and content of entries. Their advice has always been appreciated, if not always followed, and any errors remain the responsibility of the authors. Among the many who have helped us we would especially mention Dr J. A. Alexander, Dr F. R. Allchin, Dr G. H. S. Bushnell, Dr T-K. Cheng, Dr. I. W. Cornwall, J. Graham-Campbell, Dr F. R. Hodson, B. Kemp, Miss J. Liversidge, Dr I. H. Longworth, Dr P. A. Mellars, P. Parr, Dr F. H. Stubbings and Dr J. Waechter.

RADIOCARBON DATES

The entry on this technique (p. 194) refers to its recent drastic reassessment. At the time of writing (August 1969) the implications of this for prehistoric chronology have yet to be worked out. Several authorities are now working on a correction graph, which will eventually allow the conversion of radiocarbon dates into true calendar dates. We have recorded to the best of our ability the situation as it stands now, retaining the half-life of 5570 years in general usage. It is already clear that dates AD are slightly more recent than radiocarbon has suggested, and that for the centuries BC radiocarbon has underestimated the true age. It has proved possible to check dates only as far back as 4500 BC, by which time the discrepancy is as much as 800 years. Relative dates are, however, still fully valid, but only where both are based on radiocarbon analyses.

ABBREVIATIONS USED IN THE TEXT

adj = adjective	pl = plural
anc = ancient	pron = pronounced
bibl = biblical	◊ = see (another entry)
lit = literally	◊◊ = see also (another entry)
mod = modern	

SMALL CAPITALS are used in the text to indicate a cross-reference. Numbers in square brackets refer to the text figures.

A

Abbevillian The name given to the earliest (pre-ACHEULIAN) HANDAXE industries of Europe. The type site, on the 45-metre terrace of the river Somme at Abbeville, is a gravel pit from which crudely chipped handaxes [82a] were collected in C19 (◊ CHELLEAN). The Abbevillian material probably dates to the MINDEL GLACIATION.

Abercromby, Hon. J. Best known for his study of the BEAKERS of the British Isles, published in 1912. He was also responsible for founding the chair of prehistoric archaeology at the university of Edinburgh.

Åberg, Nils (1888–1957) A scholar of wide interests who wrote about most aspects of European archaeology, from the COPPER AGE of Iberia to the CELTS and the ANGLO-SAXONS. Like his fellow Swede MONTELIUS, he was concerned with the setting up of a detailed chronological system on the basis of TYPOLOGY and CROSS-DATING. The results were published in 1935–9 in the volumes of his *Bronzezeitliche u. früheisenzeitliche Chronologie.*

abri ◊ ROCK SHELTER

Abri Pataud A recently excavated site in France, in the Vézère valley, near Les Eyzies, Dordogne. It has a very rich Upper PALAEOLITHIC sequence, beginning with AURIGNACIAN deposits containing saucer-shaped living-hollows with central hearths, then Upper PÉRIGORDIAN, and finally a single proto-MAGDALENIAN level which yielded a human skull.

Abu Simbel The site in NUBIA of two temples carved from the rock by the pharaoh RAMSES II C1250 BC [1]. The façade of the larger consists of four colossi, over 60 ft high, representing the king. Chambers within the rock extended for 180 ft. Many schemes were suggested to save the temples from the drowning that would have resulted from the completion of the Aswan High Dam. Eventually the whole monument was sawn into blocks and re-erected on a new site above

Fig. 1. The Abu Simbel temple

the reach of the rising waters where it was revealed to the public in January 1968.

Abydos A city of Upper Egypt famous as a pilgrimage centre for worshippers of the god OSIRIS. Beginning with the pharaohs of the 1st dynasty, many sought to be buried there, or at least commemorated at the site. The most famous of its temples was built by Seti I of the 19th dynasty C1300 BC.

acculturation The adoption by one society of a TRAIT or traits from another society. The term is usually employed in anthropological contexts, and considers the change from the point of view of the recipient society. cf DIFFUSION

Achaeans In Homer, the name by which the Greeks of heroic times spoke of themselves. Culturally we should call them MYCENAEANS. They have been identified with both the Ahhiyawa, mentioned by the HITTITES as one of their western neighbours, and the Akawasha, listed by the Egyptians among the PEOPLES OF THE SEA. In historical times the name was limited to the Greeks of southeast Thessaly and the north Peloponnese.

Achaemenid The name of the Persian royal family, descendants of Achaemenes. CYRUS II (559–530 BC) overthrew the empire of the MEDES to found a Persian empire, conquering Lydia, Babylonia, the whole of the Iranian plateau and Palestine. His son, Cambyses II, added Egypt in 525. The throne then passed to DARIUS, of another branch of the family, who set up an efficient administration of an empire now extending from the Nile to the Indus. But at Marathon in 490 he failed to conquer the Greeks, as his son Xerxes failed at Salamis in 480. Thereafter their successors, notably Artaxerxes, fought to consolidate a waning empire. This was finally overthrown in 331 BC by Alexander of Macedon [2].

Fig. 2. Gold cup from Hamadan

The period is an important one, the high-water mark of Iranian civilization. It was also one of the richest for mutual contacts between the classical civilizations of Europe and the east. It saw the appearance and spread of Zoroastrianism, at its time the most advanced religion outside Judaism. Its most famous monuments are both the work of Darius; his new capital of PERSEPOLIS is outstanding for its architecture and monumental reliefs [141], and his rock inscription at BEHISTUN [28] for the key it gave to the translation of the cuneiform script.

Acheulian In Europe the term Acheulian

is used for the later (ie post-ABBEVILLIAN) stages of the Lower PALAEOLITHIC HANDAXE tradition. The conventional borderline between Abbevillian and Acheulian is marked by a technological innovation in the working of stone implements, the use of a flaking tool of soft material (wood, bone, antler) in place of a hammerstone. In African terminology the entire series of handaxe industries is called Acheulian, and the earlier phases of the African Acheulian equate with the Abbevillian of Europe (◊ KALAMBO FALLS, OLDUVAI, SWANSCOMBE, TORRALBA) [82b]. The type site is in France at Saint-Acheul, Amiens, where the implements were found in deposits of the early part of the RISS glaciation.

Adena A WOODLAND culture of the Ohio valley in the United States. It is characterized by large houses, complex mortuary practices involving the construction of burial mounds, and by a high level of craftwork. It began by c1000BC and is ancestral to the Ohio variant of the HOPEWELL culture.

Adlerberg ◊ ÚNĚTICE

adobe American term for sun-dried MUD-BRICK. Adobes were used in many parts of the New World for the construction of houses, temples and enormous solid platforms in the shape of truncated pyramids.

adze A flat and heavy cutting tool of stone, metal or shell in which the plane of the blade is at right angles to the haft [3].

Fig. 3. Adze.

Where the method of hafting is not obvious, the adze is distinguished from the AXE by its asymmetric cross-section. It may be used for tree felling, but its main purpose, before the introduction of an efficient saw, was for trimming timbers. It would have been particularly useful for jobs such as hollowing out a dug-out canoe.

Agade ⟡ AKKAD

agger Most Roman roads were raised on a slight causeway, especially where they crossed wet ground, in order to provide drainage. This low bank or agger can often be traced even if the surfacing material (rammed chalk, gravel, iron slag or the like) has long since been denuded or covered by vegetation.

Aguada The culture of northwest Argentina in the period AD 700–1000. It is best known for its decorated copper plaques and polychrome pottery (Draconian Ware) with designs of felines, birds, human beings and trophy heads.

Ahar ⟡ BANAS culture

Ahichchatra An ancient city site of imposing size near Bareilly in the Ganges plain of north India. Its ramparts, 3½ miles in circuit, were built c 500 BC, when PAINTED GREY WARE was still current, and rebuilt in the period of NORTHERN BLACK POLISHED WARE, 500–200 BC. Building levels, nine in all, brought the history of the site down to its abandonment about AD 1100.

Ahmose, Ahmosis The prince of Thebes who drove the HYKSOS from Egypt in 1580 BC and became the first pharaoh of the 18th dynasty and the New KINGDOM. His campaigns in Palestine were designed to prevent further threats from that direction. He was succeeded by his son AMENHOTEP I in 1555 BC.

Ahrensburgian A culture of the LATE GLACIAL PERIOD in northern Germany and the Low Countries. The most typical implements are small, tanged arrowheads [4], and the Ahrensburgian can be correlated with the Younger Dryas period (c 8850–8300 BC). At Stellmoor the Ahrensburgian deposit contained abundant reindeer bones, together with wooden arrow shafts, barbed harpoons, and antler adzes.

'Ai A site near Jerusalem which was found

to have had a triple circuit of walls in the Early BRONZE AGE, c 2900–2500 BC. A small temple and another larger building, either a temple or a palace, were excavated within it.

air photography This technique, which often gives spectacular results, is really only an extension of the principle that a high viewpoint gives clearer appreciation of the relationship between details, as through a camera held above the head, raised on scaffolding, or flown aloft on a captive balloon. The vertical photograph is usually taken from a high level, and is particularly effective when two adjacent prints are studied stereoscopically to reveal their relief. The result is an unconventionalized map, convertible to a drawn map by the principles of photogrammetry. More commonly taken for archaeological purposes are low-level obliques. These are easier to interpret, being little different from a high level ground view.

Air photographs can give a new meaning to already known sites (STONEHENGE and MAIDEN CASTLE are famous examples); they can make sense of features visible but incomprehensible from ground level, and they can reveal features too vague to be noticed from ground level at all.

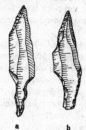

a   b

Fig. 4. (a) Ahrensburgian point; (b) Hamburgian point

Such features are shown in three ways [5]. Low relief is strongly emphasized when photographed in low sunlight – **shadow marks**. Ancient remains, even if com-

pletely levelled, often show by reason of
the different soil of which they consist –
soil marks. The most surprising results,
however, come from the varying effect of
buried features on the vegetation growing
over them – **crop marks**, or more generally, vegetation marks. Sensitive crops such

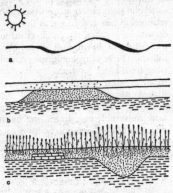

Fig. 5. (a) Shadow mark; (b) soil mark; (c)
crop mark

as the cereals will grow shorter, and turn
yellow earlier, over hard features like wall
foundations or road surfaces. Over buried
ditches or pits cut in a dry subsoil they will
grow taller and ripen later. Features can be
revealed in extraordinary detail by these
means.

The pioneers of this technique were
O.G.S. CRAWFORD and Major Allen in
Britain and Père Poidebard in Syria between the wars, though its first use goes
back to 1906 at Stonehenge. Since 1939
much new evidence has been produced,
notably by J. Bradford in Italy and J. K.
St Joseph in Britain.

'Ajjul, Tell el- A TELL near Gaza on the
Palestinian coast. It was excavated by
PETRIE 1930–34 and 1938. The site was
founded in the Middle Bronze Age, though
important cemeteries of the Chalcolithic
period and of the Intermediate Bronze Age
were discovered nearby. At its peak, the

town had walls, a plastered glacis of
HYKSOS type and a fosse. Five successive
palaces were excavated within the walls.
Several important hoards of gold jewellery
were discovered.

Akhenaten, Ikhnaton, Amenhotep IV
The Heretic Pharaoh of Egypt. He reigned
with his queen Nefertiti for 17 years towards the end of the 18th dynasty of the
New KINGDOM, c1369–52 BC. He attempted to replace the multifarious religions of
Egypt, particularly that of AMEN-Ra, with
a monotheistic worship of the sun, represented as the ATEN or Aton. His object
may have been more political than religious, to free the PHARAOH from the
strongly entrenched priesthood of Amen,
as is suggested by Akhenaten's removal of
his capital from THEBES to a new site at
Tell el-AMARNA. Here a remarkable
flowering of art and literature, in what is
known as the Amarna style, took place,
emphasizing naturalism and light in contrast to the static formalism of Egyptian
art in general.

His religious reforms were carried out
with a fanaticism which diverted all his
attention from foreign affairs. His reign
saw the collapse of the Egyptian Asiatic
empire built by earlier rulers. Even in
religion, his work survived a short while
only, his successor and probable brother,
TUTANKHAMEN, returning to the worship
of Amen. Later pharaohs attempted to
obliterate all record of Akhenaten's heresy
and name.

Akkad, Akkadian Akkad or Agade, an
unidentified site near Babylon, was founded by SARGON c2370 BC as his capital.
His Semitic-speaking dynasty saw three
major developments: the beginning of the
absorption of SUMERIANS by SEMITES; a
trend from the city state to the larger
political unit of the territorial state; and
imperial expansion. Akkad gave its name
(1) to the northern part of Sumer, the
whole country henceforward being known
as Sumer and Akkad, and (2) to the Semitic

dialects of Old Akkadian (3rd millennium) and Assyrian and Babylonian (2nd and 1st millennia). Akkadian, which was written in a CUNEIFORM script borrowed from the Sumerian, was the *lingua franca* of the civilized Near East for much of the 2nd millennium.

Alaca Hüyük (pron Alaja) A TELL near BOGHAZ KÖY in north central Turkey, with Chalcolithic and Copper Age phases dating to the 4th-3rd millennia BC. It is most famous for a cemetery of 13 tombs of c2500 BC. The bodies were accompanied by copper figurines of bulls and stags, intended as 'standard' mounts [6], and by

Fig. 6. Standard from the royal cemetery, Alaca Hüyük

sun discs, ornaments, weapons and vessels. The quantity of gold, as well as copper, implies that this was a royal cemetery. The site was reoccupied under the HITTITES, who erected a monumental gateway with sphinx reliefs.

Alalakh ◊ ATCHANA

alignment Single or multiple rows of standing stones. In the British Isles they are found in the highland zones and are often associated with, or aligned on, CAIRNS, STONE CIRCLES or HENGE monuments. The stone rows do not usually yield datable finds, but they were probably set up in the 2nd millennium BC during the final Neolithic and the Bronze Age. The other region famous for its alignments is Brittany (eg CARNAC) where the date is again Late Neolithic to earlier part of the Bronze Age.

Ali Kosh A site near Deh Luran in the southern Zagros, southwest Iran. Its three phases of occupation, between 7000 and 5700 BC, span and illustrate the transition from food gathering to food production. Wild seeds were replaced by cultivated wheats and barleys, and domesticated sheep and goats played a progressively larger part in the economy beside the hunting of wild game. At the same time the quality of the house-building improved steadily, and in addition to the flintwork, ground stone and pottery made their appearance. ◊ KARIM SHAHIR and JARMO.

Alishar A TELL near Kayseri in central Turkey which yielded four occupation levels from Chalcolithic (4th millennium) to Phrygian (1st millennium BC). However, the period of the HITTITES (later 2nd millennium), was not represented, there being a hiatus in the occupation.

allée couverte ◊ GALLERY GRAVE

Allen, Major G. ◊ AIR PHOTOGRAPHY

Allerød oscillation A temporary increase in warmth during the cold LATE GLACIAL PERIOD, allowing forest trees to establish themselves for a time in the ice-free zones. This period is dated c9850–8850 BC in Europe, and radiocarbon dates for the TWO CREEKS INTERVAL show that similar conditions prevailed in North America at about the same time.

alloy A mixture of metals, often having properties superior to those of the ingredients separately. BRONZE was much the most important alloy in antiquity. ◊ TUMBAGA

Almeria A coastal province in southeast Spain with rich prehistoric material. The name Almerian is particularly applied to a group of Neolithic material c4500–3500 BC. It is best represented by the village of El GARCEL. Agricultural communities lived in open villages of huts with storage pits. Burials were in CISTS under round mounds. Equipment included plain baggy pottery, round or pointed based, and trapezoidal flint arrowheads. The pottery comes within the WESTERN NEOLITHIC tradition, and may possibly derive from North Africa. A later phase was formerly included in the term, but is better called Millaran, after its type site of Los MILLARES.

alphabet A system of written symbols each of which represents a single sound. The first alphabets were devised in the Levant around 1500 BC; one at UGARIT used cuneiform letters, one further south invented new signs for the purpose. It was the PHOENICIANS who developed and diffused the latter, the ancestor of all modern alphabets. Since these scripts were for writing Semitic languages, only the consonants were represented. The Greeks added vowels when they adopted the alphabet in C8 BC, using the letters for Semitic consonants not occurring in Greek, eg the ' of 'aleph became the a of alpha. The total number of letters required for an alphabet varies between 20 and 30 according to the language; a SYLLABARY uses 70–90 symbols, a complex script like HIEROGLYPHIC or CUNEIFORM several hundred, and a script like Chinese, of which every sign is an IDEOGRAM, several thousand.

Altai A mountain range in central Asia rising above 13,000 ft and dominating the eastern STEPPES and their people. ◊ PAZYRYK

Altamira One of the finest painted caves, and also one of the earliest to be discovered (in 1879). The site is south of Santander, in northeast Spain, and is famous for its polychrome animals [40], which include deer, bison and wild boar painted in red, black and a range of earth colours. Most of the art in the cave was produced by MAGDALENIAN peoples. ◊ CAVE ART

Altheim (near Landshut, Bavaria) A small settlement enclosed by three concentric rings of ditches and palisades, which gives its name to the Late Neolithic-Copper Age culture of the upper Danube basin.

Al 'Ubaid ◊ UBAID

Amarna, Tell el- The site of the city Akhetaten, the 'Horizon of the Sun-disc', built by the pharaoh AKHENATEN in Upper Egypt as his capital and the centre of his reformed religion of the ATEN C1365 BC. It consisted of a group of palaces and temples, residential quarters and surrounding fields and gardens, bounded by the cliffs of the desert and delimited by a series of carved and inscribed stelae. It was abandoned soon after Akhenaten's death and its remains have preserved the record of this short but fascinating period of history.

Particularly important was a correspondence in CUNEIFORM between the Egyptian pharaoh and kings of the HITTITES and of the MITANNI and governors of Egyptian possessions in western Asia. This shows clearly the decline of Egyptian influence in that area. The presence of MYCENAEAN pottery revealed links with the Aegean, as hinted at by the frescoes. Contemporary statuary is in the lively, naturalistic Amarna style, which interrupted briefly the formal and traditional art of pharaonic Egypt.

amber Fossilized pine resin. It was much appreciated in antiquity not only for its beauty but for its supposed magical properties – of attracting small particles when warmed and rubbed. The major source in Europe is along the southeast coast of the Baltic. There are lesser sources elsewhere around the Baltic and North Sea, and minor ones even in southern Europe. However, the distribution of finds strongly supports the view that there was an important trade in amber following specific routes up the Elbe and Vistula, across the upper Danube to the Brenner Pass, and so down to the Adriatic and the countries bordering it. Other objects and ideas travelled by the same route, which made it an important factor in European prehistory. The trade began in the Early Bronze Age (⟡ ÚNĚTICE) but expanded greatly as a result of the MYCENAEANS' interest. Even Britain was brought into this trading area, as witnessed by amber SPACER PLATES in BARROWS of the WESSEX CULTURE. Later, amber was very popular with the Iron Age peoples of Italy, particularly the PICENES.

Ambrona ⟡ TORRALBA

Amen, Amon or **Amun** The god of THEBES in Upper Egypt who came into prominence with the rise of Theban dynasties in the Middle and New Kingdoms of Egypt. Many of the pharaohs from the 11th dynasty on include his name in theirs, eg Amenemhet, TUTANKHAMEN. Though represented in human form, he is associated with the ram, and in later times came to be assimilated to the sun god RA.

Amenemhet, Amenemmes The name of four pharaohs of the 12th dynasty, under whom the Middle Kingdom of Egypt reached its peak of development, c1990–1785 BC.

Amenhotep, Amunhotep, Amenophis Alternative names for four pharaohs of the 18th dynasty of Egypt, 1580–1304 BC. Amenhotep III was the most powerful of the line, Amenhotep IV (better known by his adopted name of AKHENATEN) the most interesting.

Amlash ⟡ MARLIK Tepe

Amon ⟡ AMEN

Amorites (anc **Amurru**) A branch of the SEMITES who moved out of the desert margins to overthrow the Sumerian civilization of UR c2000 BC and dominate Mesopotamia in its stead. They were, however, rapidly assimilated culturally. In the west they conquered the Early Bronze Age towns of Syria and Palestine, eventually settling and amalgamating with the CANAANITES of the Middle and Late Bronze Age.

amphora A storage jar, usually fairly large

in size, plump in shape and with a narrow mouth. It always has two handles.

Amratian An Egyptian predynastic culture named from the site of El Amrah dating c3800–3600 BC. Settlements are poorly known, but large cemeteries, such as that of NAQADA, imply that they were permanent and sizable, based on cultivation and animal husbandry. Flint was quarried for a variety of delicately worked daggers, points and tools. Copper was coming into use for simple objects like pins and harpoons as well as beads. Wide trading contacts are also implied by finds of materials from Ethiopia, the Red Sea and Syria. Several pottery wares were current, in a wide range of shapes; Black-topped Red Ware continued from the BADARIAN period, with White Cross-lined now added. This is a red ware painted in white with various forms of hatching and often with figured scenes. The dead were buried crouched, with rich grave goods of pottery, personal ornaments, ivory combs and figurines, probably intended to act as servants in the after life.

Amri A village site near the Indus river excavated by Majumdar 1929 and Casal 1959–62, probably dating to the early 3rd millennium (no radiocarbon dates are available). Its name has been given to a style of painted pottery found in its Chalcolithic levels and on tells over much of Sind and up into the hills of BALUCHISTAN. Tall globular beakers of fine buff ware are painted with strictly geometric designs such as chequered panels and looped fringes in black between red horizontal bands. At Amri chert and, more rarely, copper were used for tools. Architecture was in mudbrick and FRACTIONAL BURIAL was the practice for the dead. Terracotta figurines were absent. At Amri this culture was gradually succeeded by that of the INDUS CIVILIZATION. The uppermost levels contained JHUKAR and Jhangar material, the last probably of historic date.

Amudian An industry characterized by BLADES and BURINS, and apparently contemporary with the later stages of the ACHEULIAN in the Middle East. Amudian material has been recognized at the cave of et-Tabūn (MOUNT CARMEL), and at sites like JABRUD, Adlun and the Abri Zumoffen in the Levant. A rather similar industry has been reported from the HAUA FTEAH, in Cyrenaica. It has been suggested that the Amudian may have been ancestral to subsequent Upper PALAEOLITHIC industries of the Middle East, hence the name 'pre-Aurignacian' which has sometimes been given to industries of Amudian type.

Amun ◊ AMEN

Amuq A swampy plain at the foot of the Amanus mountains and beside the Orontes river near the northeast corner of the Mediterranean. Its most important sites were Tayanat (Neolithic-Chalcolithic), ATCHANA (Copper Age to Hittite) and Antioch (Hellenistic and Roman).

Anasazi Around the beginning of the Christian era, some DESERT CULTURE groups along the Arizona-Utah border took their first steps towards settled life. Pottery was unknown but basketry was well developed – hence the name 'Basket Maker' given to these early stages. By the Basket Maker III (or Modified Basket Maker) period (cAD 400–700) sedentary life had been achieved, intensive agriculture was practised and pottery was in use.

With the addition of certain new traits, the Basket Maker culture developed into that of the Anasazi people. In the early (Pueblo I and II) stages of the Anasazi culture the first black-on-white pottery was made, and the first PUEBLOS and KIVAS constructed. The Anasazi climax (Pueblo III) came between c1100 and 1300 when towns like Pueblo Bonito and those of Mesa Verde reached their fullest extent and fine polychrome pottery was manufactured. At this time the MOGOLLON people to the south adopted the Anasazi way of life, and their HOHOKAM neigh-

bours were strongly influenced from the same source.

From 1300 until the arrival of the Spaniards in c16 and the end of native resistance in 1692, the Anasazi culture entered a period of regression (Pueblo IV). Although some individual towns, such as Pecos, were larger than ever before, the area of Anasazi occupation dwindled and the homeland in northern Arizona was abandoned. With the encroachment of nomadic Apache and Navajo tribes, and with the arrival of Europeans from the south and east, Anasazi territory shrank still further, although some pueblos continue in occupation until the present day.

Anau A TELL in the Merv oasis of Russian Turkestan excavated by Pumpelly and Schmidt in 1904. Its development in the 4th millennium BC appears to parallel that of sites like SIALK and HISSAR in Iran. That it played some part in diffusing the techniques of food production, pottery, etc, to India and China seems likely but is not yet clearly documented.

anchor ornament An anchor-shaped object of terracotta with a perforation through the shank [7]. Such objects were

Fig. 7. Anchor ornament

widespread in the Early Bronze Age of Greece, and appear rather later in Sicily and Malta. The grooving sometimes visible on their shoulders, as if from the wear of a thread, suggests they may have formed part of a LOOM.

Andersson, J. G. A Swedish geologist working in China who in 1921 first demonstrated the presence of prehistoric material in that country. He is best remembered for his work on the YANG SHAO Neolithic culture on the middle Yellow river, and the PAN SHAN cemeteries further west in Kansu. He also carried out the first excavations at CHOUKOUTIEN, though the significance of his finds only became apparent later.

Anghelu Ruju (Alghero, Sardinia) A Copper Age necropolis of 36 rock-cut tombs, some of them decorated with carved bulls' heads. The tombs contained material of the local OZIERI CULTURE and BEAKER pottery of west Mediterranean type.

Angkor The capital of the KHMER empire, in Cambodia, founded in C9 AD. Most of the surviving ruins date from C12. They were lost in jungle and rediscovered in the last century. The city of Angkor Thom was $1\frac{3}{4}$ miles square and moated, with the fantastically sculptured temple of the Bayon at its centre. Other temples such as Ta Prohm and Angkor Vat cluster in the neighbourhood.

Angles A Germanic people first heard of on the Baltic coasts of Jutland. On the evidence of their pottery found at a number of late Roman settlements in England, they were certainly present as FOEDERATI in the late C4 AD. In C5 they took part in the Anglo-Saxon migrations across the North Sea to settle the eastern parts of England after the breakdown of Roman rule. The archaeological evidence is treated under ANGLO-SAXONS since by this period the distinction between the two peoples had all but disappeared. Their name survives in East Anglia and England.

Anglo-Saxons A compound name used from the early C5 AD after movements of the ANGLES and SAXONS from their homelands had led to a merging of their separate identities. This took place in the Elbe-Weser region of the North Sea coast, whence they crossed to settle in England after the breakdown of Roman rule. Other Germanic peoples who took part in the migrations, such as the JUTES and the FRISIANS, have become included under this name. The language, culture and settlement pattern of medieval and later England can be traced directly to them.

The movement probably began in C4 with the arrival of barbarian FOEDERATI to serve with the Roman army, a situation mirrored in the legendary invitation of Vortigern to Hengist and Horsa to settle in Thanet in exchange for their military support. The main immigration began in the middle of C5. Bede, writing early in C8, gives the only reliable historical record for this period, though incidental information can be found in the Old English literature, particularly the poem of Beowulf.

By late in C6 this movement was coming to an end and the English kingdoms were taking shape. Though they were traditionally seven in number (the Heptarchy) there were more than this to begin with, the less powerful gradually being absorbed by NORTHUMBRIA, MERCIA and WESSEX [8]. East Anglia ($\diamond$ SUTTON HOO) and Kent retained their independence longest. The increasing number of detailed contemporary documents shows the varying fortunes of these kingdoms. Wessex became the nucleus of an increasingly unified England between 886 and 927. In 1016, however, the kingdom fell to the Danes under Canute, and then to William of Normandy in 1066, the date generally accepted as marking the end of the Anglo-Saxon period.

Archaeologically the period can be divided into three, not counting the poorly documented preliminary phase overlapping the Roman occupation. The Early or Pagan Saxon period ends with the general acceptance of Christianity in the first half of C7, following the arrival of St Augustine at Canterbury in 597 and of St Aidan at Lindisfarne in 635. Its remains are limited largely to burial deposits, these

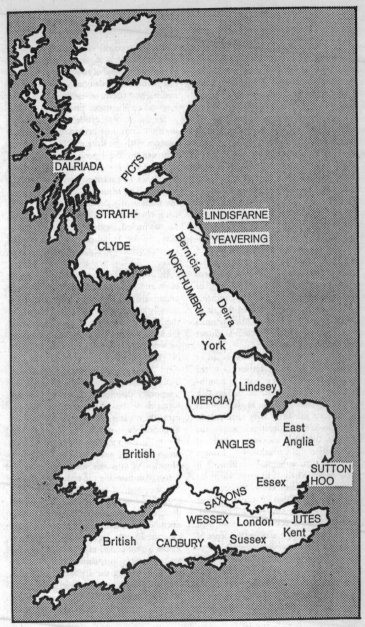

Fig. 8. The Anglo-Saxon kingdoms

often being very rich. Burial was by cremation in urns, or by inhumation in cemeteries of trench graves or occasionally under barrows. Grave goods often include knives, a sword or spear, a shield boss, and occasional brooches and buckles with the men, brooches, beads, girdle-hangers and pottery with the women. Recently villages have come to light at West Stow, Suffolk, and Mucking, Essex.

The Middle Saxon period is less well known since the practice of burying grave goods with the dead went out with the advent of Christianity. Few buildings have yet been identified, the most outstanding being the royal palaces at YEAVERING in Northumberland.

The invasions of the Vikings or Danes in c9 introduce the Late Saxon period. Grave goods are again not found but more is known of the doubtless commoner and more substantial dwellings. Large timber-built town houses have been studied at Thetford, Winchester and Southampton, and some stone-built churches survive (Bradford-on-Avon, Earl's Barton, Escomb, etc). The pottery of the period is also beginning to be understood, with the recognition of distinct fabrics made by industries based on St Neots, Thetford and Stamford.

ankh The Egyptian HIEROGLYPH for 'life', consisting of a loop surmounting a T [9]. It represents a sandal strap, the

Fig. 9. The hieroglyph, ankh

word for which had the same phonetic value. It is commonly shown carried by gods and pharaohs, and figures frequently in personal names, eg Tutankhamen.

Anlo A site on the heathland of Drenthe, Holland, with a long sequence of occupation. A settlement of the FUNNEL BEAKER culture was followed by a wooden cattle enclosure of the Late Neolithic (PROTRUDING FOOT BEAKER) people, then by a cemetery of five flat graves containing protruding foot beakers and bell beakers with CORD ORNAMENT. The next phase was a settlement with late varieties of BEAKER pottery, followed by a Middle Bronze Age plough soil and a Late Bronze Age URNFIELD.

ansa lunata A handle on a cup or bowl bearing on its top two diverging projections. The variation in the form it takes is enormous. The name (= lunate handle) comes from the Italian, where it is applied to handles occurring in TERRAMARA pottery and the APENNINE CULTURE, of the Middle to Late Bronze Age. It is found at the same period over a much wider area of central Europe. [11]

Anse au Meadow, L' The site lies on the northern tip of Newfoundland and is the only Viking settlement known in the New World. Excavation revealed traces of turf-walled houses of a type never built by Eskimos or Indians but similar to those from Viking sites in Iceland and Greenland. Norse origin is confirmed by the finding of a spindle whorl, iron nails and a smithy with pieces of bog-iron and several pounds of slag. Radiocarbon dates range from AD 700–1080 with a concentration in the late c10 which is the period when, according to the sagas, Norsemen led by Leif Eriksson sailed west from Greenland and explored the coast of America, which they named Vinland.

Antelian industry ◊ MOUNT CARMEL

Antequera (Malaga, southern Spain) A town famous for its three Copper Age chambered tombs, the Cuevas de Menga, de Viera and Romeral. All are built tombs, partly recessed into the rock. The first is of ORTHOSTATS throughout, its chamber 48 ft long and 10 ft high. This is roofed by only five capstones, and has the additional support of three central pillars. Schematized human figures are carved on its walls. The second tomb has a long orthostat-lined passage with PORT HOLE SLABS and a small square chamber. The third is a magnificent dry-stone THOLOS, with a passage over 100 ft long and a chamber 16 ft high. Nearby is a cemetery of rock-cut tombs of the Bronze Age imitating the tholos form.

antler sleeve A section of deer antler carved into a mortice at one end to hold a stone AXE head [10]. It was either set into

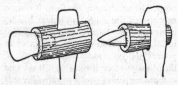

Fig. 10. Shaft-hole and tenon forms of antler sleeve

a socket in a wooden haft, or perforated to take the haft. The antler, being more resilient than wood, distributed the shock of the axe blow, and so lessened the risk of splitting the haft.

Antonine Wall A defensive fortification on the frontier of the Roman empire built by Lollius Urbicus for Antoninus Pius c145 AD. It ran for 37 miles between the Firths of Forth (Bridgeness) and Clyde (Old Kilpatrick) with 19 forts on its line and others forward and in the rear, particularly to protect its flanks. The wall itself was mainly turf-built, 14 ft wide, approximately 10 ft high, and with a substantial ditch along its north side. It was abandoned temporarily in a revolt c155 AD and permanently before the end of C2.

Anu The SUMERIAN sky god and chief divinity, whose seat was at URUK. He was, however, considered remote from earthly matters, which were more immediately supervised by EA or later MARDUK.

Anubis The jackal-headed god of ancient Egypt, primarily responsible for guarding the tombs and the underworld.

Anyang At the village of Hsiao T'un near this city in northern Honan, China, lay the last capital of the SHANG dynasty. It was founded according to tradition by Pan Keng in C14 BC, was overthrown by the Chou in 1027 BC, and excavated 1927–36 and again in recent years. It lay in the loop of a river, 320 yds by 157, apparently without further defences. The buildings were represented by rammed earth floors, the largest up to 100 ft long. Many foundation sacrifices of men, animals and chariots were found under them. Large numbers of deep storage pits yielded archaeological material, in particular inscribed ORACLE BONES.

The most important finds came from the cemeteries, which included many royal tombs. A 45 ft square pit some 13 ft deep was entered by two or four sloping ramps. At its centre a 23 ft square pit contained the body of the king in a large wooden coffin. The shelf round this pit and the ramps held more grave goods and the skeletons of the king's retinue, scores of men and horses. A small pit beneath the coffin usually held the bones of a dog. Our knowledge of the Shang dynasty derives in large measure from the settlement and cemetery of the 'Great City Shang'.

Apennine culture A Bronze Age culture which developed c1600 BC in the Italian peninsula, with some influence from the Balkans. Several of the sites imply transhumance and an emphasis on stock breeding, lying high in the mountains which give the culture its name. Others, like ARIANO, LIPARI and TARANTO, show that trade was important also, though bronze, of TERRAMARA workmanship, was rare until late in the period. Inhumation cemeteries are known. The characteristic pottery is handmade, dark burnished, decorated with band designs filled with white inlay. The numerous carinated bowls have a single handle, often fantastically elaborated [11]. The importance of this culture to the development of the PIAN-

Fig. 11. Apennine carinated bowl with ansa lunata

ELLO urnfields of c1000 BC, and of the Iron Age cultures of the 1st millennium, is a matter of debate.

Apis The sacred bull of ancient Egypt. Its chief sanctuary was at SAKKARA.

Aramaeans A branch of the SEMITES who moved out of the Syrian desert to conquer the CANAANITES of Syria and set up their own city states in C13–C12 BC. Culturally they were absorbed by their victims; politically they fell under the domination of ASSYRIA in the succeeding centuries. But their language, Aramaic, written in the script of the PHOENICIANS, became the international language of the Near East in place of the long-lived AKKADIAN. It was the vernacular speech of the Holy Land at the time of Christ.

Arawak At the time of Columbus, Arawak peoples inhabited the Greater Antilles and parts of mainland South America. Since languages of the Arawakan family are not found in North or Mesoamerica it is likely that these people reached the islands from the south. In support of this view, pottery of SALADOID type is found in a great arc from western Venezuela to the West Indies, and in the northern islands there seems to be a ceramic continuity from Saladoid ware to insular Arawak. In the Lesser Antilles the Arawaks were replaced by CARIB tribes before the

Conquest. Spanish sources describe the Arawaks as settled farmers with an elaborate religion based on a ZEMI cult.

archaeology The study of man's past by means of the material relics he has left behind him. It is therefore a technique, the story so obtained being better described as PREHISTORY or, when supplementing documentary evidence, PROTOHISTORY. The methods appropriate to different periods vary, leading to specialized branches of the subject, eg classical, medieval, industrial, etc, archaeology.

archaeomagnetism When a magnetic oxide of iron is heated above a certain temperature its magnetism is obliterated. It returns on cooling, its orientation and strength determined by the magnetic field (the earth's) in which it lies. Such oxides occur naturally in nearly all clays. When baked, they in effect fossilize the earth's magnetic field at the moment of their last cooling, this being their archaeo-, or remanent, magnetism. If the sample has not been moved since, as in a kiln or hearth, the three factors of the field – declination (the angle between true north and magnetic north), dip (the angle between the direction of the field and the horizontal) and intensity – can be determined. These all vary with time, and in well studied areas such as England the resulting curves have been calculated for approximately the last 2000 years. Within this span, any sample may now be dated within about 50 years.

archaic Of early form.

Archaic period A term used to describe an early stage in the development of civilization. Specifically, in Egypt it covers the first two dynasties, c3200–2800 BC, in which the country was unified and came to its first flowering of culture. In Greece it describes the rise of civilization from c750 BC to the Persian invasion in 480 BC. As used by Americanists, the term refers to a stage of development rather than a chronological period. It is characterized by a hunting and gathering way of life in a post-PLEISTOCENE environment similar to that of the present. Under special circumstances there may be settled life, pottery, and even agriculture as long as this is subsidiary to the collection of wild foods. The term was coined for certain cultures of the woodlands of eastern North America dating from c8000–1000 BC but usage has been extended (sometimes uncritically) to all sorts of unrelated cultures which show a similar level of development but may be of widely varying dates.

archaistic Deliberately imitating an earlier style.

ard ⟡ PLOUGH

Arene Candide A cave at Finale Ligure on the Italian Riviera. Its excavation by Bernabò Brea revealed a stratigraphy from the Upper Palaeolithic (an Italian facies of the GRAVETTIAN), through epi-Palaeolithic, Early Neolithic (IMPRESSED WARE, radiocarbon dated c4400–4200 BC), Middle (SQUARE-MOUTHED POTS of the Chiozza culture) and Late Neolithic (LAGOZZA), poor levels of the Bronze and Iron Ages, to Roman. There were rich burials in the first, second and fourth of these levels.

Argar, El An Early Bronze Age settlement on a hilltop near Almeria, the type site of a culture covering the southeast

Fig. 12. Argar pot forms

corner of Spain. Little could be recovered of its rectangular houses, and less of its walls, but some 950 interments were discovered within it. Two phases can be distinguished. The first is characterized by CIST burial, the rivetted DAGGER, HALBERD, WRISTGUARD, prismatic button with V-PERFORATION, etc. In the second, the rite was JAR-BURIAL and swords and late daggers, flat axes and FAIENCE appear. The pottery is undecorated, with a simple bowl, often sharply carinated, and high-pedestalled fruitstands, especially in the later phase, as common forms [12]. The Argaric culture was in trading contact with the east and may, indeed, owe its origin to immigration from western Greece. Its dates run c1800–1000·BC.

Argissa A long-lived site in Thessaly. Its excavation by Milojčić 1956–8 added much new information on the early phases of the Greek Neolithic. Huts consisted of shallow pits walled and roofed with branches or the like. There was ample evidence of all the early staple crops and domestic animals, and OBSIDIAN was already being traded, at a date which must lie before 6000 BC. Thereafter the site remained in occupation throughout the Neolithic, with a valuable stratigraphy, and well into the Bronze Age.

Arikamedu A site near Pondicherry in southern India where Wheeler in 1945 found BLACK-AND-RED Iron Age wares associated with ARRETINE pottery of the AD CI imported from the Mediterranean. More recently Casal has shown that the Black-and-red Ware began well before the period of Roman contacts.

Ariuşd A Late Neolithic site of the CUCUTENI culture in Romania.

Arpachiyah A TELL of the HALAF and UBAID periods near Mosul on the Tigris, excavated by Mallowan in 1933. The Halaf settlements yielded a long pottery sequence and a series of ten circular buildings of PISÉ on stone foundations, 12 to 31 ft in diameter, some having rectangular antechambers. These structures have been likened to the Mycenaean THOLOS tombs but their function is unknown.

Arras An Iron Age cemetery northwest of Hull (Yorkshire) with at least 90 burials. There are several related sites (eg Danes'

Graves), all of them in east Yorkshire, and all with similar grave goods. These define the Arras culture, distinguished by flat graves or small BARROWS, occasionally containing CHARIOT burials, and sometimes with square enclosure ditches. The chariot gear includes a distinctive three-link horse bit. Associated material dates the Arras culture to between C5 and C1 BC, and the Arras people seem to have been intruders from the continent. Their artifacts suggest links with east France and the Rhineland, and they can perhaps be identified with the tribe of the Parisii which gave its name to the city of Paris.

Arretine Ware A ware being produced at Arretium (mod Arezzo) in Tuscany to supply the Roman markets in C1 BC–AD C1. It is clearly based on metal prototypes in shape and decoration, the relief designs of silver work being imitated on the pottery by means of moulds. It was widely traded outside the empire as well as within it, examples having come from BELGIC tombs in pre-Roman Britain and from the port of ARIKAMEDU in southern India.

arris The ridge formed by the junction of two smooth surfaces, especially on the MIDRIB of a dagger or sword.

arrowhead A small object of stone, bone or metal tipping an arrow to give it greater powers of penetration. The earliest known are SOLUTREAN points of the

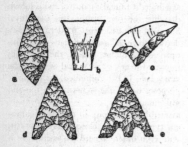

Fig. 13. Common varieties of arrowhead: (a) leaf-shaped; (b) tranchet; (c) tranchet derivative; (d) hollow-based; (e) barbed and tanged

Upper Palaeolithic. They are often the only evidence of archery, since the arrow shaft and BOW rarely survive. A few of the more common forms are illustrated. [13]

arrow straightener A stone with a straight groove on one face. The name is a poor one since the purpose is thought to have been smoothing, rather than straightening, arrow shafts. The concave SCRAPER had a similar function.

arsenic A metal found together with COPPER in some ore deposits, particularly in central Germany. It appears that arsenical copper, containing up to 3 per cent arsenic, was valued and deliberately produced to improve casting properties and hardness. It ceased to be important with the development of tin BRONZE.

Arthur The legendary Christian king who rallied the British against the Anglo-Saxon invaders. Behind the legend recounted by Malory, Geoffrey of Monmouth and Nennius there may be a sub-Roman warleader (Artorius is a Roman name) who filled such a role. Though his name does not survive in the contemporary records, he may have led the British at the battle or siege of Mount Badon (Mons Badonicus, perhaps Badbury Rings in Dorset) which checked the Saxon advance for some fifty years from about AD 490. Merlin, Lancelot, Guinevere and the rest are medieval accretions so far with even less corroborative support. How far Camelot itself can be regarded as historical should appear from the present investigation of its supposed site at South CADBURY.

artifact or **artefact** An object made by man. The line is sometimes hard to draw between a natural object and one used by man (with an EOLITH this may be particularly difficult), but there is no doubt when it can be shown that he shaped it in any way, even if only accidentally in the course of use.

Aryans The people of the RIGVEDA, who invaded Iran and India from the northwest in the later 2nd millennium BC. By one theory they were responsible for the downfall of the INDUS CIVILIZATION. Their language was an early form of SANSKRIT, the most easterly of the INDO-EUROPEAN tongues, but the use of their name to describe other Indo-European speakers is to be strongly deprecated.

aryballus A diagnostic INCA pottery form [90]. It is a large jar with a conical base, tall narrow neck and flaring rim, and was intended for carrying liquids. It was designed to be carried on the back by means of a rope which passed through two strap handles low down on the body and over a nubbin at the base of the neck. Miniature copies were also made. The name is taken from the classical Greek pottery form, a small jar for oil or perfume with globular or pyriform body, narrow neck and single handle.

Ascalon ◊ ASKELON

Ashoka or **Asoka** ◊ MAURYAN EMPIRE

Ashur ◊ ASSUR

Ashurbanipal King of ASSYRIA 668–627 BC. His many brilliant military campaigns served only to hold what had been already won by previous kings, and not even all that. Egypt regained its independence and ELAM was only retained by complete devastation. Of more importance to posterity was the library of over 25,000 clay tablets he collected in his palace, and in that of his grandfather Sennacherib, in NINEVEH. Their value for recovering the achievements of ancient Mesopotamia in art, science and religion is incalculable.

Ashurnasirpal II King of ASSYRIA 883–859 BC, the real architect of the last period of Assyrian power. His military expeditions took him as far as the Mediterranean, setting the standards of military achievement and brutality which made the Assyrians so widely feared throughout the Near and Middle East. He refounded NIMRUD as a military capital beside ASSUR and NINEVEH. His palace there was excavated by LAYARD 1845–51 and Mallowan a century later.

Askelon The only city of the PHILISTINES yet to be excavated, by Garstang 1920–21, on the coast of Palestine near Gaza. Even here, only a small stratigraphic cut penetrated the Roman levels to reveal Philistine deposits. A destruction level, the work of the PEOPLES OF THE SEA c1200 BC, separated these from the underlying Late Bronze Age of the CANAANITES.

askos An asymmetric vessel, often duck-shaped, with mouth off-centre and single handle. The form was popular in the Aegean area from the Early HELLADIC into the classical period, and appears from time to time elsewhere. [71]

Asmar, Tell ◊ ESHNUNNA

Asprochaliko A PALAEOLITHIC cave near Ioánnina, in Greek Epirus. Occupation began with two MOUSTERIAN phases, the earlier one with carefully retouched tools and use of the LEVALLOIS TECHNIQUE, the later phase with a predominance of small tools. This was followed by a very different industry of Upper Palaeolithic type, with backed BLADES, and a carbon date of 24,000 ± 1000 BC. In the final stage (11,700 ± 260 BC) geometric MICROLITHS and MICROBURINS appeared alongside the backed blades. Occupation ceased around 9000 BC.

ass There are two wild asses. In Asia the onager, *Equus hemionus*, was domesticated as a draught animal c3000 BC, and is shown drawing the war wagons on the Royal Standard of UR. The modern donkey derives from *E. asinus*, a native of Ethiopia and the Sudan, whence the Egyptians imported it as a pack animal at about the same date. It has continued for humbler purposes beside the HORSE from the 2nd millennium on.

assemblage A group of objects of different types found in closed ASSOCIATION with each other. Where the assemblage is frequently repeated, and covers a reasonably full range of human activity, it is described as a CULTURE; where it is repeated but limited in content, eg flint tools only, an INDUSTRY.

association When two or more objects are found together and it can be proved that they were deposited together, they are said to be in genuine or closed association, or to form such an association. An open association is one in which this can only be assumed, not proved. No significance, of course, attaches to accidental juxtaposition. The importance of any find is greatly increased by association with other finds, which may help with its interpretation – dating, cultural connexions, original function, etc. Good examples of closed associations are provided by a single interment grave, the material within a destruction level, or a HOARD.

Assur or **Ashur** A solar deity, the chief god of the city of Assur and ASSYRIA. With the latter's conquests, he was given supremacy over the other gods of Mesopotamia. His city, the religious capital of the Assyrian empire, lay 60 miles south of Mosul. It is first recorded as a frontier post of the empire of AKKAD, becoming in turn an independent city state and the capital of a powerful empire, whose collapse in 612 BC it failed to survive. It was briefly revived under the Parthians. It was excavated by Andrae and the Germans 1903–14. Not only were areas of the palaces, temples, walls and town cleared, but a SONDAGE pit was cut beneath the Temple of Ishtar to reveal the 3rd and early 2nd millennium levels, the first use of this technique in Mesopotamian excavation.

Assurbanipal, Assurnasirpal ◊ ASHURBANIPAL, ASHURNASIRPAL

Assyria Originally the city-state of ASSUR, it expanded northwards during the early 2nd millennium BC to include the area around modern Mosul. NINEVEH and NIMRUD later became co-capitals, and KHORSABAD briefly also. From this home territory it periodically sent out its armies to Syria, Turkey, Iran, and particularly lower Mesopotamia. Despite its almost

constant enmity with BABYLON, culturally it followed the latter very closely. Ashurbanipal's royal library shows clearly the respect felt for the earlier civilization. The main achievements, outside the field of warfare, were in architecture and sculpture, particularly the protective genii in the form of winged bulls, etc [14], which

Fig. 14. Guardian of the palace, Nimrud

guarded all palace entrances, and the magnificent reliefs of battles, hunts and military processions which adorned the walls. Many of the smaller carvings in ivory from Nimrud are Syrian rather than true Assyrian work.

But it is as a military power, armed with weapons of iron, that Assyria is best remembered. Its period of greatness, 883–612 BC, was an almost uninterrupted succession of wars waged to win, and – even less easy – to hold, an empire which at its widest extended from the Nile to near the Caspian, and from Cilicia to the Persian Gulf. Its greatest kings were all warriors, ASHURNASIRPAL II, SHALMANESER III, TIGLATHPILESER III, SARGON II, SENNACHERIB and ASHURBANIPAL, who made the name of Assyria feared throughout the Ancient East partly by their military skill, partly by their sheer brutality.

Astarte or **Asherah**, Hebrew **Ashtoreth** [15] The mother and fertility goddess of the PHOENICIANS and CANAANITES before them. She is variously equated with

Fig. 15. Terracotta votive plaque of Astarte

Egyptian ISIS, Babylonian ISHTAR, Carthaginian TANIT, and Greek Aphrodite, Cybele and Hera.

Aswan The town at the First Cataract of the Nile, where the High Dam has been erected. International cooperation has rescued the more important of the antiquities which would have been flooded, like the temples of ABU SIMBEL, and has explored those which could not be saved, like the Egyptian frontier fortress of Buhen and many others through ancient NUBIA.

Atchana, Tell (anc **Alalakh**) A mound on the AMUQ plain beside the river Orontes near the Turkish-Syrian border. It was excavated by WOOLLEY before and after the Second World War. Seventeen building phases spanned from c3400 to 1200 BC, covering a long prehistoric Copper Age, a period as an independent state, and finally as a provincial capital of the HITTITES. Its main interest comes from the mixture of cultural influences, from Mesopotamia to the east and the Aegean to the west. Its wealth derived from through trade and from the timber of the Amanus mountains which overlook it.

Aten The sun's disc, introduced as the sole god by the Heretic Pharaoh, AKHENATEN, of the 18th dynasty of Egypt, 1350 BC. It

was represented as a circle with rays ending in tiny hands. [16]

Fig. 16. The aten sun-disc

Aterian An evolved Middle PALAEOLITHIC industry centred on the Atlas mountains of North Africa, but with extensions into Libya and deep into the Sahara. Some tools (such as side scrapers and LEVALLOIS flakes) resemble MOUSTERIAN types, but the tanged points [17] and bifacially worked leaf-shaped points are distinctively Aterian.

Fig. 17. Aterian point

Athens Material going back to the Late Neolithic has come from this long-lived site, but because of the continuous occupation and its resulting disturbance of the earlier levels, a coherent story can begin only with the occupation of the MYCENAEANS in the Late Bronze Age. The city at that time was of minor importance, though its citadel on the Acropolis was walled. The Theseus legend, however, suggests that it was a rival to KNOSSOS in C15, and it was strong enough to resist the DORIANS in C12, unlike even MYCENAE. The Kerameikos cemetery (so called as it lay in the potters' quarter) documents the city's Iron Age (C11–C8), after which archaeology and history combine to tell of its brilliance through the classical period. **Atlantic Bronze Age** otherwise, and preferably, known as the **carp's tongue sword complex**. A bronze industry which developed on the west coast of France from Brittany to the Gironde c1000–500 BC. It had close connexions with Britain and the western half of Iberia. Typical products include the CARP'S TONGUE SWORD itself [186e], end-winged AXE, bugle-shaped object (of unknown use) and hog-backed RAZOR. In Iberia the double-looped PALSTAVE was added. The unifying factor was the very active trade along the Atlantic seaways.

Atlantic period ◊ POSTGLACIAL PERIOD and ZONES, VEGETATIONAL

Atlantis An earthly paradise described by Plato in his *Timaeus*, quoting Solon, and through him the Egyptian priests, as his authorities. He describes a circular island that developed a high level of civilization, but when this degenerated, it sank beneath the sea as punishment. The dates he gives for this are impossibly early, and the dimensions of the island are too large for the Mediterranean to have accommodated. Many improbable interpretations have been offered, the likeliest being that Plato's Atlantis is a philosophical abstraction, like other Utopias, never intended to be considered as fact. However, the tale may combine folk memories of the civilization of the MINOANS and of the cataclysm which destroyed Santorin (anc Thera) c1470 BC.

atlatl New World term for SPEAR-THROWER.

Atlitian ◊ MOUNT CARMEL

Aubrey, John (1626–97) An antiquarian who did much to foster the tradition of studying and describing the field antiquities of the English countryside. For example it was he who first recognized the circle of pits we now know as the Aubrey holes within the bank at STONEHENGE. Less fortunate was his suggestion that the building of that site should be attributed to the DRUIDS, although one must grant this a better guess than the Phoenicians,

Romans, Saxons or Danes variously suggested by others.

auger A tool used for extracting a small sample of deposit from a depth without actual excavation. In simple versions soil is brought up in the thread of a drill bit. In more elaborate ones a chamber can be opened to collect a core after the drill has bored to an appropriate depth. It is much used for collecting peat samples for POLLEN ANALYSIS. cf PROBE

Aunjetitz German form of the name ÚNĚTICE.

Aurignacian A flint industry of Upper PALAEOLITHIC type. In France it is stratified between the CHÂTELPERRONIAN and the GRAVETTIAN, but industries of Aurignacian type are found eastwards to the Balkans, Palestine, Iran and Afghanistan. Bone points with split bases are diagnostic of the earliest Aurignacian, and in

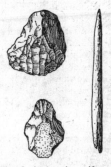

Fig. 18. Aurignacian artifacts

the west this is the period of the first CAVE ART. At the ABRI PATAUD there is a radiocarbon date of pre-31,000 BC for the Aurignacian, but it seems to have begun earlier in central Europe (42,350 ± 1,900 at Istállóskö Cave in Hungary). [18]

Australopithecus The oldest and most primitive genus of man. The australopithecines were of small size (around 4 ft tall and 50 lb weight), had small brains (within the size range of the anthropoid apes), were chinless, with massive jaws, and had strongly marked eyebrow ridges and sloping foreheads [87b]. But the shape of the palate and the arrangement of the teeth were more man-like than ape-like, and Australopithecus walked upright. The evidence from OLDUVAI and other sites suggests that some, if not all, species of Australopithecus were capable of making simple PEBBLE TOOLS. There is considerable variety within the genus, and the following species may be recognized: *A*

boisei (formerly ZINJANTHROPUS *boisei*), from Olduvai; *A. africanus* from South African sites of Early PLEISTOCENE date; *A. robustus* (formerly PARANTHROPUS), a larger form than *africanus*; HOMO HABILIS, known from Bed I at Olduvai. The *habilis* lineage may be ancestral to HOMO ERECTUS. Australopithecine remains have also been discovered near Lake Chad, at Ubeidiya in Israel and in deposits formed c2.5 million years ago at Kanapoi (Kenya). The oldest known examples are

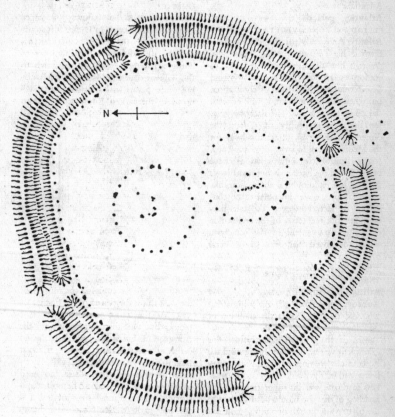

Fig. 19. Ground plan of Avebury (missing stones shown by dots

from Koobi Fora, Kenya (more than 2·6 million years) and the Omo Valley, Ethiopia (c. 3 million years old.

Avebury lies 5 miles west of Marlborough, Wiltshire, and is one of Britain's finest HENGE monuments [19]. It is also one of the largest ceremonial structures in Europe. The ditch and outer bank enclose about 28½ acres, and are broken by four equally spaced entrances. Round the inner lip of the ditch is a circle of SARSEN stones, and on the central plateau are two smaller circles each a little over 300 ft in diameter. The northern circle contains a U-shaped setting of three large stones, and the southern inner circle once had a complex arrangement of stones at its centre. From the bottom of the ditch came sherds of Neolithic WINDMILL HILL, PETER-BOROUGH and RINYO-CLACTON styles, while higher up in the fill were fragments of South British (Long Necked) BEAKER and Bronze Age pottery.

The south entrance of the henge marks the start of the Kennet Avenue, consisting of two parallel rows of sarsens forming an avenue 50 ft wide and 1½ miles long, which ends at a ritual building (the so-called Sanctuary) on Overton Hill. All these monuments are of about the same date, and form part of a single architectural complex. Burials with Beaker and Rinyo-Clacton wares have been excavated at the bases of some of the stones. Near the southern end of the Avenue was an occupation site with Neolithic and Beaker sherds, while the Sanctuary has a complicated history with several stages of reconstruction covering a similar period.

Avebury, Lord (formerly Sir John Lubbock) He influenced the development of archaeology mainly through his book *Prehistoric Times*, first edition 1865, seventh 1913, and a best-seller throughout. It popularized PREHISTORY both as a term and as a subject, and introduced the words 'palaeolithic' and 'neolithic' to describe the two main subdivisions of the Stone Age. In this book he interpreted cultural change as evidence of invasion from the east, and the development of society as the result of economic advance, views which helped forward the study of prehistory but which require considerable modification today.

awl A point of bone, flint or metal used for piercing holes.

axe A flat and heavy cutting tool of stone or metal in which the cutting edge is parallel to the haft. Its main function was for wood working (cf ADZE) but it could have served, indeed sometimes it is clearly designed to serve, as a weapon of war, the BATTLEAXE. Variation of form is largely the result of differences in materials used and the methods of hafting. The figure [20] illustrates some of the more important types, with the terms for the various parts.

axe factory Certain outcrops of fine-grained rock in the highland parts of Britain yield stone particularly suitable for polished axes, and at these sites axe-manufacture became an important industry during the Neolithic period. The tools were roughed out at the factory sites and traded, either as blanks or as finished axes, over most of the country. The chief centres were in Cornwall, the Lake District (Langdale), north Wales (Graig Llwyd) and at Tievebulliagh in northern Ireland. A similar pattern of exploitation and trade has been recognized in northwest France.

axe-hammer A shaft-hole axe having a hammer knob in addition. It was primarily a weapon of war, combining the functions of BATTLEAXE and MACE. [20b]

Ayampitín A site in northwest Argentina which produced crude grinding stones and leaf-shaped projectile points chipped on both faces. A similar assemblage was found in the lowest levels at Intihuasi Cave where two radiocarbon dates suggest occupation around 6000 BC. ◊ LAURICOCHA

Aylesford A cremation cemetery 2 miles northwest of Maidstone in Kent. It was excavated in 1890 by Sir ARTHUR EVANS who correctly identified the grave goods as belonging to the Iron Age BELGAE. Aylesford (together with a similar site at Swarling, dug in 1925) has become the type site of Belgic culture in southeastern England, and other rich graves, including

unurned cremations in pits, have been found in Hertfordshire, Essex and Cambridgeshire. Diagnostic features of the Aylesford culture are the custom of urned cremation in flat graves, and the use of wheel-made pots with pedestal bases [21]

Fig. 21. Pedestal urn from Aylesford cemetery

and horizontal cordon ornament. The culture started in CI (or perhaps late C2) BC, and survived as a native tradition for some time after the Roman conquest in AD 43.

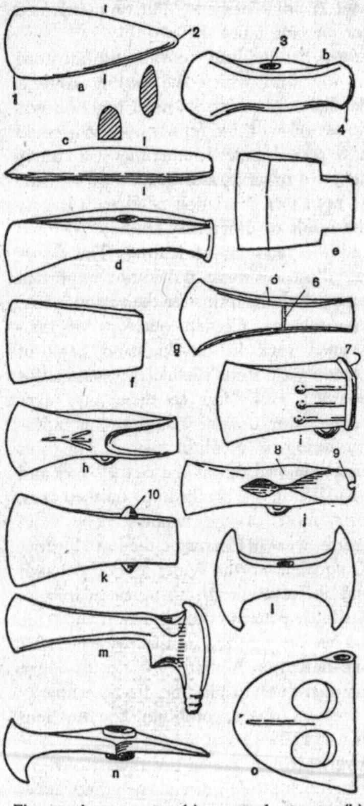

Azilian A terminal PALAEOLITHIC culture of northern Spain and southwest France, where its origins seem to lie in the Late MAGDALENIAN of the area. In date it falls within the LATE GLACIAL PERIOD, and can perhaps be correlated with the

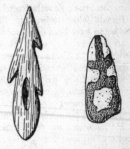

Fig. 22. Azilian harpoon and painted pebble

Fig. 20. Axe types: (a) ground stone; (b) battleaxe; (c) shoe-last celt; (d) Scandinavian boat-axe; (e) s.e. Asian shouldered axe; (f) flat copper; (g) flanged; (h) palstave; (i) socketed; (j) winged; (k) trunnion; (l) Minoan double axe; (m) Hungarian battleaxe; (n) Hungarian axe-adze; (o) Near Eastern scalloped axe

Axe terms: (1) cutting edge; (2) pointed butt; (3) shaft-hole; (4) hammer butt; (5) flange; (6) stop-ridge; (7) socket; (8) wing; (9) notch; (10) trunnion

ALLERØD OSCILLATION of the 10th millennium BC. The diagnostic artifacts are flat bone harpoons and pebbles painted with schematic designs. [22]

Aztec The last of the barbarian tribes to enter the Valley of Mexico after the collapse of TOLTEC civilization in C12 was the group we call the Aztecs, although they referred to themselves as the 'Mexica' or 'Tenochca'. For a while they lived miserably around the shores of Lake Texcoco, but in 1345 they were allowed to found a town, which they called TENOCHTITLÁN, on some unoccupied islands. The Aztecs joined in the game of politics and war in the Valley, and played it so successfully that by 1428 Tenochtitlán had become an independent state in alliance with Texcoco and Tlacopan. This Triple Alliance soon controlled the entire Valley and, with Tenochtitlán as the dominant partner, started on a programme of military expansion which was still unfinished at the time of the Spanish conquest. The Aztecs and their allies in 1519 ruled over most of present-day Mexico from the desert zone in the north to Oaxaca in the south, with extensions as far as the Guatemalan border.

This vast territory was not organized as a unified empire. Subject states, provided they remained loyal and paid their tribute regularly, were left to themselves, and no attempt was made to force their people into the Aztec mould. War, however, was basic to the Aztec way of life. By inclination and training the Aztecs were militaristic, and a man's status depended largely on his success as a warrior. The chief god of the Aztecs, Huitzilopochtli, was a war god who required the blood of sacrificial victims, and only constant warfare could ensure a supply of captives to be slain on the altar.

As the Aztecs became more powerful they became more civilized, learning from the older and culturally more advanced tribes of the Valley. From a collection of reed huts, Tenochtitlán became a great imperial city, so large that it was no longer self-sufficient but had to rely on tribute from the provinces. Luxury goods as well as necessities entered the city, and schools of craftsmen (often of MIXTEC origin) produced jewellery, turquoise mosaics, objects of featherwork and carved stone. It is difficult to recapture the splendour of Tenochtitlán because little architecture or painting survived the Spanish conquest of 1521. Copies of several books have been preserved (◊ CODEX), and Aztec sculpture has strongly influenced the work of such modern artists as Henry Moore. Mould-made clay figurines were in common use [64], and the grey-on-orange pottery was decorated with geometrical designs and stylized creatures.

B

Baal The most important god of the CANAANITES, depicted as a young warrior, armed and with bull's horns springing from his helmet. His name means simply 'Lord'. His worship was continued by the PHOENICIANS, who carried it west to CARTHAGE where he appears as Baal Hammon.

Babylon The ancient capital of Mesopotamia, 50 miles south of Baghdad. It first reached prominence c1792 BC, under HAMMURABI, who made it the capital of his empire. It was destroyed by the HITTITES c1595, and then ruled by the KASSITES until c1157. There followed a period of further decline under short-lived dynasties, punctuated by frequent wars with ELAM and ASSYRIA, until the 11th and last dynasty (626–539), when the city reached its highest development and largest size. Politically this neo-Babylonian dynasty was instrumental in destroying Assyria, and conquered an empire from the Persian Gulf to the Mediterranean before being overthrown by CYRUS the Persian in 539. It continued in existence, though with much reduced importance, until the Christian era.

The city of the neo-Babylonian period covered some 500 acres, with a population c100,000. Time has dealt very hardly with its ruins, mainly because its baked brick was highly prized for later building in a region where there is no local stone. The excavation by the Germans under KOLDEWEY, 1899–1917, has revealed the city's plan, the scanty remains of its ZIGGURAT (the original Tower of Babel), temples, especially of its patron god MARDUK, fortifications, palaces, and the substructure of what has been interpreted as the original Hanging Gardens. The finest surviving monument is the Ishtar Gate [23] and Procession Street, still standing to some 36 ft, decorated with bulls, dragons and lions in coloured relief on the blue-glazed tiles.

Fig. 23. The Ishtar Gate

Bactria The district of Turkestan around the upper Oxus river. It formed a SATRAPY of the ACHAEMENID empire and was conquered by Alexander the Great in 329 BC. A century later it was cut off from the Greek world by the PARTHIANS, but continued as a powerful Hellenistic state into c2. Its importance lies in the influence it had on ideas and art in India, through its province of GANDHARA.

Badarian A predynastic culture of the early 4th millennium named after the site of El Badari in Middle Egypt. It extended over much of Upper Egypt also. It was a local development, with some evidence of trade and the simple beginnings of a copper metallurgy. These showed themselves particularly in beads of foreign stone, shell and copper. A distinctive and very fine pottery was employed, the thin, ripple-burnished Black-topped Brown Ware later becoming red [24]. This effect was produced by firing it inverted to prevent the air from circulating inside and over the upper rim, keeping these areas black whereas the base and lower wall externally were oxidized to brown or a good red colour.

Fig. 24. Badarian Black-topped Red Ware

Baden or **Baden-Pécel** The final Copper Age culture over much of central Europe, known from Poland, Czechoslovakia, Austria, Hungary and parts of Germany. Metal tools include axe-hammers and TORCS of twisted copper wire. Pottery is normally plain and dark, but sometimes has channelled decoration and handles of ANSA LUNATA type. The horse was domesticated, and carts mounted on four solid disc-wheels were now introduced into central Europe. Radiocarbon dates suggest that the culture belongs in the middle part of the 3rd millennium BC, but some authorities point to similarities with the Early Bronze Age cultures of the Aegean, and prefer a date around 3000.

Bahía An Ecuadorian culture of the REGIONAL DEVELOPMENT PERIOD (500 BC–AD 500). Bahía shares many traits (platform mounds, polychrome painting, metallurgy and abundance of figurines) with other cultures of the period, but elements new to the archaeological record include models of houses with saddle roofs, pottery head-rests, figurines with one leg crossed over the other, Pan pipes graduated towards the centre and ear plugs shaped like golf tees. All these new items have parallels in southeast Asia, and it has been suggested that they were introduced into Ecuador by voyagers from across the Pacific.

Bahrain An island on the south coast of the Persian Gulf. It is possibly the island referred to in Mesopotamian records under the name of Dilmun, and has been shown by excavation to be an important link in the sea trade between that region and the INDUS CIVILIZATION.

Balearic Islands A group consisting of Majorca (Mallorca), Minorca, Iviza and Formentera, off the east coast of Spain. Their most interesting period is the Bronze Age, to which in the main belong their three typical monuments, the NAVETA, TALAYOT and TAULA.

balk ◊ BAULK

ball-court ◊ BALL-GAME

ball-game A game played in Mexico and Guatemala from the PRE-CLASSIC period until the Spanish conquest. The players, who were sometimes heavily padded, were allowed to use only their hips and thighs in propelling a rubber ball around the court. The ball-court itself was shaped like a capital I with exaggerated endpieces, and in the POST-CLASSIC period stone rings or macaw heads were fixed to the side walls. AZTEC records tell us that the team which passed the ball through one of these rings won the game outright. The ball-game had a ritual as well as a sporting significance. It was at various times played over a wide area of the Americas from Paraguay to Arizona and the West Indies.

Baluchistan A mountainous region separating the desert plateaus of Afghanistan and Iran from the Indus plains of the Punjab and Sind. ◊ KULLI, MEHI, NAL, QUETTA

Banas A river in Rajasthan, India, giving its name to a culture revealed at the sites of Ahar and Gilund. BLACK-AND-RED WARE was dominant, often with designs painted in white, and other related red wares occurred also. Copper and bronze were very common, stonework rare, reflecting the local wealth in metal. Agriculture was attested by querns. Stone and mud were the standard building materials. Occupation at Ahar lasted c 1800–1200 BC.

Bandkeramik The pottery of the DANU-BIAN I culture. It consists of hemispherical bowls and globular jars, usually round-based and strongly suggesting copies of

Fig. 25. Bandkeramik vessel

gourds. The name refers specifically to the standard decoration, ribbons of parallel lines forming spirals, meanders, chevrons, etc [25]. Pits are sometimes added on the lines, giving an effect that resembles musical notation.

Baradostian ◊ SHANIDAR

barbotine The practice of adding trails or incrustations of thick SLIP to the surface of a pot for decorative effect. Sometimes the result is simply a roughened surface, sometimes careful designs are produced, as in the NENE VALLEY WARE 'hunt' cups.

Barkaer (north Jutland, Denmark) A village of the final Early Neolithic period (Phase C of the TRB CULTURE). It consisted of a cobbled street separating two parallel timber buildings, each some 260 ft long and divided into 26 one-room dwellings. Offerings in pits below the houses included pottery, amber beads and copper objects.

barley With WHEAT, the staple cereal of the temperate Old World. Two groups are recognized. The two-row barley, *Hordeum distichum*, was derived from the wild *H. spontaneum*, distributed from the Aegean to the Hindu Kush. It is recorded from JARMO, and spread as far as Neolithic Switzerland before being ousted by the second group. Six-row barley, *H. hexastichum*, arose from *H. distichum* in cultivation. (*H. agriocrithon* is now dismissed as a hybrid descendant, not an ancestor.) Its

distribution extended from China to Egypt and Switzerland, and it is still occasionally grown. Modern barleys are otherwise all *H. tetrastichum*, a development from *hexastichum* recorded as early as the Neolithic in Britain and Denmark. The wild species are of the hulled form, with the seed held firmly in the glume, and have a fragile stalk to the ear; the cultivated ones all have a stronger spike which does not break during harvesting, and may be either hulled or naked, the latter making threshing much easier.

Barrancas The type site (on the lower Orinoco river, in Venezuela) of a pottery style in use from C9 BC. Related styles, making up the **Barrancoid** SERIES, are found from northern Colombia to eastern Venezuela, persisting in some areas of Venezuela until AD 1000 or later. On the lower Orinoco, it was intrusive Barrancas people who brought the SALADERO phase to an end. Some makers of Barrancoid wares eventually spread to Guyana and Trinidad, and their ceramics influenced the post-Saladoid pottery of the Lesser Antilles.

barrow A round or elongated mound raised over one or more burials [26]. The mound is often surrounded by a ditch, and the burials may be contained within a CIST, MORTUARY ENCLOSURE, MORTUARY HOUSE or CHAMBER TOMB. In Britain, earthen (or unchambered) long barrows belong to the Early and Middle Neolithic (WINDMILL HILL CULTURE). Other long barrows were constructed over MEGALITHIC tombs of GALLERY GRAVE types. Most of the British round barrows, some of them incorporating circles of stakes, belong to the Bronze Age, though burial under a round mound was occasionally practised during the Roman, Anglo-Saxon, and Viking periods. Of the varieties of Bronze Age barrow the bell, disc, saucer and probably also the pond type are associated with the WESSEX CULTURE. Bowl barrows are more widely distributed and last throughout the Bronze Age.

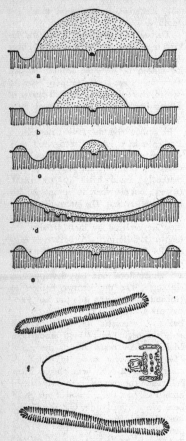

Fig. 26. Types of British barrow. Sections of:
(a) bowl barrow; (b) bell barrow; (c) disc
barrow; (d) pond barrow; (e) saucer barrow ;
(f) plan of Nutbane long barrow

Barumini (Sardinia) A NURAGHE which
began as a single tower (with a radiocarbon date of 1470 BC ± 200), but which
soon grew into a complex of towers and
perimeter walls surrounded by a village of
huts. In the late c6 the nuraghe was
sacked by the CARTHAGINIANS, but some
of the survivors returned and re-occupied

the site. The latest phase is dated by imported Roman material. [134]

Basarabi culture A rich Iron Age culture
present in cemeteries and settlement sites
over much of Romania. The type site is on
the Danube. It is a local version of the
HALLSTATT culture, dating to c800–650
BC.

Basket Maker The culture of the early
(ie pre-PUEBLO) stages of the ANASAZI
tradition in the American southwest.

basketry The weaving of containers from
vegetable fibres, twigs or leaves is so
widespread amongst all peoples at the
present day, and is basically so simple a
technique, that it probably goes back to a
very early origin. The earliest recorded
examples in the Old World are from the
FAYUM in Egypt c4000 BC, but, consider-
ing the perishability of basketry, even these
may be comparatively late in the history
of this technique. In America it was known
before 7000 BC in Mexico, and even earlier
in Oregon.

Basques A people resident in the Biscayan
provinces of Spain and France. They are
distinguished partly by an unusual pattern
of blood groups, very high in the Rhesus
negative factor, and by their language,
quite unrelated to any other known one.
They probably represent one of the
peoples who inhabited Europe before the
arrival of the INDO-EUROPEANS.

Bastis or **Bastet** The cat goddess of Lower
Egypt, whose principal cult centre was at
Bubastis in the Delta.

bâton de commandement The conventional name for an object of unknown use
found on Upper PALAEOLITHIC sites
from the AURIGNACIAN period onwards,
and consisting of an antler rod with a hole
through the thickest part of the head
[111c]. The finest and most highly decorated examples belong to the MAGDALEN-
IAN culture.

batter The slope back from vertical given
to a wall or trench face to increase its
stability.

battleaxe An AXE designed as a weapon of war. It is always of the SHAFT-HOLE variety, and frequently has a hammer, knob or point at the opposite end from the cutting edge [20b]. In stone, they are common throughout most of Europe in the Late Neolithic and Copper Age, associated with CORDED WARE and BEAKERS. Further east more elaborate ones of copper or gold are often obviously ceremonial rather than functional [20m]. In iron, the axe was a popular weapon with the VIKINGS, and continued well into the Middle Ages.

baulk A strip of earth left standing between the trenches of an EXCAVATION so that a sample of the STRATIGRAPHY remains available for study until the last possible moment.

beaker As a general term, a pottery drinking vessel deep in comparison with its diameter, normally without a handle.

Specifically, a type of pottery widely distributed in Europe from Spain to Poland, and from Sicily to Scotland, in the years around 2000 BC. In many northern and western areas its users were the first to introduce copper metallurgy, which may explain their rapid spread as traders. Their material equipment includes the west European tanged dagger [52d], bow with barbed-and-tanged arrows (note also the associated WRISTGUARD), and later the BATTLEAXE, apparently adopted from the CORDED WARE culture. Burial was by contracted inhumation in a trench, or under a round BARROW, or as a secondary BURIAL in some form of CHAMBER TOMB. Each burial was accompanied by a beaker, presumably to hold drink, prob-

ably alcoholic, for the dead man's last journey.

The origins of this important and intriguing group are still uncertain. Either Spain or Hungary seems the most likely, or indeed both. Some scholars suggest there may have been a primary eastward spread, characterized by the bell-beaker of international form [27a] followed by a westward reflux movement.

In Britain and the Low Countries, a Beaker culture can be recognized as a separate entity. Here it was perhaps introduced by an immigrant population with markedly round heads (◊ CEPHALIC INDEX), but elsewhere in Europe the distinction is less clear. The international bell-beakers are uncommon in Britain, where they are replaced by local variants, the long-necked (formerly A) beakers of eastern England and the short-necked (formerly C) beakers of Scotland [27]. There are similar local and late developments elsewhere, like the Veluwe beakers of Holland. ◊ FUNNEL BEAKER and PROTRUDING FOOT BEAKER

beans A vegetable important to man since the beginning of food production. Most modern beans are of the genus *Phaseolus*, different species of which occurred wild in both hemispheres. Their cultivation commenced at an early date in both. *Vicia faba*, the ancestor of our broad bean, was confined to the Old World, and was already being grown in the Neolithic period.

Behistun or **Bisutun** A rock face on the Kermanshah-Hamadan road in Iran on which DARIUS the Great in 516 BC recorded the victories which gave him the ACHAEMENID empire. A bas-relief shows Darius, under the protection of the god Ahuramazda, receiving his defeated enemies [28]. The inscriptions were carved in the CUNEIFORM script, and repeated in the Old Persian, Elamite and Babylonian languages. The rock face below them was then cut back to the vertical to prevent any

Fig. 27. Beakers: (a) bell; (b) long-necked; (c) short-necked

attempt at defacement, which rendered their copying by RAWLINSON 1835–47 an extremely difficult operation. The effort was repaid fully because it provided him

Fig. 28. Darius and his captives

with the key of the cuneiform script, opening to scholars the whole written material of the Mesopotamian civilizations.

Beit Mirsim, Tell (anc **Debir**) A TELL in the hills of southern Palestine. It was dug by Albright 1926–32. A small walled town, it gave important stratigraphic evidence of occupation from the late 3rd millennium (end of the Early Bronze Age) to its final destruction by the Babylonians in 587 BC.

Bel ◊ MARDUK

Belgae A group of tribes of mixed CELTIC and Germanic origin described by Caesar in mid-CI BC. In his day they held much of Belgium, and parts of northern France and southeast England. Their origins on the continent can be traced back to the LA TÈNE period in C5 BC, but their immigration into England, which was a gradual process, did not begin until C100 BC. Archaeologically the invaders can be identified with the bearers of the AYLESFORD-Swarling culture, otherwise known as Iron Age C. The tribal territories soon took on the trappings of states, each with an OPPIDUM as its capital. These were the first towns in Britain, and were fortified against intertribal raids. Coinage and the potter's wheel were introduced by the Belgae, and during the century before the Roman occupation of AD 43 the culture of the Belgic aristocracy was considerably Ro-

manized. In their richly furnished tombs are amphorae which once contained imported wine, and the Italian bronze vessels from which it was drunk. In exchange, Strabo records, the Belgae traded corn, cattle, gold and silver, skins, slaves and hunting dogs.

bell barrow ◊ BARROW

Belzoni, Giovanni A picturesque and unprincipled collector of Egyptian antiques in 1817–19, who enriched European collections enormously, but by the worst possible methods, destroying in two years almost as much as time alone had done in two thousand.

berm The flat space which separates the central mound of a BARROW from its encircling ditch, a rampart from the ditch outside it, or a spoil heap from its trench.

Bes A demi-god of ancient Egypt, appearing only in the New Kingdom, represented as an ugly dwarf [29]. He later became popular with the Phoenicians.

Fig. 29. Terracotta of Bes, from the Phoenician town of Tharros

Bethel A site near Jerusalem excavated by Albright in 1934 and by Kelso during the 1950s. It was occupied from before 2000 BC to C6 BC. The most important levels were of the Late Bronze Age, a particularly well-built town of the CANAANITES which was violently destroyed early in C13 BC, probably by the ISRAELITES, after a life of some 200 years.

Beth Shan (mod **Beisan**) A very large TELL in northern Palestine where the Plain of Esdraelon joins the Jordan valley. It was excavated by the University of Pennsylvania 1921–33. A deep sounding showed that occupation had begun with pit dwellings of the Chalcolithic, continuing unbroken from then on. A wider area was cleared down to level IX, c1400 BC. It revealed a succession of temples of the CANAANITES, Late Bronze to Iron Age. The heavy fortifications, absence of destruction levels and number of Egyptian imports suggest it was garrisoned as a frontier post of Egypt. Higher still were a Hellenistic temple and a Byzantine church. All these periods were also represented in the surrounding cemeteries.

Beth Shemesh A TELL on the edge of the plain near Jerusalem, excavated 1911–12 and 1928–31. The site was occupied successively by the CANAANITES (Middle–Late Bronze Age), PHILISTINES and ISRAELITES (Iron Age). It was abandoned at the time of the Babylonian invasions in C6 BC.

betyl A sacred stone, often a standing stone trimmed to a conical shape.

Beycesultan A TELL on the upper Meander river, western Turkey, which has given useful evidence on the local Bronze Age cultures contemporary with, but outside, the empire of the HITTITES. It may have belonged to the state known from Hittite records as Arzawa.

bird, boat and sun disc A decorative motif in HALLSTATT art combining these three features [30]. It must have had some religious significance at which we can now only guess.

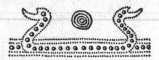

Fig. 30. Bird, boat and sun disc motif

Biskupin An Early Iron Age village, of c6 and c5 BC, near Znin, in northwest Poland. The island site was ringed by a breakwater of piles and fortified by a rampart of timber compartments filled with earth and stones. Inside were more than a hundred wooden cabins arranged along parallel streets surfaced with logs. In response to a rising water level, the site was twice reconstructed. Biskupin belongs to a late stage of the LUSATIAN CULTURE.

bits, horse The domesticated HORSE was apparently first controlled with a simple halter. Bits with CHEEK-PIECES of antler did not appear in central Europe until after 1500 BC, to be replaced later by examples in bronze. Bits without a cheek-piece, in 2-piece or 3-piece form, were introduced in the Iron Age. Particularly fine examples show the plastic modelling of CELTIC ART, and these were always show-pieces.

Black-and-red Ware A red pottery with black rims and interiors (◇ BADARIAN) current in the Indian peninsula in the Iron Age. It first appeared on late sites at the southern edge of the INDUS CIVILIZATION, like LOTHAL. It was a standard feature of the BANAS culture. In the 1st millennium it became widespread in association with iron and megalithic monuments in south India (◇ BRAHMAGIRI).

Blackwater Draw (near Clovis, New Mexico) The type site for the CLOVIS POINT and the Llano complex. In the basal stratum were Clovis points associated with mammoth bones. Above this was a level with FOLSOM points and bison bones; then, in succession, came Agate Basin points, those of the CODY COMPLEX, a Frederick point, and tools of the ARCHAIC period.

blade A long parallel-sided FLAKE struck from a specially prepared CORE. A blade may be a tool in itself, or may serve as the blank from which another artifact (eg BURIN or SCRAPER) can be manufactured. Industries in which many of the tools are made from blades become prominent at the start of the Upper PALAEOLITHIC period [31]. A 'backed blade' [75a] is a blade with one edge blunted by the removal of tiny flakes.

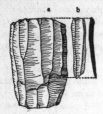

Fig. 31. (a) core; (b) blade

bleeper A survey instrument based on the same principle as the MAGNETOMETER. When two detector bottles are used, one near ground level and one about 6 ft above, small magnetic anomalies underground affect the lower, nearer, bottle more strongly than the upper. The signals from the two get out of step, and their sound signal is broken into a series of beats or 'bleeps'. It is unaffected by large scale disturbance, an advantage over the magnetometer, and is much simpler, cheaper and more portable than either magnetometer or gradiometer, from which it was developed.

bloom The slaggy material resulting from the smelting of an iron ore. To produce useful IRON, it must be hammered at red heat to expel the stone and add a proportion of carbon to the metal.

Boat-axe culture A subgroup of the Nordic SINGLE-GRAVE CULTURES from Sweden, Finland, Bornholm and the east Danish islands. The characteristic weapon is a slender stone BATTLEAXE shaped like an upturned boat. [20d]

boat burial This is a north European practice, common among the VIKINGS until burial in churchyards became customary in CII. In ANGLO-SAXON Britain there are three C7 examples from Suffolk, including the enormously rich burial at SUTTON HOO.

boats Navigation has always been important to man, for communication, transport and fishing. The earliest evidence is indirect, OBSIDIAN from the island of Melos in Upper Palaeolithic levels of the caves of Francthi in mainland Greece. Over most of Europe there is plentiful evidence of inland waterways from Mesolithic times on, beginning with one from Perth and paddles from MAGLEMOSIAN contexts in Denmark. Plank boats appeared in the Middle Bronze Age, either carvel-built (the planks joined edge to edge) or clinker-built (the planks over-lapping). Lashing or stitching was usually used to hold them together, as in the HJORTSPRING boat [86]. Nails appeared only in the Roman period, as at NYDAM.

Much less is known of sea-going vessels, beyond the fact that they must have existed. Skin boats, like the Irish curragh, are most probable. But the classical writers show that plank-built boats with sails of leather were known on the Atlantic before the Romans arrived. Full documentation here begins only with the VIKINGS.

In the Near East other types were known. Plank boats appeared alongside ones made of bundles of reeds on the Nile by 3000 BC, when the sail too was introduced. They plied the Mediterranean as well as the river, and supported the sea power of the MINOANS, MYCENAEANS and PHOENICIANS successively. Less is known of Mesopotamia and the Persian Gulf. Circular hide-covered boats are shown on some Assyrian reliefs, and plank boats must surely have been used for the trade between the Tigris-Euphrates and the Indus. Elsewhere in the world, dug-outs were the standard form, but the Americas have yielded two regional pre-conquest types of craft: the reed *caballitos* of the Peruvian coast and Lake Titicaca, and the sea-going balsa rafts from the Gulf of Guayaquil.

Bodrogkeresztur An east Hungarian cemetery with at least fifty inhumation graves. It is the type site for the middle stage of the Hungarian Copper Age (c3100–

2700 BC), noted for its metal battleaxes and axe-adzes of shaft-hole type [20 n]. ⟡ TISZAPOLGÁR, BADEN

Boghaz Köy or **Keui** (anc **Hattusas**) The capital of the HITTITES stood in the loop of the Halys river in central Turkey. It was excavated by Winkler 1906–12 and Bittel 1931–9. A site which had been occupied since the Copper Age became c1500 BC the citadel of Hattusas. As the Hittites' power grew, so did their capital, eventually covering over 300 acres, all within a massive defensive wall of stone and mudbrick. Three of its gates were decorated with monumental reliefs, showing a warrior, lions and sphinxes. Four temples have been excavated within the walls, each grouped round an open porticoed court, and the rock sanctuary of YAZILIKAYA lies only a short distance outside [32]. Few secular buildings have

Fig. 32. Warrior frieze in the Yazılıkaya shrine

been found, the most important being some insignificant store chambers which yielded over 10,000 inscribed clay tablets, from which has come much of our evidence on the Hittites. A cemetery close to the city held large numbers of CREMATION burials, a surprisingly early occurrence of this rite, but the grave goods were on the whole modest. The city fell at the same time as the empire, c1200 BC.

Boian A Middle Neolithic culture of eastern Romania and Bulgaria c3500–2700 BC. Settlements become larger, even forming small tells. The pottery has geometric designs filled with white paste. Copper begins to appear in the deposits.

Bølling Oscillation ⟡ LATE GLACIAL PERIOD

Bologna A city on the southern edge of the Po valley in north Italy. Villages of the APENNINE CULTURE, in trading contact with the TERRAMARA culture to the west, were succeeded in C9 by others of the VILLANOVANS, which rapidly grew into a very important bronze-working and trade centre [174]. This developed further under the ETRUSCANS to become the city of Felsina. It fell to the Gauls (⟡ CELTS) in C4 BC and to Rome in C2.

Bonampak A MAYA CEREMONIAL CENTRE in Chiapas, Mexico, famous for its polychrome wall-paintings of the late CLASSIC period (around AD 800) which depict a fight and various ceremonial activities.

Boreal period ⟡ POSTGLACIAL PERIOD and ZONES, VEGETATIONAL

bosing A technique for locating buried ditches or pits in a chalk subsoil. The surface is struck with a billet of wood or an ordinary pick helve, a duller note being emitted over any disturbance.

bossed bone plaque An object made from an animal long bone on which is carved a row of round or oval bosses [33].

Fig. 33. Bossed bone plaque from Castelluccio

The finest have engraved decoration also. Examples with flat bases from LERNA and TROY II date to the 3rd millennium. A series from CASTELLUCCIO in Sicily, with outliers in Italy and Malta, are curved in cross-section and belong a little before 2000 BC. The function of these objects is problematical. The decoration, it has been suggested, may represent a female figure.

Botta, Paul-Emile French consul in Mosul, Iraq, 1840–43. After some unrewarding trenches on the mound of Kuyunjik, he turned his attention to

KHORSABAD, which he believed to be the ancient NINEVEH. Here in 1843 he revealed for the first time the startling art of the ASSYRIANS in the great winged bulls and relief wall slabs. Of the many subsequent excavations by others in Mesopotamia, few revealed so much so rapidly, due to his good fortune, adroit diplomacy (essential in the face of Turkish officialdom in his day) and a brusque approach to the problems of digging, with loot the sole object.

Boucher de Crêvecoeur de Perthes, Jacques (1788–1868) His researches in the gravel pits of Menchecourt and Moulin-Quignon, on the terraces of the river Somme, produced some of the first evidence of man-made tools of chipped stone (HANDAXES in modern terminology) in association with the bones of extinct PLEISTOCENE animals. In his two books, *De la Création: essai sur l'origine et la progression des êtres* (1838–41) and *Antiquités Celtiques et Antédiluviennes* (1847), he argued that the crudely chipped tools belonged to a very remote age, long before the arrival of the Celts. At first his conclusions were scorned, but gradually he began to make converts. In 1858 the English geologist Falconer visited the Somme gravels and was so impressed that he persuaded John EVANS and John Prestwich to examine the excavations during the following year. They too were convinced, and supported Boucher de Perthes's claims in a series of papers and lectures. ◊ PENGELLY

The original finds were undoubtedly authentic, but the 'Moulin-Quignon jaw' found in 1863 is of Neolithic or still more recent age, and was planted by a workman in response to an offer of 200 fr to the finder of fossil human bones.

bow An offensive weapon with a long history in hunting and war. Actual examples as early as the Mesolithic have been preserved in peat-bogs, but our evidence is more often circumstantial. Where the bow

and string have long since decayed, the ARROWHEAD is more durable, and the WRIST GUARD may also be present. What must be arrowheads of flint from the SOLUTREAN and MAGDALENIAN show that the weapon was known in the Upper Palaeolithic, and there are representations in EAST SPANISH ROCK ART. Cultures not using the bow can sometimes be shown to have employed the SLING instead.

bowl barrow ◊ BARROW

box flue A brick consisting in effect of four tiles joined at their edges, open top and bottom, to conduct the hot air of a Roman HYPOCAUST system up the walls to escape at the eves [89]. The exposed faces of the box flue tiles were often decorated in relief to provide a key for the wall plaster which normally covered them.

Boyne In the bend of the river Boyne, about 25 miles north of Dublin, is the finest group of prehistoric ritual monuments in Ireland. Several are still unexcavated, but the complex includes five HENGES, a number of untested mounds and the three great PASSAGE GRAVES of NEWGRANGE, Dowth and KNOWTH. The term 'Boyne culture' is sometimes used to describe the material found inside passage graves all over Ireland. Its diagnostic traits include the highly decorated Carrowkeel style of pottery and bone pins with poppy- or mushroom-shaped heads.

bradisism Relative movements of land and sea produced by earth movement, up or down, as opposed to alterations brought about by ice (◊ EUSTASY, ISOSTASY). Such changes are often quite local.

Brahmagiri An important settlement site and cemetery excavated by Wheeler in 1947 in northern Mysore, southern India. There were three levels: (1) Chalcolithic, with abundant microliths, polished stone axes, and poor pottery. Radiocarbon dates from related sites place it c2200–1000 BC. (2) Iron Age, with iron and BLACK-AND-RED WARE, of the 1st millennium BC. To this period belong the 300 tombs, stone circles containing 6 ft square CISTS with PORTHOLE entrances, ossuaries for bones exposed elsewhere. Related monuments in southern India include dolmenic cists with many-legged terracotta sarcophagi, and the 'umbrella-stones', like giant mush-rooms. (3) CI AD, with Rouletted Ware and other traces of Roman contact.

Brak A TELL near the Khabur river in eastern Syria excavated by Mallowan 1937–8. Its occupation ran from the early prehistoric period until the middle of the 2nd millennium BC. Its most important remains were the 'Eye Temples' of the JEMDET NASR period, c 3000 BC. They are so called after the enormous number of flat alabaster figurines of which the eyes are the only recognizable features [34].

Fig. 34. 'Eye' figurine from Brak

They are roughly of human shape and often only an inch or two high. Later the site became a frontier post of the kingdom of AKKAD, with a palace built by Naram-Sin c 2280 BC.

breccia A rock consisting of angular frag-ments of more ancient rocks held together by a matrix of natural cement.

Breuil, Henri (1877–1961) was ordained priest in 1900, but he never took up parish duties and was allowed to spend his time on archaeology. He was a fine draughts-man, and his greatest contributions lay in the recording and interpretation of CAVE ART. On the basis of superpositions Breuil worked out a sequence of art styles, and he was the main proponent of the sympa-thetic magic theory according to which the act of painting represents an attempt by magical means to ensure success in hunting. Not until after his death were Breuil's views seriously challenged.

Another of his achievements was the fitting of the AURIGNACIAN culture into its right place within the French PALAEO-LITHIC sequence. The Abbé visited sites in England, Romania, Spain (where he accompanied CARTAILHAC to ALTAMIRA, and studied the EAST SPANISH ROCK ART), Portugal and Italy, where he per-sonally excavated one of the NEANDER-THAL skulls at Saccopastore. He worked in North Africa, visited China twice, copied paintings in Ethiopia in the company of Teilhard de Chardin, and spent the years 1942–5 in southern Africa collecting flint tools and copying rock art of all periods.

brick A building material consisting of individual blocks of clay or mud, with some tempering of sand or straw. Bricks are usually but by no means always rec-tangular in form. They may be baked to TERRACOTTA or only sun-dried, when they are referred to as MUDBRICK or ADOBE.

broch A circular dry-stone tower 45–70 ft in diameter serving as a fortified home-stead. Over 400 are known in the north and west of Scotland. The hollow walls, 12–15 ft thick, contain chambers and a staircase to an upper floor or roof walk [35]. The central court, up to 35 ft across,

Fig. 35. Section of the Broch of Mousa

was surrounded by timber lean-to buildings against the enclosing wall, which might reach a height of 40 ft. They were a local development around the turn of the Christian era from the stone DUNS, an offshoot of the west European fort-building tradition. Their material content points to strong influence, probably immigration, from southern England or western France. The Broch of Mousa on Shetland is the best preserved and most famous example.

Broken Hill (Zambia) A cave which produced a fossil skull with characteristics similar to those of NEANDERTHAL MAN. The skull was found on a ledge, and has therefore no definite evidence for date, but all the artifacts in the Bone Cave were of African Middle Stone Age type. It seems likely that the skull and the tools were contemporary, and, if so, Rhodesian man would be about 30,000 years old. ◊ FAURESMITH

bronze An alloy of COPPER and TIN, the optimum proportion being about 9 parts copper to 1 of tin. It had many advantages over pure copper: it had a lower melting point, was harder and, above all, was easier to cast without flaws. Its main disadvantage was the comparative scarcity of tin. In Eurasia it succeeded pure copper as the main material for man's tools and weapons, defining the BRONZE AGE of the THREE AGE SYSTEM. It was rapidly replaced by the commoner and more efficient IRON for such uses, but continued alongside the latter for many decorative purposes right down to the Roman and Saxon periods. Because of its economic value the metal is often found in HOARDS, which have helped enormously in the study of the developing artifacts of the period. Shaping was achieved in three main ways – casting in a one or two piece MOULD, casting by the CIRE PERDUE method, and hammering out, with repeated annealing to avoid brittleness. All sheet metalwork, for shields, helmets, vessels, etc, would

have required the third method, separate plates often being joined by riveting.

Bronze Age The second 'age' in the THREE AGE SYSTEM, when BRONZE was the main material used for man's tools and weapons. The advantage of bronze over copper was such that trade in the scarce but necessary tin had to be organized. This trade led in turn to the rapid diffusion of ideas and technological improvements. As a result, far more emphasis has been placed on TYPOLOGY for the study of this age than the others. The rapid change of tools and above all of weapons, and their frequent recovery as components of a HOARD, make particularly detailed analysis possible.

In Asia the period coincides with written history, so the awkward archaeological name may be abandoned. In Europe, centres of metal-working were established in the Aegean (the MINOANS and MYCENAEANS, the first European civilizations), central Europe (ÚNĚTICE), Spain (El ARGAR), Britain (Ireland and the WESSEX CULTURE) and Scandinavia. The later Bronze Age is the period of the great folk movements which led to the spread of the URNFIELDS. It was brought to a close by the introduction of iron. In America true bronze was used in northern Argentina before AD 1000, and the knowledge spread to Peru shortly afterwards. Certain Mexican nations, including the AZTECS, occasionally alloyed copper with tin, but bronze was never as important in the New World as in the Old, and we cannot use the term Bronze Age in America.

brooch A piece of decorative metalwork attached to a garment by a pin, either as fastening or ornament. The word is most often used in post-Roman contexts, for late forms of the FIBULA and other types such as the saucer and penannular brooches. [36]

Bubanj A Late Neolithic culture of Yugoslavia, its type site on the river Morava close to Niš. It derives from the VINČA culture and is closely related to SĂLCUȚA in Romania. 3rd millennium.

Fig. 36. Dark Age brooches: (a) square headed; (b) penannular; (c) saucer; (d) small long; (e) cruciform

bucchero A fine grey pottery with a black, or less commonly grey, shiny surface produced by the ETRUSCANS in C8–C4 BC.

bulb of percussion A bulb, or swelling, left on the upper part of the face of a BLADE or FLAKE [65] directly below the point of impact on the STRIKING PLATFORM.

burial The laying of a body in the ground or in a natural or artificial chamber or urn. In collective burial a single chamber accommodates more than one corpse, usually successively. A primary burial is one for which a burial monument such as a BARROW was erected, the secondary burials being added subsequently, usually in the edges of the mound. The term secondary burial is also used for the rite of collecting the bones of a skeleton after the flesh has been removed by exposure, and placing them in some form of OSSUARY. In fractional burial, only some of the bones are so collected and interred. The term is used generally for both INHUMATION and CREMATION. ◊ CHAMBER TOMB

burin A pointed tool made of chipped flint or stone and used to engrave bone, antler, ivory and (presumably) wood. In its most characteristic form the working tip is a narrow transverse edge formed by the intersection of two flake scars produced by striking at an angle to the main axis of the BLADE. Sometimes one facet is made by simply snapping the blade, or by truncating it with a steep retouch. There are many variations on this theme [37]. The use of the burin is one of the hallmarks of Upper PALAEOLITHIC industries.

Fig. 37. Burins

burnish A polish given to the surface of an artifact. On bronze it was done to improve the appearance; even mirrors could be produced in this way. On pottery, where it had to be carried out after drying but before baking, the main purpose was probably to compact the clay, rendering the vessel more watertight. The decorative effect was doubtless also valued. In pattern burnish, for example, the surface is left matt as a background to a design of polished lines. In stroke burnish, the surface is completely polished, but the marks of the burnisher, a pebble or bone slip, remain distinct.

Burzahom A Neolithic site near Srinagar in Kashmir. Its pit-dwellings, bone work, absence of blades, use of pierced rectangular knives, coarse pottery and association of dog skeletons with human burials, all seem to point to connexions with Mongolia rather than with the rest of the Indian subcontinent. Hunting seems to have been the main basis of the economy. Radiocarbon dates run from c2375–1400 BC.

Butmir A Late Neolithic culture related to the VINČA culture, with its type site near Sarajevo in Bosnia, Yugoslavia. Its pottery made lavish use of incised meander designs.

buttons Small objects of stone, bone or metal sewn on to garments to fasten two edges together, or purely as decoration. They are known from the Copper Age onwards in Europe, developing in the Mediterranean area and being spread along with BEAKERS. The presence of buttons is taken to imply a fashion for tailored garments, draped ones being better fastened with a PIN or FIBULA.

Byblos, Gebal or **Gebail** (adj Jiblite) A site on the coast of Lebanon north of Beirut. It has been under excavation by Dunand since the 1930s. After a modest start in the Neolithic, it grew in size and complexity, becoming by the Bronze Age the major port through which Egypt imported timber from the Lebanon from 3000 BC on. From soon after 2000 a temple to Ba'alat Gebal, The Lady of Byblos, the local version of ASTARTE, stood at the centre of the city. Noteworthy is the group of obelisks representing the deity. To C13 (or to C10 according to many scholars) belongs the sarcophagus of King Ahiram [38], bearing a famous early alphabetic inscription. At the end of the Bronze Age occupation moved to the site of the modern village and is thus irrecoverable, but by then the town's importance had declined in the face of the rivalry of Arad to the north and TYRE and SIDON to the south.

Fig. 38. Sarcophagus of Ahiram from Byblos

Bylany (Kutná Hora, Bohemia, Czechoslovakia) A village of the DANUBIAN CULTURE in the LOESS lands about 40 miles east of Prague. The settlement covered more than 65,000 square metres, and there were many phases of occupation by Danubian I peoples and later by those making STROKE-ORNAMENTED POTTERY.

C

Cadbury The name of three hillforts in Somerset, the most important being South Cadbury near Wincanton. Tradition equates it with the Camelot of King ARTHUR, and excavation in 1966-70 has shown that it was indeed occupied in C5 AD. Extensive remains of pre-Roman Iron Age occupation, and even a settlement of the Neolithic, are also being discovered.

cairn A heap of stones covering a burial. The word is often used as a synonym for BARROW in areas where burial mounds were normally of stone.

Cajamarca An area in the middle Marañon valley of the north Peruvian highlands which developed a strong regional civilization of its own. Cajamarca pottery is decorated with linear running patterns (hence the name 'Cursive') or with stylized creatures and animal heads in brownish black over a cream background. During the Cajamarca III phase this ware was exported to HUARI, and to the north coast during the Huari expansion.

calendar A cyclical system of measuring the passage of time. The basis amongst nearly all peoples is the movement of the sun, giving the units of the day and, sometimes more, sometimes less accurately calculated, the year. The moon provides the lunar month. Various methods of reconciling the three units, made difficult by the fact that none is made up of an exact number of either of the others, were employed by different peoples. Our own leap year is one such method. In Egypt (♢ SOTHIC CYCLE) no reconciliation was attempted, the two calendars remaining in use concurrently and independently.

The commonest method of identifying a particular year was by reference to the reign of a king or other official, eg the nth year of King So-and-so of the nth DYNASTY. Numbering years from a fixed point in time began only in classical times ('x years A.U.C.' *ab urbe condita* – from the founding of Rome, 753 BC, or 'in the year of the yth Olympiad' – every fourth year from c776 BC). The Christian era was not instituted until C4-C5 AD.

In America the origins of Mexican calendrics are still obscure, but evidence from MONTE ALBÁN suggests that the 52-year Calendar Round (see below) was known by C6 BC. Elsewhere the Long Count system was in use by CI BC if not before (♢ OLMEC and IZAPA). In the course of time all the civilized peoples of Mexico adopted the Calendar Round, but the use of the Long Count was confined to the MAYA zone and adjacent territories.

The Calendar Round is a combination of two cyclic calendars:

(a) The 260-day Sacred Calendar (AZTEC *tonalpohualli*, MAYA *tzolkin*) was for ritual purposes only, and had nothing to do with astronomical phenomena. It was based on the numbers 1 to 13 and the 20 named days, each of which had its own title and GLYPH. Every possible combination of one day with one number gives a total of 260 pairings before the cycle starts all over again.

(b) The Solar Year Calendar of 365 days, divided into 18 months each of 20 days plus a period of 5 'unlucky days'.

Any given day can be expressed in terms of both these cycles, and it will be 52 years (ie 73 Sacred cycles or 52 Solar ones) before the two calendars are in phase again and the same combination is repeated. This 52-year period is called the Calendar Round.

A more obvious way of measuring time, as in the Christian calendar, is to count from a fixed date. This was the principle of the MAYA Long Count (also called Initial Series because its HIEROGLYPHS occupy the beginning of Maya inscriptions). This system measures the number of days which have passed since an arbitrary fixed point in time. For some reason, perhaps mythological, the Long Count starts from a date in our year 3113 BC, well before there is evidence of advanced culture in Mexico.

The Maya Secondary Series is a calendar-correction formula, rather like our leap year correction, and was designed to prevent the 365-day Solar Calendar from running ahead of the true year of $365\frac{1}{4}$ days. On inscribed STELAE the date expressed in terms of the official Calendar Round was qualified by a Secondary Series addition, showing by how many days this 52-year cycle lagged behind the exact figure.

Calendar Round ⟡ CALENDAR

callaïs A greenish decorative stone occasionally used for beads from Late Neolithic to Early Bronze Age in western Europe. Its natural source has not been traced but probably lay in Brittany.

camel The two-humped camel, *Camelus bactrianus*, is native to central Asia. Its bones have appeared rarely on scattered sites such as ANAU, TRIPOLYE and MOHENJO-DARO, and it was certainly fully domesticated by the 1st millennium BC. The single-humped dromedary, *C. dromedarius*, was domesticated much earlier in Arabia, but the records of it are very scanty – its nomad owners have left little evidence, and the scribes and artists of the settled lands were not interested in it.

camp A word which occurs frequently in British topographical names, and is used loosely for almost any kind of ditched and embanked enclosure from Neolithic CAUSEWAYED CAMPS to Iron Age HILLFORTS and Roman fortifications.

Camulodunum ⟡ COLCHESTER

Canaanites The branch of the SEMITES related to the HYKSOS who occupied the Levant from the Middle to the Late Bronze Age, c2000-1200 BC. In the south they were displaced by the ISRAELITES and PHILISTINES; in the north they became

the PHOENICIANS. Their main significance in history lies in their role as middlemen and traders, through whose hands passed cultural influences between Egypt, Mesopotamia and the HITTITES. They were the originators of the ALPHABET. Their sites included LACHISH, MEGIDDO, BYBLOS and UGARIT.

cannibalism The eating of human flesh by men. This may be done either because of dire want or for ritual purposes, when parts of deceased relatives or enemies may be eaten so that their power can be magically acquired. The practice is not easy to prove from the archaeological record. The splitting of human long bones and the opening of the skull may be the result of the extraction of marrow or brain, but may often equally well be accidental.

canopic jar In the funeral rites of the ancient Egyptians the organs were removed from the MUMMY and placed in separate containers, one each for the liver, lungs, stomach and intestines. These were each under the protection of a goddess and had the lids carved as the heads of the sons of HORUS. The jars or urns were then placed beside the mummy in the tomb, to be reunited in spirit, subject to the appropriate spells and rituals having been performed.

Cape Krusenstern (Alaska) An area with a HORIZONTAL STRATIGRAPHY covering the whole of north Alaskan prehistory. Spread over 114 ridges representing ancient beach lines were the campsites of 10 successive cultures, beginning with the DENBIGH FLINT COMPLEX, followed by the Old Whaling culture, then by the ESKIMO cultures known as Trails Creek-Chloris, Chloris, Norton, Near Ipiutak, IPIUTAK, Birnirk, Western THULE, and late prehistoric. On the terrace behind the beaches were two more phases (Palisades I and II) which may carry the sequence back to c8000 BC. ⟡ ONION PORTAGE

Capsian A culture of MESOLITHIC type named after Gafsa, in Tunisia. Its oldest phase can be little earlier than 8000 BC, and is best represented in middens and ash heaps in Tunisia and eastern Algeria, but Capsian industries soon spread to replace those of ORANIAN type over most of Mediterranean Africa from Cyrenaica (HAUA FTEAH) to Morocco. Tools include BLADES, BURINS, scrapers, backed bladelets, MICROLITHS and MICROBURINS. Shortly after 5000 BC pottery and domesticated animals were introduced, and we can speak of a 'Neolithic of Capsian Tradition' which lasted until at least the 2nd millennium BC. The so-called 'Kenya Capsian', a blade and burin industry of East Africa, is much older than the Capsian proper and is not related to it.

capstone A horizontal roofing slab covering a CIST or a MEGALITHIC CHAMBER TOMB.

carbon^{14} dating ◊ RADIOCARBON

Carchemish Excavation of this great TELL where the Euphrates crosses from Turkey to Syria was carried out by the British Museum in 1878–81 and again 1911–14. Occupation of the site began in the Chalcolithic with HALAF ware and continued throughout the Bronze Age, but it was only under the empire of the HITTITES that it reached importance. With their downfall, it succeeded to the hegemony of the Syro-Hittite city states. The site included a great citadel controlling the river crossing, with annexed to it an extensive town, also walled. The city gates, temples and palaces all bore considerable numbers of carved reliefs and inscriptions of the period. These last help greatly with piecing together its history down to its annexation by Assyria in 716 BC.

cardium The Latin name for the cockle. In prehistory as today it was used for food. Its serrated edge was used to decorate the Mediterranean IMPRESSED WARE, the cardial technique.

cardo (pl cardines) The second major road of a Roman camp or town, intersecting with the DECUMANUS MAXIMUS. [53]

Carib Carib tribes were living in the Lesser Antilles and parts of South America when the Spaniards arrived. Their origin seems to have been on the mainland, from which some groups moved out into the islands and conquered territory at the expense of the ARAWAKS. By C15 these insular Caribs had adopted the Arawak language. They were a belligerent people, notorious for eating war captives (the word 'cannibal' is a corruption of 'Caribal', the Spanish form of 'Carib').

carination A sharp beak in curve of a vessel's profile, resulting in a projecting angle or ARRIS. [11]

Carnac (Morbihan, France) The site of the finest monuments of ALIGNMENT type. Nearly 3,000 MENHIRS still remain, arranged in three groups, each consisting of multiple rows, 10 to 13 in number, which ended originally at semicircles of standing stones. The area is also noted for a series of long cairns, of mid Neolithic to Early Bronze Age date, covering funerary chambers and secondary CISTS. The grave goods included beautiful polished axes of rare stones such as JADEITE and fibrolite.

carnelian, cornelian A red semi-precious stone used for beads and seal stones. In the INDUS CIVILIZATION designs were occasionally etched into the beads.

carp's tongue sword A SWORD current in the Late Bronze Age in western Europe, characterized by a broad slashing blade drawn into a narrower tip for thrusting [186e]. ◊ ATLANTIC BRONZE AGE

Cartailhac, Émile (1843–1921) One of the founders of archaeology in France. He edited the journal *Matériaux pour l'histoire primitive et naturelle de l'homme*, wrote books on French and Mediterranean prehistory, and was one of the most influential figures to speak against the authenticity of CAVE ART. After visiting ALTAMIRA with the Abbé BREUIL, Cartailhac changed his opinion and in 1902 published an article subtitled *Mea culpa d'un sceptique* in which he admitted the antiquity of the cave paintings. This statement by a leading prehistorian helped to sway public opinion towards the acceptance of the art as genuine.

Carter, Howard achieved fame by his discovery of the tomb of TUTANKHAMEN in November 1922. Working for Lord Carnarvon, his patient and long unrewarded study of the VALLEY OF THE KINGS at Thebes eventually brought to light the only unrifled Egyptian pharaoh's tomb, and the richest treasure ever to be discovered. He therefore ranks with LAYARD, SCHLIEMANN and WOOLLEY for the enormous boost his work gave to public interest in archaeology.

Carthage (adj Carthaginian or Punic) This colony of TYRE was founded 814 BC on a promontory 8 miles from Tunis. When the homeland fell under the domination of Assyria, Carthage combined the colonies of the PHOENICIANS in the west Mediterranean into a trading empire. This brought her into conflict, particularly in Sicily, with the Greeks, a conflict that continued for many years with varying success. But she lost both that island and Sardinia to Rome in 241 at the close of the First Punic War. From an enlarged domain in southern Spain, the Carthaginian general Hannibal in 218 led his army across the Alps to victories in Italy, but was recalled to Africa, to be defeated by Scipio Africanus at Zama in 202. Though humiliated, Carthage survived, until it was utterly destroyed by Rome in 146 BC.

Her culture is represented mainly by material excavated from her cemeteries and sacred sites (the upstanding remains all date from the much later Roman reoccupation). It derived mainly from Phoenicia, with steadily increasing Greek influence. The Punic language and its distinctive ALPHABET remained in use long after the city's destruction, but inscriptions are nearly all short. We have no surviving literature which would allow us to compare its cultural achievement fairly with that of, for example, contemporary Rome. This is only part of the explanation of the unsympathetic impression these people give. Their artistry, except perhaps in jewellery, is meagre, and the charges of infant sacrifice laid to them by the Romans have been amply confirmed by the excavation of the precinct of the goddess TANIT within the city. Her consort BAAL Hammon is little more attractive.

cartouche An oval frame with a straight stroke tangential to one end, employed by the Egyptians to enclose the HIEROGLYPHS of a royal name. [84]

cashel ◊ RATH

Cassibile A cemetery of some 2,000 rock-cut tombs near Syracuse in Sicily, the type site of a Late Bronze Age phase (= PANTALICA II). The characteristic pottery is buff with irregular all-over arcading in brown to black paint, well described by the names 'feather-painted' or 'plumed' ware. It is dated c 1000–850 BC.

Castelluccio An Early Bronze Age village and cemetery of rock-cut tombs excavated by Orsi 1891–2 near Syracuse in Sicily. One tomb had a carved façade and several were closed by slabs with carved double spirals [39]. The characteristic pottery was

Fig. 39. Tomb stela from Castelluccio

a buff ware painted simply with black lines, triangles, etc. Shapes included splay-necked cups and pedestalled bowls. Its origins have been sought in Middle HELLADIC Greece. The discovery of fine examples of the BOSSED BONE PLAQUE supports this link.

casting jet A plug of bronze which originally filled the aperture or gate into a MOULD. In finishing the object, the jet would be knocked off. Examples are occasionally present as components of a founder's HOARD, awaiting melting down.

casting seam Where objects are cast in a closed MOULD of more than one piece, the molten metal will run a short distance into the joint between the pieces of the mould. This sharp ridge or seam would normally be smoothed off by grinding when the object is being finished, but may remain visible.

Castor A Roman settlement on the north bank of the Nene, 4 miles west of Peterborough. A distinctive pottery ware once named after the site is now generally, and more accurately, described as NENE VALLEY WARE.

castro Portuguese term for a fortified site, ranging from the small walled citadels of the COPPER AGE (eg VILA NOVA DE SÃO PEDRO) to the HILLFORT settlements of the Celtic Iron Age.

catacomb An underground cemetery of Imperial Roman date, consisting of galleries, burial niches and chambers cut into the rock. Catacombs came to be associated particularly with the Christian and Jewish communities. The name was first applied to the very extensive ones of Rome itself, but they are widely known elsewhere, especially around the Mediterranean. Further north there are examples in Germany and Hungary. The inappropriate term 'catacomb grave' has been coined for the tombs of an Early Bronze Age phase of the south Russian KURGAN culture. These tombs are distributed from the Dniestr to the Caucasus, and are in fact SHAFT-AND-CHAMBER TOMBS covered by barrows.

Çatal Hüyük (pron Chatal) One of the world's earliest towns, it stands on the edge of the Konya plateau in south central Turkey, and was excavated by Mellaart in the 1950s and 60s. Twelve building levels have been dug so far, spanning the millennium from c6150 BC (a radiocarbon date). Though pottery had apparently only just been introduced, it was associated with a fully developed agriculture, using EMMER, EINKORN, bread WHEAT, BARLEY, peas and vetches. Sheep and cattle were bred and hunting continued. Trade in such materials as OBSIDIAN and seashells was extensive. The flaked stone tools were particularly fine, and polished obsidian mirrors also noteworthy.

The architecture was curious, the mud-brick buildings being rectangular and completely juxtaposed, so that access was only possible through openings in the roofs, across which all movement round the settlement took place. Shrines were very frequent, containing modelled bulls' heads with actual horn cores incorporated, recessed outlines of animals, a rich series of wall frescoes, painted or in relief, and a number of carved stone figurines portraying the mother goddess or, more rarely, her male consort. The dead were buried beneath plastered platforms within the shrines.

cattle These were widely distributed in the wild state, and are beautifully portrayed in some of the Palaeolithic CAVE ART. This wild species, the aurochs or *Bos primigenius*, was brought into domestication in a number of centres. The earliest occurrences so far reported are in northern Greece before 6000 BC. Thereafter, different breeds were developed, notably *B. longifrons* in southwest Asia and Europe, and the humped zebu, *B. indica*, in India.

cauldron A large metal bowl for cooking purposes. It is usually round based, with a heavy flange rim, and with three or four handles for suspending it over the fire. The best known examples date from the European Late Bronze Age, with their origin in a magnificent series from URARTU. [202]

causewayed camp The characteristic

enclosure of the south British Neolithic (◇WINDMILL HILL, HEMBURY) [210]. The normal situation is a hilltop which is enclosed by a series of concentric ditches with internal banks. The ditches range from one to four in number, and are not continuous but are interrupted by solid causeways. There is little evidence for houses or permanent structures inside the enclosure, but pottery, animal bones and domestic refuse stratified within the ditches show that the camps were visited throughout the entire Neolithic period. Their function is far from clear. The multiple causeways and the fact that the ditches were allowed to silt up would have made the earthworks unsuitable as defences or cattle enclosures. Perhaps the ditches, like those of the HENGE monuments, were intended to demarcate an area rather than to prevent passage. The current theory, in fact little more than a guess, has it that the camps were meeting places used at intervals by the population of a wide area, rather like the seasonal fairs of the Middle Ages.

cave art The Upper PALAEOLITHIC period saw the development of man's oldest surviving art. It can be divided into MOBILIARY ART (on small objects) and cave art proper (paintings and engravings on cave walls). The subject matter of cave art is predominantly animals, and above all the large herbivores (mammoth, horse, ox, deer and bison) which were hunted during the Late PLEISTOCENE. Human figures are relatively uncommon and are poorly drawn, but non-representational 'signs' are frequent. There are no landscapes, or naturalistic scenes involving figures or animals in a setting. The artist used a range of reds, blacks, yellows and browns derived from ochres and other naturally occurring mineral pigments. The greatest concentration of painted caves is in southwest France and northeast Spain, but outlying sites have been discovered in Portugal, Italy, Greece and the Ural mountains.

The purpose and meaning of cave art are still obscure. It cannot be purely decorative, for much of the art is found in dark and inaccessible parts of the caves, far away from the entrance zones where the people lived. Moreover, paintings and

Fig. 40. Painted bison from Altamira

engravings often overlap each other, or are superimposed in a way that spoils the decorative effect. One school of thought believes that the key to the interpretation lies in the concept of sympathetic or hunting magic, the belief that the act of drawing an animal will help the hunter to go out and kill one. In support of this view, some of the abstract 'signs' have been interpreted as arrows, wounds, or traps. On the basis of the same evidence other scholars have reached widely different conclusions, some preferring a totemistic interpretation of the art, others believing that it symbolizes the complementary male and female principles, each of which is represented by certain species of animal in association with particular signs. None of these explanations is completely convincing, and the study of recent primitive peoples shows that art can have many different functions in society. It is unlikely that we shall ever know the truth. ◊ ALTAMIRA, LASCAUX and [40]

Cayla de Mailhac A hilltop settlement and a series of cemeteries near Narbonne, providing the key sequence for the Late Bronze Age and Early Iron Age of southwest France. Occupation began just before 700 BC with an URNFIELD culture of final Bronze Age type. During Phase II (c600–550) iron became fairly common, and a cart burial from the cemetery of La Redorte shows connexions with the HALLSTATT Iron Age cultures. Phase III belongs to the full Iron Age, and is dated to the second half of c6 by imports of Greek Black Figure Ware and Etruscan pottery. The settlement of Phase IV was enclosed by a rampart, and had houses of sun-dried brick. Datable material included Greek Red Figure pottery and FIBULA brooches of Hallstatt D/early LA TÈNE types. The fifth, and last, phase belonged to a middle stage of the La Tène culture, no later than 100 BC.

celt (I) with soft 'c'. The usual name in the last century for an AXE, ADZE or HOE blade of stone or bronze. The term has largely died out except for special cases, such as the DANUBIAN shoe-last celt [20c]. Its passing should not be regretted as it was a mistake in the first place, a misreading of the Latin text of the Vulgate. (2) with hard 'c' ◊ CELTS

Celtic art (otherwise known at least in its early stages as LA TÈNE art) An art style, one of the most impressive in antiquity, which developed amongst the CELTS soon after 500 BC. It was first created for the chieftains of an area centred on the middle Rhine, extending to the upper Danube and the Marne (◊ WALDALGESHEIM). Thence it spread widely [41] but never as widely

Fig. 41. Horn cap from Brentford in the Waldalgesheim style

as the Celts themselves. Many of its finest achievements were produced in the British Isles in CI BC and AD, after the Celts had lost control of their continental territories. Indeed in Ireland, beyond the reach of the Roman armies, it survived to return after the Roman withdrawal and fertilize the artistic revival in NORTHUMBRIA in C7 AD.

The main factors in its development were the love of the Celtic aristocracy for ostentation, and the introduction by way of the Rhône or Alpine passes of classical exemplars, notably the bronze jugs and other appurtenances of the new fashion for wine drinking. To this was added a taste for animal design, often fantastic animals, derived from the SCYTHIANS of the steppes. But behind it all lies the artistic genius of the Celtic craftsmen, building on the tradition of HALLSTATT geometric and abstract design. The result is the bold, curvilinear La Tène style, both linear and plastic, with a fascinating blurring of the distinction between naturalistic and abstract, and a strong taste for balance without symmetry. It appears most commonly in bronzework, war and horse gear, and eating and drinking vessels – just those fields of activity emphasized by the Celts. There are also, however, notable examples of monumental stone carving, many with religious intent. [60]

Celtic field Traces of ancient field systems may still be visible on the ground in areas where later agriculture has not removed them. The oldest examples in Britain are the so-called Celtic fields which are blocks of arable land (sometimes associated with farmsteads, HOLLOW WAYS, stockades and enclosures) divided into a patchwork of more or less square units. Individual fields are usually about half an acre in area, and never more than two acres. They are defined by LYNCHETS at the upper and lower edges, and by slightly raised ridges at the sides. The term 'Celtic' is a misnomer. The oldest fields go back to the Early Bronze Age (around 1500 BC), but most of the extant groups belong to the later part of the Bronze Age (from c1000), the Iron Age, and even the Roman era, when native methods of farming persisted outside the areas of VILLA agriculture. Similar fields are known from Scandinavia and the Netherlands.

Celts (adj Celtic) An important protohistoric people of central and western Europe, also known as the Gauls and Galatians. The classical writers from Hecataeus (c500 BC) and Herodotus (c450) distinguished them from neighbouring peoples by their appearance, customs, language and political organization. They spoke of them as tall, fair, excitable, ostentatious in dress and action, and fierce warriors. They are portrayed by themselves and others with wavy swept-back hair, heavy moustaches, and wearing the TORC or neck-ring [42]. In the early c4 BC Gauls invaded Italy from their homeland north of the Alps, sacked Rome, and

Fig. 42. Self portrait of a Celt, Mšecké Žehrovice

settled in the Po valley. A century later the Galatians invaded Greece and sacked Delphi, while others crossed to ravage Anatolia and finally settle there. From 225 BC on, Rome gradually extended control over their territories, first northern Italy, in c2 Spain and Provence, in 58–52 BC Gaul, from AD 43 Britain. Only Scotland and Ireland remained unsubjugated.

Linguistically, a branch of the INDO-EUROPEAN group of languages can be firmly associated with this people from the evidence of personal and place names, supported by a few inscriptions in the Latin alphabet but vernacular tongue. Of its two branches the Q-Celtic or Goidelic survives in the Old Irish and Gaelic, and P-Celtic (the names reflect a major consonant change) or Brythonic in Welsh and Breton.

Archaeologically, a close correlation with certain cultural groups is possible, but there is no single Celtic culture one can point to. The Gaulish cemeteries in Italy have been identified and studied. In Spain the URNFIELD cemeteries and areas with Celtic place names tally closely. In central Europe aristocratic burials of the HALLSTATT culture, often containing wagons or horses, were certainly Celtic, if some doubt attaches to the humbler urnfields there. The problem is at its most acute in Britain, where the BEAKER folk of c2000 BC and the MARNIANS of c250 have both been claimed as the first Celtic inhabitants. The most notable material evidence for the Celts is provided by the LA TÈNE or CELTIC ART. The implications of this and of the aristocratic burials agree well with the literary traditions of Celtic culture as it survived particularly in Ireland. A clear picture emerges of a Heroic Age, with emphasis on courage on the numerous battlefields, unstinting hospitality in the home, and a brave show everywhere.

cenote A kind of natural well on the arid plateau of Yucatan, Mexico, formed by the collapse of the surface limestone which exposed the ground water below. Without this source of water the MAYA civilization could never have flourished in Yucatan. At CHICHÉN ITZÁ and other sites, rich offerings have been recovered from the cenotes.

centuriation The practice of dividing up the country around a newly planted Roman colony by roads or lesser boundaries into square blocks, normally 776 yds a side, as allotments to the colonists. This pattern has survived, at least partially, in many places on the Continent but has not yet been convincingly demonstrated anywhere in Britain.

cephalic index One of the most frequently recorded anthropological criteria in man is the shape of his skull [43]. The index is obtained by expressing the maximum breadth as a percentage of the maximum length, measured from a point just above the eyebrow ridges. A figure below 75 is described as long-headed or dolichocephalic, 75 to 80 meso- or mesati-

cephalic, above 80 round-headed or brachycephalic. More strictly, the term should be applied to measurements taken on the living head, -cranial being more appropriate on the skull than -cephalic.

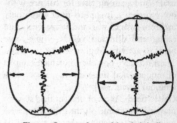

Fig. 43. Long and round-headed skulls

ceramic analysis Several techniques are important for the detailed study of pottery. Colour should be objectively described by reference to the MUNSELL SOIL COLOR CHARTS. Examination of a thin section under the microscope may reveal the technique of manufacture and allow the identification of mineral grains in the tempering. Refiring experiments will show how the original baking was carried out.

ceremonial centre An architectural complex which differed from a village or true town in consisting wholly or mainly of religious and governmental buildings which were used at prescribed times by the people of a wide surrounding area, who most of the year lived dispersed in farms throughout the countryside. This pattern of settlement was common in parts of the New World.

Chagar Bazar A tell near the KHABUR river in eastern Syria excavated by Mallowan 1934–7. It yielded an important sequence of prehistoric wares, particularly HALAF, and remained in occupation until c1400 BC.

chalcedony A hard stone, related to quartz, used in antiquity for beads, seals, and even on occasion as a substitute for FLINT where the latter was scarce. Varieties include agate and CARNELIAN.

Chalcolithic ⧈ COPPER AGE

Chaldaea An alternative name for Babylonia in the last period of its power (626–539 BC), deriving from the Kaldu, the name of the tribe of ARAMAEANS from which its ruling dynasty sprang. Its more important rulers were Nabopolassar, NEBUCHADNEZZAR and Nabonidus, who ruled an empire from the Mediterranean to the Persian Gulf from their capital at BABYLON. It was instrumental in the destruction of ASSYRIA in 612, but itself fell to CYRUS the Persian in 539.

chalice ⧈ FRUITSTAND

chamber tomb A stone-built tomb, often MEGALITHIC in construction, which served as a vault in which successive burials were made over a long period. The term is also used for a rock-cut tomb, especially the SHAFT-AND-CHAMBER TOMB, with a similar burial rite. Chamber tombs were built in many parts of the world and at many different times. For the European varieties ⧈ CORBELLING, COURT CAIRN, DOLMEN, DOMU DE JANAS, DYSS, ENTRANCE GRAVE, GALLERY GRAVE, GIANTS' GRAVE, HUNEBED, HYPOGEUM, PASSAGE GRAVE, PORTAL DOLMEN, THOLOS, TRANSEPTED GALLERY GRAVE, SEVERN-COTSWOLD TOMB, WEDGE-SHAPED GALLERY GRAVE

Champollion, Jean-Francois ⧈ HIEROGLYPHS

Chancay ⧈ CUISMANCU

Chan Chan The capital of the CHIMÚ empire, situated near the modern Peruvian city of Trujillo. It covers about 14 square miles, had an estimated population of 40–50,000, and includes 9 large rectangular walled enclosures separated by irrigated gardens and cemeteries. Each enclosure was probably the headquarters of a clan, and contains storehouses, reservoirs, adobe platforms and palaces whose walls are decorated with plaster reliefs.

Chanhudaro A double TELL on the east bank of the Indus in Pakistan, south of MOHENJO-DARO. It was excavated by

Mackay in 1935–6. Mound I contained material of the INDUS CIVILIZATION only. The three lowest levels reached in mound II yielded the same. They were overlain by poor levels of JHUKAR and Jhangar type, the latter probably of historic date.

channelled With broad INCISED or GROOVED decoration.

chape The metal case protecting the tip of a SWORD scabbard. [186 h–j]

charcoal identification Charcoal is frequently found in archaeological contexts, and identification of the type of tree from which it came can give useful results. The method is to examine it in transverse, radial and tangential sections, each wood having a characteristic structure. The information may be of interest for environmental studies (⧈ POLLEN ANALYSIS), but its main value will be for showing the use made of different resources by ancient man.

chariot A light vehicle of war, usually carrying two men, a warrior and a driver. A clumsy prototype with four solid wheels and drawn by four asses, goes back to the URUK period in Mesopotamia, and is figured on the standard of UR, but this is

Fig. 44. Chariot painted on Greek geometric vase, C8 BC

better described as a war wagon. Only with the introduction of the light version, with two spoked wheels and horses to draw it, does the chariot become important. It first appears in the Near East in C17 BC, associated with the immigrant peoples from the north who became the HYKSOS, KASSITES and HURRI. The ARYANS carried it to India, and in China it formed the core of the SHANG army. The MYCENABANS introduced it to Europe, where it spread widely and rapidly [44].

It revolutionized warfare by allowing warriors to be transferred rapidly from one part of a battlefield to another. But the cost of its upkeep kept it an aristocratic prerogative, and its popularity as a funeral offering may be explained by this. Graves containing chariots have been found in Shang China, in Cyprus from C7 BC, and among the LA TÈNE CELTS. The earliest Celtic chariot burials are in the Rhineland and eastern France with dates around 500 BC, but slightly later burials are known from east Yorkshire (C3 and C2) and Europe as far east as Hungary, Bulgaria and south Russia.

The chariot was finally replaced by the mounted warrior or knight when horses of sufficient strength had been bred in the late and post-Roman periods.

Charsada (anc **Pushkalavati**) The capital of the ACHAEMENID SATRAPY of GANDHARA, near Peshawar in the North-West Frontier Province of Pakistan. Excavations in 1958 on the Bala Hisar identified the defences overrun by Alexander the Great in 327 BC. A separate mound nearby was the Indo-Greek city of C2 BC.

Chassey A Neolithic culture, with many regional subgroups, found over most of France. By c3500 BC Chassey pottery had superseded IMPRESSED WARE in the Midi, and the new style is found in caves, village sites, CISTS, pit graves and MEGALITHIC CHAMBER TOMBS. In this area the earliest Chassey pottery is often decorated with scratched geometric patterns, whereas the later wares tend to be plain and provided with FLÛTE DE PAN lugs [45]. In north and central France, where the culture cannot be recognized before about 3000, it is impossible to make distinctions between early and late Chassey. In many areas the

Chassey people were the first NEOLITHIC farmers, and the Mediterranean version of the culture was modified to suit local conditions. The Jura has lake villages and fortified sites (like the type site, the Camp de Chassey, in the Côte d'Or), while the

Fig. 45. Chassey pot with flûte de Pan lug

pottery and flintwork of the Paris basin differ in many ways from those of the Midi. One distinctive form of vessel, the vase support with scratched decoration, is confined to the Paris basin and western France.

Châtelperronian The earliest industry of Upper PALAEOLITHIC type in south-west and central France. It owes something to the preceding MOUSTERIAN tradition. Its diagnostic implement is the Châtelperron knife [46], a blade with a straight

Fig. 46. Châtelperron knife

cutting edge and a curved, blunted back. The Châtelperronian has radiocarbon dates of 31,690 BC ± 250 and 31,550 ± 400 at Grotte du Renne (Arcy-sur-Cure, Yonne), but it may have started as early a 35–34,000. ⟷ PÉRIGORDIAN

Chavín, Chavín de Huántar A CEREMONIAL CENTRE 10,000 ft up in the north Peruvian Andes. The buildings, which show several periods of reconstruction, consist of various temple platforms containing a series of interlinked galleries and chambers on different levels. In the oldest part of the complex is a granite block, the Lanzón, on which is carved a human figure with feline fangs and with snakes in place of hair. Relief carvings in a similar style decorate the lintels, gateways and cornices at the site, and human and jaguar heads of stone were tenoned into the outside wall of one of the platforms.

The origins of the Chavín culture are still obscure. Comparisons are hampered by the lack of a reliable chronology: the first (Rocas) pottery at Chavín itself may be older than 1200 BC, and the culture might end anywhere in the period 600–200 BC. Whatever its origins and date, the Chavín style quickly spread over the whole of northern Peru, both in the highlands (KOTOSH) and along the coast, where the local style is called 'Cupisnique'. On the coast, where stone is scarce, the highland architecture is replaced by work in adobe. Stone sculpture is also absent, but Chavín symbolism and jaguar designs appear on pottery, textiles, metalwork and bone objects all the way to the central coast. Further south, the PARACAS culture shows strong and continuing Chavín influence, and Chavín must be considered the first great HORIZON style of Peru.

cheek-piece (1) A bone or metal rod at either end of a horse-BIT for the attachment of the reins. (2) A plate of bronze or leather attached to the lower rim of a HELMET to hang over and protect the cheek.

Chellean Term once used for the early stages of the European Lower PALAEO-LITHIC HANDAXE tradition. The name was an unfortunate one, for the type site (Chelles-sur-Marne) has yielded only late and evolved tools of the kind now called ACHEULIAN. The phrase 'Chelleo-Acheulian' was at one time used for the succession of African handaxe industries as a whole, but has now been superseded by 'Acheulian'. ⟡ ABBEVILLIAN

Cheng Chou (Honan, north China) The site of the SHANG dynasty capital from C15 to C13 BC when it was succeeded by ANYANG. Following villages of the YANG SHAO and LUNG SHAN cultures, four phases of Shang occupation were traced. The city was surrounded by a wall of rammed earth 66 ft thick and originally 23 ft or more high, enclosing a rectangular area 1,900 by 2,200 yds. Cemeteries of pit graves were found but no royal tombs like those of Anyang.

Cheops, Kheops, Khufu The pharaoh of the Egyptian 4th dynasty who erected the Great PYRAMID of Giza. He reigned c2570 BC.

Chephren, Khephren, Khafra, Kaph-re The pharaoh of the Egyptian 4th dynasty who erected the second PYRAMID of the Giza group. The Great SPHINX was also his work. He reigned c2540 BC.

chert A poor quality FLINT.

chevaux de frise A defence work consisting of closely set spikes or upright stones, and serving to impede or break up a cavalry charge. Sometimes found as the outer defence of a HILLFORT.

Chibcha or **Muisca** A confederation of peoples with an advanced culture who were occupying the Bogotá and Tunja basins of the Colombian Andes at the time of the Spanish conquest. Each new chieftain, when he took office, coated his body with gold dust which was washed off in the sacred lake Guatavita, the custom which may have inspired Spanish legends of El Dorado (which means 'the gilded man').

Chichén Itzá A MAYA CEREMONIAL CENTRE in the northern part of the Yucatan peninsula, Mexico. There are traces of early occupation at the site, but the oldest surviving buildings are in the Puuc style of c9 and early C10 AD. During the late C10 TOLTEC influence becomes so strong as to suggest an actual invasion. The new buildings (including BALL-COURTS and temples with columns depicting the god QUETZALCÓATL) have their closest parallels at TULA, and offerings thrown into the Sacred CENOTE, or Well of Sacrifice, show widespread trade contacts. Chichén Itzá remained an important centre until about 1200, when it was superseded by MAYAPÁN.

Chichimec The name given collectively to the barbarian tribes who invaded central Mexico from the northwest. In origin they may have been farming peoples who had spread into marginal land, from which they were driven back by climatic deterioration.

Some of these groups may have entered the Valley of Mexico after the fall of TEOTIHUACÁN, and there is a Chichimec constituent in TOLTEC culture. By convention, however, the Chichimec period proper begins after the destruction of TULA and the decline of Toltec influence in about AD 1200. In 1224 a band of NÁHUATL-speaking Chichimecs entered the northern part of the Valley and established a kingdom at Tenayuca. After their arrival the barbarians settled down again to farming life, learned the arts of civilization and were eventually absorbed into the AZTEC confederation; but on the inhospitable plateau to the north independent Chichimecs maintained their nomadic and hunting way of life until the Spanish conquest.

Childe, V. Gordon (1892–1957) One of the leading archaeologists of the mid C20, successively professor at Edinburgh and London. He died in his native Australia shortly after his retirement. His most significant contribution was perhaps his emphasis not so much on the detailed study of artifacts as on the human society, or at least CULTURE, which could be recognized from them. His grasp of the prehistoric material from the whole of Europe was unequalled. As well as many works of prehistory (*Dawn of European Civilization*, 1st edn 1925), he added several on methodology (*Social Evolution*, 1951, *Piecing Together the Past*, 1956) which also represented a significant advance on previous work.

Chimú The most powerful state (◇ CUISMANCU and CHINCHA) to emerge on the Peruvian coast after the decline of HUARI influence. The Chimú empire stretched from Tumbez in the north to a point near Lima in the south, and was a despotic and urban state (◇ CHAN CHAN), with great cities, fortresses, road systems, and vast irrigation works which sometimes combined the resources of several valleys. Crafts were organized on an industrial scale, and the best known products are objects of gold and silver, and black pottery with moulded reliefs. Other vessels are in the shape of animals, houses and everyday objects. Legend records that the Chimú state as a political entity was the creation of Ñançen-pinco, thought to have reigned in about AD 1370, but archaeology shows that Chimú material culture developed gradually during the centuries after 1000 from the final Huari-derived culture of the north coast. The Chimú kingdom was conquered by the INCA and absorbed into their empire in about 1470.

Chincha The chronicler Garcilaso de la Vega mentions a powerful state on the south coast of Peru from the Cañete to Nasca valleys at the time when the CHIMÚ empire was flourishing in the north. This report seems greatly exaggerated, and archaeology suggests that Chincha was at best a small state which grew up in the valley of the same name after the decline of HUARI influence. Chincha reached the height of its power in the early C15 when it also controlled part of the Pisco valley, and it retained a certain prestige under the INCA after their conquest of the area in 1476.

chip-carving A form of EXCISED DECORATION in which small chips, usually triangular and always rectilinear, are cut from the surface. It is found in both woodwork and pottery, when it has to be done before the clay is fired. FALSE RELIEF is a special version of this technique.

chipping floor A workshop area marked

by a scatter of debris from the manufacture of chipped stone tools.

Chiriquí An area of Panama best known for its fine gold objects and elegant pottery decorated with NEGATIVE PAINTING and polychrome patterns. On the coast the Chiriquí phase has been dated AD 1100 to the Spanish conquest, but it may have begun some centuries earlier in the highlands.

chloromelanite ◊ GREENSTONE

Choga Zanbil (anc **Dur-Untash**) A city near SUSA in southwest Iran. It was built as a capital for ELAM by Untash-Gal in C13 BC. Between 1951-62 Ghirshman excavated a massive and well preserved ZIGGURAT with surrounding temples and cult installations, three palaces, a reservoir and the fortification walls.

Cholula (Puebla, Mexico) One of the greatest cities and religious centres of ancient Mexico. The site was first occupied c600-300 BC by villagers of the PRE-CLASSIC period, but soon afterwards Cholula came within the orbit of the TEOTIHUACÁN civilization. During the Teotihuacán period at the site, a major pyramid was built and subsequently enlarged three times to produce the biggest pyramid in Mexico, a vast structure 180 ft high and covering 25 acres. Tunnelling has revealed the older pyramids nesting inside the final version. Around AD 8-900, after the decline of Teotihuacán, Cholula became a centre of the Mixteca-Puebla culture (◊ MIXTEC) whose art influenced that of most of the other Mexican POST-CLASSIC cultures. Cholula polychrome wares were highly prized by the AZTECS. When the Spaniards reached Cholula they found a splendid city dominated by the ruins of the Great Pyramid.

chopper A large PEBBLE TOOL with the cutting edge flaked from one side only. ◊ CHOPPING TOOL

chopping tool A CORE tool with a transverse cutting edge made by flaking from two faces [140] (cf CHOPPER). It is especially characteristic of Middle PLEISTOCENE industries in Asia (eg CHOUKOUTIEN).

Chou The Chinese dynasty which overthrew that of SHANG in 1027 BC and was itself destroyed by the Ch'in in 256. Its capital in the Western Chou period was at Tsung Chou in Shensi, moving to LOYANG in Honan in 771, to initiate the Eastern Chou period. Political decline followed, the central power being constantly eroded by the feudal states. The archaeological evidence, mainly from the excavation of tombs, gives a rather different picture. The main technological advance was the introduction of IRON c 500 BC, both forged and cast (Europe did not learn of the latter until the Middle Ages). An important group of tools for agriculture and carpentry were found in a tomb at Hui Hsien. Bronze remained the material for weapons. Other cultural innovations included the sword (late C6), the crossbow, and the use of roof tiles (c C4). The chariot is more fully documented now, as many as nineteen coming from a single tomb at Liu Li Ko. Otherwise there was little change from the Shang period.

In art, the Chou bronzes begin by continuing the Shang style in rather simpler form, with more stylized motifs and freer use of inscriptions. In C7 shapes become more flamboyant, interlace work appears, and the decoration is progressively more tightly compressed.

Choukoutien A locality near Pekin, China, which was the scene of one of the first discoveries of the extinct form of man now known as HOMO ERECTUS. In limestone fissures were Middle PLEISTOCENE deposits, probably of MINDEL date, some 500,000 years old, which yielded the remains of about 40 individuals, together with extinct animals, FLAKE and CHOPPING TOOLS, and traces of fire. This Middle Palaeolithic material was present at the parts of the site known as Localities 1, 13 and 15. From the 'Upper Cave' came skeletons of HOMO SAPIENS type with stone and bone tools belonging to the Upper Palaeolithic.

Christy, Henry (1810–65) A wealthy banker and businessman (one of his claims to fame was the introduction of Turkish towelling into England) who travelled widely in the years from 1850 onwards and accumulated what was in its time the greatest private ethnological collection in the world. Christy's journeys took him from Mexico to Hudson's Bay. Then in 1863 he and EDOUARD LARTET began excavations at the great series of PALAEOLITHIC caves in southwest France.

Christy died in 1865 of a chill contracted during a visit to cave sites in Belgium, but left money in his will for the publication of *Reliquiae Aquitanicae*, which embodied the results of his French research. He left the Palaeolithic material to be divided between France and Britain, and his trustees presented the rest of the ethnological collection to the British Museum together with a sum of money for further purchases. The Christy Collection now contains about 30,000 specimens.

chronology ◊ DATING

chthonic Of the underworld.

chullpa A cylindrical or square burial tower of stone or adobe found in parts of the southern Andes, especially around Lake Titicaca, just before and after the INCA conquest. Some of the cruder chullpas are associated with pottery derived from final TIAHUANACO styles, but chullpas made of dressed stone are of Inca date.

Ciempozuelos A site near Madrid in Spain which has given its name to a group of late BEAKERS on the Meseta. Most of the material comes from pit tombs or cist burials. The pottery is distinguished by its complex incised, not comb-stamped, decoration. It survived in use through the whole 2nd millennium BC.

Cimmerians A nomadic people of the Russian STEPPES who were driven thence by the SCYTHIANS in c8 BC. They retreated through the Caucasus to cause havoc in Anatolia, destroying Phrygia, Lydia and the Greek cities on the coast. Their relatives the Thracians retreated similarly into the Balkans, where they had rather more success in establishing themselves north of the Aegean.

cinerary urn An URN used to bury the ashes of the dead in after CREMATION.

cinnabar Mercuric sulphide, occurring naturally as a red ore. Like red OCHRE, it was occasionally used as a colouring matter. The Romans in particular employed it to pick out inscriptions carved in stone.

circle ◊ STONE CIRCLE

Circumpolar cultures A group of related cultures in the forest zone of Eurasia, to the north of the region where settled farming life was possible. Although contemporary with Neolithic, and even Bronze Age, communities farther south, the Circumpolar tribes remained semi-nomadic hunters and gatherers. They adopted pottery from the farming peoples and made egg-shaped bowls with pitted or comb-stamped decoration, but their characteristic tools were hunting and woodworking equipment, often of ground slate. Rock-carvings and actual finds attest the use of boats, skis and sledges, and this mobility is further demonstrated by long-distance trade. Sites, both villages and cemeteries, are usually close to water, and fishing was an important activity.

cire perdue (the **lost wax** process) A technique of casting objects in metal [123d]. It is particularly useful for a figurine or other piece too awkwardly shaped for casting easily in a MOULD. The object is modelled simply in wax, often around a clay core to economize on metal. The whole is then coated in clay and baked, vents being left for the molten wax to escape. Through the same vents liquid metal is poured in to fill the cavity thus left. When the metal has cooled the terracotta covering is broken, to leave the metal casting, an exact copy of the original wax figure. The technique was already known in Early Dynastic UR, soon after 3000 BC, and has been widely used throughout the Old World for the casting of bronze since. In South and Middle America, cire perdue casting in gold and TUMBAGA was perfected centuries before the conquest.

cist A box-shaped burial structure made of stone slabs set on edge. Cists may be either sunk below ground level or built on the land surface, in which case they are covered by a protective BARROW.

Clactonian A Lower PALAEOLITHIC flint industry principally of Great Inter-Glacial (MINDEL-RISS) date, named after discoveries at Clacton-on-Sea, Essex. Apart from the tip of a wooden spear, the artifacts consisted of trimmed flint FLAKES and chipped pebbles, some of which can be classified as CHOPPER tools. HAND-AXES were absent. At SWANSCOMBE and other sites Clactonian tools underlay gravels containing Middle ACHEULIAN hand-axes. The Clactonian seems therefore to have coexisted with Early Acheulian. Some authorities believe that the two industries are quite distinct, while others maintain that both assemblages might have been made by the same people, and that the Clactonian could in theory be an Acheulian industry from which handaxes were absent because such tools were not needed for the jobs carried out at a particular site. Clactonian and related industries are distributed throughout the north European plain, north and east of the main handaxe concentrations, and the difference in environment might perhaps account for the differences between the tool kits.

Classic period A term found only in New World archaeology. (In the Old World 'classical' is used but is restricted to Greek and Roman civilization.) It was originally coined for the stage of MAYA civilization which fell between C3 and AD 600 and was characterized by great CERE-MONIAL CENTRES, advanced material culture, and fine art. By extension, the word came to be used for other Mexican cultures with a similar level of excellence (◊ TEOTIHUACÁN, MONTE ALBÁN, EL TAJÍN). In these areas the cultural climax was roughly contemporary with that of the Maya, and the term Classic (which originally had only a qualitative sense) took on a chronological meaning as well. The expression has become a cliché of Mexican archaeology and is probably here to stay, but in many ways the concept of a Classic period is misleading. Even in the Maya zone the line between Classic and PRE-CLASSIC status is difficult to draw. Elsewhere (eg among the OLMEC) most of the traits of 'Classic' civilization appeared during the millennium before the 'Classic period' in the chronological sense. The situation is as bad for the centuries after AD 900, and the great TOLTEC and AZTEC civilizations, which are qualitatively 'Classic' by any standards, have been relegated to the limbo of a POST-CLASSIC period. Attempts have been made to apply the system to Peru and to create a Classic period for the MOCHICA and NASCA cultures.

Clava tombs A small group of PASSAGE GRAVES in Scotland on the south side of the Moray Firth. Some of the stones bear CUP MARKS, and many of the cairns are ringed by free-standing stone circles.

cleaver A heavy CORE or FLAKE tool, with a D-shaped outline and a straight transverse cutting edge [82c]. Technologically it is related to the HANDAXE, and is often found as a component of ACHEULIAN handaxe industries.

closed find ◊ ASSOCIATION

Clovis point A concave-based projectile point with a longitudinal groove on each face running from the base to a point not more than half way along the tool [47f]. Clovis points and the artifacts associated with them (grouped together as the Llano complex) are among the earliest tools known from the New World and have been found over most of North America, with a few outliers as far south as Mexico and Panama. Clovis material occurs at open air camp sites, and at butchering sites where hunters killed and cut up mammoths. Radiocarbon dating shows that Clovis

agriculture and the knowledge of pottery, forms the basis of the farming cultures of MOGOLLON and HOHOKAM which develop by C100 BC. ◊◊VENTANA CAVE

Coclé A province of Panama where very

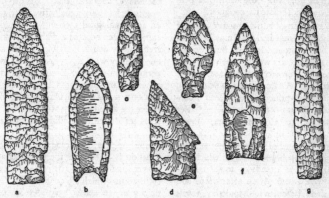

Fig. 47. New World projectile points: (a) Scotsbluff; (b) Folsom; (c) Sandia; (d) Cody knife; (e) fishtail point; (f) Clovis; (g) Eden

points were in use during the 10th millennium BC (roughly the time of the TWO CREEKS INTERVAL), though some examples may be earlier still. ◊ BLACK-WATER DRAW

Clyde-Carlingford tomb ◊ COURT CAIRN

Cnossus ◊ KNOSSOS

Cochise A local variant of the DESERT CULTURE centred on southwest New Mexico and southeast Arizona. The earliest (Sulphur Spring) stage begins in the centuries before 7000 BC and at the type site is said to be associated with mammoth and extinct horse remains. After a poorly known Cazador stage comes a third (Chiricahua, c 5000–2000) with evidence of early cultivated MAIZE from the Bat Cave. Here there is a radiocarbon date of 3655 ± 290 BC (although the geological evidence suggests a rather later figure). The final (San Pedro) stage has the first pit dwellings and, with improved

rich tombs have yielded striking polychrome vessels with flamboyant scrollwork patterns. Associated finds include jewellery of gold and TUMBAGA. The Early Coclé stage may have begun by c AD 500, and the succeeding (Late Coclé and Herrera) phases continue the tradition until the Spanish conquest.

codex (pl codices) In Mexico, any manuscript painted before the Spanish conquest or written in the native manner during the early Spanish period. The surviving codices are mostly religious or historical documents and take the form of long strips of deerskin or bark paper which are folded concertina-fashion, like a modern map. The finest of the preserved examples come from the MIXTEC territory. Codices of the Colonial period are written on paper and may resemble a book in format.

Cody complex A North American flint industry characterized by the Eden and Scotsbluff varieties of stemmed point with parallel PRESSURE FLAKING, and by a kind of oblique knife with a shoulder on one side (the Cody knife) [47]. These are usually found with bison remains, and their probable date is c7500–5000 BC.

Colchester (anc **Camulodunum**) It began life as capital of the tribe of the Trinovantes, who held roughly what is now Essex in the earlier CI BC. By AD 43 it had been conquered by the Catuvellauni and had become the capital of Cunobelinus (Cymbeline, perhaps also Old King Cole). The great Lexden barrow covered the remains of a member of his family. The Romans refounded the town as a colony for time-expired soldiers, and as the religious centre of the province. Some of the masonry of the temple to Claudius survives in the foundations of the Norman castle. A native type of shrine has been studied at Gosbeck's Farm outside the town. Camolodunum recovered from its destruction by Boudicca and flourished throughout the Roman period, possibly even surviving into Saxon and later times. It is a site difficult to investigate as it lies under the modern town.

collagen content Animal bone consists basically of calcium phosphate, associated with two organic materials, fat and bone protein or collagen. On death, the fats break down and are rapidly washed out. The collagen survives much longer, though in decreasing amounts. It can be measured by analysis of the nitrogen present. The rate of decay is neither uniform nor universal, but bones of different dates in a single deposit can be separated on the basis of their nitrogen content. The test is used mainly in association with the FLUORINE TEST and RADIOMETRIC ASSAY, as in the cases of PILTDOWN and SWANSCOMBE Man.

collared urn ⟡ URN

collective tomb A CHAMBER TOMB, either rock-cut or MEGALITHIC, built to contain many burials, often successive depositions spread over a long time.

Colt Hoare, Sir Richard An antiquarian of the early CI9 who, with CUNNINGTON, established the techniques of archaeological excavation in Britain. He dug 379 barrows, and published and classified his findings. In addition he recorded many other field monuments of Salisbury Plain. But his *Ancient Wiltshire*, 1810–21, is an admission of defeat. Despite the quantity of material recovered, he had no means of dating it. The THREE AGE SYSTEM had yet to be introduced.

comb A toothed object of wood, bone or metal with a number of uses – for hair dressing, for carding wool, for compacting the weft in weaving, for decorating pottery (⟡ COMBED ORNAMENT). It is very widely distributed in space and time.

combed ornament Pottery decoration produced by drawing a toothed instrument across the surface of the soft clay. The result is a band of parallel incisions, often wavy.

Combe-Grenal A rock-shelter in the Dordogne valley in France, near the town of Domme. The basal levels contained a late ACHEULIAN industry dating from the end of the RISS GLACIATION, and this was followed by a series of 55 MOUSTERIAN levels containing all the different varieties of the Mousterian currently recognized in France. Occupation ceased just before the end of the Mousterian period, and there is a radiocarbon date of just over 37,000 BC from Level 12, near the top of the deposit.

comets A subject more directly concerning ancient history. The brighter comets attracted considerable attention and so were likely to be mentioned in ancient records, eg the Bayeux Tapestry. Furthermore their occurrences can be calculated by astronomers, as can ECLIPSES, and ancient reports can thus be exactly dated, a useful check on the recorded chronology.

Conca d'Oro The rich plain around Palermo in northwest Sicily, in which a number of Copper Age rock-cut SHAFT-AND-CHAMBER TOMBS have been found.

Local incised wares were accompanied by BEAKERS of west Mediterranean type.

contour fort A HILLFORT in which the defensive bank and ditch follow the contour so as to enclose the entire hilltop.

convergence Similar traits may appear in different areas or at different times, and from different antecedents. They will then be examples of convergence or convergent EVOLUTION, not of DIFFUSION. For instance, ROCKER PATTERN was used for decorating pottery in widely separated contexts.

copper One of the first metals to be exploited by man because, like gold, it can be found in the native form, pure and requiring no smelting. It was later extracted from a variety of ores, the carbonate (MALACHITE), oxides and sulphides. Shaping could be done by simple hammering, which served also to harden the metal. But where smelting produced the metal in molten form, the possibilities of casting must have been soon realized. An open MOULD would normally have been used as unflawed castings are very difficult to obtain in closed ones. In the Old World these were only introduced when alloying of the copper, particularly with tin to produce BRONZE, got over this difficulty. In the New World, however, CIRE PERDUE casting of copper is first recorded in the PARACAS culture of Peru. By the time of the European conquest the technique was practised from the southwestern USA to Argentina. ◊ TUMBAGA

Copper Age According to the principles of the THREE AGE SYSTEM, it should strictly mean the period when COPPER was the main material for man's basic tools and weapons. It is difficult to apply in this sense as copper at its first appearance was very scarce, and experimentation with alloying seems to have begun very soon. The alternative names of Chalcolithic and Eneolithic, implying the joint use of copper and stone, are little better since stone continued in use beside bronze to a much later

period. However, in many sequences, notably in Europe and Asia, there is a period between the NEOLITHIC and BRONZE AGE, separated from each by breaks in the cultural development, within which copper was coming into use. For this the term is a convenient one. In Asia it saw the origins of civilization, in Europe the great folk movements of the BEAKER and CORDED WARE cultures, and perhaps the introduction of the INDO-EUROPEAN languages.

coprolite Desiccated or fossilized dung. Examples of human origin preserved in the desert parts of America have been examined to give useful evidence of diet in early times.

corbelling A technique for roofing stone chambers [132b]. In the upper stages of the wall each course of stones partially oversails the one below it until the stones eventually meet or leave only a small gap which can be spanned by a CAPSTONE (◊ THOLOS). The same method can be used for a corbelled 'false' arch, or vault, as in the architecture of the MAYA. [114]

Corded Ware A pottery ware decorated with CORD ORNAMENT found in local versions over much of the north European plain from Jutland to the Volga in the later 3rd millennium [48]. The commonest

Fig. 48. Corded Ware beaker from Saxo-Thuringia

shapes are the BEAKER and the GLOBULAR AMPHORA. The ware is always associated with primitive agriculture, the stone

BATTLEAXE, and usually with single burial under a small barrow or KURGAN. The origins and importance of this pottery are matters of long-standing controversy. It may derive from Denmark, central Germany (Saxo-Thuringia), eastern Poland or the Ukraine. It has often been suggested that its bearers were the first INDO-EUROPEANS in Europe, a reasonable but quite unprovable claim.

cordon A strip of clay applied to the surface of a pot before firing. Most commonly it will form a simple hoop round the vessel, but wavy and geometric designs are not unusual and even figured scenes can occur. The cordon often bears a series of finger or stick indentations along its course. The name is also used for horizontal ribs round beaten metal vessels, although these are produced by REPOUSSÉ, a very different technique.

cord ornament Pottery decoration produced by impressing a twisted cord into the surface of the soft clay. Sometimes short individual motifs were produced by wrapping a cord round a stick (PETERBOROUGH WARE), or cord impressions replaced simple incisions in a design, or part or the whole of a vessel was wrapped closely in cord (CORDED WARE and some varieties of BEAKER).

core A lump of stone from which FLAKES or BLADES have been removed. Sometimes a core is merely the by-product of toolmaking, but it may also be shaped and modified to serve as an implement in its own right. An object, such as a HANDAXE, made in this way is a core tool. [31a]

Cortaillod A village of PILE DWELLINGS on the edge of Lake Neuchâtel, and the type site of the oldest NEOLITHIC culture in Switzerland, with a starting date of c3000 BC. Cortaillod is noted for the fine preservation of wood, cloth, and plant remains, and for its plain round-based pottery of WESTERN NEOLITHIC type. ⬨ HORGEN

Cortes de Navarra A village site of the Late Bronze and Iron Ages near Saragossa in the Ebro valley of Spain. Narrow mud-brick houses were arranged in terraces. The finds show it to have belonged to the URNFIELD groups which entered Spain c750 BC.

cotton The earliest records of cotton are from the New World, in the TEHUACAN VALLEY of central Mexico (3500–2300 BC), and at about the same date in pre-ceramic villages on the Peruvian coast. It was grown in northeast Mexico by c1800, and was introduced into the southwestern United States during the millennium before Christ. In the Old World the first occurrence is in the INDUS valley civilization where cotton was used for both string and textiles at MOHENJO-DARO by 2500. Although the cultivated cottons of the Old World derive from African wild species, the first record in African archaeology goes back only to the culture of MEROÉ in C5 BC.

All the cottons of the Old World have 13 *large* chromosomes, while the wild species of the Americas has 13 *small* chromosomes. The fact that all the cultivated cottons of the New World have 26 chromosomes (13 large and 13 small) led to the suggestion that at some time in prehistory trans-Pacific voyagers must have introduced an Asiatic race into America where it hybridized with the native wild form. An alternative explanation is that a wild cotton with 13 large chromosomes of Old World type existed in South America in ancient times and has since become extinct.

counterscarp bank A low bank on the outer, downhill, edge of a defence ditch on sites of HILLFORT type.

coup de poing ⬨ HANDAXE

court cairn A variety of MEGALITHIC CHAMBER TOMB found in southwest Scotland and northern Ireland, hence the alternative name 'Clyde-Carlingford tomb'. Essential features include an elongated rectangular or trapeze-shaped cairn with an unroofed semicircular forecourt at one end [49]. The court gives access to the burial chamber proper, which is normally a gallery with two or more chambers separated by jambs, or by a combination of jambs and sills. This basic form, some-

Fig. 49. Plan of Browndod court cairn in County Antrim

times called a 'horned cairn', has many variants. In the 'lobster-claw', or 'full court', cairns the wings of the façade curve round until they almost meet at the front of the tomb to enclose a circular or oval forecourt. Sometimes a cairn contains more than one tomb, or subsidiary chambers are present. A few court cairns in Co. Mayo have side chambers and can be classed as TRANSEPTED GALLERY GRAVES. In Ireland cremation is the dominant rite; in Scotland inhumation is just as common. In both areas the grave goods suggest a date early in the Neolithic (sometime after 3000 BC), but court cairns continued to be used – if not actually built – until the end of the Neolithic period around 1800. These court cairns share many features with the SEVERN-COTS-WOLD TOMBS of southwest Britain and with the transepted gallery graves near the river Loire, but the relationship between these areas is not yet understood in detail.

cowrie, cowry A variety of spiral shell, genus *Cypraea*, in which the opening is reduced to a slit running the length of one side. Its popularity in antiquity seems to depend on its use as a symbol of the female vulva. It was widely traded, larger species being imported into Europe from as far off as the Red Sea.

crannog An artificial island made of brushwood, peat, stones and logs, and often surrounded by a timber palisade. Most crannogs are small, and probably represent single homesteads. The oldest examples in Ireland have yielded early Neolithic material (Bann flakes), others have BEAKER pottery. Most of them, however, are of Late Bronze Age, Iron Age, Early Christian or medieval date. One Irish crannog was still in use in C17.

crater A large open two-handled bowl used for mixing wine. It is characteristic of Greece in the Mycenaean and classical periods, but examples diffused widely in Europe. That from VIX is one of the most famous.

Crawford, O.G.S. An archaeologist with a surprising number of claims to fame – as the first clear exponent of the mapping of DISTRIBUTIONS, of AIR PHOTO-GRAPHY, of FIELD ARCHAEOLOGY, of the national mapping of antiquities (he was Archaeological Officer of the Ordnance Survey for many years), and of enlightening the public (as the editor of the popular journal *Antiquity* for its first 31 years, until his death in 1958).

cremation The practice of burning the dead. There is as much variation in the disposal of the ashes as there is of the body in the contrasting rite of INHUMATION, perhaps the commonest custom in the archaeological record being to place them in a CINERARY URN for BURIAL.

Creswell Crags The type of site of the CRESWELLIAN CULTURE. A gorge cut into Permian limestone near the Derbyshire village of Creswell contains caves which have yielded flint tools of MOU-STERIAN, 'proto-SOLUTREAN', Creswellian and MESOLITHIC types, as well as harpoons and a bone fragment with an engraved horse's head in Late MAGDALEN-IAN style.

Creswellian culture A British PALAEO-LITHIC culture found at CRESWELL CRAGS and in caves in Wales and southern England. The characteristic tools [50] are large trapezes, obliquely blunted BLADES and small backed blades – all of which are present in related industries of Tjongerian/ FEDERMESSER type in the Low Countries and north Germany. The continental evidence indicates that the Creswellian belongs mainly to the ALLERØD OSCIL-

Fig. 50. Creswellian artifacts

LATION (c9850–8850 BC), but certain objects can be paralleled in the HAMBURGIAN and MAGDALENIAN industries. Three radiocarbon dates from Anston Cave (s. Yorks) cluster around 7900 BC.

Crete ◊ MINOANS

Cro-Magnon A ROCK SHELTER in the Dordogne in southwest France. In 1868 it was the site of the first discovery of remains of HOMO SAPIENS in a deposit containing Upper PALAEOLITHIC tools.

cromlech A Welsh word used as a general term for all categories of MEGALITHIC CHAMBER TOMB. The term is now obsolete in archaeological literature but has persisted in Welsh folk usage.

crop mark ◊ AIR PHOTOGRAPHY

cross-dating In the absence of GEOCHRONOLOGY, two cultural groups can only be proved contemporary by the discovery of links between them. If in culture A an object produced by culture B is found, A must be contemporary with, or later than, B. The term cross-dating ought strictly to be used only when an object of culture A is also found in proved ASSOCIATION with culture B, when overlap of at least part of the time span of each is proved.

crucible A small coarse pottery vessel for holding molten metal during smelting or casting. It is usually easily recognizable

from the effects of the high temperatures to which it has been subjected, as well as from its shape and thickness.

cryoturbation The soil in regions close to an ice sheet contains a good deal of water, and when it refreezes after the seasonal thaw the pressure of growing ice crystals tends to rotate and rearrange the stones. The presence of such a structured soil indicates periglacial conditions. ◊ GLACIATION

Cucuteni culture The Romanian branch of the TRIPOLYE culture. There is a radiocarbon date of 3380 for an early phase and one of c3000 BC for the second phase.

Cuismancu A kingdom described by Garcilaso de la Vega as occupying the Chancay, Chillon and Rimac valleys of the central Peruvian coast in the centuries before the INCA conquest. Other chroniclers give different accounts, and archaeology offers no support for a Cuismancu state. The people of the northern valleys used pottery in the Chancay style with black linear patterns over a creamy white background, while those of the Rimac and Lurín valleys made a quite different ware with white-painted and appliqué designs.

cultivation The raising of plants for human benefit, primarily for their fruit, seed, leaf or fibre. Man must have exploited vegetable matter from the very start, but by bringing it under his direct control he greatly increased and stabilized his food supply. The process was a slow one, and as with the DOMESTICATION of animals the criterion of full cultivation should be the breeding by selection of strains most useful to man. The first staples among Old World crops were WHEAT and BARLEY, both with wild ancestors in southwest Asia, appearing as cultivated species c7th millennium BC. To these were added oats and rye in Europe, MILLET and RICE in Asia, sorghum in Africa, and of course the wide range of vegetables and fruits from many sources.

The change from food gathering to food production has been called the NEOLITHIC revolution, and was one of the most important in human development. In America the process was equally slow, and took place in widely scattered centres. Crops included beans, COTTON, gourds, MAIZE, MANIOC, POTATOES and squashes.

culture (1) Every human activity, whether represented by an ARTIFACT (material culture) or a practice or belief (non-material culture), which is transmitted from individual to individual by some kind of teaching, not by genetic inheritance. Although usually bound by strict tradition, cultural change can come about comparatively rapidly by DIFFUSION or by local development without external stimulation.

(2) If an ASSEMBLAGE recurs consistently over a restricted area and within a given period (ie has limited distributions in space and time) it is described as a culture, and taken to be characteristic of a particular human society. Here too a non-material trait is as important as a material one, though only material evidence of it can be recovered archaeologically. Cultures are the bricks of which PREHISTORY is built, and it must be conceded that the bricks are not as sound as could be wished. Examples from historical times or from ethnography show that the equation of culture with society is not perfect, though it is the best the archaeologist can achieve unaided. Problems of definition constantly crop up in separating adjacent or successive cultures.

Cumae A hill on the Italian coast west of Naples. The cemetery of an Iron Age settlement was found here in 1915. This was succeeded c750 BC by the Greek colony of Kyme (Latin Cumae), the first in the west. It had an eventful history in peace and war between the Greeks and ETRUSCANS, but was eventually eclipsed by Neapolis (Naples).

cuneiform The name for the writing developed in Mesopotamia and used 3rd–

1st millennia BC. The pictographic script of the URUK period, the oldest known in the world, was reduced to angular forms to make it more suitable for impressing in wet clay with a split reed. This gives the strokes their characteristic (cuneiform = wedge-shaped) appearance [51]. The

Fig. 51. A letter in its envelope, Kultepe

nature of the script was very like that of the Egyptians, with ideographs, phonograms and determinatives (✧ HIEROGLYPHS). The script was used for a number of languages (SUMERIAN, AKKADIAN, Elamite, Hittite, Old Persian, etc), even being adapted to serve as an alphabet at UGARIT.

The first success in its decipherment was by Grotefend, a German philologist, in 1802. In inscriptions from PERSEPOLIS he recognized the names of Darius and Xerxes and the Old Persian word for 'king'. It was not until 1844–7 that further progress came, through the accurate, and difficult, recording and study of Darius's rock inscriptions at BEHISTUN by Rawlinson. He was able to translate the Old Persian version; Westergaard in 1854 tackled the Elamite text, and Rawlinson, with others, cracked the Babylonian in 1857. This was much the most important of the three as it led directly back, through the many cuneiform inscriptions at that time coming to light, to the first written records, those of ancient Sumer.

Cunnington, William A distinguished English excavator and field archaeologist of the early C19. He worked, like his contemporary COLT HOARE, mainly on Salisbury Plain.

Cupisnique A local variant of CHAVÍN culture found in tombs in the Cupisnique valley on the north coast of Peru.

cup mark (cup-and-ring mark) A rock carving consisting of a cup-shaped pit, often surrounded by concentric circles which may themselves be cut by radial lines. This decoration occurs on natural boulders in highland Britain, on MENHIRS, on slab CISTS of the FOOD VESSEL culture, and in connexion with STONE CIRCLES. In its classic form most cup-and-ring art belongs in the Bronze Age, but the motif occurs on PASSAGE GRAVES, for example in the CLAVA TOMBS and on the capstones at NEWGRANGE, where it may show links with similar rock carvings in north-west Spain.

currency bar A strip of iron 30–35 ins long and pinched up at one end, which served as a unit of currency in Britain before the introduction of coins by the BELGAE. The bars may have originated as sword blanks or roughouts. Their distribution centres on Dorset and the Cotswolds with a related group in the Severn basin.

cursus A structure of unknown function, consisting of a long avenue defined by two parallel earthen banks with quarry ditches outside them. The ends of the avenue are closed by similar earthworks. The name was coined by the C18 antiquary William STUKELEY for the example at STONEHENGE, which he thought was intended for the celebration of funeral games and compared, quite misleadingly, to a Roman racetrack. The Stonehenge cursus measures some 3,000 yds by 110, but the longest known cursus, in Dorset, runs for more than six miles. This class of monument is found only in Britain, and belongs to the later part of the Neolithic. Some examples incorporate or are aligned on earthen LONG BARROWS, and at Thornborough in Yorkshire a cursus underlay a HENGE.

Cuzco ◊ INCA

cyclopean masonry Masonry or architecture characterized by the use of very large close-fitting irregular stones. The ancient Greeks attributed the walls of TIRYNS, built in this fashion by the MYCENAEANS, to the mythical one-eyed Cyclops. The technique occurs widely elsewhere in the Mediterranean (◊ NURAGHE, NAVETA, TALAYOT, TORRE), and was sometimes employed by the INCA and other Andean peoples.

Cyrus the Great The second of that name, he overthrew the empire of the MEDES in 550 BC, plundered its capital Ecbatana, and founded the ACHAEMENID empire with its capital at Pasargadae. Before his death in 530 he had extended his conquests as far as the Indus, Jaxartes, Aegean and the frontiers of Egypt, and absorbed these territories into the administrative scheme. He represented himself as a liberator rather than a conqueror, a marked contrast to the earlier Assyrians. His tomb at Pasargadae survives.

D

Dabar Kot A large TELL, 500 yds in diameter and 100 ft high, near Loralai in north BALUCHISTAN. A trading post of the INDUS CIVILIZATION succeeded a long occupation of the site by local cultures.

Dabban The oldest dated BLADE-and-BURIN industry of Upper PALAEOLITHIC type. It spans the period c38,000–13,000 BC and is recorded from only two sites (Hagfed ed-Dabba and the HAUA FTEAH) in Cyrenaica. It seems to have been introduced from somewhere outside this area, but its origins are still unknown.

dagger A short cutting and stabbing weapon of flint, copper, bronze, iron, or occasionally bone. The distinction between it and an inoffensive knife blade is hard to draw and may never have been clear cut.

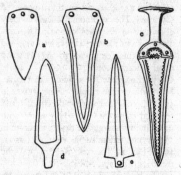

Fig. 52. Some dagger forms: (a) triangular; (b) ogival; (c) solid-hilted (central European); (d) w. European; (e) tanged (s. European)

In copper it was ancestral to the RAPIER, SWORD, SPEAR and HALBERD (♦ TYPOLOGY). Some distinctive forms are illustrated. [52]

Dálriada The kingdom founded by Fergus and his brothers when they led the Scots from Ireland to western Scotland in C5 AD. It occupied roughly the modern county of Argyll and was ruled from the rock fortress of Dunadd. In about 843 Kenneth MacAlpin extended his rule over the PICTS to lay the foundations of the kingdom of Scotland. Dalriada had already achieved importance in the religious field by providing the Celtic church under St Columba with the island of IONA as a base for the conversion of northern Britain to Christianity.

Danger Cave (Utah, USA) The lowest stratum, whose date probably falls within the range 9500–9000 BC, contained fauna of modern type, a few nondescript stone artifacts and a leaf-shaped point. The levels above this contained remains of DESERT CULTURE type spanning the period from the 8th millennium BC to the start of the Christian era, and from the top of the deposit came pottery left by more recent Indian groups.

Danilo A Neolithic village site on the Dalmatian coast. Two associated pottery styles, painted in black and broad red bands on buff ware, and incised on dark burnished ware, belong in the Middle Neolithic. The geometric designs suggest connexions with contemporary wares in Italy, particularly RIPOLI and SERRA D'ALTO.

Danubian culture The first farming culture of much of central and eastern Europe. During the Danubian I stage, starting by c4500 BC, a single culture based on SLASH AND BURN cultivation of the easily tilled LOESS lands can be recognized from the Dniestr to the Rhine, and from Yugoslavia to Belgium and eastern France. Characteristic of Danubian I are the SHOE-LAST CELT, objects of SPONDYLUS shell and the use of BANDKERAMIK [25]. Villages (♦ BYLANY, KÖLN-LINDENTHAL) contained many substantial timber longhouses, but were abandoned once the fertility of the soil was exhausted. After the land had lain fallow for a sufficient time the site was reoccupied and the village rebuilt. This cycle was repeated several times. During the early 4th millennium the unity of the Danubian I stage broke down, with the emergence of regional Danubian II cultures (◊ RÖSSEN, STROKE-ORNA-MENTED WARE, LENGYEL, TISZA).

Danzantes Figures of nude men carved on the retaining slabs of a temple built during Period I at MONTE ALBÁN. Some of the figures are mutilated, and many of the others are arranged in distorted postures. Several of the slabs bear hieroglyphs which cannot yet be read.

Darius I (521–486 BC) The most powerful ruler of the ACHAEMENID empire. The details of his accession, which extinguished the rule of the senior branch of his family, are clouded by the fact that we have only his side of the story, notably in his great rock inscription at BEHISTUN [28]. His removal of the royal capital from Pasargadae to PERSEPOLIS underlines the break. Undoubtedly his main right to the throne was by conquest, which explains the strengthening of the central power in his reorganized empire. He also extended its limits in India and Thrace, but his designs on Greece were repulsed at the battle of Marathon in 490. His tomb survives, carved in the cliff face at Naqsh-i-Rustam, near Persepolis.

dating or **chronology** The time factor is obviously of paramount importance in archaeology, and many methods of recording it are employed. Relative dating, in which the order of certain events is determined, must be distinguished from absolute dating, in which figures in solar years, though often with some necessary margin of error, can be applied to a particular event.

Unless tied to historical records, dating by archaeological methods can only be relative (◊ STRATIGRAPHY, TYPOLOGY, CROSS-DATING and SEQUENCE DATING). Many techniques have been made possible by GEOCHRONOLOGY. Absolute dating, with some reservations, is provided by DENDROCHRONOLOGY, VARVE DATING, THERMOLUMINESCENCE, POTASSIUM-ARGON DATING, and, most important of all at present, RADIOCARBON dating. Some relative dating can be calibrated by these or by historical methods to give a close approximation to absolute dates – ARCHAEOMAGNETISM, OBSIDIAN DATING and POLLEN ANALYSIS. Still others remain strictly relative – COLLAGEN CONTENT, FLUORINE TEST and RADIO-METRIC ASSAY. Many of these techniques are so recently developed that others may be expected to appear at any moment.

daub Clay smeared on to some rigid structure, usually of interwoven twigs (wattle), to exclude draughts and give a smooth finish. It is rarely preserved unless accidentally baked.

Dead Sea Scrolls Texts recovered from the caves in which they had been hidden from the Romans at the northwest corner of the Dead Sea. They are the religious writings of the Essenes, a sect who in CI BC and CI AD dwelt in a monastery at Qumran, excavated by de Vaux. The relevance of this material to the origins of Christianity is enormous and still under active study.

Déchelette, Joseph (1862–1914) The author of one of the finest works of synthesis in the history of European archaeology. His *Manuel d'Archéologie Préhistorique, Celtique, et Gallo-romaine*, published between 1908 and 1913, was at that time unique in its range and scholarship, and still puts most of its more recent competitors to shame.

decumanus maximus The main street of a Roman camp or town (the square grid layout of the two was basically identical, though it is debatable which came first), usually running from the gate in the middle of one wall to the gate opposite. The main transverse street was known as the CARDO, the administrative block or FORUM being placed at the intersection of the two. Other decumani parallel to the decumanus maximus cross the transverse cardines to divide the area into insulae. [53]

Fig. 53. Caerwent. Layout of Roman town

deep sea cores Samples in the form of cores up to 20 metres long have been obtained by drilling from the Globigerina ooze which accumulates on the ocean floors. In a few of the cores the deposits are continuous, with no sign of disturbance or interruption. The proportion of the oxygen isotopes O^{18} and O^{16} in the calcium carbonate of the ooze is dependent upon the sea temperature, which has varied over the period deposits were forming. Later levels of the ooze can be dated directly by RADIOCARBON or thorium^{230}, and dates for the earlier levels extrapolated backwards. A close correlation with the temperature changes of the last GLACIATION has been obtained, but correlations with the earlier Ice Ages are more debatable. The date of 300,000 has been claimed for the onset of the first glaciation.

Deir el-Bahri A site on the west bank of the Nile opposite THEBES in Upper Egypt. In a bay of the cliffs two great funerary temples were erected. That of Mentuhotep I of the 11th dynasty (Middle Kingdom, c2050 BC) consisted of a chamber tomb and a pyramid set in elaborately planned colonnades and terraces. That of Queen HATSHEPSUT, on a similar plan but without the pyramid, belongs to the 18th dynasty (New Kingdom, c1480 BC). It is famous for a series of reliefs including one portraying a trading expedition to PUNT.

delta The flat alluvial tract built up by the deposition of silt at the mouth of a river, in particular that of the Nile. Its name comes from the Greek letter which resembles it in shape. The Nile Delta, Lower Egypt, is in marked contrast with the valley, Upper Egypt. Though it has an equally important history, its remains are now lost, buried beneath many feet of the silt which has accumulated since ancient times.

demography ♦ POPULATION ESTIMATION

demotic An Egyptian cursive script for secular use derived from HIEROGLYPHS by way of HIERATIC. Although more easily written, its structure was identical with that of the original hieroglyphic. It first appeared in C7 BC, surviving until C5 AD. It was used for the central of the three inscriptions on the ROSETTA STONE.

Denbigh Flint complex A flint industry found at Iyatayet, CAPE KRUSENSTERN, ONION PORTAGE and other Alaskan sites. The typical artifacts are BURINS, MICROLITHS (bladelets, small crescents) and bifacially pressure-flaked points. The Denbigh complex had developed by c2500 BC. It is one of the industries grouped within the **Arctic Small Tool tradition**, which spread eastwards over the whole Arctic zone from Alaska to Greenland, and contributed to the earliest ESKIMO cultures.

Dendera A site in Upper Egypt with

a temple of HATHOR founded in the Middle Kingdom and frequently added to by later rulers down to the Roman emperors.

dendrochronology Where trees grow in a variable climate, in certain years growth rings thinner or thicker than average will be formed. In 1929 A. E. Douglass showed how this variation could be used to date archaeological material. By matching the ring pattern of timbers collected from a restricted area in the southwest United States, and therefore controlled by the same climatic variation, he built up a master plot extending from the present back to the period of the pre-Columbian PUEBLO villages. Any timber recovered from a site, preserved there by the near-desert conditions, could be dated exactly by matching its rings against the plot. The method has some similarities to VARVE-DATING.

It is limited to areas where climatic variation (of rainfall or temperature) was sufficiently large, where timber was much used, and where enough of it has been preserved (by desiccation, waterlogging or charring) to be worked on. Despite these restrictions it has given many useful results, notably in the southwestern USA, Alaska and Scandinavia. Some floating chronologies, not continued up to the present, have been produced elsewhere. These allow relative DATING between sites or structures, even if they cannot provide absolute dating. Recently a much longer series has been prepared from the Californian bristlecone pine, going back some 6,500 years. This has allowed useful, if disturbing, checks to be made on the validity of RADIOCARBON dating.

Der Tasa ◊ TASIAN

Desert culture A way of life adapted to the post-PLEISTOCENE conditions of the arid and semi-arid zones of the American West from Oregon to California, and with extensions into similar areas of Mexico. Agriculture was unknown or unimportant, and the small nomadic bands lived by collecting wild plant foods and hunting game. Typical artifacts include grinding slabs for cracking seeds, together with mats, baskets, SPEAR-THROWERS and DIGGING STICKS. This mode of subsistence was established by 8000 BC and lasted until agriculture had developed sufficiently to permit settled life (◊ MAIZE). In the Mexican states of Puebla (◊ TEHUACAN) and Tamaulipas the first attempts at cultivation began early, but village life and subsistence patterns based on domesticated plants do not appear until 3400–2200. This stage was not reached in the southwestern USA until the last few centuries BC (◊ COCHISE and MOGOLLON), and some tribes, like the Utes and Paiutes, were still living a 'Desert' life in C19. ◊◊ DANGER CAVE and VENTANA CAVE

Deverel–Rimbury culture As originally defined, this was a local culture of southern England during the second half of the Middle Bronze Age (C12–C10 BC). It was named after two sites in Dorset, and was characterized by CELTIC FIELDS and palisaded cattle enclosures, and by burial in cremation cemeteries, either in flat URNFIELDS or under low BARROWS. Sometimes Deverel–Rimbury cremations were also inserted into the mounds of pre-existing barrows. The distinctive pots were globular vessels with channelled or fluted decoration, and barrel or bucketshaped URNS with cordoned ornament. More recent work has demonstrated that Deverel–Rimbury is not a unified culture at all, but is made up of a number of distinct regional groups of roughly the same date but of diverse origins.

Dhimini A small fortified Late Neolithic site at Volos in Thessaly, central Greece. Within the multiple walls are a MEGARON palace and smaller buildings. The typical pottery, largely confined to eastern Thessaly, includes spirals and meanders painted in black or white on a yellow or buff ground [54]. Their connexions are probably with the Cyclades rather than, as was for long assumed, with the DANUBIAN of central Europe.

Fig. 54.   Dhimini painted jar.

diffusion The spread of a cultural TRAIT from its point of origin. The bearers of the CULTURE in which it first appeared may carry it by folk movement, war or trade, or it may be adopted by another culture by simple imitation. Diffusion has played a major part in human development by spreading ideas and techniques more rapidly than they could have spread had they been independently invented, but it has on occasion been credited with far too much. Multiple origins, even within Europe, for such traits as metal-working or megaliths, are now happily accepted, whereas influence from Egypt was insisted upon by ELLIOT SMITH and his school forty years ago. The onus of proof is on the diffusionist, to show that the trait is the same in the two areas, that communication between the two was possible, and that there are no difficulties in the relative dates. In a great number of cases these criteria can be met.

digging stick A straight wooden tool for loosening the ground. It served in food-gathering economies to turn up roots or burrowing animals, and in Neolithic communities for cultivation until displaced by the HOE and later (in the Old World only) by the PLOUGH. Efficiency could be increased by forcing a perforated stone, a digging stick weight, on to the shaft near the lower end, in order to give greater thrust to the downward blow.

disc barrow ⟡ BARROW

distributions One of the archaeologist's most useful tools is the distribution map, covering a site, a region, a country or a continent. This is the visual representation of the distribution of some archaeologically significant trait or traits. Most commonly, each findspot is marked by a single symbol, though enlarged symbols for many occurrences at one site are usual. For comparison, other traits may be represented by different symbols. Where there are too many examples to be shown separately, differential shading may be used to show frequency of occurrence. The proportions of two traits can be represented similarly. The proportions of more than two traits will require 'sliced cake' diagrams to show their relative frequency in different areas.

An explanation is then sought. The distribution should show the extent of a CULTURE of which the traits are distinctive, outlying occurrences being explained by DIFFUSION, especially if strung along natural routes. The origin of more localized traits may be defined. Concordant distributions, where trait A is found only over the same area as trait B, suggest the association of two traits. Exclusive distributions, where trait A is confined to the area where trait B is absent, may give evidence of contemporaneity. Significant correlations may appear with soil maps or vegetation types, with linguistic patterns or historically recorded peoples. A word of warning: negative evidence on a distribution map must always be treated with caution – if something is not there, it may be missing only because it has not been looked for.

Distributions in time can be similarly represented by bars on a time chart, an effective way of showing the changing popularity of different traits, or the succession of different assemblages or cultures.

dog The first animal species to accept domestication. It has been recorded from Mesolithic contexts (eg STAR CARR, C7500 BC), and in America in a Late PLEISTO-

CENE deposit at Jaguar Cave, Idaho. Its functions were probably, in order, scavenger, watch dog, hunting assistant and, in the New World, food. Herding is probably a quite recent addition. Its wild ancestor is still not identified, but a small form of wolf seems the likeliest on present evidence.

dolmen In early antiquarian works, the word is used as a descriptive term for MEGALITHIC CHAMBER TOMBS in general. This usage is now obsolete in English but is still, quite correctly, employed in that sense in French. In English archaeological literature 'dolmen' should be used only for tombs whose original plan cannot be determined or for tombs of simple unspecialized types which do not fit into the PASSAGE GRAVE or GALLERY GRAVE categories (though ◊ PORTAL DOLMEN).

dolmen deity A mysterious personage or divinity who peers at us from megalithic and rock-cut tombs, from the SYMBOL-KERAMIK and various idols of western Europe [55]. At her simplest, she is represented by nothing but a pair of eyes or eyebrows, the OCULUS motif. Breasts and necklaces, her next most common attributes, show her to be female. Her most detailed representation is in the French STATUE MENHIR [179]. She is possibly an

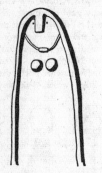

Fig. 55. Goddess carved on the wall of a tomb at Courjeonnet, Marne, France

Earth Mother, an underworld goddess of death and, probably, fertility.

Dolní Věstonice A camping site of Eastern GRAVETTIAN mammoth-hunters in the LOESS country of the Pollau mountains, in southern Moravia. Excavation revealed various phases of occupation, represented by houses, burials, flint tools, ornaments of mammoth ivory, animal figurines of baked clay and VENUS FIGURINES [205]. There is a radiocarbon date of $23,650 \pm 170$ BC.

domestication The controlling of animals so that they can be bred primarily to the advantage of man. The purpose may be for meat, milk, hides, fur, wool or power, as beasts of burden or draught animals. The breeding of animals to assist in hunting is a rather special case for which the biological term 'symbiosis' might be preferable. It is debatable whether the dog or cat, or its master, gains most from the relationship. The process of domestication was a slow one. DOG bones associated with MESOLITHIC remains suggest that it was under way by that period. Skeletal changes, and the relative numbers of bones belonging to different sexes and ages, imply that SHEEP were domesticated by 9000 BC at ZAWI CHEMI SHANIDAR in Iraq. GOATS, CATTLE and PIGS followed in the next 3000 years, all in the same area of southwest Asia. The HORSE appears in the 2nd millennium, and the camel not generally until the 1st. In the New World domesticable animals were far fewer, notably the dog, LLAMA and guinea pig. The best criterion of domestication comes from evidence of breeding – any alteration from the wild stock will imply human selection, and so full human control. The change involved, from hunting and gathering to food production (◊ CULTIVATION), was one of the most important in human development, and has been called the NEOLITHIC revolution, even though the process was a slow and gradual one.

domu de janas The Sardinian dialect name

(meaning 'house of the fairies') for a kind of rock-cut CHAMBER TOMB, often with many interconnecting rooms, current in the island during the COPPER AGE and Early Bronze Age. ◊ ANGHELU RUJU

donkey ◊ ASS

Dorak A site in western Turkey, south of the Sea of Marmara, reported by Mellaart to have produced a series of royal tombs of the Copper Age comparable to, but far richer than, those of ALACA HÜYÜK. This very important material has since vanished in a manner more appropriate to a crime thriller than to archaeological research, and little can be made of it unless it reappears.

Dorians A group of peoples recorded in Greek tradition as invading southern Greece from the north at the end of the 2nd millennium after the decline of the MYCENAEANS. They may have been responsible for the latter's overthrow. Unfortunately it has proved difficult to recognize their products in the archaeological record, and this makes it hard to discover their origins. Tradition and the linguistic evidence combine to show that they were an important component of the classical Greeks. In classical times the Dorian dialect was spoken through much of the Peloponnese and the southern Greek islands.

Dörpfeld, Wilhelm ◊ TROY

Dorset A prehistoric ESKIMO culture of the east Canadian Arctic and Greenland. It began 800–600 BC and in places lasted until AD 1300. In many areas, however, it was replaced by the expanding THULE culture which spread eastwards from Alaska after c900.

double axe A SHAFT-HOLE AXE which has two opposed cutting edges [20l]. The stone BATTLEAXE is occasionally found in this form. Better known are the examples in copper or bronze of the MINOANS of Bronze Age Crete. There it clearly acquired significance as a religious symbol of the goddess, beside its functional use. It is frequently represented in art also. The form continues sporadically in later contexts.

Douglass, A. E. ◊ DENDROCHRONOLOGY

Dowris At this site, 18 miles south of Athlone in Co. Offaly, was discovered a HOARD which has given its name to a phase of the Irish Bronze Age. Implements of the Dowris A phase (c8–c600 BC) include many gold ornaments, and a series of bronzes [56] showing great proficiency in casting and sheet metalwork. Ireland was at this time in contact with Mediterranean and Nordic lands. Bronze CAULDRONS and V-notched shields demonstrate western links, while U-notched shields,

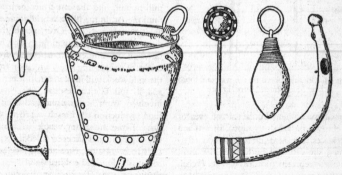

Fig. 56. Metal objects from Dowris (not to scale)

bronze buckets and horns, pins with sun-flower-shaped heads and the use of conical rivets show connexions with northern and central Europe. Some of these objects recur in the contemporary industry of HEATH-ERY BURN type in northern England. Ireland did not enter the Iron Age until just after 300 BC (ie during the LA TÈNE period in Continental terminology), though a few swords and axes show contact with HALLSTATT Iron Age cultures elsewhere. The terms Dowris B and C are used for the final Irish bronze industries (c600-300 BC) contemporary with the first part of the continental Iron Age.

dowsing A technique for discovering buried features or materials by the use of a Y-shaped hazel wand, bimetal strip or the like. The scientific principle behind it is not understood and indeed by many people its validity, at least for archaeologi-cal prospecting, is doubted.

Dragendorff The German scholar who in 1895-6 published a scheme of classification for the shapes of SAMIAN WARE.

dragon A mythical beast symbolizing cosmic forces, popular as an artistic motif throughout Chinese art. In the SHANG and CHOU periods it appears commonly in the form of a k'uei, usually in profile. Two of these confronted make a T'AO T'IEH mask [188]. In later periods it became much more variable and fanciful.

dromos The corridor-like entrance pas-sage leading into the burial chamber of a tomb of PASSAGE GRAVE or THOLOS type.

Druids The priesthood of the Gauls and Britons in CI BC and CI AD. They led the resistance to the Romans, so that when defeated (the last stand was in Anglesey in AD 47) they were exterminated, and the Latin records are usually hostile and one-sided. Archaeologically the only material securely attributable to them is a votive HOARD of bronze and iron at Llyn Cerrig Bach in Anglesey. It is no longer seriously believed that they had anything to do with STONEHENGE or AVEBURY.

dun Scottish and Irish word for a fort or a fortified dwelling place. The term has been stretched to include a wide variety of sites, from large duns of HILLFORT type to small defended homesteads as little as 50 ft in diameter. Some examples, of both ring fort and PROMONTORY FORT types, have galleries or passages within the drystone enclosure wall. In western Scotland the ramparts of some of the larger duns have TIMBER LACING. The oldest duns may belong to the Iron Age, but many are of the Early Christian and medieval periods.

Durrington Walls (Amesbury, Wiltshire) A large twin-entrance HENGE with a dia-meter of some 1600 ft. The site was first occupied during the Middle Neolithic by people who made pottery of the WIND-MILL HILL style, but RINYO-CLACTON ware of a slightly later date also occurs on the ground surface. The henge monument was built while Rinyo-Clacton and BEAKER styles were in use. Excavation has revealed POST HOLES of two complicated timber structures within the enclosure and roughly contemporary with it. The southern structure began as four concentric circles of posts with a straight façade, but this was replaced by a five-circle structure which was later surrounded by a further ring of posts. (The architecture is reminiscent of that at WOODHENGE only 80 yds away.) The northern circle had two concentric rings of posts approached by an avenue of timber uprights. This structure was later rebuilt to a similar plan. Only part of the site has been excavated, and there may be other buildings still to be found within the bank and ditch.

Duweir, Tell el- ◊ LACHISH

dyke ◊ LINEAR EARTHWORK

dynasty A line of kings, usually related by blood, who succeeded each other on a throne. Egyptian history was divided into 31 dynasties on these lines by MANETHO in c3 BC, a convenience maintained by his-torians ever since. The dynasties of Meso-potamia were distinguished by their places of origin rather than their relationships, eg those of Ur, Larsa, etc. In China the dynasties were longer-lived, those of Shang and Chou spanning twelve centuries.

dyss (pl dysser) A MEGALITHIC CIST [57] of the final stage of the Danish Early Neolithic (phase C of the TRB CULTURE). The oldest dysser are slab cists roofed with capstones and containing from one to six skeletons. The burial chamber is covered with a mound which rises to the height of the CAPSTONE and has a retaining KERB of stones. Similar but less massive cists were built by other TRB groups elsewhere in northern Europe. The dysser seem to have been a purely local invention, owing nothing to the PASSAGE GRAVES which were first introduced into this area in the middle Neolithic (TRB 'D') stage. Some of the more elaborate dysser overlap in

Fig. 57. Plan of Danish dyss

time with the earliest passage graves, and both kinds of tomb were used by the same people.

E

Ea, Enki The Sumerian god of sweet water and wisdom. His chief seat was at ERIDU, and with ANU and ENLIL he held the chief power over SUMER.

East Spanish Rock Art An art style of southeast Spain, found on the walls of shallow rock-shelters, and probably of the MESOLITHIC period. The subjects are lively scenes from everyday life, with warriors, hunters, dancers and animals. The style is quite unlike that of CAVE ART,

Fig. 58. East Spanish Rock Art

the East Spanish figures being small and painted in solid colours with no attempt at light and shade [58].

eclipses A subject more directly concerning ancient history. Eclipses are frequently mentioned in ancient records, usually as bad omens. Their occurrence can be calculated by astronomers, and where an ancient report can be correlated with a known eclipse, a useful chronological check can be obtained. ⟡ COMETS

effigy mound In the upper Mississippi region of the USA are groups of burial mounds, rarely more than 4 ft high but often several hundred feet long, and made in the shape of animals and birds. They were constructed by a group of Late WOODLAND folk in the centuries before 700–800 AD.

Egtved (east Jutland, Denmark) The site of a Bronze Age BARROW which covered the burial of a young woman in an oak coffin. Also in the grave were the cremated bones of a child. Waterlogged conditions had preserved the woman's body with its clothing and bronze ornaments, as well as the ox-hide shroud and a box and pail made of birch bark.

einkorn A primitive variety of WHEAT.

Elam The broad lower valley of the Karkeh and Karun rivers in southwest Iran, which geographically is an extension of the southern plain of Mesopotamia. Its chief site, SUSA, has revealed that culturally it followed closely parallel to Mesopotamia. For example, it early adopted the idea of writing, but devised its own pictographic script (proto-Elamite) to suit its own language. Later it used Akkadian CUNEIFORM. Politically the two regions were usually bitterly opposed. Twice Elam spread its conquests across the plains, when the Elamites overthrew the 3rd dynasty of UR shortly before 2000 BC, and when they raided as far as BABYLON in the later C13. But on each occasion they were expelled, although they continued to figure frequently in local power politics down to their absorption into the ACHAEMENID empire in C6.

El Amrah ⟡ AMRATIAN

El Argar, El Garcel, El Omari ⟡ ARGAR, GARCEL, OMARI

Elateia An important Neolithic settlement site in central Greece, excavated by Weinberg in 1959. Radiocarbon dates place its beginnings c5500 BC. Thereafter it documents fully the development of the whole Greek Neolithic. Certain curious scuttle-shaped vessels on four legs betray links with the DANILO culture of western Yugoslavia.

electrum An alloy of GOLD and SILVER used particularly for decorative vessels.

elephant There are two species today, the

African and Indian. The former has been more or less tamed on rare occasions (Carthaginian coins suggest that it was this one which accompanied Hannibal across the Alps) but its importance has always lain more in its IVORY. The Indian elephant was regularly employed for show and war as early as the Bronze Age in China. Wild herds in the Near East survived into the 1st millennium BC, when they were hunted to extinction for their ivory. Forms now extinct, especially the mammoth, were an important source of food in the PALAEO-LITHIC period, and are portrayed in CAVE ART.

Elephantine An island in the Nile just above ASWAN. It was the traditional southern boundary between Egypt and NUBIA and had famous granite quarries. Two temples recorded by the archaeologists of Napoleon's expedition have since disappeared.

Elgin, Lord (1766–1841) A British diplomat, ambassador to Turkey from 1799 to 1803, who in 1801 obtained permission to remove the marble metopes from the Parthenon in Athens. Since 1816 they have been housed in the British Museum. The rights and wrongs of whether they should remain there or be returned to Greece have long been, and doubtless will long continue to be, hotly debated. But at least the marbles have survived far better than they could have hoped to do in their original position.

El Jobo In northwest Venezuela the remains left by pre-agricultural hunting peoples have been found at more than 45 sites. Four stages of development are recognized and together make up the 'Joboid SERIES': Camare (the earliest stage, with crude CHOPPING TOOLS and trimmed FLAKES), Las Lagunas (with bifacially worked BLADES), El Jobo (with the addition of leaf-shaped points like those of AYAMPITÍN and SANTA ISABEL IZTA-PAN) and Las Casitas (with stemmed points).

Elliot Smith, Sir Grafton (1871–1937) A distinguished anatomist who, through a study of the Egyptian MUMMY, became interested in the history of mankind. He considered mummification far too complicated to have been invented on more than one occasion. The alternative was to derive all occurrences of it, as well as of metal-working, building with megaliths, and indeed all civilization, by DIFFUSION from a single source, Egypt. His theory had simplicity as its sole merit. Like all other hyperdiffusionist interpretations, it can only be maintained by rigorous selection of supporting evidence, and quite unjustifiable rejection of the many adverse facts.

El Tajín (Mexico) A CEREMONIAL CENTRE of the CLASSIC Veracruz civilization. The buildings, most of them constructed in the period AD 600–900, include a stepped pyramid with niches opening into the vertical faces, various courts and platforms, at least seven BALL-COURTS, and carved reliefs showing the curvilinear scroll patterns typical of the culture. The site was destroyed by fire c1200.

Emiran industry ◊ MOUNT CARMEL

emmer A primitive variety of WHEAT.

Eneolithic An alternative term for COPPER AGE.

Enki ◊ EA

Enkidu The wild man in the Sumerian epic of GILGAMESH.

Enkomi An important Bronze Age settlement on Salamis Bay in Cyprus. It was first founded in the Middle Bronze Age, and flourished as a result of its copper-working, trading the metal widely through the east Mediterranean. After the collapse of Late Bronze Age Greece, MYCENABANS seized the town in c13 BC. About 1200 it was destroyed again, probably by the PEOPLES OF THE SEA, but continued with declining prosperity for another two centuries.

Enlil The patron god of NIPPUR and most important god of the Sumerians until ousted by MARDUK. His particular domain was the sky and the storm.

entrance grave A type of CHAMBER TOMB which shares features of both PASSAGE GRAVE and GALLERY GRAVE. The round mound is in the passage grave tradition, but there is no clear distinction between the entrance passage and the funerary chamber, hence the alternative term, **undifferentiated passage grave**. Distribution includes southern Spain, Brittany and the Channel Isles. In southwest Cornwall, the Scilly Isles and southeast Ireland is a group of small entrance graves,

Fig. 59. Plan of entrance grave, Scilly Isles

the **Scillonian** [59] or **Scilly-Tramore** tombs, with grave goods of Bronze Age type and a date of 1500–1000 BC.

Entremont (near Aix-en-Provence, France) A Celto-Ligurian OPPIDUM built in C3 BC (middle LA TÈNE culture). It was the capital of the Salyes until destroyed by the Romans in the year 124 BC. Like nearby ROQUEPERTUSE, Entremont had a sanctuary with sculptured figures. Finds include heads and torsos carved in the round, and four-sided limestone pillars [60] with severed human heads carved in relief.

eolith A name coined from two Greek words (*eos*, dawn; *lithos*, stone) and used for what were once thought to be the oldest man-made tools. They consist of crudely chipped FLAKES and CORES from pre-Pleistocene or very early PLEISTOCENE deposits. Nowadays it is generally accepted that eoliths were chipped by natural agencies.

epi-Palaeolithic cultures Cultures which are technologically in the PALAEOLITHIC

tradition, but which represent a survival into the early POSTGLACIAL PERIOD.

Erech ⟡ URUK

Eridu The tell of Abu Shahrain, 12 miles southwest of UR, was excavated by the Iraqis 1946–9. It had already been identified as the ancient Eridu, the oldest city of SUMER. Occupation began in the UBAID period, the earliest phase of which is named after this site, in the mid 6th millennium BC. A series of temples of the Ubaid and URUK periods was found, beginning with a simple rectangular room of mudbrick. They were already decorated with typical Sumerian buttresses and niches to relieve the blank walls. Each incorporated the wall stumps of its predecessor in its platform, a development leading directly to the later ZIGGURAT. A palace of the Early Dynastic period c2500 was also excavated. The site declined in importance with the rise of Ur under its 3rd dynasty c2100 BC.

Erösd ⟡ ARIUṢD

Ertebølle The final MESOLITHIC culture

Fig. 60. Carved stone pillar from Entremont

of the west Baltic coastal region. The most conspicuous sites are the KITCHEN MIDDENS along the ancient (Litorina) shorelines, and POLLEN ANALYSIS places the start of the culture within the ATLANTIC PERIOD, after c 5000 BC. The later phases of Ertebølle are marked by the introduc-

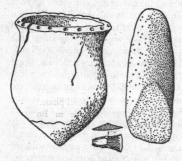

Fig. 61. Ertebølle artifacts

tion of pottery as a result of contact with the newly arrived NEOLITHIC farmers to the south. [61]

Eshnunna (mod **Tell Asmar**) A tell in the Diyala valley northeast of Baghdad excavated by the Americans 1930–36. It appears as a city-state in the Early Dynastic period (early 3rd millennium) to which belong shrines and sculpture, palaces and private houses. Politically its importance came in C19 and C18, when it was involved in a struggle for power with ASSUR (the Old Assyrian Empire), MARI, ELAM and BABYLON under Hammurabi. It is rarely mentioned in history after its conquest by the last, c 1761 BC.

Eskimo The culture of the present day Eskimos has a long history of development in the Arctic. The Eskimo way of life and certain of the distinctive tool types can be traced back before 1000 BC into the Arctic Small Tool tradition (◊ DENBIGH FLINT COMPLEX), and from that date the cultural continuity is clear. Other traits seem to have been adopted by the Alaskan Eskimos from the Siberian tribes. ◊◊ CAPE KRUSENSTERN, DORSET, IPIUTAK, THULE, OLD BERING SEA, ONION PORTAGE

Este A small town on the edge of the Po plain near Padua, north Italy. It has given its name to a rich Iron Age culture, the Atestine, in the surrounding area. This flourished down to the invasion of the CELTS in C4, and is particularly famous for its fine red cordoned vases and its magnificent SITULA art.

Etruscans A colourful but mysterious people who occupied north central Italy (anc Etruria, mod Tuscany) in the 1st millennium BC. They can first be recognized in C8, distinguished from their predecessors the VILLANOVANS by the wealth and oriental appearance of their tombs. In a remarkably short space of time they developed a high level of civilization, with extensive trade contacts with Greece and Carthage, and across the Alpine passes to central Europe. Their cities were large and well appointed: Populonia, Vetulonia, Tarquinia and Caere (Cerveteri) near the coast, Veii, Clusium (Chiusi) and Perusia (Perugia) inland, forming a loose confederation. Etruscan influence spread widely, through Rome itself down to Campania in the south, and north to the Po valley, where the city of Felsina (Bologna) was founded in C6 and Melpum (Milan) and Spina, a port near the mouth of the Po, soon after. But conflict with the CELTS in the north and Rome in the south led to conquest by the latter, beginning with Veii in 396 and completed early in C2. Despite their political extinction, the influence of the Etruscans on Roman civilization was enormous.

The hostility of Rome has given us only biased records of this people. Their own writings, in an alphabet borrowed from the Greeks, can be transliterated, but very little of their non-INDO-EUROPEAN language can be translated. Archaeology can go some way towards repairing the omission, but offers us alternative explanations for the facts it reveals. According to one theory, supported by the authority of Herodotus, the Etruscans sailed from western Turkey to impose their rule on the native Villanovans and to found the Etruscan cities of Italy. An alternative view is that the Villanovans themselves, blessed with mineral wealth and encouraged by the Greek and Phoenician merchants, acquired the trappings of oriental civilization through trade. Neither interpretation is completely convincing, and the right answer may well be some combination of the two, with oriental refugees arriving in small numbers in the 2nd millennium.

Most of our evidence comes from tombs, as the small town of Marzabotto near Bologna is the only site at which much work has been done on their settlements. The cemeteries show a rapid increase in wealth and luxury. At the same time the inhumation rite replaces cremation. Greek painted pottery was imported in great quantity, and good local copies were also produced, as well as the fine local BUC-CHERO wares. Imported metalwork stimulated local production of this too, notably of engraved bronze mirrors. More Phoenician in character is the jewellery, showing gold granulation and filigree of high skill. It is the tombs themselves which show the Etruscan genius best. The finest are mounds covering a burial vault (there is much variation, including simple trench graves and cremation burials in human-headed

urns), as in the cemeteries of Tarquinia and Cerveteri. The vaults may be elaborately frescoed with scenes from life, mythology, or the rites associated with death. We find feasts, dancers, wrestlers, or the soul being carried off by demons [62]. Even more remarkable is a tomb at Cerveteri, the walls of which are covered with stucco reliefs of everyday objects.

eustasy A world-wide alteration in sea level independent of any isostatic movement of the land ($\diamond$ ISOSTASY). At the end of a GLACIATION melting of the water previously held in the ice sheets raises sea levels (eustatic rise), and a high level can often be correlated with an interglacial period or with the postglacial phase.

Eutresis A settlement site in Boeotia, central Greece. The earliest levels go back to the Middle, Late and sub-Neolithic, but the most important occupation was of the Bronze Age, with detailed stratigraphic evidence for the three sub-phases of the Early HELLADIC, beginning c2670 BC. The Middle Helladic seems here to have carried on late, unaffected by the Late Helladic of the MYCENAEANS elsewhere.

Evans, Sir Arthur (1851–1941) Son of SIR JOHN EVANS, he turned to archaeology early in his career, becoming keeper of the Ashmolean Museum, Oxford, in 1884. His first interest was in coins and seals, and it was the latter which drew his attention to Crete. He began excavations at KNOSSOS in 1899 at his own expense, and in the next 35 years laid bare not only this Bronze Age palace of the MINOANS, but in effect their whole civilization, a remarkable achievement for one man. Careful CROSS-DATING with Egypt allowed him to put dates to his sequence, making it a vitally important link in the dating of prehistoric Europe before the discovery of RADIO-CARBON. Though he was unable to decipher the Minoans' three written scripts, his detailed study of them gave the necessary basis for later work, culminating in the reading of LINEAR B by VENTRIS in 1952.

Fig. 62. Piper from a tomb fresco at Tarquinia

Evans, Sir John One of the last and greatest of the British antiquaries, his work covered the second half of the 19th century. It included detailed studies of pre-Roman coinage (1864), and the stone (1872) and bronze (1881) implements of Britain. He was actively concerned in the controversies over the authenticity of the HANDAXE in the 1850s and the EOLITH in the 1890s. He was the father of SIR ARTHUR EVANS.

evolution The gradual change of form of living organisms throughout time, usually but not always towards complexity and functional improvement. Its great exponent was Charles Darwin, whose *Origin of Species* appeared in 1859. The principle has been applied to material objects with some success ($\lozenge$ TYPOLOGY) but must always be treated with caution. It does not follow that a society or CULTURE will automatically develop through certain stages without the need for the external stimulus of DIFFUSION, as has sometimes been maintained.

excavation Archaeological evidence if not buried is almost entirely destroyed, so excavation must play a large part in its recovery. For long it was regarded as merely a method of collecting artifacts, a glorified treasure hunt. PITT RIVERS in Britain and PETRIE in the Near East first placed emphasis on evidence rather than artifacts, not what is found but where it is found relative to the layers of deposit (STRATIGRAPHY) and to other objects (ASSOCIATION); in a word, context. It is this which explains why an excavated object has so much more value than a chance find. The methods employed vary enormously from site to site ($\lozenge$ GRID LAYOUT, QUADRANT METHOD, RABOTAGE, SONDAGE).

In excavation the deposits are perforce dug away, and so destroyed. The excavator can only justify his destruction (1) if it is done with meticulous care so that every artifact, be it an axe or a posthole, is discovered and if possible preserved, however faint the surviving traces may be; (2) if it is recorded accurately enough for all information, whether its relevance is immediately obvious or not, to remain available after the site has completely disappeared; and (3) if this record is speedily made available to all by publication. If in addition he has the skill to interpret his evidence in a way which allows us to picture in detail the activities of our ancestors on that site, and their cultural relationships with their predecessors, contemporaries and successors, then he has succeeded in his task and added new pages to the story of man.

excised decoration Pottery decoration produced by cutting strips or shapes out of the soft clay surface before firing. The resulting cavity was often inlaid with a white paste to contrast with the dark pot surface. $\lozenge$ CHIP-CARVING and FALSE RELIEF

F

fabricator A tool used to manufacture other kinds of stone implement by flaking.

faience A name applied originally to the medieval pottery of Faenza in northern Italy, an early maiolica. In archaeological literature, where it would be better defined as Egyptian faience, the name is used for a substance composed of a sand and clay mixture baked to a temperature at which the surface begins to fuse to a bluish or greenish glass. It was invented in ancient Egypt and was traded widely in the 2nd millennium BC, being widely imitated also. Its main use was for beads, seals, figurines and similar small objects. The alternative names of 'frit' or 'paste' are equally misleading.

false entrance A dummy entrance, sometimes with a forecourt, at the end of a chambered long BARROW in the place where the true entrance would normally be. The false entrance is merely for show, and the burial chambers open from the side of the mound. ⟡ SEVERN-COTS-WOLD TOMB, TRANSEPTED GALLERY GRAVE

false relief A form of EXCISED or IM-PRESSED DECORATION on pottery in which two rows of inward pointing triangles are cut from, or impressed on, the pot surface. The zigzag running between them then appears to be in relief, though it is actually no higher than the surface of the pot elsewhere. The motif was widely popular. [67]

Far'ah, Tell el- Two TELLS of this name have been excavated in Palestine, by PETRIE in 1928–30, inland from Gaza, and by de Vaux since 1946, east of Nablus. The former began with a Middle Bronze Age town provided with a plastered glacis of HYKSOS type. The CANAANITES were here succeeded in C12 by the PHILISTINES, five of whose tombs were particularly rich. The site was abandoned in the Iron Age, though the tombs included one of Achaemenid date.

The northern Far'ah (anc Tirzah) dates back to the Chalcolithic or Proto-Urban period, here very fully documented, in the 4th millennium. A town grew on the site in Early Bronze Age I, was massively walled in II, but abandoned in III, c2600. It was reoccupied from C18 to C9 (Middle Bronze II to Iron Age), when it was abandoned again. For a few years in C9 it was the capital of Israel, before Omri moved to SAMARIA.

Fat'janovo, Fatyanovo A cemetery near Yaroslavl, on the upper Volga in central Russia, of a group of people related to the bearers of the SINGLE-GRAVE CULTURES. With the dead were laid globular jars (some of them with CORD ORNAMENT), model wheels of terracotta, stone BATTLE-AXES and copper trinkets. Although the tombs are not covered by mounds, the Fat'janovo culture is a late (Copper/Early Bronze Age) sub-group within the main Single-Grave/Battleaxe tradition.

Fauresmith A Stone Age industry of south and east Africa, with tools representing a development from the final ACHEULIAN HANDAXE tradition. At Saldanha, in Cape Province, Fauresmith artifacts were probably contemporary with a NEANDERTHAL-like skull similar to the one from BROKEN HILL.

Fayum, Fayoum A depression near the west bank of the Nile above Cairo containing a lake, once much more extensive than now; also a culture found in this region. Early settlement sites here were occupied by some of the first food-producing peoples of Egypt, who cultivated emmer and barley and bred cattle, sheep and pigs. Saw-edged sickle flints, matting-lined silo pits and saddle querns were found. Hollow-based flint arrowheads, bone dart tips, stone maceheads and bone harpoons testify to hunting and fishing. Axe heads were of flaked flint or ground pebbles. Undistinguished pottery was in use. Beads of ostrich eggshell and seashells of both Mediterranean and Red Sea types were imported. A radiocarbon date of 4440 ± 180 BC has been obtained. Gerza, the type site of the GERZEAN culture of the late predynastic period, is in this region also.

Federmesser The small backed BLADES, about the size and shape of penknife blades, which were the most distinctive artifacts of the LATE GLACIAL peoples of the north European plain during the ALLERØD OSCILLATION (c9850–8850 BC). Similar bladelets occur in the related CRESWELLIAN CULTURE of Britain.

Fell's Cave (Patagonia) Here and in the nearby cave of Palli Aike the lowest strata contained bones of horse and ground sloth together with crude CHOPPING TOOLS, bone awls, discs of lava (probably for grinding wild seeds), pressure-flaked fish-tail projectile points [47e], and a single unstemmed example similar to the North American Plainview type. Radiocarbon dates of 8759 ± 300 BC (Fell's Cave) and 6689 ± 400 (Palli Aike) suggest that man had spread south to the Straits of Magellan by the 9th millennium BC.

Ferrières A style of pottery from Languedoc, named after a MEGALITHIC CHAMBER TOMB in the department of Hérault. The ware is decorated with incised chevron patterns and horizontal lines, and was one of the styles used by the PASTEURS DES PLATEAUX. The earlier variety belongs to the Neolithic period and the later style is contemporary with the Copper Age pottery of FONTBOUÏSSE. Ferrières pottery has been found in caves, village sites, PASSAGE GRAVES and cremation cemeteries.

fibula A decorative brooch of safety-pin form, usually made of bronze. The name comes from the thin pointed leg bone which served from early times as a pin.

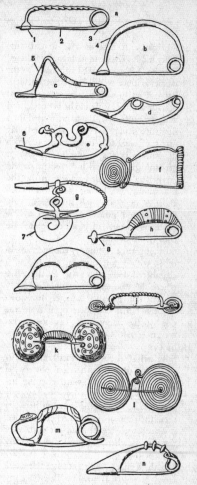

Fig. 63. Fibula types: (a) violin bow; (b) arc; (c) elbowed; (d) serpentine; (e) dragon; (f) harp; (g) disc with 'elastic bow'; (h) leech; (i) boat; (j) early northern two-piece fibula; (k) later two-piece; (l) spiral; (m) La Tène I; (n) La Tène III

Fibula terms: (1) catchplate; (2) pin; (3) spring; (4) bow; (5) stilt; (6) elongated catchplate; (7) disc catchplate; (8) knobbed (Certosa) catchplate

Like the simple PIN, the fibula implies draped garments, such as the cloak or toga. The earliest examples date to around 1300 BC, though their point of origin is still a matter of controversy. There are two main families of fibulae. In the south they were made in one piece, starting with the Peschiera or violin bow form in north Italy and Mycenaean Greece. From this developed the arc fibula north of the Mediterranean and the harp and spectacle fibulae in the eastern Alps in the years around 1000 BC. From the Certosa form was derived the long series of LA TÈNE Iron Age varieties, providing an excellent example of TYPOLOGY. Even wider variation is found among the succeeding Roman fibulae, leading on to the final forms in the Saxon and Migration periods (usually, if illogically, described by the name of BROOCH rather than fibula). In northern Europe the pin was generally made separate from the bow, though the variations followed a similar course to that in the south. The figure [63] gives only a few of the enormous range of types.

field archaeology (otherwise known, more accurately, as archaeological field survey, or, more disparagingly, as humps and bumps archaeology) The study of archaeological remains traceable on the ground without recourse to excavation. Some cannot be missed (barrows, castle mounds, hill forts), some will not be found without deliberate search (old field systems), and some are disclosed only by chance disturbance such as ploughing. All are valuable, and vulnerable, and their accurate recording is a matter of urgency. It is a study particularly suitable for amateurs as it calls for far less expenditure of time and money, and even if badly done does not harm the remains.

The technique will always be associated with the name of O.G.S. CRAWFORD, who between the wars demonstrated its methods and value. The three stages are observation (there is an obvious link with AIR PHOTO-GRAPHY), interpretation and accurate recording.

figurine A small model of a human or animal, the purpose of which seems usually to have been religious, to serve either as an object of worship itself, or as a votive offering to a god. [64]

Fig. 64. Aztec figurine

Filitosa (Taravo Valley, Corsica) A spur of rock fortified by a wall of CYCLOPEAN blocks. Inside are three buildings of Bronze Age TORRE type, one of which has a carbon date of c1200 BC. STATUE MEN-HIRS from an earlier period are incorporated in the structure of the buildings, and there are other fine examples nearby.

Fine Orange Pottery A high quality orange ware, often decorated with incised or black-painted patterns, which was traded all over the MAYA zone at the end of the CLASSIC period and throughout the POST-CLASSIC. It originated on the Gulf Coast of Mexico and was distributed as far as Guatemala.

Fiorelli, Giuseppe took over the Pompeii excavations between 1860 and 1875, and was one of the the first people to apply the methods of STRATIGRAPHY and area excavation on a large scale. Through his training school at Pompeii he passed on his methods to many other archaeologists.

First Northern culture ⟡ TRB CULTURE

Fishbourne A Roman site a mile west of Chichester discovered in 1960 and, after seven years' excavation, now confidently identified as the palace of Cogidubnus, client king of the Regnenses and Roman legate in Britain. Built c70 AD, it was one of the most lavish at that time in the empire, with a fully enclosed garden court, suites of mosaic-floored rooms and a complete set of baths.

flake A fragment removed from a larger stone (the CORE or nucleus) by percussion or pressure, which leaves characteristic marks on both the core and flake [65]. This makes it comparatively easy to distinguish human workmanship from natural accident, but the factor of design must be proved to give certainty. Flakes often

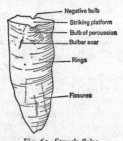

Negative bulb
Striking platform
Bulb of percussion
Bulbar scar
Rings
Fissures

Fig. 65. Struck flake

served as blanks from which more complex artifacts, or **flake tools**, could be made. ⟨⟩ BLADE

flange A transverse flattening of an edge. It is most commonly used for the sides of a bronze weapon, which are flattened to hold a grip or haft of a different material [20.5]. An external ledge round a pottery bowl is often given the same name.

flint A hard but brittle stone found in chalk or limestone. It is chemically a quartz, but differs in having a microcrystalline structure. This gives it the great advantage to man that it can be flaked readily in any direction, and so shaped to some desired useful form. It occurs widely, and where available was the basic material for man's tools until the advent of metal – it is the commonest 'stone' of the Stone Age in the THREE AGE SYSTEM. The only types of stone preferred to it were

OBSIDIAN and the tougher rocks used for ground tools in the NEOLITHIC. Flint was usually shaped by flaking [65], less commonly by grinding.

flood The SUMERIAN people preserved an account of a disastrous flood which wiped out all mankind save a single family, that of Utnapishtim. The discovery of the legend by George Smith in 1872, in CUNEIFORM tablets telling the epic of GILGAMESH, created a considerable stir by reason of its closeness in details to the Old Testament story of Noah. Both must derive from a common source, and Woolley at UR in 1929 showed that the source could have been a factual one. He revealed a depth of 8 ft of silt separating the Ubaid and Uruk levels, a deposit he could account for only by just such a flood. It should be noted, however, that flood levels have been found at other sites whose dates can be more appropriately equated with Noah's.

fluorine test The fluorine in percolating groundwater slowly replaces the calcium in buried bone. The rate at which it does so depends on the amount of fluorine present and is therefore not a universal standard, nor necessarily constant even on a single site. The change, however, is irreversible, so if bones of different geological date are found close together their relative ages can be quickly determined – the older they are, the more fluorine they will contain. The test, often in conjunction with RADIOMETRIC ASSAY for uranium, and analysis for COLLAGEN CONTENT and RADIOCARBON, has proved of great value in particular cases, notably those of SWANSCOMBE Man and PILTDOWN Man.

flûte de Pan A type of suspension lug found on pottery of the CHASSEY [45], CORTAILLOD and LAGOZZA cultures. Several vertical clay tubes, of width suitable to take a suspension cord, are set side by side on the wall of the vessel. The lug resembles a Pan pipe, or a section of corrugated cardboard.

fluting A series of broad parallel grooves,

horizontal, diagonal or vertical, on a pottery or metal vessel. Its primary purpose was decorative.

In the Americas, fluting often refers to the technique of producing channel-shaped flake scars on points of FOLSOM and CLOVIS types.

foederati Tribes beyond the frontiers of, but in treaty relations with, the Roman empire. Later the term came to be used for auxiliary troops recruited from outside the empire to support the LEGIONS in its defence.

fogou, fougou ⟡ SOUTERRAIN

Folsom (New Mexico, USA) was in 1926 the scene of one of the first discoveries in the New World of artifacts associated with extinct fauna (*Bison antiquus*). The site gives its name to a projectile point of ogival shape, with a concave base which may have ear-shaped projections at the corners. A channelled or fluted effect was produced by removing a longitudinal flake from each face, so that the flake-scars run almost to the tip of the tool [47b]. Folsom points are dated around 9–8000 BC and are a specialized development (found chiefly in the High Plains on the eastern side of the Rocky Mountains) of the fluted point tradition which began with CLOVIS.

Fontbouïsse (Villevieille, Gard, France) A Copper Age village which has given its name to a style of pottery decorated with

Fig. 66. Fontbouïsse pot

CHANNELLED ornament arranged usually in metopic or concentric semicircle patterns [66]. Fontbouïsse ware is widespread in southern France, occurring in CHAMBER TOMBS, village sites, burial caves, natural rock clefts and small cremation cists. ⟡ FERRIÈRES, LÉBOUS, PASTEURS DES PLATEAUX

Fontéchevade A cave, in the French department of Charente, which yielded fragments of a human skull in association with tools of TAYACIAN or CLACTONIAN character dating from the RISS-WÜRM INTERGLACIAL period. The remains were very incomplete but, like those from STEINHEIM and SWANSCOMBE, have been claimed as representing an early form of HOMO SAPIENS. Other anthropologists place the Fontéchevade skull near the beginning of the line which led to NEANDERTHAL MAN.

food vessel A vessel found singly in graves of the Early Bronze Age in northern Britain and Ireland, 1600–1300 BC. It is suggested that it was intended to hold food for the deceased's journey, just as the beaker is thought to have held drink [67]

Fig. 67. Food vessels: (a) Yorkshire and (b) Irish types, both showing false relief decoration

The form, however, is much more variable than the BEAKER, and may be derived from Neolithic prototypes. Associated traits, including the vessels themselves, cremation burial under a cairn, plano-convex knives and jet crescentic necklaces, enable one to speak of a Food Vessel culture.

forest clearance The natural vegetation of most of Europe is forest, so that the first NEOLITHIC farmers in the area had to make clearings before they could plant their crops. The clearings would be produced by the SLASH AND BURN method, and enlarged by the grazing of domestic animals. Clear evidence for this process is provided by POLLEN ANALYSIS, in the form of a sharp decline in the proportion of tree pollen, corresponding with a rise in the pollen of grasses, including the cereals, and weeds of cultivation, particularly the plantains and goosefoots.

Formative period ◊ PRE-CLASSIC PERIOD

forum The administrative centre and market place of a Roman town, usually placed at the intersection of the main streets, the DECUMANUS and CARDO. [53]

Fox, Sir Cyril With Wheeler, he led the development of excavational technique in Britain in the 1920s. He was also a notable field archaeologist, witness his study of Offa's Dyke. He is, however, best remembered for his geographical approach to archaeological problems, as in his *Archaeology of the Cambridge Region* (1923) and *Personality of Britain* (1932). He died in 1967.

Frere, John (1740–1807) One of the first people to recognize the antiquity of flint artifacts. In a communication to the Society of Antiquaries in 1797 he discussed the discovery at the Hoxne brickearth pit, in Suffolk, of 'flint weapons' (PALAEOLITHIC HANDAXES in today's terminology) with remains of extinct animals in an undisturbed deep stratum. Frere referred the finds to 'a very remote period indeed', but his ideas were in advance of his time, and his conclusions were ignored.

Frisians A Germanic people resident in the early centuries BC and AD in the low-lying districts of northern Holland and northwest Germany. Their coastal settlements were on artificial mounds known as TERPEN. Though mentioned in the records only in an obscure reference of Procopius, they were involved in the invasion of England by the ANGLO-SAXONS in C5 AD. To a much later date they controlled the trade of the North Sea from the port of Dorestad at the mouth of the Rhine.

fruitstand or **chalice** Convenient, if misleading, names for an open bowl on a high pedestal base. It may have had many different uses, of which holding fruit is not necessarily one.

frying pan A shallow pottery bowl with decorated base found in the Early Bronze Age in the Cyclades [68]. The handle con-

Fig. 68. Cycladic frying pan

sists of two diverging knob legs. The decoration includes spirals, very frequently the female sexual symbol, and rarely representations of a boat. The vessel's purpose is unknown, perhaps ritual, perhaps, when filled with water, as a mirror, but certainly not for frying.

funnel beaker A BEAKER with an expanded neck. The German form of the word, *Trichterbecher*, usually abbreviated to TRB [193], is used to describe the earliest Neolithic culture of northern Europe. The funnel beaker is not directly related to the bell-beaker of central and western Europe.

Füzesabony The third stage of the Hungarian Bronze Age, named after a TELL in the district of Heves (◊ TÓSZEG). The Füzesabony culture of C16–C15 BC is the Hungarian version of the Transylvanian OTOMANI culture.

G

gadroon A decorative motif in metalwork and pottery consisting of an embossed tear shape, one of a series radiating from the base of the vessel. They may cover only the lower portion of the sides, giving a blossom effect, or the whole vessel, making it look like a peeled orange. This same result was sometimes obtained through making simple vertical incised or fluted lines.

gallery grave (*allée couverte*) A form of CHAMBER TOMB [69] in which there is

Fig. 69. Plan of gallery grave

no distinction between the entrance passage and the burial chamber proper. The structure therefore resembles a MEGALITHIC corridor under an elongated mound. The many local variants of this form are distributed in Catalonia, France (♦ SEINE-OISE-MARNE CULTURE), the British Isles (♦ COURT CAIRN, SEVERN-COTS-WOLD TOMB, WEDGE-SHAPED GALLERY GRAVE), northwards as far as Sweden, and east to Sardinia (GIANTS' GRAVE) and south Italy. Most of the tombs were built during the NEOLITHIC period (roughly the 3rd millennium BC) and were still in use during the COPPER AGE when BEAKER pottery was introduced, but the Sardinian examples belong to the full Bronze Age.

Gallinazo ♦ VIRÚ VALLEY

Gandhara The ACHAEMENID SATRAPY of this name, roughly Pakistan's North-West Frontier Province, together with that of 'India', roughly the Punjab, was important in passing Persian ideas on to the civilizations of the Ganges valley in C5–C4 BC. It had even greater influence in C2 when its

rulers, the Greeks driven from BACTRIA, introduced Hellenistic art styles to India.

Gangetic hoards A group of hoards of copper objects found in the Ganges basin of India [70]. They include unexplained

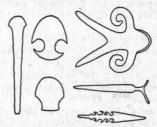

Fig. 70. Copper objects from the Gangetic hoards

anthropomorphic objects, harpoons, antenna swords, hooked spears, bar chisels and broad flat axes. A date in the 2nd millennium is likely since three hoards have provided associations with OCHRE-COLOURED POTTERY.

Garcel, El An Early Neolithic village in ALMERIA, southeast Spain, the type site of the earlier phase of the Almerian culture.

Garstang, Professor John A prominent scholar of Near Eastern prehistory, his major excavations included SAKÇE GÖZÜ 1908, JERICHO 1930–36 and MERSIN 1936–9, all of which materially advanced our knowledge of the area's past.

Gaudo A cemetery of SHAFT-AND-CHAMBER tombs at Paestum in Campania, Italy. It was discovered in bull-dozing an

Fig. 71. Askos from Gaudo

airstrip in 1943. The tombs produced up to 25 disarticulated skeletons apiece, and great quantities of unusual pots, especially asymmetric straight-necked flasks approximating to the form of an ASKOS [71] but oval, square or triangular in plan. There were also cups, open dishes, lids and double vessels. The scanty use of copper and the presence of fine flint daggers place this group in the Copper Age, with parallels at RINALDONE.

Gavrinis An island in the Morbihan, Brittany, with one of the most elaborately decorated PASSAGE GRAVES in Europe. The designs pecked into the walls include representations of polished stone axes, as well as abstract patterns.

Gawra, Tepe A TELL near Mosul excavated by the Americans 1931–8. It had been occupied from the later 5th to mid 2nd millennia BC. Its most important period was as a northern outpost of the UBAID culture in the 5th–4th millennium. Three temples planned round a court show an early spread of the developing civilization of SUMER to the north. There is evidence for surprisingly extensive trade too. A curious circular house of the succeeding URUK phase, perhaps a chieftain's residence, is also noteworthy.

de Geer, Baron G. ♢ VARVE DATING

Gelidonya A cape in southwest Turkey off which a merchant ship foundered in C13 BC. It was discovered in 1960, providing a classic example of UNDERWATER ARCHAEOLOGY and useful information on the MYCENAEANS. Its cargo had consisted of ox-hide INGOTS of copper from Cyprus.

geochronology The general term for all dating methods depending on the earth's physical changes. For examples ♢ ARCHAEOMAGNETISM, DENDRO-CHRONOLOGY, FLUORINE TEST, OBSIDIAN DATING, POTASSIUM–ARGON DATING, RADIOCARBON, THERMO-LUMINESCENCE, VARVE DATING

geophysics The study of physical properties of the earth, eg magnetism, radio-

activity, vulcanism, etc. Its applications to archaeology have been to provide dating methods (GEOCHRONOLOGY) and techniques for exploration (MAGNETOMETER and RESISTIVITY SURVEY).

Gerzean or **Nagada II** The late predynastic culture of Egypt which developed out of the AMRATIAN c3600 BC. It is named after the site of El Gerza or Gerzeh in the FAYUM and is well represented at the cemetery of NAQADA in Upper Egypt. Flintwork continued, notably magnificently ripple-flaked knives, but copper was coming into much wider use for axes, daggers, etc. FAIENCE was introduced for the first time. Ground stone vessels were popular and very finely worked. The typical pottery ware is a light coloured fabric in shapes imitating the stone vessels, decorated with red painted designs. These include imitations of stone markings, geometrical patterns and designs taken from nature. Ships were particularly common, representing the papyrus-bundle craft which plied the Nile [72].

Fig. 72. Gerzean jar painted with a boat

The most important development in this period was the strengthening of Asiatic influences, seen in wavy-ledged handles on the jars, in cylinder seals (these certainly Mesopotamian in origin), representations of mythical animals, the use of mudbrick in architecture and possibly writing at the very end of the period. These seem to have led to the advances which brought Egypt to the level of civilization at the start of the Dynastic period c3200 BC.

Getian A tribal name for peoples in the territories of modern Romania and Bulgaria. They are often referred to as Thraco-Getians or Geto-Dacians, and were strongly influenced by both CELTS and SCYTHIANS. Their culture belongs to the later Iron Age, from C4 BC until their conquest by Rome in AD 106. It is a local version of LA TÈNE.

Gezer An important TELL near Jerusalem. The site was a difficult one to interpret and the excavation, by Macalister 1907–9, too early to yield all the evidence that might have been expected had modern methods been available. Renewed excavations are currently in progress. It was occupied from the proto-Urban period before 3000 BC to the Iron Age (C10), and sporadically later. To the Iron Age belong the remains of a gateway built by Solomon. The most noteworthy finds were a potsherd with one of the earliest uses of the ALPHABET (C18–C17) and the Gezer calendar, (C11–C10), the oldest known inscription in Early Hebrew writing.

Ghassul, Teleilat A site to the northeast of the Dead Sea, excavated 1930–38, 1960, and again in 1967. It was occupied by a small village during the Chalcolithic, c3500 BC. The houses were of PISÉ and had originally had elaborate polychrome frescoes. A wide range of pottery shapes was in use, in a ware found on many other Palestinian sites. Carbonized date and olive stones are amongst the earliest evidence for the cultivation of these fruits.

ghost wall When a stone or brick building falls into disuse the building materials may be taken away to be re-used elsewhere. If the walls were removed right down to their foundations below ground level, the outline or 'ghost' of the vanished building can often be recovered by following the robber trenches of the stone-seekers. [182]

giants' grave (*tomba di giganti*) The local name for a kind of MEGALITHIC CHAMBER TOMB built in Sardinia during the mid 2nd millennium BC [73]. The burial chamber is of GALLERY GRAVE type, and is set in a long cairn with a retaining wall. Some giants' tombs have curved façades

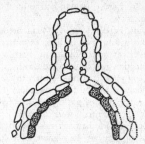

Fig. 73. Plan of Giant's Grave at Sos Ossastros, Sardinia

enclosing a forecourt, creating a superficial – and coincidental – resemblance to an Irish COURT CAIRN. For the domestic architecture of the period ◊ NURAGHE.

Gilgamesh The hero of the best-known SUMERIAN epic, which had a wide currency and very long life in the ancient world [74]. He was half god, half man, and

Fig. 74. Gilgamesh, from a seal

king of URUK, but abused his position to such an extent that the wild man Enkidu was sent by the gods to humble him. The two fought, and as a result became friends and allies. They journeyed together to overcome Humbaba, a giant of the Cedar Forest (Amanus). When Gilgamesh spurned the goddess ISHTAR's love, she punished him by killing Enkidu. Gilgamesh then went in search of Utnapishtim (the Sumerian Noah) beyond 'the waters of death', to seek the key to immortality for himself. This, in the form of a plant growing on the seabed, he obtained with many difficulties, but it was stolen from him by a snake, leaving him to the fate of all mortals.

Giyan, Tepe A long-lived TELL site south of Hamadan, western Iran, excavated by Contenau and Ghirshman 1931–2. Its foundation goes back to late HALAF, overlapping phase III at SIALK early in the 4th millennium. In the 2nd millennium it saw the native painted pottery replaced by the grey monochrome ware believed to be associated with the first INDO-EUROPEAN speaking Iranians. Its highest level shows it to have been an outpost of Assyria, with a palace of C8 BC.

Giza The cemetery region on the west bank of the Nile opposite modern Cairo. It is most famous for the Great PYRAMID, two only slightly smaller neighbours, and the Great SPHINX, erected by pharaohs of the 4th dynasty c2500 BC.

glaciation A period of cold climate during which the area covered by the ice caps increased. Several glaciations may go to make up an 'Ice Age' (◊ PLEISTOCENE and [p 183], for its main subdivisions). The periglacial zone round the margin of an ice sheet has permanently frozen subsoil, and is occupied by cold-loving plants and animals. The precise dating of the Pleistocene glaciations has still to be worked out.

glacis The open slope below the outer rampart of a fortification, where the attackers are exposed to the missiles of the defenders.

Glasinac A mountain valley near Sarajevo in Bosnia, Yugoslavia, where there are several thousand tumuli of the Late Bronze and Early Iron Age containing more than 10,000 graves. The metal and ceramic objects show connexions with Greece, Italy and the Danube valley.

glass An artificial material produced by fusing a silica sand with an alkali. It was developed from FAIENCE in the Near East shortly before 2000 BC, but was rarely used for anything larger than beads until Hellenistic and Roman times. Natural glass also occurs, OBSIDIAN.

Glastonbury (Somerset) A lake village, excavated 1892–1907 by A. Bulleid and H. St G. Gray, which has yielded more data than any other site about life in the British Iron Age. The village was built on a wooden platform keyed to the underlying peat and was enclosed by a timber palisade. Inside were more than 60 round huts with clay and plank floors. Preservation was so good that the excavators recovered baskets, iron objects (including CURRENCY BARS and tools with their original hafts), dugout canoes, fragments of spoked wheels, lathe-turned bowls and wooden tubs decorated with LA TÈNE art motifs, farming and fishing gear, and evidence that potting, weaving and metalworking were carried on in the village. Occupation lasted from C3 or C2 BC until just before the Roman conquest. On the high ground nearby is an Iron Age earthwork, a scatter of Roman pottery, and a Dark Age structure dated to C6 AD. Glastonbury, like CADBURY Castle, is linked in folklore with King Arthur.

glaze A glassy surface given to objects, usually of pottery, by coating them with powdered glass and reheating them to a temperature where the glass begins to fuse. Apart from improving the appearance, this renders the naturally porous earthenware impermeable.

globular amphora An AMPHORA of broad proportions, the characteristic pottery vessel produced by a cultural group occupying Germany and neighbouring districts around 2000 BC. The culture is closely linked with both TRB and the CORDED WARE, but the nature of the relationships has yet to be clearly determined. ◊ KURGAN

glyph ◊ HIEROGLYPH

goat *Capra hircus aegagrus*, the bezoar of the mountains of southwest Asia, was the wild ancestor of the domestic goat.

Domesticated bones are recorded from such early sites as JERICHO, JARMO and ÇATAL HÜYÜK, but the complexity of separating goats from SHEEP in skeletal material has made their early history difficult to recover.

Gobi The great desert of east central Asia. Mesolithic and Neolithic material was discovered by Swedish and American expeditions in the 1920s and 30s, proving that climatic conditions were much less extreme in the past. Finds included many microliths, together with polished stone axes and coarse pottery. Influences from Siberia and to a lesser extent China were detectable.

Golasecca An Iron Age culture of Lombardy and Piedmont in the upper Po valley named after a site near Milan. Its URNFIELD cemeteries are outshone by those of ESTE and BOLOGNA.

gold One of the first metals to be exploited by man. Occurring naturally, as nuggets or dust, it needs no smelting. It is too soft and scarce for functional use, but has been prized for its decorative value throughout human history – for beads, display vessels, ornamental trimmings, etc. Working was basically by hammering, to which more complicated techniques like casting, soldering, granulation and filigree were later added.

Gordium The capital of the PHRYGIANS, on the bank of the Sakarya river in Turkey. The site has been under excavation since 1949 by the Americans, who have made rich finds in the great tumulus tombs of its cemetery.

gourd *Lagenaria siceraria*, a plant of the melon family grown solely for its hard rind, which was much used for making vessels and containers. In some areas the shapes of pots can be explained as copies of gourd vessels, DANUBIAN I offering the best example. Gourds were cultivated in early times in both the Old and New Worlds.

Gournia A Late Bronze Age town of the MINOANS overlooking the Gulf of Mirabello in eastern Crete. A small palace was built on the site in Middle Minoan III, c1600 BC, showing features copied from the palaces of KNOSSOS and MALLIA. Through the Late Minoan period, from c1550, the town grew up round it, consisting of many modest houses mainly occupied by artisans and the like. The palace, too, had been turned into workmen's houses, and a small shrine remained the only civic building.

gradiometer ◊ BLEEPER

graffiti Any figures or inscriptions scratched into a surface. They may be found on rocks, buildings or pottery.

Graig Llwyd (Penmaenmawr, Caernarvonshire) ◊ AXE FACTORY

grain impression A cereal grain which has been incorporated by chance in clay to be baked will normally be completely consumed in the firing. The impression left in the clay, however, may be clear enough for identification to be possible, and thus provide useful evidence on the crops in cultivation at the time. ◊ PALAEOBOTANY

Grand Pressigny (Indre-et-Loire, France) A mining and workshop site from which a distinctive caramel-coloured flint was exported in the form of blocks and unfinished blanks during the Copper Age. Grand Pressigny flint has been found everywhere from the Pyrenees to Holland and Switzerland.

grave goods Objects placed with the deceased on BURIAL. They may represent personal possessions, offerings to the dead man's spirit, or provisions for the spirit in, or on its journey to, the afterlife.

Gravettian An advanced Upper PALAEOLITHIC industry which succeeds the AURIGNACIAN, and is named after the site of La Gravette, in the Dordogne. In French terminology the Gravettian is the earliest phase of the Upper PÉRIGORDIAN (Périgordian IV), and is characterized principally by small, pointed BLADES [75a] with straight blunted backs (the so-called

Gravette points). Most of the French sites are caves, but possibly related industries, known as Eastern Gravettian, are distributed through the LOESS lands of central Europe and Russia where the camp sites

a   b

Fig. 75. (a) Gravette backed blade; (b) Font Robert point

of mammoth-hunters have been excavated (◊ DOLNÍ VĚSTONICE, VENUS FIGUR-INES). The term Gravettian has also been loosely employed for all the Upper Périgordian material. The date for the Gravettian proper seems to be slightly earlier than 25,000 BC.

Great Interglacial or **Hoxnian** The warm interval between the MINDEL and the RISS GLACIATIONS.

greenstone A loose term comprising a variety of rocks which the geologist would prefer to distinguish as serpentine, olivine, jade, jadeite, nephrite, chloromelanite, etc. The general term is useful, however, as ancient man employed these materials interchangeably, mainly for high quality or ceremonial polished stone axes, figurines and the like. Jade was particularly popular in China and Middle America, being held to have magical properties.

grid layout The practice of dividing a site into squares for ease of recording features and objects excavated. Normally a square trench will be cut within each grid square, separated by a baulk from each neighbouring trench.

Grimaldi A locality just to the east of Monaco, where excavations at a number of

caves have unearthed Middle and Upper PALAEOLITHIC flint industries. The Grotte du Prince yielded a pure MOU-STERIAN deposit, and from other caves the sequence can be continued through early Upper Palaeolithic, AURIGNACIAN, Grimaldian (an industry with backed BLADES akin to those of Upper PÉRIGORDIAN, or GRAVETTIAN, type), and finally a micro-lithic industry. Several burials of the Upper Palaeolithic were also unearthed. There is no MAGDALENIAN in Liguria, where the Grimaldian persists until the end of the Palaeolithic period.

Grimes Graves Neolithic flint mines near Brandon, on the Norfolk–Suffolk border. In an area of 34 acres are the remains of 346 mine shafts, some of which were sunk to a depth of 30 ft where beds of good quality flint were followed by means of radiating galleries. The products, mainly axe blades, were roughly chipped to shape at the site and were then traded in semi-finished condition. In one shaft was found an altar of flint lumps. Around it were piled deer antlers, and at its base was a chalk lamp. In front of the altar was an offering of chalk balls, a phallus carved in the same material and a chalk figurine of a fat woman.

grooved decoration Pottery decoration in which comparatively broad lines are drawn on the firm but unbaked pot surface. No clay is removed, as it is in EXCISED DECORATION, nor is the surface itself broken, as with INCISED DECORA-TION.

Grooved Ware In British archaeology the term refers to the grooved variety of RINYO-CLACTON pottery. [161]

Grotefend, Georg Friedrich ◊ CUNEI-FORM

guilloche A decorative band of regularly interlaced ribbons reproduced on a plane surface. [76]

Gumelniţa A Late Neolithic/Copper Age culture of eastern Romania and Bulgaria c2700–2000 BC. Permanent villages of

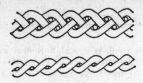

Fig. 76. Double and single guilloches

rectangular houses formed low TELLS. Copper and gold were coming into use beside flint. Gumelnita can be derived from the HAMANGIA, BOIAN and Maritza cultures which preceded it in this area.

Gundestrup A bog in northern Jutland, Denmark, in which a great silver cauldron had been placed as a VOTIVE DEPOSIT during the pre-Roman Iron Age. On the plaques which decorate both the inside and outside of the bowl are scenes from CELTIC mythology. The cauldron was probably manufactured in Romania or Bulgaria during C1 or C2 BC.

Günz glaciation The first major PLEISTO-CENE GLACIATION of the Alps [p 183]. There were probably earlier glaciations represented by the so-called Donau phase.

Habur ♢ KHABUR

Hacılar (pron Hajilar) A small but important site excavated by Mellaart in the lake region of southwest Turkey, to be compared with ÇATAL HÜYÜK. The houses were of mudbrick or wood and daub on stone foundations, with an upper storey of wood. They were finished internally in plaster, rarely painted. No pottery was found in the earliest settlement, which must represent an early phase of settled life, dated by radiocarbon to the 7th millennium BC. Crops included BARLEY, EMMER and lentils. Bones of SHEEP and CATTLE were also found, not certainly domesticated, as well as wild species like deer. Levels IX to VI were of the Late Neolithic,

Fig. 77. Painted jar from Hacılar

with more substantial houses, monochrome red to brown pottery and some use of copper. Hacılar in levels V to I was a fortified settlement, fully Chalcolithic and characterized by boldly painted red on white pottery. [77]

Hadrian's Wall A wall, in its final form entirely of stone, running for 76 miles from Tyne to Solway to defend the northern frontier of Roman Britain, built under Hadrian c AD 122–133. The wall itself was 8–10 ft thick and 12–16 ft high (this figure is not certainly known). There were 16 forts along its length, fortlets or mile-castles regularly spaced a Roman mile apart, and turrets, two between each pair of milecastles. Where the lie of the land to the north did not already give adequate protection a ditch 9 ft deep and 27 ft across was added. To the south of the wall, another great ditch with wide spaced banks, the **Vallum**, follows roughly the same line, perhaps marking the limit of the military zone. Though the whole work, with outlying forts and service roads, was a most impressive undertaking, it could only serve its purpose of excluding the barbarians when adequately manned. It was overrun in 197, rebuilt by Severus, overrun again in 296 and restored by Constantius Chlorus, overrun again in 367 and rebuilt by Count Theodosius, and finally abandoned by AD 400.

Hagia Triada A palace of the MINOANS in southern Crete 2 miles west of PHAESTOS. It seems to have replaced the latter as a royal residence c1600 BC, and survived for the two centuries of the Late Minoan I period. The small town around it continued later, and it is to Late Minoan III that the site's most famous find belongs. This is a pottery coffin painted with scenes associated with funeral ritual, the pouring of libations, bringing of offerings, etc [78]. Also well known is the Harvester

Fig. 78. Detail from the Hagia Triada sarcophagus; pouring libations

Vase, a stone RHYTON portraying in low relief a delightful and vigorous scene of a procession of celebrating harvesters.

Halaf A large TELL near the KHABUR river where this crosses from Turkey to

Syria. It was excavated by von Oppenheim 1911–14. It serves as the type site of an important stage of north Mesopotamian development, roughly the 5th millennium BC. Architecture is more competent than in the HASSUNA period, mudbrick appearing freely beside the PISÉ. At ARPACHIYAH in particular there are elaborate and mysterious circular buildings. Simple steatite stamp seals were coming into use, which imply the development of personal property. The pottery was exceptionally fine, a thin hard ware in a wide range of competent and attractive shapes bearing brilliant carpet-like designs painted in black, red and white on the buff surface [79]. A bull's head motif was par-

Fig. 79. Painted plate, Halaf

ticularly popular and, like the double axe and Maltese cross motifs, may have held some special significance. The Halaf period was succeeded by the UBAID.

halberd A weapon in which a pointed blade is mounted at right angles to, and in the same plane as, its haft and used with a chopping motion [80]. In bronze it was popular in the Early Bronze Age in Europe, particularly in Ireland and central Europe. It appears again in the Chinese Bronze Age.

Hallstatt This site, in the Austrian Salzkammergut 30 miles east of Salzburg, is noted for its salt mines and for its cemetery of almost 3,000 graves. The oldest mine galleries go back to the Late Bronze Age, though most are of Iron Age date. The salt in the mines has preserved corpses,

clothing and all sorts of mining tools. The cemetery began in Late Bronze Age URNFIELD times, when the rite was usually cremation, but most of the graves are of the full Iron Age (Hallstatt and transitional Hallstatt-LA TÈNE periods: see below).

In central European archaeology the terms Hallstatt A (C12 and C11 BC) and Hallstatt B (C10–C8 BC) are used as a chronological framework for the urnfield cultures of the Late Bronze Age. The first iron objects north of the Alps appear at the close of this period, and the Iron Age proper begins with the Hallstatt C (or I) stage of C7. The area of fullest development is Bohemia, upper Austria and Bavaria, where HILLFORTS were constructed and the dead were sometimes interred on or with a four-wheeled wagon, covered by a MORTUARY HOUSE below a BARROW. Sheet bronze was still used for armour, vessels and decorative metalwork, but the characteristic weapon was a long iron SWORD (or bronze copy of this) with a scabbard tipped by a winged CHAPE [186g and j]. These swords are found as far afield as southeast England, in the so-called 'Iron Age A' cultures. During the Hallstatt D (or II) period, in C6, the most advanced cultures are found further west, in Bur-

Fig. 80. Halberds: (a) Irish type; (b) flint copy (Italy); (c) with bronze shaft (Germany)

gundy, Switzerland and the Rhineland. Wagon burials are still prominent (◊ HEUNEBURG, VIX), and trade brought luxury objects from the Greek and ETRUSCAN cities round the Mediterranean. By the close of this period in the mid C5, elements of Hallstatt culture (though without wagon burials) are found from southern France to Yugoslavia and Czechoslovakia. ◊ CELTS, KLEIN ASPERGLE

Hama A TELL on the Orontes in Syria excavated by the Danes in the 1930s. Open to influences from all directions, its cultural levels provided valuable correlations over wide areas. A Neolithic occupation in level M comparable to that of MERSIN was succeeded by a village with HALAF pottery. Later levels continue the story through to the Iron Age, when it was an inland site of the PHOENICIANS.

Hamangia A site close to the mouth of the Danube. It has given its name to an Early–Middle Neolithic culture in the

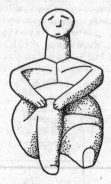

Fig. 81. Terracotta figurine from Cernavoda

Dobrudja and coastal Bulgaria which is regarded by some as a branch of the IMPRESSED WARE culture, arriving by sea from the Aegean before 3500 BC. Noteworthy are its use of spondylus shell bracelets and its famous terracotta and marble figurines. [81]

Hamburgian The culture of the first people to colonize north Germany and the Low Countries after the final retreat of the PLEISTOCENE ice sheets had made the area available for settlement. The Hamburgians may have been the descendants of Eastern GRAVETTIAN or peripheral MAGDALENIAN groups, and many of their sites fall within pollen zone I (c13,000–9850 BC – [p 186]. They were great reindeer hunters whose diagnostic tools are small, single-shouldered points [4b] and 'zinken' (small beaked implements used for working antler).

Hammurabi (1792–50 BC) The sixth king of a dynasty of AMORITES resident at BABYLON. In c1783 BC he began the series of campaigns which won him an empire from MARI and NINEVEH to the Persian Gulf. He is best remembered for his Code of Laws. These, with their emphasis on retaliation and an eye for an eye, however harsh they appear to modern eyes, still marked a considerable advance. They also yield detailed evidence on the structure of contemporary society. His 43-year reign saw the final extinction of SUMER as a political power, though its culture was dominant for far longer. His empire declined steadily after his death, until swept away by the HITTITES and KASSITES c1595 BC.

handaxe A large bifacially worked CORE tool, normally oval or pear-shaped, and from 3 to 10 ins in length [82]. It is the diagnostic implement of certain Lower

a   b   c

Fig. 82. Lower Palaeolithic tools: (a) Abbevillian handaxe; (b) Acheulian handaxe; (c) cleaver

PALAEOLITHIC industries (◊ ABBE-VILLIAN, CHELLEAN, ACHEULIAN), and of one variety of the MOUSTERIAN. In spite of the name it was not an axe at all, and probably served as an all-purpose tool. The oldest and crudest handaxes have been found mainly in Africa, where the form seems to develop out of the PEBBLE TOOL, but the finer, Acheulian, tools are known from most of Africa, Europe, southwest Asia and India.

Harappa One of the twin capitals of the INDUS CIVILIZATION, beside the Ravi river in the Punjab, 400 miles northeast of MOHENJO-DARO. Its baked bricks were looted to serve as ballast on the nearby railway line, but excavations by MARSHALL in the 1920s and Wheeler in 1946 have recovered much information from the 50 ft citadel mound on its west side. Its massive wall was of mudbrick with a facing of baked brick, 40 ft thick and enclosing an area 200 yds by 400. To the north were discovered workmen's quarters, working floors and great granaries for the city's food supply. To the south the inhumation cemetery known as R37 was contemporary with the later period of the city. Cemetery H beyond it belonged to the small population of squatters who re-occupied the site after its destruction. The rite here was inhumation or fractional BURIAL associated with black on red painted pottery very different from the Indus ware. Its motifs include peacocks, sundry animals and many geometric or floral filling designs. Deep excavation revealed a pre-Indus occupation related to that of KOT DIJI and perhaps the ZHOB valley.

harpoon A throwing spear whose head, usually of bone or antler, consists of a pointed shaft with one or two rows of backward pointing barbs [83 and 111]. It was often loosely hafted so that it would separate from its shaft after the point had struck home. A line attached to it would prevent the quarry escaping. It was particularly popular during the Upper Palaeolithic and Mesolithic. Two similar points with barbs down the inner side only could be lashed to a shaft to form a LEISTER.

Hasanlu A long-lived TELL south of Lake Urmia, northwest Iran, excavated by Dyson from 1956 on. It is best known for a gold bowl with relief decoration of weather gods and scenes from the mythology of the HURRI. This had been looted c800 BC by soldiers from URARTU who, however, were killed by the collapse of a burning roof before they could escape. The bowl is related artistically to the finds from MARLIK and ZIWIYEH.

Hassuna A TELL near Mosul in northern Iraq excavated by Seton Lloyd and Fuad Safar 1943–4. It has given its name to the pottery ware present in its lowest levels, dated to the 6th millennium. This pottery may be related to that of the upper levels at JARMO and is widely distributed from Susiana to southern Turkey (SAKÇE-GÖZÜ and the AMUQ). It was usually a buff ware in simple shapes, sometimes burnished, sometimes painted or incised with simple geometric patterns. In higher levels it was replaced by SAMARRA ware.

Hastinapura A site on the upper Ganges which has given a stratigraphy important to the later prehistory of India. The lowest level, with a poorly understood OCHRE-COLOURED POTTERY, was followed by 5 ft of deposit with PAINTED GREY WARE, mudbrick walls, etc. Over this, 10 ft with NORTHERN BLACK POLISHED WARE was capped by material of historic date.

Hathor The cow goddess of ancient Egypt, represented in either human or animal form. She was the goddess of women and childbirth.

Hatshepsut A queen of Egypt who reigned as PHARAOH 1505–1484 BC after the death of her husband. A vigorous ruler,

Fig. 83. Harpoon head of antler from Star Carr

she sent a trading expedition to PUNT, as recorded in detail in her funerary temple at DEIR EL-BAHRI. She was succeeded by her son Thothmes III.

Hattusas The ancient name for BOGHAZ KÖY, the capital of the HITTITES.

Hatvan The type site, northeast of Budapest, of the second stage of the Hungarian Bronze Age (◊ TÓSZEG). The Hatvan culture overlaps in time with the NAGYRÉV culture but soon replaces it entirely.

Haua Fteah A cave in Cyrenaica with a long archaeological sequence going back to c78,000 BC. The oldest flint industry is a Libyan variant of the PRE-AURIGNACIAN, and is followed successively by LEVAL-LOISO-MOUSTERIAN, DABBAN, ORAN-IAN, CAPSIAN and finally (from c5000) by NEOLITHIC with pottery and domesticated animals.

Hazor The largest Palestinian TELL, excavated by Yadin 1955–9, it lies southwest of Lake Huleh in the extreme north of Israel. The citadel in the southwest corner was occupied from the Early Bronze Age until the ISRAELITES drove out the CANAANITES c1220 BC. Refounded by Solomon in c10, to which period belongs a monumental gateway, it was destroyed again by the ASSYRIANS c734. There was sporadic later occupation down to the Hellenistic period. To the citadel was added in the Middle Bronze Age, c1700 BC, a town of 180 acres, enclosed by a great bank and ditch of HYKSOS type.

hearth The site of an open domestic fire (cf KILN, OVEN), represented by ash, charcoal and discolouration. There may be slight structural additions such as clay flooring or a setting of stones around it.

Heathery Burn (near Stanhope, Co. Durham) A cave, now destroyed, which was the home of a group of Late Bronze Age metalsmiths. Bronzes of the kind made at Heathery Burn occur in hoards in northern England from c8–c7 BC, and are the English counterpart of the DOWRIS industry of Ireland. The use of lead bronze,

known previously in the WILBURTON complex of southern England, now becomes general in the north of England as well.

Heidelberg ◊ MAUER JAW

Heliopolis The Egyptian city which was the centre of the cult of the sun god Ra, whose symbols were the PYRAMID and the OBELISK. It was 20 miles north of MEM-PHIS and 5 miles east of the modern city of Cairo. It was from this site that Cleopatra's Needle, an obelisk of Thothmes III, was brought to London.

Helladic The generic name for the Greek Bronze Age (cf CYCLADIC in the Cyclades and MINOAN in Crete). It is divided into Early, Middle (◊ MINYAN WARE) and Late, each further subdivided. Late Helladic is equated with Mycenaean as a period (◊ MYCENAEANS).

helmet Evidence for some form of protective headgear goes back almost as far as evidence for warfare. The troops on the Royal Standard of UR wear leather helmets. The Blue Crown worn by PHARAOH in the New KINGDOM of Egypt was a war helmet [144c]. One type covered with boar's tusks was current among the MY-CENAEANS. More obviously for parade than war are the bronze examples from the European Late Bronze and Iron Ages. Among the VILLANOVANS the cinerary urn was often covered with the helmet of the dead warrior [207]. Several fine examples from Britain are decorated with CELTIC ART. The New World has yielded helmets made of gold and of wood encrusted with turquoise mosaic.

Helwan The town on the east of the Nile Delta, the name of which is sometimes applied to the material from the neighbouring Neolithic site of El OMARI.

Hembury (near Honiton, Devon) A CAUSEWAYED CAMP which has given its name to the plain pottery of the earliest Neolithic in southern England (◊ WIND-MILL HILL CULTURE). The Neolithic earthwork produced radiocarbon dates in the 3300–3000 BC range, and an Iron Age HILLFORT was later built on the same site.

henge A type of ritual monument found only in the British Isles [19] and consisting of a circular area, anything from 150 to 1,700 ft across, delimited by a ditch with the bank normally *outside* it. Class I henges have a single entrance marked by a gap in the earthworks, while those of Class II have two such entrances placed opposite each other. Many henges have extra features such as burials, pits, circles of upright stones (eg AVEBURY and STONEHENGE) or of timber posts (as at DURRINGTON WALLS and WOODHENGE). Henges are usually associated with Late Neolithic pottery of RINYO-CLACTON, PETERBOROUGH and BEAKER types, dating from the centuries after 2000 BC. At Stonehenge some of the secondary construction is of Early Bronze Age (WESSEX CULTURE) date.

Hesi, Tell el- This TELL in southern Palestine was dug by PETRIE and Bliss 1890–92. It was occupied from the Early Bronze Age, c2600 BC, to the Iron Age. Its importance lies less in its contents than in the influence of its excavation, the first clear exposition of the correlation of pottery TYPOLOGY, STRATIGRAPHY of successive building levels, and datable imports (from Egypt), the basic principles of all Near Eastern excavation.

Heuneburg, The A great Iron Age HILLFORT of the HALLSTATT period on the upper Danube near Riedlingen, Württemberg, in Germany. There were five main building phases, but at the start of the second one (c6 BC) part of the rampart was reconstructed in the Greek manner, with bastions of mud brick on a stone foundation. Wine amphorae and Attic Black Figure pottery were imported from the Greek city of Massalia. Close by the fort are princely burials of the same date, including the Hohmichele TUMULUS. This covered a timber MORTUARY HOUSE containing the body of an archer accompanied by a wooden wagon and precious offerings.

hieratic A cursive form of the Egyptian HIEROGLYPHS arising as a result of their being written by brush pen on PAPYRUS for business and similar non-monumental purposes. It was gradually replaced by DEMOTIC from C7 BC, but survived for religious use to the end of paganism in Egypt.

hieroglyphs (lit sacred carved [letters]) In the strict sense, the signs of the earliest Egyptian script, introduced c3000 BC and remaining in use until C4 AD. The name is misleading in that the script was employed for funerary and monumental inscriptions as well as more strictly religious ones, and even more in that it was often painted or written on papyrus rather than carved. Hieroglyphs were deciphered by Champollion in 1822, through his study of the bilingual inscriptions on the ROSETTA STONE and an obelisk from PHILAE.

The script's development seems to have been so rapid that it may have been in some sense an imitation of the earliest writing of Mesopotamia in its URUK phase. In both scripts three classes of symbol were used, each a single picture or geometric figure. Pictograms or ideograms represented whole words in pictorial form. Phonograms represented the sounds of words, the picture of an object pronounced in the same way as the desired word being used in its place (this was made easier by the fact that the vowels were disregarded). Determinatives told the reader the class of word spelt by the phonograms, necessary where these were ambiguous. Often all three classes of symbol were used in conjunction. No attempt was made in its long history to simplify the basis of the writing, even when the more cursive forms of it, HIERATIC and DEMOTIC, were introduced. The result was artistic, as can be seen in the many carved and painted tomb and temple inscriptions [84], but extremely cumbrous.

More loosely the term has been applied

to other scripts based on pictograms, particularly those of MINOAN Crete, the HITTITES and the MAYA.

Fig. 84. Cartouche from Tutankhamen's tomb
with inscription in hieroglyphs

hilani or **bit-hilani** A suite of reception rooms comprising a portico with one to three columns, a rectangular throne room and usually a range of storerooms, all lying transverse to the axis of the building. A stairway to an upper floor opens from one end of the portico. This architectural unit was much employed by the Syro-HITTITES in the early 1st millennium BC, and was copied on occasion by the Assyrians. The earliest known examples are from Tell ATCHANA nearly a thousand years before.

hill figure A type of monument found on the chalk downs of southern Britain. The design, usually a horse or a human figure, is cut into the hillside and stands out white against the green turf. The oldest figure, the White Horse of Uffington, may date to the Late Iron Age and probably had some religious function. The Cerne Abbas giant is of the Roman period, and the Long Man of Wilmington may be either Roman or Saxon. All the others are of more recent date, and are usually commemorative or purely ornamental.

hillfort A fortified hilltop enclosed by one or more ramparts of stone or earth, often with external ditches. The range of size is considerable. Some hillforts contain houses and were perhaps royal residences or, in the case of large forts of OPPIDUM type, true towns; others seem to lack permanent buildings, and were probably refuges where the people and flocks from the surrounding area took shelter in times of crisis. ◊ CONTOUR FORT, DUN, RATH, TIMBER LACING

In Europe enclosed settlements are known from the 2nd millennium BC, but large scale defence works did not become common until about 1000 when the Late Bronze Age URNFIELD peoples began to construct true forts. At first these were usually PROMONTORY FORTS, but in the last four centuries BC the true hillfort, with defence works following the contours, became the predominant form. From about C2 BC hillforts were common throughout CELTIC lands until the Roman conquest. In Britain most of the great forts were built during the two and a half centuries before the conquest of AD 43, but in Ireland (which was not invaded) and highland Britain (only superficially Romanized) hillforts continued to be built and used for several more centuries.

Hissar, Tepe A TELL near Damghan in northern Iran excavated by Schmidt 1931–2. In the 4th millennium its culture seems to have been in some sense ancestral to that of Baluchistan and India. Around 2500 BC, earlier than elsewhere in Iran, the painted pottery tradition was replaced by one of grey monochrome ware. This is usually held to mark the first movement of INDO-EUROPEAN speaking peoples from central Asia into Iran. The settlement was destroyed somewhere between c1900 and 1600 (the date is debated), perhaps by new waves of Iranian invaders.

Hissarlik ◊ TROY

Hittites, Hatti or (to the Egyptians) **Kheta** A people who infiltrated Anatolia and in smaller numbers the Levant from the north c2000 BC, but the details of their origin are more than somewhat obscure. Their history falls into three periods. In the Old Kingdom (c1750–1450) they established a state in central Turkey with its capital first at Kussara, then at BOGHAZ KÖY. Mursilis I overran north Syria c1600 and pushed on as far as BABYLON, but this conquest was ephemeral. Under the empire (1450–1200) a more stable state was built up over most of Anatolia and north Syria, displacing the kingdom of the MITANNI and successfully challenging Assyria and Egypt (Battle of KADESH 1286). The end came quite suddenly c1200 BC, when the empire was overwhelmed by a folk migration, one branch of which reached Egypt as the PEOPLES OF THE

Fig. 85. Inscribed relief from Karatepe

SEA. The Hittite outposts in north Syria, however, survived as a chain of Syro-Hittite or neo-Hittite city states – KARA-TEPE, SINJERLI, SAKÇE GÖZÜ, MALATYA, ATCHANA and most important of all CARCHEMISH – down to their final annexation by the Assyrians in c8.

The Hittites have a number of points of interest. Their discovery and study provided one of the most brilliant chapters of archaeological and philological detection. Of the main languages spoken in the empire, Hittite and Hieroglyphic Hittite are largely INDO-EUROPEAN, the earliest to be recorded. Hurrian, the language of the HURRI, was non-Indo-European, as of course was the AKKADIAN much used for commercial and foreign correspondence. The Akkadian cuneiform script was generally employed too, though for monumental purposes local HIEROGLYPHS were preferred. Hittite art, particularly the carved stone reliefs, was crude but often has a pleasing and unintentionally amusing vigour [85]. It emphasizes the high round head shape which distinguishes the Hittites from their predecessors in Anatolia. Finally it was the Hittites who discovered a practicable technique for IRON smelting, a secret they guarded jealously until their downfall.

Hjortspring A small bog on the Danish island of Als in which was discovered a VOTIVE DEPOSIT of the pre-Roman Iron Age, dated c200 BC. The main finds were a BOAT [86] and many shields, spears and swords. The boat was plank-built, sewn together without the use of nails, and measured 58 ft in length, with room for about 50 paddlers. The bow and stern were upturned, and were provided with ram-like projections.

Hoabinh A little known Mesolithic or Neolithic culture of southeast Asia (the type site is in Vietnam) represented mainly by finds of chipped, pecked and polished stone axes. Its importance lies in its position between the earliest centres of rice growing in India and China, and in the part it must have played in diffusing the knowledge of agriculture into Indonesia and the Pacific.

hoard A collection of material (coins, bronzes, precious metal, rarely pottery) deposited in the ground. GRAVE GOODS

Fig. 86. Hjortspring boat

are excluded as a special case. Various classes are distinguished according to their method of accumulation. A **personal hoard** consists of an individual's personal property buried for safety and not recovered. A **merchant's hoard** will contain new objects ready for sale (he may – quite rightly – have distrusted the inhabitants of the next village he was coming to). A **founder's hoard** by contrast will contain obsolete, worn out or miscast objects, and frequently cake metal as well, all of it awaiting melting down and recasting. A **votive hoard** is rather different in that the objects were deposited, possibly over a long period of time, in temples or caves, buried, or thrown into water as religious offerings, with no intention of recovery. A **hoard of loot** is self-explanatory. Deciding to which class a hoard belongs is important as each has different value as an ASSOCIATION, and this will be crucial in a period such as the BRONZE AGE when hoards provide much of our evidence. In decreasing value, their order would be the merchant's hoard (often, however, of only a single tool type), the personal hoard, loot, the founder's hoard and the votive hoard (unless enclosed within some container).

hoe or **mattock** A digging tool consisting of a working blade at right angles to the haft. Examples in antler go back to the Mesolithic, and were probably used for digging up roots. They are more typical of the farming peoples of the Neolithic and later, for the cultivation of fields and gardens. They may have a stone blade or be of wood throughout. They succeeded the DIGGING STICK and gave rise to the PLOUGH.

Hohokam A sedentary farming culture which developed out of the COCHISE culture of southern Arizona by c100 BC. With settled life came the development of large villages and irrigation, and in the period AD 500–900 the Hohokam people adopted platform mounds and BALL-COURTS from the Mexican cultures to the

south. By c1000 the first copper artifacts were being imported, and from about 1100 certain groups began to construct PUEBLOS under ANASAZI influence. After c1400 the story is less clear. The Hohokam territory along the Gila and Salt rivers seems to have been largely abandoned, and such groups as remained may have been ancestral to the historic Pima and Papago Indians.

hollow way A track cut down below the level of the surrounding fields. The cutting is due more to water erosion than to deliberate excavation. Some hollow ways are ancient and are associated with CELTIC FIELDS, where they were used to mark the boundary between neighbouring estates, but many tracks are of fairly recent date.

Holocene, Recent or **Postglacial period** The time from the end of the PLEISTOCENE Ice Age (c8300 BC) to the present day.

home art ◊ MOBILIARY ART

Hominidae The family which includes both extinct and modern forms of man.

Homo The genus which includes modern man (HOMO SAPIENS), NEANDERTHAL MAN (*H. neanderthalensis*) and, in most recent schemes, HOMO ERECTUS (*Pithecanthropus*).

Homo erectus (also *Pithecanthropus, Pithecanthropus erectus*) An extinct form of man. In the older classifications he is generally listed as a distinct genus of the family HOMINIDAE, but nowadays is usually considered a species of the genus HOMO. *Homo erectus* lived during the Middle PLEISTOCENE, about half a million years ago. He was short (just over 5 ft tall), walked upright, had a receding forehead, prominent eyebrow ridges and no chin. His brain size (c800–1200 cc) was intermediate between those of AUSTRALOPITHECUS and NEANDERTHAL MAN [87c]. The best known discoveries are from the Far East (in Java, and at CHOUKOUTIEN, near Pekin), but skeletal remains have been found in East Africa (Bed II at OLDUVAI), in North Africa (Ternifine and Sidi Abderrahman) and in Europe (◇ MAUER JAW and VÉRTESSZÖLLÖS). On the African sites *Homo erectus* made HANDAXES, but at Choukoutien and Vértesszöllös his remains were found with PEBBLE TOOLS and CHOPPERS. At Choukoutien there was proof that he knew the use of fire.

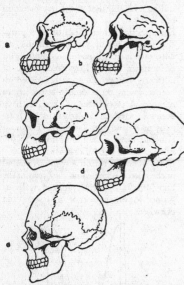

Fig. 87. Comparative hominid skulls: (a) Gorilla; (b) Australopithecus; (c) Homo erectus; (d) Neanderthal man; (e) Homo sapiens

Homo habilis An early form of man, whose remains were discovered in the same stratum as those of ZINJANTHROPUS (*Australopithecus boisei*) at OLDUVAI. The excavator, Dr Louis Leakey, maintained that the *habilis* skeletons showed certain features (eg greater brain size, opposable thumb, shape of skull) which distinguished them from those of other AUSTRALO-PITHECUS forms, and which placed them closer to the line of descent leading to HOMO ERECTUS and the advanced forms

of man. He also suspected that *H. habilis* was the maker of all the tools found in the deposit. Most anthropologists now believe that *H. habilis* falls within the range of variability of the *Australopithecus* genus, although *H. habilis* may represent a separate species.

Homo neanderthalensis ◇ NEANDER-THAL MAN

Homo sapiens Modern man first appears in the fossil record during the later part of the Upper PLEISTOCENE around 35,000 BC, or a little earlier if the radiocarbon date from NIAH CAVE is accepted. In Eurasia the oldest flint industries associated with *Homo sapiens* are always of Upper PALAEOLITHIC BLADE-and-BURIN type. Modern man replaced (or evolved out of) NEANDERTHAL MAN, and the new Upper Palaeolithic technology replaced that of the MOUSTERIAN period.

Still unresolved are the problems of the origin of *Homo sapiens* and of his relationship to Neanderthal man. Some authorities believe that one strain of Neanderthal man evolved into modern man, and their view can be supported by stressing certain elements of continuity between Mousterian and Upper Palaeolithic flintworking. Other scholars have maintained that *Homo sapiens* originated in a homeland somewhere outside Europe (the exact region is still unlocated, though southwest Asia has been suggested), and from there moved westwards to eliminate Neanderthal man and introduce the new blade-and-burin flint industries. This theory once seemed to be confirmed by the existence of a hybrid *sapiens-neanderthal* population in the caves of MOUNT CARMEL during the Mousterian phase, but more recent work has tended to discredit this interpretation of the Carmel remains. Skeletal material from the critical period is so scanty that the question must, for the time being, remain an open one. [87e]

homostadial Archaeological cultures are said to be homostadial if they represent the same level of technological advance, regardless of their absolute dates. This is the principle behind the THREE AGE SYSTEM.

homotaxial Objects are homotaxial if they appear in the same relative position in different sequences. The assumption that they are therefore contemporary is usually valid in geology, with its enormous time spans, but certainly not in archaeology, where time lag must be allowed for.

Hopewell A WOODLAND culture centred on the states of Ohio and Illinois. Hopewell is one of the most advanced Indian cultures of North America, with conical or dome-shaped burial mounds, large enclosures with earthen walls, and fine pottery with corded or stamped decoration. Farming was practised, and trade brought exotic raw materials from many parts of the continent. Hopewell is noted for its minor art objects, such as carved tobacco pipes, ornaments cut out of sheet copper or mica, and ceremonial obsidian knives. The culture probably developed during the closing centuries BC and ended C AD 400.

Horgen The type site, on Lake Neuchâtel, of the Middle Neolithic (post-CORTAILLOD) culture of Switzerland. The pottery consists of rough bucket-shaped vessels with decoration limited to a few appliqué cordons. In both shape and ornament it resembles that of the French SEINE-OISE-MARNE CULTURE.

horizon A horizon is represented by the spread of identical traits or artifacts over a wide area. Provided that these 'horizon-markers' were diffused rapidly and remained in use for only a short time, the local regional cultures in which they occur will be roughly contemporary (⟡ CROSS-DATING). An art style (eg TIAHUANACO or CHAVÍN) which fulfils these conditions is called a 'horizon style' in American archaeology.

horizontal stratigraphy STRATIGRAPHY is by definition obtained from superposed deposits, but something like it can some-

times be recognized in other circumstances. Horizontal stratigraphy has been found useful in studying ancient cemeteries. The oldest burials are likely to be those nearest the settlement, the top of a hill, or some other favoured position. The later ones will be progressively further out as the cemetery expands. The concept must naturally be used with caution, but can still be a helpful tool in the interpretation of a site.

horn (musical) Horns of cattle were probably used to produce music, or noise (the difference merely a matter of taste), from early times. In the Late Bronze Age of northern Europe these were copied in bronze, giving them a much better chance of survival. A number of examples have been recovered, particularly from the peat-bogs of Ireland and Denmark. The most elaborate form is the Danish LUR. ⟡ [56]

horned cairn ⟡ COURT CAIRN

horns of consecration A religious symbol of the MINOANS based on the horns of the bull [88]. It frequently topped walls or shrines in the palace of KNOSSOS and elsewhere.

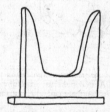

Fig. 88. Minoan horns of consecration

horse Widespread in temperate regions in the PLEISTOCENE, it subsequently became confined to the Asiatic steppes and forests. In America it was hunted to extinction, to be reintroduced only in recent centuries. In the steppes the horse was brought into domestication by the nomads much later than CATTLE, SHEEP, etc, had been brought under control by the settled peoples further south. Early in the

2nd millennium BC it is recorded in the TRIPOLYE culture of the Ukraine. It spread rapidly through the Near East with northern peoples like the HURRI, HYKSOS, KASSITES and ARYANS, particularly after the invention of the CHARIOT in Syria. Only later, as a heavier stock was bred, did the practice of riding become important. Its use for commercial draught and general agricultural purposes came much later still.

Horus The falcon god of Hieraconpolis in ancient Egypt, represented in either human or bird form. Later he became thought of as the son of ISIS and OSIRIS, the reigning pharaoh being his incarnation.

Hötting A Late Bronze Age URNFIELD culture of the North Tyrol and Upper Austria. The Hötting people controlled the huge copper mines of Mitterberg, and must have been the principal suppliers of the metal throughout the east Alpine region.

hour-glass perforation With a primitive technology, a drilled hole tends to be conical in section. Two such holes drilled from opposite faces will give a perforation of hour-glass, or biconical, form.

Housesteads (anc **Vercovicium** or **Borcovicium**) A Roman fort near the mid-point of HADRIAN'S WALL. It is one of the best examples in Britain of a permanent military CAMP, with its defences, street plan, administrative buildings and barrack blocks, and, what is rarely demonstrable elsewhere, a small civil settlement for traders, etc, at its gates.

Hsia The name of the first Chinese dynasty. It cannot yet be connected with any archaeological material, as its successor SHANG can, but is believed to be not entirely mythical.

huaca or **guaca** A Quechua word implying sanctity, now applied indiscriminately in some Latin American countries to ancient mounds, ruins, tombs or their contents (eg HUACA PRIETA).

Huaca Prieta This site, on the desert coast of north Peru, was the first pre-ceramic village to be excavated in that country, and was also one of the first sites ever to be dated by the RADIOCARBON method. The inhabitants lived in sub-terranean houses, used gourd containers, made patterned cotton textiles by TWINING without the aid of a loom and relied for subsistence on sea food supplemented by wild plants and by cultivated squashes, beans and peppers. The settlement was established c2500 BC. The latest stages are marked by the use of CUPISNIQUE pottery and the introduction of MAIZE agriculture.

Huari A large and powerful city in the central Peruvian Andes near Ayacucho. Round about AD 600 the local culture came under TIAHUANACO influence, and Huari acted as a secondary centre from which modified Tiahuanaco traits were spread to the Pacific coast. The first contacts may have been peaceful, but seem to have been followed by conquest which brought about the downfall of the NASCA and MOCHICA states in about c7. The Huari empire collapsed a century later. The city itself was abandoned and the Ayacucho region entered a period of depression, but Huari influence remained strong in the local pottery styles of the coast until the end of the 1st millennium. It was followed by the re-emergence of the coastal tradition and the creation of new states (◊ CHIMÚ, CUISMANCU and CHINCHA).

Huelva A town in southwest Spain. In 1923 a Late Bronze Age HOARD of bronzes, probably the cargo of a wrecked merchant ship, was dredged from its harbour. It included a remarkable range of types, not only local products like the CARP'S TONGUE SWORD but an Irish lunate SPEARHEAD and a Cypriot type of elbowed FIBULA. It fits remarkably well, in fact, with what we are told of the traders of TARTESSOS in just this area. The date is c700–500 BC.

hunebed The Dutch name for the MEGALITHIC CHAMBER TOMBS of the north Netherlands. The tombs are built of large stones, and consist of a round or oval mound surrounded by a KERB and covering a rectangular burial chamber with its entrance on one of the long sides. A few examples have an entrance passage, giving them a T plan which suggests a relationship with the PASSAGE GRAVES of Denmark. The Danish tombs are slightly later than the oldest Dutch ones, but in both areas they were built by the bearers of the TRB CULTURE during the Middle Neolithic.

Hurri A people first recognized to the southwest of the Caspian Sea c2300 BC. Thence they moved down into Syria, where they set up several kingdoms, notably that of MITANNI c1500. They had a pantheon, distinct from that of their neighbours, which was recorded in the rock sanctuary of YAZILIKAYA by the HITTITES. Their language is known from a number of religious texts and a letter among the archives of Tell el-AMARNA. It is not related to any of the major language families. The Syrian part of their territory was absorbed into the Assyrian empire, but the district of URARTU remained independent until much later.

hut circle A circular depression, wall, or ring of boulders, marking the footing of a vanished hut whose superstructure was of perishable material.

hüyük Turkish for TELL.

Hvar An island off the Dalmatian coast with caves which have yielded a striking Late Neolithic pottery painted with red scroll and spiral patterns on a dark surface. It is found in neighbouring areas of the mainland, where it is known as the Lisičiće style.

Hyksos The desert nomads often known as the Shepherd Kings, but more correctly as the Princes of Foreign Lands, who infiltrated Egypt towards the end of the Middle KINGDOM. They can be traced in Middle Bronze Age Palestine, in towns characterized by great plastered scarps outside the walls. From 1640 to 1570 BC they dominated the Nile Valley from their capital of Avaris in the Delta. Their breaking of Egyptian isolation opened the way for the flowering of culture in the New Kingdom, which immediately followed their expulsion. They were responsible for the introduction of the HORSE and CHARIOT, and perhaps the upright loom, olive and pomegranate.

hypocaust A floor of tile and concrete, sometimes with MOSAIC, supported on low tiled pillars to allow the hot air from a furnace to circulate beneath it – the very efficient Roman equivalent of central heating [89]. The gases escaped up BOX

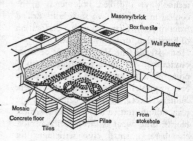

Fig. 89. Roman hypocaust system

FLUE tiles at intervals round the walls, thus warming these also.

hypogeum An underground chamber or vault, usually for burial.

Iberians The people of the eastern and southeastern Spanish coastal regions in the 1st millennium BC. Although their archaeological material falls into separate cultural groups a basic unity is shown by the inscriptions. These have a common script based on Greek but with some syllabic signs in addition to the letters, and a common language, a non-INDO-EURO-PEAN one which cannot yet be translated. Notable among their products are their jewellery and statues, of which the Dama de Elche is the most famous. This people's origins are obscure, perhaps North African. They disappeared as a separate group under the Roman occupation, partly by fusion with the CELTS of the interior, partly through displacement of their distinctive language by Latin.

Ibero-Maurusian ◊ ORANIAN

Ice Age ◊ PLEISTOCENE

Idaean Cave A sacred cave high on Mount Ida in central Crete. Votive offerings were made here by the MINOANS, but the most important were a magnificent series of decorated shields of C8–C7 BC, showing artistic influence from Syria and Assyria. The cave was one of those claimed to be the birthplace of Zeus.

ideogram A single written symbol conveying the meaning of a whole word.

impressed decoration Pottery decoration produced by pressing something into the surface of the clay when still soft. Stamped decoration is a special form of this, in which a stick or bone is previously carved to give the impression its design. Intermediate in form are the impressions of natural objects like bird bones or serrated sea shells.

Impressed Ware The pottery of the first Neolithic farmers to spread round the west Mediterranean, c 5000–3500 BC. It is found on the east coast of Italy, whence it was carried by sea to Sicily (STENTINELLO [180]), Liguria (ARENE CANDIDE), Provence (Châteuneuf-les-Martigues and Spain. Its origins have been sought at MERSIN, or in the STARČEVO culture of Yugoslavia. Similar material in North Africa may be of independent origin, coming from the Sudan across the Sahara. The ware is characterized by simple shapes bearing profuse impressed decoration. The serrated edge of the CARDIUM shell was particularly popular. ROCKER DECORATION is found in the Italian province and stamped impressions in the Sicilian.

Inca A group of Quechua-speaking tribes from the Cuzco area of the south Peruvian Andes. Their ultimate origins are uncertain, but C16 records suggest that the dynasty was established at Cuzco by Manco Capac in about AD 1200. During the next two centuries the Inca engaged only in local wars with neighbouring tribes, but under three able rulers, Pachacuti (1438–71), Topa Inca (1471–93) and Huayna Capac (1493–1525), they rapidly expanded their territory. The highlands were conquered first, then upland Ecuador (where Quito became an important Inca city) and the coastal states of CHIMÚ, CUISMANCU and CHINCHA. By 1525 the Inca empire stretched from the northern frontier of Ecuador, southwards through Peru and Bolivia, into parts of Argentina and northern Chile.

This vast area was unified into a single state with a centralized organization. At its head was the ruler, 'Son of the Sun', worshipped as a god in his own lifetime. As a divine king he was above the law, and as a despotic ruler he was very much the political head of state. Administration was in the hands of officials drawn from the Inca nobility and from the chiefs of conquered tribes. An efficient road system, along which relays of messengers could travel 150 miles in a day, ensured that Cuzco was kept informed of developments all over the empire. These same roads allowed Inca forces to be quickly moved into any province which showed signs of rebellion, and, if necessary, dissident populations were transplanted wholesale to other parts of the empire and replaced by more loyal subjects.

This centralization was both the strength and the weakness of the Inca state. The unifying force was the ruler in person, and the death of Huayna Capac precipitated a crisis. Civil war broke out when two of his sons, Huascar and Atahuallpa, disputed the succession. Atahuallpa won the war, but before he could consolidate his position he was seized and murdered by Pizarro's Spaniards in 1532. Without a leader the Inca system could not function. Most of the empire was quickly brought under Spanish control, but an independent Inca group held out in the Urubamba valley until 1572.

Archaeologically, highland Inca culture is characterized by fine quality stone

Fig. 90. Inca pottery aryballus

masonry, agricultural terraces, mass-produced and standardized pottery forms (ARYBALLUS) [90], and certain metal objects. Writing was unknown, but the QUIPU was used for keeping records.

Agriculture was based on plant foods, especially POTATO, quinoa, and (at lower altitudes) MAIZE. Domesticated animals included DOG, LLAMA, guinea pig and alpaca. Fine textiles were woven using a simple backstrap LOOM. ◊ KERO, MACHU PICCHU

incense cup or **pygmy vessel** A small subsidiary vessel found with the skeleton or cinerary urn in barrows of the WESSEX CULTURE, C1400 BC. Several forms are recognized, as shown in [91]. Their origin is somewhat obscure – the CHASSEY culture of France and local RINYO-CLACTON wares have both been suggested – and their function is quite unknown. The

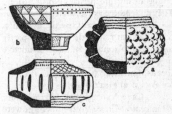

Fig. 91. Wessex culture cups: (a) Manton or 'grape' type; (b) Aldbourne type; (c) 'slashed' type

name is an archaeological label only, arising from the holes some of these vessels have through their walls.

incised decoration Pottery decoration in which the soft surface of the clay is cut with a sharp instrument.

Indo-European A group of languages originating in the region of the steppes. They diffused, largely through folk movements during the second millennium BC, into Europe, the Near East (temporarily, among the HITTITES and Hurrians of MITANNI), Iran and India. Nearly all modern European languages, and in India Sanskrit and its descendants, are thus related, as was first recognized by Sir William Jones in 1786. The name should be used only in this linguistic sense, since its groupings correlate at best poorly with the racial and cultural evidence.

Indus Civilization One of the greatest civilizations of antiquity, and the least understood, was that of the Indus valley, largely in West Pakistan. It was revealed in excavations by Sir John MARSHALL, Sir Mortimer Wheeler and others since its discovery in 1921. The twin capitals were HARAPPA and MOHENJO-DARO, smaller sites extending over much of the Punjab, Sind and Kathiawar, with a few outlying trading posts. Over this enormous area there is a surprising and rather depressing uniformity of culture.

Certain sites, such as Harappa itself, overlie settlements related to the hill villages of BALUCHISTAN, from which in some sense the civilization must derive. Influences from the Middle East (◊ MUNDI-GAK) are also probable. So far, however, its origins are little more than supposition. The challenge of the Indus floodplain must have been a major factor, demanding and supporting cultural advance. Certainly by around 2300 BC the Indus Civilization was fully developed and in trading contact with Sargonid SUMER, typical seals having been found there.

Radiocarbon dates from several sites support this date, and suggest that by 1700 BC the civilization was in marked decline. The Indus river seems to have played a significant part too. Many sites, Mohenjo-daro above all, show deposits left by frequent catastrophic floods. Over-exploitation of the vegetation, particularly for the baking of enormous quantities of brick, aggravated the decline of the countryside. The final collapse seems to have been due to hostile attack, probably the upheavals preceding or associated with the arrival of the ARYANS.

The Indus cities were open (KALIBAN-GAN may have been an exception), though many had walled citadels. A few inhumation cemeteries have been found associated with them. Gridiron town planning was

general, the oldest recorded, and elaborate drainage systems also. Burnt brick was employed throughout. Large civic granaries have been identified and the best explored site, Mohenjo-daro, had a great bath, assembly hall and other monumental buildings as well. The type of organization this implied is not known; temples and palaces have alike escaped discovery. The widespread use of an undeciphered HIEROGLYPHIC script and standard weights and measures argue that the state was centralized and powerful.

The economy was based on mixed agriculture. Wheat, barley and vegetables were grown, also rice, at LOTHAL, and cotton, the earliest recorded use of the last. Humped cattle were the most important domestic animals. Trade overland through Baluchistan and by sea along the Persian Gulf is well attested. In metalwork the Indus people were curiously backward. Their copper and poor bronze flat axes and spears show no great competence and CHERT knife-blades were still general. A bronze statuette of a dancing girl on the other hand is of high quality, as are the few figures in stone, that of a bearded man being the most famous. Of the many terracotta figurines the commonest are of women, shown wearing the shell or clay bangles and FAIENCE, copper or stone (notably LAPIS LAZULI and etched CAR-NELIAN) beads which are also frequently found. The pottery was mass-produced and on the whole unimaginative. The finer ware was elaborately painted in black on red with animals, birds and leaves. Artistically the finest products were square STEA-TITE seals, carved with local or mythical animals and brief inscriptions [92].

These go some way to correct the general impression of monotony and regimentation. Our inability to read the script, indeed the absence of records to read, prevents a fair assessment. Man's control over the environment was always precarious here, and order, at the expense of individuality, must have been prized. The Indus Civilization, despite its shortcomings, was an achievement of some

Fig. 92. Indus seals

substance. More work is needed to determine how lasting was its effect on the later culture and religion of India.

industry An ASSEMBLAGE of artifacts including the same types so consistently as to suggest that it is the product of a single society. If more than one class of objects (eg flint tools or bronze weapons) is found, we can talk of a CULTURE.

ingot Metal cast into a particular shape, determined by custom rather than function, for trade. Often it will be of a standard weight, sometimes of a guaranteed purity. Examples include the ingot of the Mycenaeans (c65 lbs of copper) in the shape of an ox-hide, the bronze ingot TORC of the European Bronze Age, the iron CURRENCY BAR of the English Iron Age and the Roman lead pig stamped with the smelter's name.

inhumation The practice of burying the dead, contrasting with CREMATION and exposure. BURIAL may be in a dug grave, or in a natural or built chamber. Terms commonly used to describe it are: extended (with spine and leg bones more or less in a straight line), flexed (with the leg bones bent, but by less than 90°) or crouched (with the hip and knee joints bent through more than 90°). Extended burials may be supine (on the back), prone (on the face), or on the side.

Initial Series ◊ CALENDAR

insula (lit island) A block of buildings in a Roman camp or town planned on the grid principle. [53]

intaglio Design cut into a hard stone or metal, especially as on a SEAL.

Integration Period The last stage of Ecuadorian prehistory (AD 500 to the INCA conquest) when there was a tendency for regional developments to give place to greater uniformity of culture over wide areas. In many parts of the country there is evidence for urban centres, class distinction, intensive agriculture and high quality metallurgy.

interglacial A warm interlude between two GLACIATIONS. The ice sheets diminish in area, and the improved climate allows the growth of temperate types of vegetation. cf INTERSTADIAL [p 183]

interment The practice of, or an example of, the BURIAL of the human dead.

interstadial A period of milder climate within a GLACIATION. An interstadial period, unlike a true INTERGLACIAL, is either too cold or too short to permit the growth of vegetation of present-day type.

Intihuasi Cave (Argentina) ◊ AYAMPITÍN

Iona An island in the Inner Hebrides granted by Connal of DÁLRIADA to St Columba in 563 for the foundation of a monastery. It was the base from which the Celtic church, under Columba, Aidan and their successors, converted northern Britain to Christianity. LINDISFARNE was its most important daughter house.

Ipiutak (Alaska) A coastal ESKIMO village with about 600 houses and many burials accompanied by finely carved bone and ivory objects. The art style includes animal forms which show links with Siberia and northern Eurasia. Ipiutak is the largest Eskimo settlement ever discovered, and radiocarbon dates from the type site place it in the centuries around AD 300. ◊

CAPE KRUSENSTERN, ONION PORTAGE

iron Meteoric iron, containing a high percentage of nickel, is found naturally and, since its heavenly origin was realized, it was highly prized for its supposed magical properties. There are scattered records of smelted earth iron from early times, but the technique of iron-working was not mastered until c1500 BC under the HITTITES. When they were overthrown and their secret leaked out, iron spread rapidly to replace bronze for man's basic tools and weapons, thus opening the IRON AGE of the THREE AGE SYSTEM. The pre-Columbian New World, however, never developed iron technology.

The technique of smelting is more complicated than with copper or tin, since the first smelt gives only an unpromising slaggy lump, the bloom. Hammering at red heat is then required to expel stone fragments and combine carbon with the iron to make in effect a steel; pure iron is too soft for functional use. But once the technique is discovered, it replaces earlier metallurgies; iron ores are much commoner than those of copper or tin, and the resulting metal is far superior. Unfortunately for the archaeologist it corrodes much more rapidly. The two basic methods of working it are by forging – hammering into shape at red heat – and casting. The Chinese used the latter method as early as c5 BC, but it was not employed in Europe until the Middle Ages. For most purposes it is less suitable than forging because the metal, though harder, is brittle.

Iron Age IRON had such manifest advantages over bronze that its spread was rapid. Indeed, in parts of the world like Africa, it overtook the earlier metal, excluding a BRONZE AGE altogether. In America iron was not introduced until the arrival of Europeans. In most of Asia the Iron Age falls entirely within the historic period. In Europe it begins at earliest c1100 BC, when the collapse of the HITTITES allowed the secret of iron-working to

escape. Highlights are provided by the VILLANOVANS in Italy and the cultures of HALLSTATT and LA TÈNE in central and western Europe. It is the period of the startling CELTIC ART. Beyond the Mediterranean shores the age closes with the appearance of the Roman legions in c1 BC and c1 AD. Outside the imperial frontiers, it is conventionally taken to end with the Migration Period, c c4–c6 AD. Because of its overlap with history – strictly it should last at least until the Industrial Revolution – the period is even more anomalous than the others of the THREE AGE SYSTEM.

Ishtar or **Inanna** The Sumerian goddess of the planet Venus, like her classical counterpart having jurisdiction over love and procreation. Her husband was TAMMUZ. She was worshipped equally by Sumerians, Akkadians, Babylonians and Assyrians, and as ASTARTE by the peoples of the Levant.

Isis The moon goddess of ancient Egypt, wife to OSIRIS and mother of HORUS. She is represented as a woman with the moon's disc on her brow.

isostasy An alteration in the height of the land relative to the sea. The weight of ice in an ice sheet causes a local sinking of the land beneath it, but when the ice melts during an INTERGLACIAL period this pressure is eased and the land rises again. ◊ EUSTASY

Israelites That branch of the SEMITES sprung from the KHABIRU-Hebrews which returned from Egypt under Moses, and won a footing in the Promised Land under Joshua in c13 BC. By c10 under David and Solomon they had conquered the CANAANITES and PHILISTINES to become a powerful monarchy with its capital at JERUSALEM. But soon after, this split into the kingdoms of Judah and Israel, and remained divided until the destruction of the latter by the Assyrians in 722 and of the former by the Babylonians in 587.

ivory Animal tusk, usually from the elephant, occasionally from the walrus, in the Upper Palaeolithic from the mammoth.

Elephant ivory was used throughout the Near East for decorative work of various kinds. The ivories from NIMRUD, fittings for furniture, are a famous example. [133]

Izapa A CEREMONIAL CENTRE in Chiapas, Mexico. Occupation began c1500 BC, but Izapa is famous as the type site of a culture known chiefly through its art style, which is distributed in Veracruz, Chiapas and parts of Guatemala (◊ KAMINAL-JUYÚ). The relief art, carved on altars and STELAE, is a development of the OLMEC tradition but at the same time looks forward to early MAYA work. The style falls within the Late PRE-CLASSIC PERIOD (300 BC–AD 300), intermediate in time between Olmec and Maya. Dates were written in the LONG COUNT system; a pure Izapan stele from El Baul, Guatemala, carries a figure equivalent to AD 36.

J

Jabrud (Syria) A locality with three rock-shelters which between them have yielded a long series of PALAEOLITHIC industries, as well as some NATUFIAN and Neolithic material. Jabrud is the type site of the Jabrudian industry, which is broadly contemporary with the AMUDIAN and Late ACHEULIAN of the Middle East. The Jabrudian is distinguished by well-made side SCRAPERS of MOUSTERIAN type and, in some cases, by BLADES similar to those of the Amudian. In some instances (eg at MOUNT CARMEL and Abri Zumoffen) there may be HANDAXES. In its typical form, at Jabrud, the industry bears a strong resemblance to some Mousterian industries from France. The dating is uncertain, but probably falls within the RISS-WÜRM INTERGLACIAL or the first Würm INTER-STADIAL.

jadeite ◊ GREENSTONE

jar burial An INHUMATION BURIAL within a pottery vessel. Contrast URN burial which, being for a cremation, requires a much smaller pot. The rite is reported sporadically over much of the Mediterranean area, going back to the Early Bronze Age in Anatolia.

Jarlshof A settlement site on Sumburgh Head at the southern tip of Shetland. The earliest occupation was a Late Neolithic village comparable to SKARA BRAE. It was followed after an interval by oval houses of the Late Bronze Age, a round house and WHEELHOUSE with SOUTERRAIN of the Iron Age, a BROCH, a Viking settlement, and finally a medieval fortified farmhouse. The name is not an ancient one, but was invented by Sir Walter Scott.

Jarmo A village site in the ZAGROS mountains east of Kirkuk in northern Iraq excavated by Braidwood 1948–55. Carbonized wheat and barley show it to have been a settlement of farmers, but of the animal bones found only those of the goat

were certainly domesticated. The first 11 of its 16 levels had no pottery, though clay-lined pits were baked *in situ*. Square houses of PISÉ were built, with clay ovens. Flaked and ground stone were freely used for tools and utensils. The radiocarbon dates from the site have been unfortunately erratic, but a date c6500 BC is generally accepted, placing it amongst the world's earliest food-producing settlements.

Java man An old, and now long obsolete, name given to the remains of HOMO ERECTUS from Java.

Jemdet Nasr A pottery ware found in a late phase of the URUK period of Mesopotamia, distinguished by black and red painting on large buff jars. The type site is between Baghdad and Babylon. The phase it represents, in which writing was becoming much more common and sculpture makes its appearance, was followed immediately by the Early Dynastic period of SUMER.

Jericho (Tell es-Sultan) commands the route crossing the Jordan valley at the north end of the Dead Sea. Excavation by the Germans 1907–9, Garstang 1930–36 and Kenyon 1952–8 have revealed the great importance of the site. Camping occupation of the Mesolithic c8000 BC developed in the pre-pottery Neolithic c7000 into a walled town of modest but competent mudbrick houses which is amongst the earliest permanent settlements known. To this period belongs the famous series of plastered skulls [93]. Scrappy evidence continues to the proto-Urban c3200, after which successive walled towns with their cemeteries carry the story down to c1580, when the HYKSOS settlement was destroyed by the Egyptians. Its great plastered glacis is noteworthy, as are its tombs for their preservation of woodwork and basketry as well as pottery, bronze, bone, etc. The Late Bronze Age town captured by Joshua's ISRAELITES has left very few traces. The fallen walls found by Gar-

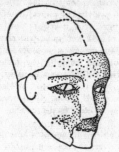

Fig. 93. Neolithic plastered skull, Jericho

stang are now known to be a millennium too early to be associated with Joshua's attack. There was some reoccupation during the Iron Age.

Jerusalem Archaeological investigation of this site, so important to world history, has proceeded on and off from 1864 to the present day. Its story begins in the proto-Urban period, to which belong several tombs, but the first true settlement was the town of the Jebusites, a branch of the CANAANITES, in the Late Bronze Age. This stood on the ridge of Ophel, now outside the city to the southeast. It was captured by David and the ISRAELITES c1000 BC, who covered Ophel with their town. Solomon added the Temple immediately to its north. The western ridge, beyond the Tyropoeon valley, was not incorporated until c1. The city fell to the Babylonians in 587 and was rebuilt after 538. The present plan of the city, excluding the two ridges to the south, goes back to Herod the Great (37–34 BC) and the rebuilding under Hadrian.

jet A soft black stone, related to lignite, used for decorative purposes (beads, buttons, etc) in the British Bronze Age. The main source is in Yorkshire around Whitby.

Jhukar A Chalcolithic culture of Pakistan which succeeded the INDUS CIVILIZATION on certain sites in Sind, of which Chanhudaro is the best known. Its material shows a mixture of elements from the Indus, Baluchistan and the Middle East, the last represented by compartmented seals, copper dress pins and a shafthole axe. It probably falls about the middle of the 2nd millennium BC.

Jōmon An early culture of Japan, its relics surviving in shell mounds of KITCHEN MIDDEN type round the coasts of the Japanese islands. A radiocarbon date of around 7000 BC shows that these settlements began very early, but evidence for food production – cattle, millet, buckwheat and some vegetables – does not appear until Middle Jōmon times, roughly the 4th millennium. Pottery, however, was known from a very early date, heavy but surprisingly elaborate, especially in the modelling of its castellated rims [94].

Fig. 94. Jōmon pottery

Other artifacts, of stone and bone, were simple. Light huts, round or rectangular, have been identified. Burials were by inhumation, crouched or extended. The Jōmon was succeeded by the YAYOI period in c3 BC.

Jordanova, Jordanów, Jordansmühl A settlement and cemetery near Nimptsch, in

Polish Silesia, Jordanova is the type site for a sub-group of the LENGYEL culture. Its pottery is incised or painted, and copper objects were beginning to be used.

Jorwe A site in India east of Bombay. It has been chosen from a large and well-studied group (Nevasa, Chandoli, Prakash, etc) as the type site of a generally wheel-made red ware painted in black, including distinctive long-spouted vessels. Radiocarbon dates place it 1375–1050 BC.

Judeidah A TELL in the AMUQ plain inland from the northeast corner of the Mediterranean. Its lowest level, XIV, was of the Neolithic MERSIN type, with a long series of succeeding deposits.

Jutes The branch of the Germanic peoples loosely grouped as ANGLO-SAXONS who settled Kent, the Isle of Wight and the Southampton area in C5 AD. Their earlier home appears to have been northern Jutland. The proximity of their settlements to the continent led to a development of cross-Channel trade and close cultural links with the Franks of the lower Rhine. One result was the increase in wealth of Kent, as typified by the justly famous garnet-inlaid jewellery. St Augustine was welcomed to their capital of Canterbury in 597, but shortly afterwards they declined in political importance, eventually passing under the sway of Mercia and later of Wessex.

K

Kadesh or **Qadesh** A strategically placed site on the river Orontes in Syria. It achieved fame as the scene of the inconclusive battle between RAMSES II of Egypt and Muwatallis of the HITTITES c1286 BC. Both sides claimed the victory but the result was to confirm the frontier on the former line and to initiate a period of friendlier relations between the two states.

Kalambo Falls A site on the Zambia–Tanzania border at the southeast end of Lake Tanganyika, Kalambo Falls has yielded one of the longest archaeological sequences in sub-Saharan Africa, as well as important pollen and radiocarbon data. The oldest deposit contained Late ACHEULIAN tools. This phase ended c60,000 BC. Preservation was unusually good, and the excavators recovered wooden objects (a club and digging sticks), food remains (wild fruits) and evidence that man was already using fire. The sequence continued with SANGOAN, followed by Early Middle Stone Age (Lupemban) industries related to those of the Congo, then MAGOSIAN, and a MICROLITH-using Late Stone Age culture of WILTON type, and finally (from mid C4 AD) remains of early agricultural and iron-using peoples who were probably of Bantu stock.

Kalibangan A site in India near HARAPPA on the banks of the extinct Ghaggar River. A Chalcolithic settlement similar to KOT DIJI and the site underlying the Indus city at Harappa has given radiocarbon dates of c2150 BC. About 1950 (further radiocarbon dates) a small town of the INDUS CIVILIZATION was built over it. The citadel had a brick wall with square bastions, and traces of another wall are reported around the lower town. In all other respects the town was typical, with its brick architecture, grid layout and material contents. It flourished to c1750 BC.

Kamares Cave A sacred cave of the MINOANS on the slopes of Mount Ida overlooking PHAESTOS in Crete. The votive offerings of Middle Minoan pottery, 1900–1600 BC, painted in red and white on black, were so rich as to give their name to this attractive style of pottery.

Kaminaljuyú This site, on the outskirts of Guatemala City, has been much damaged, but once had more than 200 mounds. As the greatest centre in the highland MAYA zone, Kaminaljuyú has a history of occupation dating back to c1500 BC, but it reached its first climax during the Miraflores phase in the centuries after 300 BC. The Miraflores people buried their dead with rich offerings, carved STELAE in the IZAPA manner, and used a hieroglyphic script with glyphs unlike those of the lowland Maya. C2 and C3 AD were a period of decline and partial ruin, but there was a revival in c400 when new people arrived from Mexico, and Kaminaljuyú became an outpost of the TEOTIHUACÁN civilization. From this time onwards, archaeology and documentary evidence suggest that various Mexican dynasties ruled over the Maya population until the Spanish conquest.

Karanovo A TELL in eastern Bulgaria. It disclosed 40 ft of stratigraphy, with seven phases of occupation running from the Early Neolithic (cf STARČEVO) to the Bronze Age, 6th to late 2nd millennium BC. The development of the architecture, all in wattle and daub, was particularly interesting. The 50 to 60 early, scattered, square huts were replaced by rectangular, larger, porched, plastered and painted ones in later phases.

Karatepe A site on the Ceyhan river, Cilicia, southern Turkey, excavated by Bossert in the 1940s. It was founded by Asitawad, king of the Danuna (perhaps to be equated both with one of the PEOPLES OF THE SEA and with the Danaoi of Homer) c740 BC. He had set up a series of carved reliefs which, if not of the first rank aesthetically [85], still tell us a great deal of the strains, classical Hittite, Assyrian, and Phoenico-Egyptian, which went into the making of the art of the Syro-HITTITES. More important still is the great bilingual inscription on the gateway, Hittite on the right, Phoenician on the left, which has added enormously to our knowledge of the Hittite language. The site was abandoned after a short life.

Karim Shahir A hilltop site near Kirkuk in northern Iraq occupied in the period when hunters were beginning to control the animals and plants on which they depended for their food. No buildings were identified. Its material is closely related to that of ZAWI CHEMI SHANIDAR.

Karnak A modern village, adjoining LUXOR, which has grown up around the ruins of the great temple of AMEN at THEBES, the ancient capital of Upper Egypt.

Kassites A people of the central ZAGROS mountains who occupied BABYLON after the Hittite raid c1595 BC. The four centuries they held the city cover a period of comparative stagnation, of which little detail has been recovered, ending with the city's conquest by ASSYRIA and ELAM c1157. The Kassites may or may not have been themselves INDO-EUROPEANS, but the invocation of Indo-European gods such as Shuriash (= Surya) shows that their rulers certainly were.

Kaushambi An impressive city site 4 miles in circuit, 30 miles from Allahabad in the Ganges valley. Its earliest wall, of mudbrick faced with baked brick 40 ft high, was built about 500 BC. Within it is a Buddhist monastery said to be of c5 BC, soon after the Buddha's death.

Kennet Avenue ◊ AVEBURY

Kenniff Cave (Queensland, Australia) One of the oldest sites yet discovered in the continent. The basal strata contain an industry of CORE and FLAKE SCRAPERS dated by radiocarbon to c14,000–13,000 BC. These tools were later joined by small BLADES, MICROLITHS, delicate points, wood-working flakes, and (around 1900 BC) by backed blades.

Kensington Stone A stone slab found in Minnesota at the end of the last century with an inscription in RUNES purporting to record the arrival of a party of exploring Vikings. An object of controversy from the beginning, it is now dismissed as a forgery, despite recent confirmation of the Viking visits to the eastern American coast (◊ ANSE AU MEADOW).

Kent's Cavern A cave one mile east of Torquay, Devon, which was first seriously excavated by MACENERY in 1825–9, and later by PENGELLY and others. The main occupation is of the Middle and Upper PALAEOLITHIC periods and includes artifacts of the MOUSTERIAN, AURIGNACIAN, 'proto-Solutrean' and the CRESWELLIAN CULTURE, as well as harpoons and a needle of MAGDALENIAN appearance. The sequence compares closely with that from CRESWELL CRAGS.

kerb A retaining wall built round the edge of a CAIRN or BARROW.

Kerbschnitt ◊ CHIP-CARVING

kernos A jar bearing small cups around its lip. It is an east Mediterranean form, of uncertain function.

kero A large wooden beaker with straight or concave flaring sides. Keros decorated with incised geometric patterns were used in INCA times, but examples with scenes painted in lacquer are of post-conquest date. In pottery the shape started earlier and was especially popular in the TIAHUANACO culture.

Khabiru or **Habiru**, Egyptian **Apiru** (generally accepted as cognate with Hebrews) A nomadic people, a branch of the SEMITES and probably related to the HYKSOS, who are recorded as infiltrating Palestine in the course of the Middle Bronze Age. They were ancestral to the ISRAELITES.

Khabur A tributary of the Euphrates in eastern Syria. Its basin, a strategic area for communications between Mesopotamia, Syria and Turkey, contains such important sites as Tell HALAF, CHAGAR BAZAR and BRAK.

Khafajah (anc **Tutub**) A group of TELLS on the Diyala river northeast of Baghdad excavated by the Americans 1930–38. It has given the best evidence for the three-fold subdivision of the Mesopotamian Early Dynastic period. A temple with ten building levels of the JEMDET NASR and Early Dynastic periods was dedicated to the moon-god Sin (= Sumerian NANNAR). A second Early Dynastic rectangular mud-brick temple faced onto a square court round which were grouped storehouses and priests' quarters, separated from the town by a massive wall oval in plan.

Khirbet Kerak (anc **Beth-yerah**) lies just west of the river Jordan where it leaves the Sea of Galilee. Excavations were carried out 1945–6 on a small walled town occupied throughout the Early Bronze Age in the 3rd millennium BC. It has given its name to a distinctive pottery ware of c2600 which has been found on many sites throughout the Near East, from JUDEIDAH in the Amuq to LACHISH in the south. This highly burnished ware with red or black slip is often decorated in relief, grooving or fluting. Its origins lie up in the southern Caucasus, whence it was carried south by an emigration perhaps, as WOOLLEY suggested, of the ancestors of the HITTITES.

Khirokitia An Early Neolithic village near the south coast of Cyprus excavated by Dikaios in the early 1950s. It consisted of round houses of mudbrick on stone footings. Agriculture was attested, though no actual grain was recovered; evidence for stock breeding was inconclusive. No pottery was made, stone bowls and prob-ably vessels of organic materials serving instead. The site yielded a radiocarbon date of c5800 BC.

Khmer An empire destroyed by the Thais about AD 1400 after it had ruled a large part of southeast Asia for some five cen-turies. Its capital was ANGKOR in Cam-bodia.

Khorsabad (anc **Dur Sharrukin**, Fort of Sargon) near Mosul. Founded by SARGON II in 717 BC, it included a magnificent palace within a city a mile square. It did not survive its founder's death in 705. Re-discovered in 1843 by BOTTA, who thought it to be NINEVEH itself, it yielded a rich collection of sculptured slabs and cuneiform inscriptions now in the Louvre. Further work was carried out by Place 1852–4 and the Oriental Institute of Chicago 1928–35.

Kidder, Alfred Vincent (1885–1963) A pioneer figure in archaeological studies of the American southwest. He carried out stratigraphical excavations (notably at the PUEBLO of Pecos), and combined STRATI-GRAPHY with pottery TYPOLOGY to produce the first – and best – synthesis of southwestern prehistory (*Introduction to the Study of South-western Archaeology*, 1924). Kidder's research forms the basis of nearly all later studies in the area.

In 1929 he began work in a new field and became director of the MAYA programme for the Carnegie Institution of Washing-ton. Under Kidder's chairmanship the Institution brought together archaeolo-gists, ethnologists and natural scientists in a great interdisciplinary study which had published more than sixty volumes of data by 1950, the year in which Kidder retired. He personally made several recon-naissance expeditions, excavated at the site of KAMINALJUYÚ, and studied the arti-facts from UAXACTÚN.

kiln A built chamber designed to produce high temperatures for industrial purposes, particularly the baking of pottery. In the simplest forms the fuel itself may form the chamber, or a single chamber of sods may hold both the fuel and the pots (a clamp kiln). In the updraught kiln a firebox pro-vides the heat, which passes up through firebars into the pottery chamber. This was only a temporary structure of clay that had to be demolished to extract the contents after each firing. Higher temperatures were possible where the fire was to one side of the chamber, the heat being introduced at its top and allowed to escape near its base (the down-draught kiln). Other versions were designed for different purposes such as glass-making or the parching of corn (to dry it and prevent it from sprouting) where the flames could not touch the contents. The kiln, like the POTTER'S WHEEL, implies craft specialization, and appears only at advanced stages of economic development.

Kingdoms, Old, Middle and **New** The names conventionally applied to the three peaks of development in the history of ancient Egypt, separated by periods of decline and disorder. They include the 3rd to 6th dynasties, c2700–2200 BC; the 11th–13th dynasties, 2100–1650; and the 18th–20th dynasties, 1580–1075 BC respectively.

Kingsborough, Lord An English nobleman who set out to prove that the civilized peoples of Mexico and Central America were descended from the ten lost tribes of Israel. His main thesis was nonsense, but in *Antiquities of Mexico* (published in nine huge volumes, 1830–48) he reproduced manuscripts of CODEX type together with early accounts of native life. The books lost money, and their author, who had spent his own fortune on them and could no longer pay the printer's bills, was put into a debtors' prison where he died.

Kisapostag A cremation cemetery in western Hungary. The metal objects link Kisapostag with other Early Bronze Age cultures (eg HATVAN and ÚNĚTICE), while related sites are found in Slovakia and in Hungary west of the Danube.

Kish A city state of ancient SUMER near Babylon excavated by the French in 1912 and by an Anglo-American expedition (Oxford–Chicago) 1923–33. Occupation began in the JEMDET NASR period, suc-

ceeded by Early Dynastic levels containing the remains of a royal palace of the period when Kish was a leading state in Sumer. Though the supremacy passed to UR c2600 BC, Kish remained in occupation right through to the Sassanian period in the early centuries AD.

kitchen midden Literally any heap of domestic or food refuse, but often used in a more limited sense for the huge mounds of sea shells left by some food-gathering peoples. ◊ ERTEBØLLE, JŌMON, SAMBAQUÍ

kiva An underground chamber (generally circular, sometimes rectangular) found in PUEBLO villages. Kivas were used as men's clubhouses and for the performance of religious ceremonies. ◊ ANASAZI

Kivik (Skåne, south Sweden) The site of one of the largest grave mounds in Scandinavia. The barrow is some 70 yds in diameter and covers a central CIST made of slabs with carvings on their inner faces [95]. The designs include processional

Fig. 95. Grave slab from Kivik

scenes, a CHARIOT with rider, ships, horses, fish, axes, sun-wheels and human figures. The contents of the tomb were plundered at the time of discovery in 1748, but the carvings that remain are of Bronze Age style and may date to about c10 BC.

Klein Aspergle (Ludwigsburg, Württemberg, Germany) The site of a rich CELTIC burial of the early LA TÈNE period. Funerary offerings included an ETRUSCAN bronze vessel, a native copy of an Etruscan beaked flagon, gold mounts for a pair of drinking horns and two imported Attic cups dated around 450 BC. In the same village is a slightly earlier tumulus burial, of the late HALLSTATT D period, with imported ivories (including a sphinx) as well as bronzes.

Knossos, Cnossus The chief palace of the MINOANS, near Herakleion at the centre of the north coast of Crete. Its excavation was the life's work of Sir Arthur EVANS, from 1899 to 1935. More work has been done on the Neolithic levels by J. D. Evans since 1958. A long-lived Neolithic settlement built up what was in effect a TELL at least 23 ft high on the crest of a hill. Further deposits of unknown thickness were added in the Early Minoan period, but were cut away to level the site for the palace at the beginning of the Middle Minoan period, c2000 BC. This covered an area c400 by 450 ft, with a central court 87 by 174 ft. Around this were grouped the main buildings, the Throne Room, reception halls and shrines to the west, with magazines behind, and on the east the Domestic Quarter of at least three storeys. Comparatively minor alterations were made throughout the life of the palace, the associated deposits allowing Evans to subdivide the Middle and Late Minoan periods in detail. Unlike the other Cretan palaces, Knossos survived the violent eruption of Santorin/Thera c1450 BC, but under new rulers, MYCENAEANS. The legend of Theseus and the Labyrinth (= the House of the Double Axe, ie Knossos) must refer to this period.

The internal fittings and contents speak of a high level of comfort, or even luxury. Floors were neatly paved in stone, and the drains beneath were far in advance of sanitary engineering anywhere else in the ancient world. Walls had a dado of gypsum at the base and carried delightful frescoes above. These show amongst other things the bull sports which took place in or near the palace, the courtiers who watched them [96], others in ceremonial procession

Fig. 96. Detail from the Miniature Fresco, Knossos

carrying offerings, and the priest-king himself. Shrines contained highly artistic figurines of a snake goddess, etc, and tell us something of Minoan religion. Finds of clay tablets with inscriptions in LINEAR A and B show the careful accounting which supported this show. From them, too, we learn that in the last phase of occupation the rulers of the palace were themselves Greeks.

It should be remembered that the Palace of Minos was only the greatest building in a sizeable town. Other smaller but equally well-appointed mansions have been investigated nearby, and some humbler houses have been disinterred. The viaduct and caravanserai to the south should also be mentioned, as should the cemeteries of CHAMBER TOMBS, especially the so-called Temple Tomb, combining grave and shrine.

Knovíz culture An URNFIELD culture of central and northwest Bohemia, where it followed the decline of the TUMULUS BRONZE AGE. Except for the burial rite, the Knovíz culture is similar to that of the neighbouring MILAVČE group.

Knowth One of the principal sites in the great funerary and religious complex of the BOYNE valley, Co. Meath, Ireland. The central cairn measures almost 100 yds in diameter and was carefully built up from layers of turf, stones, clay, shale and earth. The stones forming the kerb around the cairn are decorated in the passage grave style. Opening from opposite points on the round barrow are two tombs. The first is a large but simple PASSAGE GRAVE, with several decorated stones but no evidence of CORBELLING. The second tomb, also a passage grave, has a corbel-vaulted burial chamber from which open three niches. One of these contained a stone basin ornamented with grooves and circular designs, and there is further carving on the walls of the tomb itself. The central mound was surrounded by at least 15 smaller tombs, each under its own cairn, and these 'satellite' tombs included both ENTRANCE GRAVES and passage graves of cruciform plan. Knowth was later reoccupied in the early historic period when SOUTERRAINS were constructed within the mound.

Koldewey, R. In charge of the Deutsche Orient Gessellschaft excavations at BABYLON 1899–1914. Like his colleague Andrae at ASHUR, he aimed at exposing a whole city plan (previous work had failed to give the layout of a single building) and at recovering the STRATIGRAPHY of a long-lived site. For the purpose, the techniques perfected by the Germans at Olympia were adapted to Mesopotamian needs, in particular by learning to identify and follow walls of MUDBRICK. This opened the way for all further progress, and was brilliantly exploited by Koldewey himself in, for example, the recovery of Babylon's Sacred Way and Ishtar Gate.

Köln-Lindenthal A village of the DANUBIAN CULTURE on the outskirts of modern Cologne, Germany. The excavation, in 1929–34, was a pioneer attempt to strip a large settlement in order to reveal POST HOLES and house plans. In the original report the rubbish-filled quarry pits were interpreted as pit dwellings, while the longhouses were dismissed as barns. This view is now discredited, and Köln-Lindenthal is recognized as a typical Danubian site with seven widely separated phases of occupation covering the Danubian I and II periods.

Körös The Hungarian form of the culture known as STARČEVO in Yugoslavia and Cris in Romania. The Körös variant is distinguished by its footed vessels and relative lack of painted wares.

Koszider Koszider bronzes [97] take their name from three hoards found at Dunapentele-Kosziderpadlás, on the Danube

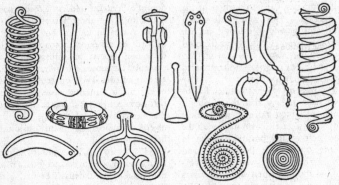

Fig. 97. Koszider bronzes

south of Budapest. The contents were characteristic of an early phase of the TUMULUS BRONZE AGE, and serve to document the expansion of that culture eastwards into Hungary. Similar hoards (with ivy-leaf pendants, spiral anklets with rolled ends, shaft-hole battleaxes decorated with spiral and geometric patterns, belt-plates, socketed axes and tanged sickles) have been found all over east central Europe from the Baltic to the Sea of Azov, and mark a Koszider HORIZON, of early Tumulus influence, around 1400 BC.

Kot Diji A TELL 25 miles east of MO-HENJO-DARO in West Pakistan excavated by Khan in 1955–7. At about 2100 BC (a radiocarbon date) a fortified settlement using only mudbrick was destroyed and replaced by one of the INDUS CIVILIZA-TION. The Kot-Dijian pottery was a thin pinkish ware decorated with horizontal black lines, perhaps related to that of the ZHOB valley. Comparable wares have been found in pre-Indus levels at HARAPPA and KALIBANGAN.

Kotosh A site on the eastern slopes of the central highlands of Peru. In the earliest, pre-ceramic, levels were remains of a plat-form on which stood a temple with crossed hands modelled in plaster relief on an inner wall. The next (Waira-jirca) period has a radiocarbon date of 1850 ± 110 BC and saw the introduction of the first pottery, a grey ware with incised designs and post-fired painting in red, white or yellow. In the following (Kotosh) stage there is evidence of MAIZE cultiva-tion, and the pottery, with grooved designs, graphite painting and STIRRUP SPOUTS, has CHAVÍN-like features. Radio-carbon dates suggest that this period is centred on C1000 BC and was closely followed by a pure Chavín stage with the typical pottery and ornament. Next in sequence came levels (Sajara-patac and San Blas phases) with white-on-red pot-tery, and the uppermost strata (Hiqueras period) were characterized by red vessels,

rare NEGATIVE PAINTING and copper tools. Occupation ended around AD 1.

Kroeber, Alfred Louis (1876–1960) One of the small group of scholars whose work laid the basis of New World archaeology as a scientific discipline. Kroeber was a man of wide interests, and his publications range over the whole field of ethnology, folklore, linguistics, archaeology and anthropological theory. In 1915 he began to make a typological SERIATION of potsherds from Zuñi sites of the American southwest, and his work, together with that of KIDDER and Nelson in the same area, showed how archaeological methods could reveal time depth and cultural change in North America. From 1921 onwards Kroeber applied the same tech-niques to the splendid collections of Peruvian material sent to California by Max UHLE. By 1926 he had worked out a scheme for Peruvian archaeology which formed the basis of all studies of the subject for the next twenty years, and is still not entirely superseded. After a brief interlude in Mexico, where he made stratigraphic tests at early sites, he made his first field trip to Peru where TELLO became his friend and collaborator. In 1925–6 Kroeber explored much of the Peruvian coast, especially the NASCA valley where he made the first ever stratigraphic excava-tion of a Peruvian midden. Kroeber con-tinued to write about the ethnology of North American Indians, but from 1917 onwards he developed a concern for the theoretical aspects of anthropology, in particular the processes of culture change.

Kuban culture The Copper Age culture of the north Caucasus, distinguished by rich KURGAN graves (◊ MAIKOP), use of the BATTLEAXE and a range of metal objects including the 'Pontic' hammer-headed pin. [149d]

k'uei (◊ DRAGON) The word is also used for a handled bowl to contain food, a com-mon form in CHOU dynasty bronze-work.

Kujavish grave A type of grave constructed in the lower Vistula region of Poland during the middle part of the local Neolithic (TRB CULTURE). Each tomb consists of a triangular or trapeze-shaped mound, sometimes more than 100 yds long, which covers a single flat grave containing an inhumation burial. Occasionally the number of graves is increased to two or three, but the Kujavish graves are in no way COLLECTIVE TOMBS.

Kulli An important Chalcolithic culture and pottery style widespread in south BALUCHISTAN called after a site excavated by Sir Aurel STEIN in the Kolwa region. The pottery is mainly buff and wheel made, painted in black with friezes of elongated humped bulls [98], felines or

Fig. 98. A Kulli bull

goats and spiky trees between zones of geometric ornament. Terracotta female and bull figurines were plentiful, the latter with painted bars on the flanks. The culture is further distinguished from that of AMRI-Nal in the same area by the practice of cremation burial. Mudbrick architecture and small tell sites are common to the two cultures. There are signs of INDUS CIVIL-IZATION influence on later Kulli material, particularly at MEHI. The carved stone vessels from that site are identical with examples from Early Dynastic Meso-potamia, where the pottery too has paral-lels in the SCARLET WARE. A date in the early 3rd millennium is therefore indicated.

Kültepe (anc **Kanesh**) A TELL near Kay-seri in Cappadocia, central Turkey. Its importance lies not in the Bronze Age city which built up the mound but in a canton-ment at its foot excavated by Hrozny in 1925 and Özgüç since 1948. Here through C19 BC a colony of Assyrian merchants had set up a trading organization, the *karum*, to control and foster the trade between Anatolia and Mesopotamia. Their cor-respondence is remarkably illuminating. It was written in Assyrian CUNEIFORM on clay tablets and constitutes the oldest surviving records from Turkey. Supple-mented by the evidence from the houses and burials revealed by excavation, it throws invaluable light on the country immediately before the rise of the HIT-TITES. For example, among the proper names mentioned are already some of INDO-EUROPEAN form.

kurgan The Russian word for a mound or barrow covering a burial in a pit grave, MORTUARY HOUSE or CATACOMB grave. The earliest kurgans appeared during the 3rd millennium BC among the COPPER AGE peoples of the Caucasus (KUBAN, MAIKOP), and soon afterwards in the south Russian steppe and the Ukraine. Shortly after 2500 the influence of the kurgan cultures affected most of east, central and northern Europe. The local Late Neolithic and Copper Age communities adopted such new traits as GLOBULAR AMPHORA vessels, CORDED WARE, asymmetrical stone BATTLEAXES copying metal forms already in use to the southeast, domesticated horses and burial of a single body (often sprinkled with ochre) in a pit, or more rarely a mortuary house, covered by a barrow. It has been argued – though not all scholars accept the view – that these intrusive traits were brought by invaders from the Pontic region, and that the newcomers were the people who introduced INDO-EUROPEAN dialects into Europe. From the start of the 2nd millennium this underlying unity broke down, and several regional kurgan-derived cultures can be recognized (◊ SINGLE GRAVE CULTURES). In Russia the kurgan tradition persisted late (◊ CATA-COMB grave), and in a somewhat altered form was still practised by the historical SCYTHIANS and Sarmatians of the steppe zone (◊ PAZYRYK).

Kuyunjik ◊ NINEVEH

L

Lachish Identified at **Tell ed-Duweir** west of Hebron and overlooking the coastal plain of Palestine. Excavation, begun in 1932, was called off on the murder of its director, J. L. Starkey, in 1938. Occupied caves and burials of the Chalcolithic period onwards were found, occupation of the town apparently beginning in the Early Bronze Age. A massive plastered glacis of HYKSOS type belonged with the Middle Bronze Age settlement, destroyed by the Egyptians c1580 BC. In the fosse at its foot the CANAANITES built three successive temples, C15–C13. Occupation by the ISRAELITES ended with a violent destruction, probably that of the Babylonians in 588 BC. There were later levels of Achaemenid and Hellenistic date.

The site is most famous for three vital groups of inscriptions. To C18 or C17 belongs a dagger bearing four symbols [99], with the GEZER potsherd and

Fig. 99. The Lachish inscribed dagger

SHECHEM plaque the earliest alphabetic letters known. Four inscriptions on vessels from the third Fosse Temple illustrate a later stage in the history of the alphabet. A group of inscribed sherds beneath the Babylonian destruction level have been interpreted as the documents in a court-martial case.

La Ferrassie A site 4 miles southwest of Les Eyzies in the Dordogne, France. Occupation began in the MOUSTERIAN period, to which belong four NEANDERTHAL skeletons, two adults and two children, buried in shallow trenches. The sequence continues with CHÂTELPERRONIAN, AURIGNACIAN and finally a thin GRAVETTIAN level.

Lagash (mod **Telloh**) A TELL north of UR, excavated by the French under de Sarzec 1877–1900, and sporadically thereafter. Its period of greatness lay in the 3rd millennium, particularly under Eannatum c2500 and Gudea c2100, a contemporary of the 3rd dynasty of Ur. Lagash fell soon after to LARSA. Its archaeological importance rests mainly on the vast number of cuneiform tablets excavated from its ruins, mostly by clandestine diggers. These throw light particularly on the economic, social and legal aspects of the Early Dynastic period in Sumer, in contrast to the literary texts from NIPPUR. Better known perhaps are the remarkably fine statues of Gudea himself [184], a typical SUMERIAN prince.

Lagozza A lake village site at Besnate near Milan in north Italy. It is the type site of a WESTERN NEOLITHIC culture related to, and possibly derived from, CHASSEY and CORTAILLOD. It is characterized by dark burnished round-based bowls and dishes [100], some carinated. Decoration is rare, consisting of radiating lines on the lower walls or scratched cross-hatched triangles. Instead of proper handles, simple and multiple perforated lugs were used, including the FLÛTE DE PAN. Scratched pebbles are reported from some sites.

Spindle whorls and loom-weights witness to textile production. Flint microliths formed the stone industry. The culture was established before 2850 BC (a radiocarbon

Fig. 100. Lagozza vessel shapes

date) in the north, whence it spread slowly down the Adriatic side of Italy to the Marche and RIPOLI in the Late Neolithic, and to Ariano by the Copper Age, surviving there to give rise to the APENNINE CULTURE of the Bronze Age.

Laibacher Moor ◊ LJUBLJANSKO BLAT
lake village ◊ PALAFITTA, PILE DWELLING, CRANNOG, GLASTONBURY

lamp A vessel to hold liquid fuel to feed a light-giving flame. Simple saucers of stone or chalk for this purpose go back to the Upper Palaeolithic. In pottery, the use can rarely be proved unless a special spout or pinched lip was provided to support the wick, or signs of burning have survived at the rim.

lancehead A missile point of stone, bone or metal, larger than an ARROWHEAD, smaller than a SPEARHEAD, so assumed to have armed a light lance or javelin.

Langdale ◊ AXE FACTORY

lapis lazuli A semi-precious stone of an intense blue colour. It was very popular in the ancient Near East for decorative inlays, beads, seals, etc. Its main source was Badakhshan, northern Afghanistan, from which it was traded in surprising quantities as far as Egypt.

Larco Hoyle, Rafael (1901–66) A landowner and businessman whose studies formed the basis of north Peruvian coastal archaeology. He did much to help other scholars working in the area, while he himself defined the cultures of CUPISNIQUE and SALINAR, broke down MOCHICA into a number of sub-periods, and amassed the finest private archaeological collection in Peru.

larnax A terracotta coffin.

Larnian culture A MESOLITHIC culture, named after Larne in northeast Ireland, and found only on sites close to coasts and estuaries. The characteristic tool is a leaf-shaped point made on a FLAKE, the oldest unambiguous implement in Ireland.

Larsa (mod **Senkera**) A TELL near UR, representing one of the city states of SUMER. It has never been properly explored, most of its history being recovered from documents from other sites. Its period of greatness was in the early 2nd millennium, when it contested the supremacy of Mesopotamia with Isin, ASSUR and ESHNUNNA. Its greatest ruler, Rim Sin, destroyed Isin c1794 BC but was himself overthrown by HAMMURABI of Babylon c1763.

Lartet, Edouard (1801–73) was one of the pioneers of PALAEOLITHIC archaeology. Originally a palaeontologist, he turned to cave excavation, at first alone, then from 1863 onwards in collaboration with his English friend Henry CHRISTY. These two carried out the first systematic study of south French caves, and excavated many of the most famous sites in the Dordogne (LAUGERIE – HAUTE, LE MOUSTIER, LA MADELEINE, etc). They realized that several distinct stages were represented and, on the basis of associated fauna, Lartet divided the cave material into an earlier group with cave bear and mammoth (MOUSTERIAN, or Middle Palaeolithic in today's terminology) and a later one (Upper Palaeolithic) in which reindeer bones predominated. In addition, Lartet and Christy were the first to discover objects of MOBILIARY ART in a properly documented cave excavation. Their results appeared in several important articles, and also, during the decade 1865–75, in the volumes of *Reliquiae Aquitanicae; being contributions to the Archaeology and Palaeontology of Périgord and the adjoining provinces of southern France.*

Lascaux (Montignac, Dordogne) One of the most famous painted caves in France. It was discovered in 1940, and proved to contain a fine series of Upper PALAEO-LITHIC paintings and engravings (◊ CAVE ART). Once the cave had been opened and visitors allowed inside, the delicate atmospheric balance was disturbed and the paintings were attacked by fungus. The disease is now responding well to treatment.

Late Glacial period The closing stages of the PLEISTOCENE Ice Age, when the glaciers had begun their final retreat and when much of northern Europe was tundra. This period lasted from c13,000 to 8500 BC [p 186]. The sub-stages in northern Europe are the *Oldest Dryas* (13,000–10,450), the *Bølling oscillation* (10,450–10,050), the *Older Dryas* (10,050–9850), the ALLERØD OSCILLATION (9850–8850), and the *Younger Dryas* (8850–8300). Cultures of the Late Glacial period include AHRENSBURGIAN, CRESWELLIAN CULTURE, FEDERMESSER cultures, and HAMBURGIAN.

La Tène The site of a great Iron Age VOTIVE DEPOSIT in the shallow water at the east end of Lake Neuchâtel, Switzerland. Excavations in 1907–17 revealed wooden piles, two timber causeways and a mass of tools and weapons of bronze, iron and wood. Some of these objects bore curvilinear patterns which are the hallmark of La Tène art everywhere from central Europe to Ireland and the Pyrenees. ◊ CELTIC ART

La Tène has given its name to the second period of the European Iron Age, which followed the HALLSTATT period over much of the continent and lasted from mid c5 BC until the CELTS were subdued by

Roman conquest (though ◊ BELGAE). The highest development, and the birth of the art style, took place in west central Europe from the Rhineland to the Marne. Contact with the Greek and ETRUSCAN worlds brought wine, metal flagons and Attic drinking cups into lands north of the Alps (◊ KLEIN ASPERGLE), and La Tène art shows links with that of the SCYTHIANS to the east. In Britain, contact with the continental La Tène cultures is shown by CHARIOT burials (◊ ARRAS) and the presence of La Tène art motifs on metalwork and pottery (eg at GLASTONBURY). British cultures showing La Tène influence are sometimes grouped within an Iron Age B complex, but this does not imply either invasion from the Continent or the contemporaneity of all cultures within the group. In Ireland, which the Romans never invaded, a Celtic culture and an art style with La Tène elements persisted into the Early Christian period.

Latians An Iron Age people of southern Latium, the region south of Rome. Their cremation cemeteries are known particularly from the Alban mountains, and from Rome itself. The Latians seem to have developed from the PIANELLO urnfielders, notably those who buried their dead in the cemetery at Allumiere, and were certainly the ancestors of the Romans. The first huts on the Palatine Hill were built by these people in c9.

Laugerie–Haute A rock shelter in the Vézère valley near Les Eyzies, Dordogne, France, which has yielded the richest Upper PALAEOLITHIC sequence ever recorded. It starts with Upper PÉRIGORDIAN (nowadays Périgordian VI), followed in order by 'proto-Magdalenian', final AURIGNACIAN (Aurignacian V), several rich layers of Early, Middle and Late SOLUTREAN, and finally by Early MAGDALENIAN.

Lauricocha The three excavated caves lie at an altitude of 13,000 ft in the central Peruvian Andes. The earliest level, with a radiocarbon date of c7500 BC, yielded the skeletons of people who hunted deer and guanaco with spears tipped with leaf-shaped points. Above this was another hunting culture with better-made points of willow leaf shape of a kind found at AYAMPITÍN, where they are dated c6000–3000. At Lauricocha, however, radiocarbon dates for this phase range from c3200 to 2300 BC. The second culture at Lauricocha was replaced by a third one with smaller leaf- and diamond-shaped points. This lasted until 1200 or later, and the later part of this period overlaps in time with the earliest farming villages on the Peruvian coast, where points of Lauricocha type have been found in rubbish heaps. Stages IV and V represent pottery-using cultures. Other caves in the area have engravings, some of which include motifs employed by about 1000 BC on pottery at KOTOSH, only 50 miles away.

Lausitz culture ⇨ LUSATIAN CULTURE

La Venta (Tabasco, Mexico) The greatest of the OLMEC CEREMONIAL CENTRES. The site occupies a small island, entirely surrounded by swamps, and lacking both farmland and building stone. The principal monument is a huge lobed pyramid of clay, and subsidiary structures include platforms and courtyards spread over some $1\frac{1}{2}$ miles of country. La Venta is famous for its stone sculpture, its buried pavements of serpentine blocks brought from about 100 miles away, and its offerings of carved jade. The important buildings were constructed from c1000 BC and the site was violently destroyed five or six centuries later.

Layard, Sir Austen Henry (1817–94) excavated for the British Museum on a number of Mesopotamian sites 1845–7 and 1849–51. His most important discoveries were at NIMRUD, which he identified wrongly as Nineveh. The Assyrian winged bulls and reliefs he excavated there are now in the British Museum. At NINEVEH proper, modern Kuyunjik, he recovered from Sennacherib's palace a great library of CUNEIFORM tablets. His book on his finds, *Nineveh and its Remains*, ranks as one of the first archaeological best-sellers.

leaf-shaped Pointed at the ends and with convex sides, as in a willow leaf. Applied to an ARROWHEAD, the blade of a slashing SWORD or the flattened bow of a FIBULA.

Lébous (St-Mathieu-de-Tréviers, Hérault, France) A fortified village of the Copper Age FONTBOUÏSSE people. The site is surrounded by a stone wall with towers at intervals, and has a radiocarbon date of 1920 ± 250 BC.

legions The military units forming the backbone of the Roman army. They numbered at the time of the invasion of Britain about 6,000 men each, and were supported to an increasing extent by more mobile, lighter armed, auxiliary units. Each was based on a legionary fortress, a larger and more permanent version of the Roman military camp. Three legions were stationed in Britain, at Gloucester (later at Caerleon), Chester and Lincoln (later at York).

leister A fish spear having two bone or antler heads with barbs pointing inwards and backwards. When found singly the heads are indistinguishable from HARPOON points. They are recorded from Mesolithic and lakeside Neolithic settlements.

Leland, John One of the early antiquarian topographers, who included useful information on ancient remains in his descriptions of the countryside. He had the distinction of being appointed the King's Antiquary in 1533, an office unfortunately soon extinguished.

Le Moustier A rock shelter some 10 miles from Les Eyzies, Dordogne, France, and the type-site for the MOUSTERIAN industry.

Lengyel A late DANUBIAN CULTURE, with many regional variants, in western Hungary, parts of Austria and much of Czechoslovakia and Poland. It is closely linked to the TISZA culture of the Hungarian plain, and it may have been from this area that the Lengyel people adopted painted pottery and the occasional use of copper. Date: first half of the 4th millennium BC, and perhaps as late as 3000.

Lepenski Vir An unusual village settlement on the banks of the Danube above the Iron Gates in Yugoslavia. Trapezoidal houses were occupied by fishermen with an advanced Mesolithic economy. Many

Fig. 101. Stone head, Lepenski Vir

carved stone human heads were found, often with 'fishy' features [101]. Radiocarbon places it in the 7th millennium BC. The site was later occupied by a STARČEVO village.

Lerna A long-lived coastal settlement site near Argos in the Peloponnese, southern Greece. It was excavated by Caskey 1956–9. Middle and Late Neolithic villages were succeeded by a fortified township of Early HELLADIC II. After a conflagration, this was rebuilt in Early Helladic III, when the first pieces of MINYAN Ware appear. Following a peaceful transition to the Middle Helladic, the site remained in occupation throughout that period. Scattered imports from Crete assist in the dating. Two royal graves contemporary with the earlier (Circle B) shaft graves at MYCENAE, c1600 BC, were the latest material on the site.

Levallois technique A technique of flint flaking (named after C19 discoveries at Levallois-Perret, a suburb of Paris) in which the face of the CORE is trimmed to shape in order to control the form and size

of the intended FLAKE. Characteristically the preparatory flaking is directed from the periphery of the core towards the centre. The residual core is shaped rather like a tortoise, with one face plane and the other domed, while the flake shows the scars of the preparatory work on one face and is plane on the other [102]. The Leval-

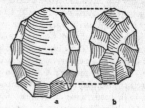

Fig. 102. (a) Levallois tortoise core; (b) Levallois flake

lois technique was employed by certain late Lower PALAEOLITHIC HANDAXE makers, and throughout the Middle Palaeolithic by some MOUSTERIAN communities. It lasts into the Upper Palaeolithic of the Levant, and in the epi-Levalloisian industries of Egypt.

Levalloiso-Mousterian ◊ MOUSTERIAN

Le Vallonet (Roquebrune-Cap-Martin, Provence, France) A cave on the Mediterranean coast which has yielded what may be the oldest tools in Europe. In sediments with fauna of Upper VILLAFRANCHIAN type were five PEBBLE TOOLS and four FLAKES. Both the animal bones and the tools suggest a correlation with the early part of the OLDUVAI sequence, and raise the hope that skeletal remains of AUSTRALOPITHECUS, the most primitive form of man, will one day be found in Europe.

levigated Purified by sedimentation. When clay is mixed with water and allowed to stand, the coarser grains will settle to the bottom, and water and any vegetable impurities can be strained off the top. The layer between gives a particularly fine clay for delicate or high quality pottery.

Levkas or **Leucas** One of the Ionian Islands off the west coast of Greece. The cave of Chirospilia has yielded Neolithic material, but more important are the Early and Middle Bronze Age cemeteries. The former included the rites of JAR BURIAL and partial CREMATION under barrows. Two groups of tombs of the Middle Bronze Age contained some MINYAN Ware, and show some links with the shaft graves of MYCENAE, as also with burial mounds in Albania.

li A vessel shape common in the Chinese Neolithic and Bronze Ages in both pottery and bronze [103]. It is a small jar the base of which divides into three hollow legs.

Fig. 103. Li tripod

limes The frontier zone of the Roman empire, under direct military rule. It is particularly used of the defences holding the gaps between the Rhine and Danube in central Germany, and between the Danube and the Black Sea in the Dobrudja.

Lindisfarne Otherwise known as Holy Island, it is connected to the coast of Northumberland only at low tide. A monastery founded here in AD 635 by St Aidan from IONA soon became the leading centre of the Celtic church and was in its turn parent to important religious houses at York, Jarrow and Hexham. After the Celtic church acknowledged the supremacy of Rome (the Synod of Whitby in 663 was the main step towards unity), it was the centre of a cultural renaissance in NORTH-UMBRIA around AD 700. This is best demonstrated by the superb illuminated

manuscripts, such as the Lindisfarne Gospels. The monastery flourished until 793 when it was the object of the first Viking raid on England.

Linear A and B Scripts in use by the MINOANS and MYCENAEANS in Crete and Greece in the Bronze Age, so called by Sir Arthur EVANS to distinguish them from the HIEROGLYPHIC which preceded them. Each is a SYLLABARY, and was written with a sharp point on clay tablets [104]. Linear A (Middle Minoan III–Late Minoan

Fig. 104. Clay tablet inscribed with Linear B

I in Crete, c2000–1500) cannot yet be read. Linear B (Late Minoan II in Crete and Mycenaean IIIA–B on the mainland, 1500–1100) was brilliantly deciphered by VENTRIS in 1952. It is an early form of Greek, and its reading has thrown much light on the continuity between Bronze Age and classical Greece, although the only texts are bare inventories and the like.

linear earthwork, dyke An earthwork consisting of a bank and ditch, or multiple banks and ditches, which does not curve round to form an enclosure but continues more or less straight across country. Such dykes may be anything from a few hundred yards to more than 50 miles in length, and vary greatly in date and purpose. Some Bronze and Iron Age examples may be ranch boundaries with no defensive value, but in the later Iron Age and the post-Roman Dark Age it is often difficult to distinguish boundary markers from defence works. Many of these later dykes cut across communication routes or lines of easy access, and would have been an effective obstacle against CHARIOTS or wheeled vehicles. Sometimes literary references supplement archaeological evidence, as in the case of Offa's Dyke, constructed by this c8 king as a boundary between his kingdom of MERCIA and the Welsh. The post-Roman Wansdyke seems to have been built as a barrier against invading SAXONS.

linear pottery ♢ BANDKERAMIK, DANUBIAN CULTURE

lion An animal now found wild only in East Africa and the Saurashtra peninsula of west India. Being so popular as a symbol of power and royalty, ancient representations are a poor guide to its early distribution. It seems to have survived into the Christian era in the Near East, lingering particularly in Turkey and Iran. It is not certainly known whether its range extended into Greece and the Balkans. [126, 127]

Lipari The chief of the Eolian (or Lipari) Islands, a group lying 20 miles off the north coast of Sicily at its northeast corner. All are volcanic (Stromboli and Vulcano are still active), and Lipari has extensive deposits of the volcanic glass OBSIDIAN highly prized in antiquity. Largely in consequence of this it was continuously occupied from an early date. In addition the deposits on the obvious site for settlement, the Castello, have been constantly incremented with volcanic dust. The result is one of the finest stratigraphies of archaeological deposits anywhere. It was revealed by Bernabò Brea 1950–60.

IMPRESSED WARE of STENTINELLO type was found only inland, the first level on the Castello being Middle Neolithic, with connexions in southern Italy (Capri and SERRA D'ALTO) and Dalmatia (DANILO). The Late Neolithic Diana Ware followed, red-slipped and trumpet-lugged. In the Copper Age, Piano Conte and Piano Quartara cultures (from other sites in the group) succeeded each other, the latter in particular with Aegean links. Capo Graziano, Milazzese and Ausonian cultures span the Bronze Age, the first with some MYCENAEAN II imported sherds, the second (related to THAPSOS in Sicily) with

Mycenaean IIIA and B and APENNINE CULTURE imports, the third an offshoot of the Apennine culture. A later version of Ausonian continued through the Iron Age, with Calabrian and Campanian links. A Greek colony, Lipara, was founded in 580 BC, and Greek, Hellenistic, Roman and later levels were all present.

Little Woodbury An Iron Age farmstead, one mile south of Salisbury, revealed by air photography and excavated by Gerhard Bersu in 1938–9. This excavation, together with Wheeler's at MAIDEN CASTLE, set new standards in British Iron Age studies, and Little Woodbury was more intensively examined than any previous site of its kind. It consisted of a circular timber hut 45 ft in diameter, surrounded by corn-drying frames, granaries and silo pits for grain storage, all enclosed within a wooden stockade some 400 ft across. The site may have been inhabited for as long as three centuries without changing its basic character. The house was rebuilt on several occasions, and at some time of crisis was surrounded by a defensive ditch which was never finished.

Ljubljansko Blat A marsh near Ljubljana in Slovenia, Yugoslavia, on which a number of village sites have been found. These have yielded Late Neolithic to Copper Age material, including copper and moulds for casting it. The culture is related to others throughout the East Alpine area, such as VUČEDOL, and was in contact with northern Italy.

llama A domesticated animal exploited by the ancient Andean civilizations as a beast of burden and, to a lesser extent, for its meat and wool. It is related to the camel, though smaller in size and lacking a hump. Its wild ancestor, the guanaco, is still found in the Andes. The centre of domestication was probably the highlands of southern Peru, Bolivia and north Chile, perhaps as early as the 6th millennium BC.

Llano complex ♢ CLOVIS POINT

lobster–claw cairn ♢ COURT CAIRN

lock rings Small penannular ornaments of gold or bronze popular in the Early to Middle Bronze Age in northern Europe. They are thought to have been used as hair ornaments.

loess A wind-borne rock dust carried from outwash deposits and moraines, and laid down as a thick stratum during periglacial conditions in the steppe country surrounding the ice sheets (◊ GLACIATION). It provided good grazing for the animals on which PALAEOLITHIC man fed, and was later settled by NEOLITHIC farmers who found it easy to till with primitive equipment.

long barrow ◊ BARROW

Long Count ◊ CALENDAR

longevity Man's expectation of life is one of the simplest ways of measuring his ability to cope with his surroundings. It can rarely be calculated for an ancient population because too few skeletons are usually found to provide an adequate statistical sample for skeletal analysis. Even then the results may be biased, since infants often failed to qualify for ceremonial burial and so may not be represented. But the age distribution of even a few skeletons may give useful results, by comparison of the numbers reaching, say, the age of 30, 50 and 70 years.

loom The apparatus required for weaving cloth. Normally the variety of loom employed can be deduced only from surviving fragments of the resulting cloth. These show, for example, that the horizontal loom was the more usual in ancient Egypt, the vertical loom in Syria and Mesopotamia. Through Europe the evidence is clear that the vertical loom with weighted warps was standard until classical times. The weights employed, disc-shaped, quoit-shaped or pyramidal, are frequently found on sites from the Late Neolithic on, being particularly frequent in the Bronze Age. They reappear with the Anglo-Saxons. In the Americas the most common form was the belt or backstrap loom, in which a continuous warp thread passed between two horizontal poles. One was attached to a support whilst the other was attached to the seated weaver, who could adjust the tension of the warps simply by leaning forward or backward.

Los Millares ◊ MILLARES, LOS

lost wax ◊ CIRE PERDUE

Lothal The most important of the southern INDUS CIVILIZATION sites, it lies at the head of the Gulf of Cambay, north of Bombay. Besides typical Indus structures like a walled citadel, granary, drains and a grid street plan, it had a dock faced with baked brick. The importance of the site undoubtedly lay in its sea trade, as shown by the discovery there of a seal from the Persian Gulf. There were also contacts with the Chalcolithic cultures of the Deccan peninsula and the practice of rice cultivation had been introduced from even further east. Radiocarbon dates place it early in the 2nd millennium BC. It yielded the earliest evidence to date of rice cultivation, by C18 BC.

lotus A water-lily, the bud and flower of which were much used as motifs in the arts of ancient Egypt and countries under its immediat· influence [105] and at a later date in Buddhist Asia.

Fig. 105. Lotus bloom with two buds

Lough Gur Round the shores of this lake, 11 miles south of Limerick, is one of the greatest concentrations of sites in Ireland. At Knockadoon were Neolithic huts, and at the Spectacles site were huts of the Early Christian period with their associated fields. Ritual or funerary monuments include MENHIRS, a WEDGE-SHAPED GALLERY GRAVE, a flat-topped cairn with URN burials, and a circle of contiguous stones which yielded Late Neolithic and Early Bronze Age pottery. There are also several CASHELS and a CRANNOG.

Loyang A city was founded here, near the south bank of the Yellow river in Honan province, north China, early in the CHOU dynasty. From 771 BC it became their capital, following the loss of Tsung Chou in Shensi. It finally fell to the Ch'in in 256. Traces of its rammed earth walls have come to light, and one of its cemeteries of pit graves also.

lug A knob handle on pottery. If perforated, the hole, vertical or horizontal, is too small to take a finger, but would hold instead a loop of cord or thong.

Lung Shan A Late Neolithic culture of the lower Yellow river in China, characterized by a fine black burnished pottery, usually made on the wheel. Polished stone was common, and much use was made of bone for arrowheads, etc. Two traits pointing forward to the SHANG Bronze Age are the use of rammed earth for defensive ramparts and of ORACLE BONES for divining. In Honan, where its distribution overlaps that of the YANG SHAO culture, Lung Shan is stratified above the former and below Shang material. The relationships of the three need clarification.

Fig. 106. Gold lunula

lunula A crescent-shaped sheet of gold some 8 ins across, probably worn as an ornament on the chest [106]. Their chased decoration suggests they were copied from the JET necklace. They were made by the FOOD VESSEL people of Ireland and Scotland in the Early Bronze Age, and traded not only to southern England but also across to northern Europe.

lur (pl lurer) A large musical HORN of bronze, having a double curve and a disc-shaped bell or mouth [107]. Lurer come from the peatbogs of Denmark and are almost invariably found in pairs, suggesting that they were VOTIVE DEPOSITS. They date to the Late Bronze Age.

Fig. 107. Lur from a Danish peatbog

Luristan The region of the central Zagros range between Iran and Iraq, where a distinctive bronze-working industry flourished 1100–700 BC. It is characterized by a free use of animal and demonic human forms as decoration on weapons, horse-bits, pins, etc [108]. Its origins are attributed to an immigration of people from the

Fig. 108. Luristan bronze, a decorative pin head

Caucasus, grafted onto a population of KASSITES who had already developed a bronze industry in the area in the centuries around 2000 BC. The newcomers included Indo-European speakers, and were culturally, perhaps also ethnically, ancestral to the MEDES and PERSIANS.

Lusatian culture An URNFIELD culture which had formed by C1200 BC in east Germany, northern Czechoslovakia and much of Poland. It is noted for its bronzework and its fine dark pottery, sometimes graphite-burnished and generally decorated with bosses and fluted ornament. In the northern part of its range (◊ BISKUPIN) the Lusatian culture persisted, with the adoption of iron tools, throughout the earlier, HALLSTATT, part of the Iron Age, and did not become extinct until c300 BC. In some classifications the Middle Bronze Age 'pre-Lausitz' phase is considered the first stage of the Lusatian culture proper.

Luxor The modern town on the site of ancient THEBES of which KARNAK is now a part.

Lyell, Sir Charles (1797–1875) Although primarily a geologist, his work had a bearing on the development of archaeology at two points. His *Principles of Geology*, 1830–33, in stating that geological events must be explained by still occurring processes, not by universal floods or other catastrophes, opened the way for the acceptance of a vastly longer time-scale for the world than the traditional 6000 years. His *Antiquity of Man*, 30 years later, dealt in detail with man and geology, bringing in the implications of Darwinism.

lynchet A bank of earth which accumulates on the downhill side of an ancient ploughed field as the disturbed soil moves down the slope under the action of gravity.

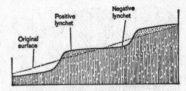

Fig. 109. Section through lynchets

The denudation at the top edge of the field creates a negative lynchet [109]. Lynchets are conspicuous in the square CELTIC FIELDS (Bronze Age to Romano-British in date) and in the long rectangular fields, the so-called strip lynchets, laid out on sloping terrain in post-Roman and medieval times.

M

Maat The ancient Egyptian goddess of truth and divine order. Her symbol was the ostrich feather.

mace A weapon designed to give a crushing blow, usually made of stone and hafted by means of a SHAFT-HOLE. It is very variable in form, as the illustration shows. [110]

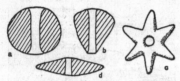

Fig. 110. Some types of mace: (a) spheroid; (b) pyriform; (c) star-shaped; (d) discoid

MacEnery, Father J. In 1825 he began excavations at KENT'S CAVERN, near Torquay, and soon started to find PALAEOLITHIC flint tools alongside the bones of extinct animals in an undisturbed stratum sealed by a stalagmitic layer. He drew the obvious conclusion that man and these ancient animals must have coexisted, but these views found little acceptance in the geological and religious climate of the day. MacEnery died in 1841 without publishing his results, and it was left to William PENGELLY in 1869 to publish the report of MacEnery's excavations.

Machu Picchu An INCA town discovered in the Urubamba valley by Hiram Bingham in 1911. It contains some fine stone buildings, but what has captured popular imagination is the situation of the town, on a saddle of the Andes overlooking a drop of 1,500 ft on either side.

Mad'arovce ◊ ÚNĚTICE

Maes Howe (Orkney) A fine PASSAGE GRAVE, roofed by CORBELLING and covered by a circular CAIRN surrounded by a ring ditch. The plan is unusual in having a squared burial chamber with three rectangular cells opening from it through doorways placed about 3 ft above the level of the chamber floor. Nothing was found inside the tomb when it was explored in 1861, but scratched on the wall is a C12 inscription in RUNES stating that the grave was looted by Vikings who carried off a great treasure. Other graffiti include a C12 dragon.

Magdalenian The final PALAEOLITHIC culture of much of western Europe, named after the site of La Madeleine in the Dordogne. Its centre of origin was southwest France and the adjacent parts of Spain, but elements characteristic of the later stages are represented in Britain (CRESWELL CRAGS), and eastwards to southwest Germany and Poland. Magdalenian culture,

Fig. 111. Magdalenian bone objects: (a) and (b) harpoons; (c) bâton de commandement

like that of earlier Upper Palaeolithic communities, was adapted to the cold conditions of the last (WÜRM) GLACIATION, and reindeer were an important source of food. The Magdalenians are famous for their CAVE ART (eg from ALTAMIRA), and for beautiful decorative work in bone and ivory (◊ MOBILIARY ART). One of the most diagnostic tools of the later Magdalenian is the barbed harpoon [111]. The time range is c15,000–10,000 BC.

Maglemosian The first MESOLITHIC culture of the north European plain. The way of life was adapted to a forest and lakeside environment. The tool kit included MICROLITHS, wood-working tools such as chipped axes and adzes, spear heads of bone or antler and fishing gear [83, 112]. Wooden bows, paddles and dugout canoes

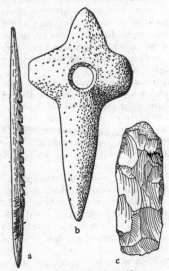

Fig. 112. Maglemosian artifacts

have been found, and the dog was already domesticated. The earliest stages (eg at STAR CARR) reach back to c8000 BC (PRE-BOREAL pollen zone), but the culture persisted through the succeeding BOREAL period, to end c5000 BC.

magnetometer An instrument for measuring the intensity of the earth's magnetic field at any point. When a current is passed through a coil in a bottle of water or alcohol the protons of the hydrogen atoms align themselves to its magnetic field. When the current is cut off the protons

realign themselves according to the earth's field, its strength being indicated by the frequency of their gyration on realignment. This sets up a weak current which is transmitted back from the bottle to the instrument and there registered on dials. The resulting figures are plotted to reveal anomalies in field strength. These are usually due to buried iron, to kilns, hearths or the like (◊ ARCHAEOMAGNETISM), or to pits or ditches (topsoil is more magnetic than subsoil). These features can thus be rapidly located without disturbance of the ground, and subsequent excavation can be directed immediately to the most promising areas. ◊ BLEEPER and RESISTIVITY SURVEY

Magosian A stone industry found in the eastern part of sub-Saharan Africa, where it is dated c10,000–6000 BC. Diagnostic tools include small points, MICROLITHS and small BLADES, which make their appearance alongside the heavier tools of the preceding phase. ◊ KALAMBO FALLS

Maiden Castle The site, 2 miles southwest of Dorchester, Dorset, was dug by Wheeler in 1934–7, and is one of the largest and most completely excavated HILLFORTS in Britain. The oldest structure on the hilltop is a Neolithic CAUSE-WAYED CAMP, followed after an interval by an earthen LONG BARROW, 1,800 ft in length, which is partly built over the ditches of the earlier camp. Occupation resumed in the Early Iron Age with the construction of a hillfort which was later extended to fortify the entire hill and enclose an area of 45 acres. Maiden Castle was by this time a permanent settlement with stone and wooden huts linked by surfaced trackways. In the next stage the site was occupied by new people who twice rebuilt and strengthened the defences. The entrances were remodelled, and the old UNIVALLATE fort converted into a massive stronghold with four concentric ramparts. This defence in depth may be connected with SLING warfare, for piles containing up to 22,000 sling shot were found in place at strategic points. Sometime before 50 BC the site came under the control of the BELGAE and became the tribal capital of the Durotriges, with coinage and imported Gallo-Roman luxuries. During the Roman conquest the fort was sacked by Vespasian's legion, and the slain defenders were buried in a cemetery near the east gate. The Romans moved the remaining population to a new site at Durnovaria (Dorchester), and the hillfort was abandoned until C4 AD when a Romano-Celtic temple was built there.

Maikop (Kuban valley, northern Caucasus) The site of one of the richest KURGAN burials ever discovered. The barrow covered a timber MORTUARY HOUSE divided into three sections. In the central one was a royal burial of a man sprinkled with ochre and laid under a canopy with gold and silver supports. The corpse was accompanied by tools and weapons of copper, a profusion of gold ornaments, gold vessels and silver vases engraved with animal scenes. The metalwork shows links with Mesopotamia and southwest Asia. Maikop belongs to the Early Kuban culture, or oldest stage of the Caucasian Copper Age, with a date in the middle-late 3rd millennium BC.

Mailhac ◇ CAYLA DE MAILHAC

maize The original centre of maize cultivation was probably northern Mesoamerica. Its wild ancestor (now extinct) may have grown in the Mexican highlands some 80,000 years ago, but the first archaeological evidence comes from the TEHUACAN VALLEY, in south central Mexico, where maize pollen and a few chewed cobs of wild maize occur in deposits of the El Riego phase (7000–5000 BC). A little cultivated maize appears in the succeeding Coxcatlán period (c 5000–3500) although wild foods still provide about 90 per cent of the diet.

Maize may have been domesticated independently in a number of places. The Nal-tel race was cultivated in the Sierra de Tamaulipas, northeast Mexico, by c 2500 BC, and the COCHISE people of the southwestern United States had begun to grow maize between 3600 and 2000. The plant did not reach the eastern USA until about the time of Christ. Further south, maize was probably grown by 3000. In Peru it appeared on the north central coast in the late pre-ceramic period (2500–1800) and soon afterwards along the entire coast. In the Andes a primitive form is found in caves near Ayacucho sometime during the period 3500–3000. At the start of the CHAVÍN period sometime before 1000 BC, an improved variety was introduced into Peru from Mexico, and maize then became a staple food.

malachite The green carbonate of COPPER. It was first employed as a cosmetic and ointment for the eyes, to cut down the glare of the sun and discourage flies. The discovery that metal could be obtained from it was probably accidental. The extensive deposits in SINAI were much exploited in antiquity.

Malatya The mound of Arslantepe (anc Milid), near the upper Euphrates in central Turkey, was excavated by the French in the 1930s. It was an important site of the Syro-HITTITES, best known for the reliefs of its Lion Gate and the colossal statue of one of its kings.

Mallia A palace and town of the MINOANS on the north coast of Crete 15 miles east of KNOSSOS. The site has been under excavation by the French for over 30 years. The palace is large and well planned around a central court. Its life spanned the Middle Minoan and Late Minoan I periods (c 1900–1450 BC) though rebuilding was needed after an earthquake c 1750. Among notable individual finds are a great bronze sword and a battleaxe carved in the form of a leopard. The town was established by Early Minoan I, but most of the buildings so far studied are Middle and Late Minoan, and extremely well-appointed. The royal cemetery had already been looted, but yielded a very fine gold pendant showing two bees on a berry or honey comb.

Malta A Mediterranean island some 60 miles south of Sicily. A settlement of the IMPRESSED WARE culture at Skorba has recently been radiocarbon dated to c4000 BC. Further immigrants arrived from Sicily c3200. These people from c2800–1900 BC erected a startling and unique series of megalithic temples [113], some 30 still surviving, of sophisticated plan and construction. The goddess appears as an

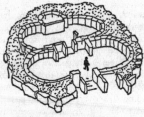

Fig. 113. A Maltese temple, Mnajdra

obese figure with fertility and death aspects. These people were succeeded by warlike immigrants, possibly from western Greece, who dug an URNFIELD into the ruins of the TARXIEN temples and planted villages on all naturally defended hilltops. It is to this period that the mysterious 'cart-ruts' belong. The island was finally brought under the control of the PHOENI-CIANS c C9 for the sake of its harbours, and passed by conquest to Rome in 216 BC.

Malwa A district in India 300 miles north-east of Bombay. Important sites include NAVDATOLI, Nagda and Kayatha (Ujjain). The name is particularly applied to a red slipped, black painted ware of c1600 BC, the influence of which has been noted over much of central India.

Manetho A Graeco-Egyptian who wrote a history of his country in C3 BC. Though the work is lost, quotations from it in later writers are extremely important for re-constructing the dynastic lists of the PHARAOHS. It is to him indeed we owe the system of dividing the pharaohs into successive DYNASTIES.

manioc (also called **cassava** and **yuca**) The plant is native to the tropical lowland zone of South America, where there seems to have been an independent focus of culti-vation based on manioc and other root crops. Venezuela has been suggested as the area where manioc agriculture began, prob-ably before 2000 BC, but the plant will tolerate varied climates. It became estab-lished in the Andes and had reached the Peruvian coast by about 1500 BC. Under good conditions MAIZE is a more produc-tive crop, and in areas where it could be grown successfully it became the staple food, even replacing manioc in parts of Colombia and Venezuela. Only in the lowland forest did manioc retain its posi-tion as the main food plant.

There are several varieties, of which the bitter types are poisonous unless carefully processed. On archaeological sites, large clay discs are often interpreted as griddles on which were baked flat cakes made of a flour prepared by roasting grated manioc roots after squeezing out the prussic acid they contain. There are, however, other ways of dealing with manioc and the absence of discs in a given area does not prove that the plant was unknown there.

mano In American archaeology the upper (ie hand-held) stone used when grinding MAIZE on a METATE, or stone slab. ⟡ QUERN

Marajoara A style of pottery made on Marajó island at the mouth of the Amazon from about C5 AD until just before the European conquest. The elaborate poly-chrome decoration of the urns has affinities with that of other wares along the river Amazon and in eastern Ecuador.

Marduk or **Bel** The god of BABYLON who in C13–C12 BC ousted ENLIL as the most prominent god in the Sumerian pantheon.

Mari (mod **Tell Hariri**) A TELL on the

right bank of the Euphrates near the Syrian–Iraqi border. It was excavated by the French under Parrot 1933–8 and from 1951 on. It was the chief city of the middle Euphrates until its destruction by HAMMURABI C1759 BC. The palace of Zimri-Lim, its last king, is the best preserved of the period in Mesopotamia, its well-planned layout covering 5 acres. Its archives of about 25,000 CUNEIFORM tablets, too, illuminate brilliantly the international politics of the period and the administrative and economic organization of the kingdom.

Marlik Tepe A site southwest of the Caspian Sea, excavated by Negahban, 1961–2. Its royal tombs have produced a great wealth of gold and silver vessels, jewellery and weapons, dated to the late 2nd millennium BC. The relief decoration on the beakers and bowls is in the form of vigorous animals and humans, linking it with the art of the steppes to the north and LURISTAN to the south. Clandestine digging at the neighbouring site of Amlash has produced closely comparable work.

Marnians The name formerly used for those CELTS, possessing a rich LA TÈNE culture, who occupied a region centred on the Marne valley in north central France in C3 and C2 BC. They were held to have formed a conquering aristocracy in England but, apart from those who brought the ARRAS culture to Yorkshire, the evidence for them is now thought to indicate trade rather than invasion.

Marschwitz ◊ ÚNĚTICE

Marshall, Sir John Director-General of Archaeology in India in the 1920s and 30s, the period when India's long prehistory was first revealed. HARAPPA and MOHEN-JO-DARO were discovered in 1921. In the years following, besides the work on those sites, many others of the INDUS CIVILIZATION were found and much was learnt of the Chalcolithic cultures which preceded it in Sind and Baluchistan.

Masada A great rock fortress west of the Dead Sea where the last survivors of the Jewish revolt of AD 70 defied the Roman army, whose siege works can still be traced. Excavations have revealed monumental remains of Herod the Great's buildings.

mastaba The mudbrick superstructure over a tomb in early Egypt, originally intended to copy the house of the living. Mastabas were introduced in the 1st dynasty, becoming steadily more elaborate, with progressively greater use of stone, through the Old KINGDOM. The PYRAMIDS were a direct development from them.

Matera A small city in southern Italy northwest of Taranto. The name is applied to a Middle Neolithic ware from many sites in its neighbourhood, notably the ditched villages of Murgecchia and Murgia Timone and a cave site, the Grotta dei Pipistrelli. A dark burnished ware with curved bowls and straight-necked jars, it is characterized by rectilinear geometric designs scratched after firing and filled with an inlay of red ochre. It is widespread in southern Italy and may derive from a late version of the IMPRESSED WARE. A quite different ware, thin, buff-coloured and painted with broad bands of scarlet, is sometimes included in the term.

mattock ◊ HOE

Maudslay, Alfred Percival (1850–1931) A British scholar who was one of the first people to visit and make a scientific record of the great MAYA sites. Inspired by travellers' accounts of the ruins, he visited Guatemala and the neighbouring republics, and by 1894 had made seven expeditions at his own expense, photographing, making casts, plans and drawings at such sites as Quirigua, PALENQUE and CHICHÉN ITZÁ. He was also the first archaeologist to see the important ruins of Yaxchilan. He published the results of his journeys as part of a series entitled *Biologia Centrali-Americana, or, Contributions to the Knowledge of the Flora and Fauna of Mexico and Central America*, issued in 1889–1902.

Maudslay's work was remarkable for its accuracy and objectivity. His records are still a valuable source of information, and the texts which he transcribed formed the basis of early studies of Maya hieroglyphs.

Mauer jaw A lower jaw of HOMO ERECTUS type found in the Mauer sands near Heidelberg, Germany. No tools were recovered from the stratum, but on the basis of associated fauna the Mauer jaw is placed either within the GÜNZ-MINDEL INTERGLACIAL or else in an INTERSTADIAL of the Mindel glaciation. The presence of fossil hyaena and elephant bones makes the former date the more likely one.

Mauryan empire The first fully historic period of Indian history. Chandragupta, king of Magadha in Bihar, led the movement which expelled the Greeks from India after the death of Alexander the Great in 323 BC. His capital at Pataliputra (mod Patna) became a centre where the art of ACHAEMENID Persia was absorbed and Indianized. His grandson Ashoka accepted Buddhism, an even more important element of later Indian culture. The dynasty subsequently declined and was deposed by the Sunga in 187 BC.

Maya A civilized people who occupied the peninsula of Yucatan and British Honduras, the lowland jungle zone immediately to the south of it, and the highlands of Guatemala and western Honduras. Mayan origins must lie in the local Formative cultures (◊ PRE-CLASSIC PERIOD) which were stimulated by contact with the OLMEC and IZAPA regions, but by c200 BC (at sites like TIKAL and UAXACTÚN) the first pyramids were being built in the central lowlands of Guatemala. CORBELLING appears not long afterwards; the first dated STELA was erected at Tikal in AD 292, and by about 300 we can talk of a CLASSIC Maya civilization.

The Early Classic period (c3–600) began the golden age of Maya culture in the lowlands. The peasantry lived scattered throughout the jungle, but the great CEREMONIAL CENTRES acted as foci for administration, religion and the arts. Architecture, sculpture and painting were highly developed; records were kept in HIEROGLYPHIC writing; elaborate ceremonies were carried out in the temples on top of their pyramids. A class of astronomer-priests observed the sun, moon and planets, and had evolved a calendrical system more accurate than the Julian calendar used in Christian Europe (◊ CALENDAR). In mathematics the priests used a vigesimal system with the concept of zero and with a positional notation. The southern region (highland and Pacific Guatemala) was aberrant in many respects, and never adopted such typical Maya traits as corbel vaults and LONG COUNT dates.

The Late Classic period (c600–900) shows an aesthetic development. Sculpture and architecture became more flamboyant, and regional styles can be recognized [114].

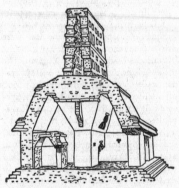

Fig. 114. Maya temple at Palenque

Northern Yucatan began to come into its own at sites like CHICHÉN ITZÁ and Uxmal, where fine buildings in the Puuc style were erected during C9. For reasons not fully understood, the later part of this period witnessed the end of civilization in the lowlands where the great centres were abandoned during C9 and early C10.

The Post-Classic period (c900 to the Spanish conquest) is best represented in Yucatan where the factors which brought about the collapse of lowland Maya culture seem to have been less effective. This period began with strong Mexican influence, particularly at Chichén Itzá where buildings were constructed in the TOLTEC style of central Mexico, and the art shows representations of Toltec warriors overpowering Maya chiefs. Maya legends are confusing and contradictory, but they contain references to a group of Mexicanized foreigners, the Itzá, who conquered Chichén and ruled much of Yucatan from that city. Another legend records the arrival of Kukulcan with a group of foreigners in the years 967–87. Since the name Kukulcan is synonymous with QUETZALCÓATL, the feathered serpent god well known to the Toltecs, this story may refer either to a full scale invasion or to the introduction of the worship of Quetzalcóatl, whose image now appears prominently in Yucatan.

Sometime around 1200 the Itzá were driven from their capital, and MAYAPÁN became the leading city of Yucatan. The great days of the Maya were over. Mayapán was a mean city, and during its period of dominance artistic standards deteriorated still further. In about 1440–50 Mayapán was overthrown and there followed a time of disunity and warfare which lasted until the Spaniards conquered Yucatan in 1541. The Maya kingdoms of highland Guatemala were subdued in 1525, but in the lowlands the descendents of the exiled Itzá held out until 1697. ◊> BONAMPAK, KAMINALJUYÚ and PALENQUE

Mayapán A late MAYA city in Yucatan. Excavation showed it to be a walled town covering about 2½ square miles and containing more than 3,000 houses. Although the quality of building is often poor, urbanism is a new concept in the Maya zone and here replaces the earlier pattern of CEREMONIAL CENTRES. After the decline

of CHICHÉN ITZÁ in c1200 AD Mayapán became the dominant city of Yucatan until sacked by the forces of a neighbouring state in about 1450.

Mazapan ware Orange-or-buff pottery decorated with parallel straight or wavy lines produced by a multiple brush [115]. It was made by the TOLTECS of Mexico.

Fig. 115. Mazapan bowl

meander A running design consisting of a single line or band twisting regularly. The spiral meander is a simple running spiral, the square meander a rectilinear form of the same thing.

Medes An INDO-EUROPEAN speaking people, related to the PERSIANS, who settled in northwest Iran. Between c8 and c6 BC they played an active part in the complicated power politics of the Middle East, their greatest achievement being the destruction of ASSYRIA in 612, under Cyaxares. Though the initiative was seized by the Persians under Cyrus, the Medes remained ruling partners in the ACHAEMENID empire he set up. They are well illustrated in the friezes of PERSEPOLIS. [141]

megalithic Built of large stones. Megalithic structures include MENHIRS and ALIGNMENTS, STONE CIRCLES, certain HENGE monuments and many kinds of CHAMBER TOMB. The phrase 'megalithic tomb' is often used loosely for any above-ground chamber tomb, whether built of large or small stones.

megaron A hall consisting basically of a

rectangular room with the side walls projecting beyond the forward end to form a porch, which may be pillared [116]. A large central hearth in the hall is usual, and extra rooms at the rear end, still between the

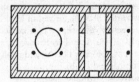

Fig. 116. The megaron at the centre of Nestor's palace at Pylos

same side walls, are common. The form is recorded at TROY in the middle of the 3rd millennium, and continued to be used in Turkey until much later. It appears as early as the SESKLO period in Greece, and formed the nucleus of the MYCENAEANS' palaces.

megger earth-tester ◊ RESISTIVITY SURVEY

Megiddo A large TELL standing above the Plain of Esdraelon in northern Palestine, commanding the pass across the Carmel range from the Plain of Sharon. Between 1925 and 1939 the Oriental Institute of Chicago attempted a complete excavation, but below level V the area of work had to be restricted drastically. A town in the Early Bronze Age was built c 3000 BC on a site sporadically occupied since the Neolithic. It became a great fortified centre through its vital strategic position on the land route from Egypt to Syria. It survived frequent sackings almost without break of occupation down to c 350 BC, yielding very full evidence of the cultural changes throughout its long life. Notable were a hoard of ivories of C13, a rock-cut shaft and 70 yd passage of the same period to give the CANAANITES access to a spring from inside the walls, and elaborate stables of the Israelite kings c 850 BC.

Mehi (Mashkai, south BALUCHISTAN)

A TELL which yielded a mixture of KULLI and INDUS CIVILIZATION material. The latter probably represents a trading post planted in Kulli territory. A cremation cemetery, exceptionally rich in copper objects, lay immediately outside the settlement. The most noteworthy finds were a series of small carved stone vessels with incised decoration. Identical examples have come from Mohenjo-daro to the east and southern Persia and Early Dynastic Mesopotamia to the west, where they date from around 2800 BC.

Melkarth or **Melqart** One of the gods of the PHOENICIANS. His name means 'ruler of the city', and in origin he was probably the patron deity of TYRE, the political rise of which gave him wider power (cf MARDUK). For example, CARTHAGE, a Tyrian colony, also venerated him. He was later equated with the Greek Herakles.

Melos One of the Cyclades in the Aegean, famous as a major source of OBSIDIAN, trade in which brought wealth to the island. At Phylakopi three successive settlements were discovered, of roughly Early Cycladic II, Middle Cycladic and Late Cycladic respectively. They show increasing influence from the MINOANS of Crete, so much so that the third is better regarded as a provincial Minoan town than a native Cycladic one. Nevertheless the island maintained close contact with the Greek mainland, and with the collapse of Crete it came fully into the sphere of the MYCENAEANS.

Memphis One of the leading cities of Lower Egypt, on occasion the capital of the whole country. It stood near the key point where the Nile begins to divide its waters at the head of the DELTA. The only surviving remains are the cemeteries west of the city, most notably the pyramids and sphinx of GIZA.

Menes According to Greek record, the pharaoh who united Egypt and founded the 1st dynasty, c 3200 BC. Perhaps to be equated with NARMER.

menhir A single vertical standing stone. Menhirs are difficult to date, but in Ireland and southwest England a few examples mark burials dating from the BEAKER period to the Middle or Late Bronze Age. A similar or slightly earlier date is attested for some of the Breton menhirs. In all these areas, a few of the stones bear CUP MARKS. Other menhirs are undoubtedly later than the ones discussed above, and the idea of setting up large stones has occurred to many peoples at different times. ⟡ ALIGNMENT, STATUE MENHIR

Mercia A province of the ANGLO-SAXONS in central England, on the frontier with the British. It rose to hegemony over the other kingdoms during C7 and C8 AD. Its most famous kings were Penda (632–54) and Offa (757–96). Thereafter it declined and disappeared under the encroachments of the Danes and of WESSEX.

Merimde A site on the west bank of the Nile Delta representing one of the earliest cultures of Egypt, similar to that of the FAYUM. It yielded a radiocarbon date of 4180 BC. Three occupation phases showed progressively more substantial shelters, beneath which the dead were buried in a crouched position. Barley and emmer, cattle, sheep and pigs are attested. Sickle flints and hollow-based arrowheads, pyriform and spherical maceheads, sling stones, fishhooks, spindle whorls and simple stone axeheads have been found. The pottery was poor, plain, straw-tempered and often covered with a slip.

Meroe A city site in the Sudan which succeeded Napata as the capital of a vigorous state flourishing from 750 BC to AD 350 in NUBIA. Its court was much influenced by Egypt, and it rose to power with the latter's decline. Indeed its king Piankhi conquered Egypt to found the 25th dynasty in C8 BC.

Mersin The 80 ft high TELL of Yumuk-tepe lies in the coastal plain of Cilicia, on the south coast of Turkey. It was dug by GARSTANG before and after the Second World War. The lowest levels he reached were of an Early Neolithic characterized by monochrome impressed wares, radiocarbon dated to 6000 BC. A long series of Chalcolithic levels were tied into the Mesopotamian sequence (HASSUNA, HALAF, UBAID, etc) by imported sherds. Noteworthy was the fortress of level XVI. Subsequently the site was occupied by peoples of the Anatolian Bronze Age, the HITTITES, the early Greeks, and finally the Byzantines and Arabs.

Mesolithic (Middle Stone Age) The period of transition between the PALAEO-LITHIC and the NEOLITHIC, with persistence of the old Palaeolithic hunting and collecting way of life in the new environment created by the withdrawal of the PLEISTOCENE ice sheets around 8300 BC. Glacial flora and fauna were replaced by modern forms, but agriculture was still unknown. Mesolithic flint industries are often distinguished by an abundance of MICROLITHS. The period came to an end with the gradual invention and diffusion of the 'Neolithic' manner of life based on farming and stock-rearing. In the Near East, which remained free of ice sheets, climatic change was less significant than in northern Europe and agriculture was practised soon after the close of the Pleistocene. In this area the Mesolithic period was short and poorly differentiated, but it became longer as one moves further away from the centres of early farming. In Britain the Mesolithic-Neolithic transition did not come until the fourth millennium BC.

metate In American terminology, the flat or concave stone slab on which maize was ground. ⟡ MANO, QUERN

Michelsberg A Neolithic culture of Belgium, north France, the Rhineland and parts of Switzerland. It occupies a frontier zone on the borders of the DANUBIAN CULTURE, TRB CULTURE and WESTERN NEOLITHIC complex, and shares traits with all three. There are many regional sub-groups. The Belgian one has leaf-shaped arrows, antler combs, flint mines, and enclosures similar in construction to CAUSEWAYED CAMPS, and may have links with the WINDMILL HILL CULTURE of Britain.

microburin A by-product of the manufacture of MICROLITHS. A BLADE is notched, and then snapped off where the chipping has narrowed and weakened it. One piece becomes a microlithic tool,

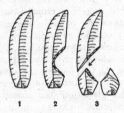

Fig. 117. Stages in the manufacture of a microburin

while the residue (the 'microburin') still shows traces of the original notch and fracture [117]. Certain trapeze-shaped microliths were made from the central part of a double-notched blade, in which case both ends have the appearance of microburins.

microlith A very small tool made on a BLADE or FLAKE. Often less than an inch

Fig. 118. Microliths hafted as arrows

long, microliths sometimes occur in geometric shapes (eg triangles and trapezes), and few of them could have been used without hafting. Some served as barbs and tips of arrows; others were set edge to edge in grooved hafts of bone, wood or antler [118]. Microliths are characteristic of, though not limited to, the MESOLITHIC period in the Old World.

midden A heap or stratum of refuse (broken pots and tools, ashes, food remains, etc) normally found on the site of an ancient settlement. ◊ KITCHEN MIDDEN

Middle Mississippi culture This culture came into existence in the central Mississippi valley and its tributaries around AD 700 and lasted until the historical period in C16 and C17. The most notable features are elaborate pottery, large and often fortified villages, and CEREMONIAL CENTRES with temple platforms and courtyards. The influence of the SOUTHERN CULT can be recognized in the later stages. From the nuclear area, cultures of Mississippi type spread outwards until they had overrun most of the eastern United States. In the north, Mississippi culture encroached on and blended with the WOODLAND cultural tradition.

midrib A thickening of the centre-line of a bronze weapon to add the strength which that material normally lacks.

Milavče, Milaveč (near Domalžice, Czechoslovakia) The type site of a south-west Bohemian culture which stems from the TUMULUS BRONZE AGE but shows elements of the new URNFIELD rite. Corpses were burned but the ashes not placed in urns, and most graves were still covered by BARROWS. Milavče itself is such a site; the ashes of the dead were laid in a wheeled cauldron of cast bronze, and then buried under a mound. ◊ KNOVÍZ

Mildenhall A town in Suffolk famous for the treasure of silver ploughed up there in 1942. It comprised the household silver of a wealthy Roman family, probably buried to save it from Saxon raiders in C4–C5 AD but not recovered. The finest dish alone weighs 18 lbs and measures 2 ft across, with magnificent relief designs of Bacchus and attendants.

Millares, Los A walled township, with projecting bastions and four outlying forts, near the coast in Almeria, southeast Spain. It was dug by Siret at the turn of the century. At a date fixed by radiocarbon c2345 BC the wall was rebuilt after a collapse. The cemetery outside includes some hundred PASSAGE GRAVES of THO-LOS type with PORTHOLE SLABS. The pottery consisted of plain ware of AL-MERIA type, now including tronco-conic vessels and carinated forms, and also much decorated ware, notably the SYMBOL-KERAMIK. The same symbolism reappears on a variety of 'idols' [119] in pottery,

Fig. 119. Stone idol of Millaran type

stone and bone. Arrowheads were bi-facially worked, leaf-shaped, rhomboid and barbed-and-tanged (concave-based ones are restricted to the southwest). Copper was in common use.

Whether one looks on this site, and others like it, as colonies from the east Mediterranean, or as local developments under the stimulus of urbanization and trade, or as something between the two, they exerted a powerful influence on the whole of southern Spain and Portugal. Their culture was succeeded by that represented by BEAKERS.

millet Four cereals are grouped under this name. *Panicum miliaceum* was the most important, first securely recorded at JEM-DET NASR in Mesopotamia. It was widely grown in Neolithic Europe and was the staple crop in early China. Its source is not certainly known. *Setaria italica* was possibly developed in southern Europe, and even there was never as common as *Panicum*. It was also known in China in the Neolithic. Grains of the *Setaria* genus were an important item of diet in parts of Mexico as early as c6500 BC, but were possibly collected from wild plants. *Eleusine* and *Pennisetum* are of more recent origin, largely confined to tropical Africa, and introduced thence to India.

milpa American word for a MAIZE field, often a plot used for only a few years in a cycle of SLASH AND BURN cultivation.

Mindel glaciation The second major PLEISTOCENE GLACIATION of Alpine Europe. [p 183]

Minoans The people of Bronze Age Crete. The name was coined by Sir Arthur EVANS from that of the legendary ruler Minos. They stand out as the first civilized Europeans, with a highly sophisticated way of life and material equipment, in many ways surprisingly modern. They emerged as a cultural group c2500 BC, probably representing a fusion between Anatolian immigrants and the native Neolithic population, with at least sporadic trading contacts through the east Mediterranean. At c2000 BC, the Middle Minoan period, urbanization became apparent, towns appeared and, a Minoan speciality, the first of the great palaces, KNOSSOS, MALLIA and PHAESTOS. Overseas trade was greatly expanded too. The height of this development was reached at the end of the Middle Minoan and beginning of the Late Minoan periods, c18–c15, when Crete controlled the south Aegean, with a number of island settlements. On the destruction of the palace sites c1450, probably by the cataclysmic eruption of Santorin, Greek-speaking MYCENAEANS gained control of

Knossos and the island, and held them for a half-century. The final fall of Knossos c1400, whether from native revolt, assault from the mainland, or another natural disaster, marks the end of Crete's period of greatness.

'Minoan' is strictly a cultural term. Surviving bones show that the Bronze Age Cretans were a racially mixed group. Linguistically more evidence is needed. Of their written scripts, the hieroglyphic cannot yet be tackled. Attempted decipherments of LINEAR A, whether as a Semitic or an Anatolian language, are unconvincing. LINEAR B has been successfully translated as an early form of Greek, written in a SYLLABARY, but belongs only to the period of mainland domination, and is therefore more relevant to Mycenaeans than Minoans.

The cultural brilliance of the Minoans was outstanding. Though many of their traits and ideas can be traced back to Anatolia, Syria and Egypt, their civilization as a whole is not only quite different from, but in many ways superior to, that of their contemporaries elsewhere. Their palaces were magnificently appointed, with lavish wall frescoes and advanced drainage, designed more for comfortable living than for show. This luxury extends down to at least the larger town houses, and was not a prerogative of royalty only. Their pottery

Fig. 120. Minoan bull-leaping (from a seal impression)

is amongst the most artistic of any place or time, using abstract curvilinear, floral and, most notably, marine designs. Vessels, figurines and magnificent seal stones were also carved in stone. Bronze and gold were competently worked. Minoan religion is somewhat obscure, but includes a Mother Goddess who was worshipped in many shrines equipped with figurines, VOTIVE DEPOSITS, the sacred DOUBLE AXE and HORNS OF CONSECRATION, and also in cave and hill-top sanctuaries, but not in temples. A noteworthy feature of Minoan life is the bull sports. Frescoes, seals and figurines show athletes leaping on, or somersaulting over, charging bulls in what were clearly exciting and exacting events, though whether religious or secular is not clear. [120]

Minyan Ware A grey or yellow wheel-made ware of high quality first appearing at TROY VI and in Greece towards the end of the Early HELLADIC, c C19 BC. It was ancestral to MYCENAEAN pottery, and may represent a movement of new peoples into the Aegean area, the first Greek speakers.

Mitanni A kingdom which arose in the foothills between the Tigris and Euphrates c1500 BC. Its capital of Wassukkanni has not been identified. It flourished for a little over a century, treating on near-equal terms with EGYPT and the HITTITES, until overthrown by the latter c1370. Its people were mainly HURRI, but its ruling dynasty, from the form of their names and more especially from the gods they invoke in an extant treaty, were INDO-EUROPEANS related to the roughly contemporary ARYANS of India.

Mithras Originally a Persian demigod, he achieved independence and importance during the Roman empire. Especially in military circles, his worship challenged early Christianity. He is portrayed as a young man in a Phrygian cap, usually in the act of kneeling on the back of a bull to despatch it by a sword thrust in the neck. A **Mithraeum** is a building, often semi-subterranean, containing a passage between broad shelves on which the worshippers reclined during the ceremonies. The end wall may hold a fresco or relief of Mithras himself.

Mitla The site (25 miles southwest of Oaxaca, Mexico) was first occupied in the centuries before 600 BC, after which it became an outpost of MONTE ALBÁN civilization. After the parent site was abandoned in C8–10 AD, a fortification wall was built at Mitla and pyramids were constructed there. The town was now an important religious centre. Most of the surviving palaces are of late date (Monte Albán Period V) and were still in use at the time of the conquest, when Mitla was said to be the residence of the ZAPOTEC high priest. Certain frescoes were painted in pure MIXTEC style, although Mitla itself may have remained under Zapotec control.

Mixtec A people living in the mountainous country of Oaxaca, in southern Mexico. Several books (◊ CODEX) have survived, and allow the history of the Mixtecs to be traced back to AD 695. For a long time their activities were confined to their homeland, but in C14, by a mixture of force and political manoeuvring, they infiltrated into ZAPOTEC territory and occupied much of the Valley of Oaxaca (◊ MONTE ALBÁN, MITLA). The Mixtecs were great craftsmen, famous for their metalwork, painting, stone-carving and turquoise mosaic. The influence of their art is apparent as far north as CHOLULA, in the state of Puebla, where a regional Mixteca-Puebla style came into being, and was in turn one of the formative influences on AZTEC art. Many of the finest objects from Aztec territory were probably the work of Mixtec artisans. Parts of the Mixteca were soon conquered by the Aztecs, but in the south some Mixtecs remained independent until the arrival of the Spaniards.

Mixteca-Puebla culture ◊ MIXTEC

mobiliary art or **home art** General term used to describe the small and portable objects produced by artists during the Upper PALAEOLITHIC period (◊ CAVE ART). Artifacts include figurines, engraved and sculptured fragments of bone, ivory or stone, artists' trial pieces, decorated weapons, tools and ornaments. The distribution extends from Siberia to Spain.

Moche, Mochica A culture which originated in the Moche and Chicama valleys on the north coast of Peru and was later spread by conquest as far south as the Santa and Nepeña rivers. Mochica is best known for its irrigation works, its massive adobe temple-platforms, and for its pottery. Especially famous are the modelled vessels and portrait vases in the shape of human heads, and the jars, often with STIRRUP SPOUTS [121], painted in reddish brown

Fig. 121. Mochica stirrup-spouted pot

with scenes of religion, war and everyday life. The Mochica culture developed at about the start of the Christian era, and was brought to an end by the spread of the HUARI culture from further south in C7.

Mogollon A culture which flourished in southeast Arizona and southwestern New Mexico from C100 BC until C14 AD. Its roots lie in the COCHISE version of the DESERT CULTURE in this area, but the Mogollon folk were settled agriculturalists who lived in villages of pit houses. From c1000 the Mogollon people came under the influence of their northern neighbours, the ANASAZI, and began to build PUE-BLOS. To this late period belongs some of the finest pottery of the American south-west, Mimbres ware, painted with stylized black animals on a white background.

Mohenjo-daro One of the twin capitals of the INDUS CIVILIZATION, on the west bank of the Indus 400 miles southwest of HARAPPA. It was excavated by MARSHALL in the 1920s, Mackay in the 1930s, with more recent work by Wheeler and Dales. The city, covering approximately a square mile, was laid out on a grid plan, the oldest recorded. The larger blocks, separated by broad streets with elaborate drains, were irregularly subdivided and

Fig. 122. The 'priest-king' statue, Mohenjo-daro

closely built over in baked brick. A block in the middle of the west side stood higher than the rest, forming a 35 ft citadel. Traces of mud and baked brick defences were found. Within these an assembly hall, 'college', great bath and granary were excavated. The highest point is covered by a Buddhist STUPA of much later date.

Excavation could not reach the lowest levels of the site owing to the high water-table. Recent drilling has brought up cultural material from as much as 39 ft

below the modern plain surface, with the mounds rising 35 ft above this level. Much of this depth is made up of flood deposits, which many times overwhelmed the city. The highest levels showed a distinct cultural decline, and the final collapse is marked by groups of unburied skeletons. There was no reoccupation like that of Harappa.

The dating of this extraordinary site is still debated. Radiocarbon dates and con-nexions with Mesopotamia suggest a span from 2300 to about 1750 BC.

Molfetta A town on the Italian Adriatic coast near Bari. 1½ miles inland lies the Pulo, an enormous collapsed cave. A Neolithic village and cemetery beside this provide a type site for the south Italian IMPRESSED WARE, for which radiocarbon dates around 4300 BC have been obtained. In about 1500 BC other people, bringing an early version of the APENNINE CUL-TURE, occupied the floor of the depression and caves in its walls.

molluscs (more loosely **snailshells**) These occur quite freely in calcareous deposits, and may give useful information if asso-ciated with archaeological remains. Some species are fussy about where they live and many have marked preferences. A group from a single deposit will often give a clear indication of prevailing environmental conditions, eg standing water, damp vege-tation, dry grassland, etc. The results could be archaeologically significant in studying, for example, the silting of a ditch or siting of a barrow. More tentatively, general climatic conditions can be deduced from the presence of cold or warm climate species. Still more tentatively, a deposit containing molluscs may be dated against the geological scale.

Marine molluscs have been less often used in this way, though they document clearly the past history of the Baltic, from fresh water to salt to brackish. Their importance derives rather from the fact that they were a source of food for early man ($\lozenge$ KITCHEN MIDDENS), and were used for decorative purposes, for which they were often widely traded ($\lozenge$ COWRY and SPONDYLUS).

Mondsee culture The Copper Age culture of Upper Austria, noted for its villages of PILE-DWELLINGS and for its decorated pottery with white-inlaid circles and stellar designs. The Mondsee people were the first to smelt the local copper ores.

Monte Albán (Oaxaca, Mexico) The major CEREMONIAL CENTRE in ZAPOTEC territory, it is a site with a long history.

Period I (c600–100 BC): The first buildings were constructed on the hilltop. Hieroglyphic writing was known, bar-and-dot numerals were employed, and dates expressed in terms of the CALENDAR Round ($\lozenge$ DANZANTES).

Period II (100 BC–AD 150) shows a good deal of continuity from the previous stage, with the addition of new elements taken from the PRE-CLASSIC cultures of the MAYA zone. To this period belongs the Observatory, a building carved with glyphs depicting the conquest of enemy cities. This stage is followed by a short transitional period (AD 150–300) during which appear the first signs of contact with TEOTIHUACÁN.

Period IIIA (c300–600) is marked by strong influence from Teotihuacán. Native and foreign traits combine to create a distinctive Zapotec culture. After a second, poorly defined, Transitional phase, Monte Albán reached the height of its power during Period IIIB. Most of the surviving buildings belong to this time, but a period of decadence and decline led to the abandonment of the site sometime be-between AD 700 and 950.

Period IV: No occupation, though burials continued to be made there ($\lozenge$ MITLA).

Period V: Early in C14 this part of Oaxaca was controlled by the MIXTEC tribes who re-used the tombs of Monte Albán for their own dead. To this period belongs the treasure from Tomb 7, with gold and silver ornaments, lapidary work, and bones carved with hieroglyphic and calendrical inscriptions.

Montelius, Oscar (1843–1921) A Swedish archaeologist who divided European prehistory into numbered periods (four for the Neolithic, three for the Bronze Age). To these periods he succeeded in giving absolute dates by extending CROSS-DATING from Egypt right across Europe. His scheme was an improvement on the epochs of de MORTILLET, but was in turn displaced by the concept of cultural groups, each with its own space/time distribution.

Monteoru A fortified hilltop near Bucharest, the type site of a Middle to Late Bronze Age culture, c1600–1300 BC, which covered much of eastern Romania. It was of local origin, but absorbed influences from both the south (notably FAIENCE in trade) and the steppes. It had a rich and varied repertoire of pot and metal forms.

Mortillet, Gabriel de (1821–98) A pupil of LARTET, and founder in 1864 of one of the earliest archaeological journals, *Matériaux pour l'Histoire positive et philosophique de l'Homme*. His greatest contribution lay in classification, especially of the PALAEOLITHIC. For the palaeontological criteria of LARTET he substituted archaeological ones based on tool forms rather than faunal remains. He extended into prehistory the geological system of periods, or epochs, each characterized by a limited range of TYPE FOSSILS. Each period was named after a 'type site' where the diagnostic material was well represented. By 1869 de Mortillet's scheme for the Stone Age had the following sub-divisions: Thenaisian (for the now discredited EOLITHS), followed by CHELLEAN, MOUSTERIAN, SOLUTREAN, AURIGNACIAN, MAGDALENIAN, and (for the Neolithic) Robenhausian, named after a lake village.

With further modifications, this classification was widely adopted and remained the standard terminology for European archaeology until well into C20. It had, however, one important defect: de Mortillet saw his epochs as periods of time or as stages of development with a universal validity, and his scheme was basically a refinement of the THREE AGE SYSTEM. He did not allow for purely local variants within a single epoch, and once archaeologists had begun to think in terms of CULTURES instead of periods de Mortillet's classification (and all similar systems) proved inadequate. His nomenclature remains in use, but such terms as Magdalenian, etc, are nowadays used only in a restricted sense for localized cultures.

mortuary enclosure A structure made of earth, stone or wood, and used for the storage of bodies prior to their COLLECTIVE BURIAL. Remains of such enclosures are sometimes found under BARROWS. ⟡ MORTUARY HOUSE

mortuary house A wooden or stone copy of an actual dwelling, buried under a BARROW or KURGAN, and used as a tomb for the dead. There is sometimes an overlap between the definitions of mortuary house and MORTUARY ENCLOSURE, but very different ritual ideas may be involved. A mortuary house often contains only a single corpse, and serves primarily as a sepulchre rather than as a charnel house in which bodies were accumulated.

mosaic A technique of decoration used mainly on floors or walls involving the setting of small coloured fragments of stone or glass, each called a TESSERA, in a cement matrix [89]. It was employed by Roman and later craftsmen with as much artistry as painting or tapestry work.

mouflon A wild sheep of southwest Asia, *Ovis orientalis*, found from Cyprus through Syria to Iran. It was the breed first domesticated, being found at ZAWI CHEMI SHANIDAR c9000 BC and JARMO 6000. Later it was largely replaced by the URIAL.

A second species of mouflon, *O. musimon*, still occurs wild on Corsica and Sardinia.

mould Molten metal poured into a concavity will solidify into a corresponding shape, a fact readily apparent to all metalworkers. The concavity has only to be given the shape of the required artifact. Such moulds can be made of stone, pottery, or metal with a melting point higher than that of the alloy being cast. The simplest type of mould is a one-piece or open one, from which the casting emerges with one flat face, requiring further hammering to give it a symmetrical form [123]. Two-piece moulds allowed proper bifacial tools

Fig. 123. The principal types of mould: (a) one-piece (or open); (b) two-piece; (c) three-piece with sprue cap; (d) cire perdue

and weapons to be cast, a third piece, or core, being added if a socket was required. These technical advances had been made before the end of the Early Bronze Age. Multi-piece moulds were used in SHANG China, but elsewhere the CIRE PERDUE method of casting was preferred.

Moulds were also used for making figurines, and occasionally for relief-decorated pottery (eg SAMIAN ware in the Roman empire). Pressed relief decoration is found in northern Peru, where moulds were also used to produce the elaborate asymmetrical vessels of the MOCHICA and CHIMÚ styles.

Mount Carmel (Palestine) The caves on the flanks of the biblical Mount Carmel have between them yielded a long STRATIGRAPHY which embraces most of the PALAEOLITHIC. The sequence begins with coarse FLAKE tools of TAYACIAN type, followed by ACHEULIAN HANDAXE industries. Associated (and perhaps inter-stratified) with the final Acheulian were Jabrudian artifacts (◊ JABRUD) and eventually also BLADE tools of AMUDIAN type. The next industry, the Levalloiso-MOU-STERIAN, was represented at two caves, et-Tabūn and es-Skhūl, and was associated with human remains whose evolutionary position is still a matter for controversy. Taken all together, the skeletons show a wide taxonomic range with the character-istics of both NEANDERTHAL MAN and HOMO SAPIENS. It was once suggested that they represented a hybrid population, but more detailed analysis shows that all the skulls from et-Tabūn fall within the Neanderthal range while all those from es-Skhūl are of sapiens type. Examination of the associated fauna shows that the remains from es-Skhūl could be as much as 10,000 years later than those from et-Tabūn.

The sequence continues with the so-called Emiran industry, followed by the Palestine AURIGNACIAN (also called Antelian), by a blade, scraper and burin industry (the Atlitian) known only from this site, and finally by NATUFIAN.

Mousterian The flint industry associated with NEANDERTHAL MAN. Flintwork of Mousterian type (with RACLOIRS [124],

Fig. 124. Mousterian flintwork: (a) racloir; (b) point

triangular points made on FLAKES, and – in some variants – well-made HANDAXES) has been found over most of the unglaci-ated parts of Eurasia, as well as in the Near East and North Africa. In these areas it constitutes the Middle PALAEOLITHIC. In certain industries, called Levalloiso-Mou-sterian, the tools were made on flakes produced by the LEVALLOIS TECHNIQUE. The earliest Mousterian goes back to the RISS GLACIATION, but most of it comes into the earlier part of the final, WÜRM, glaciation, giving a total lifespan from before 70,000 BC until c 32,000.

mudbrick (in the New World ADOBE, and ◊ PISÉ) Unbaked brick. In a dry climate, where fuel for baking BRICK is in any case scarce, bricks were, and are still, commonly sun-dried only. A building constructed of these can expect only a limited life, perhaps 30 years. When it collapses, the roof timbers would be worth the effort of salvaging but the decayed brick would not. New brick would be brought in for any new building, which would be superimposed on the levelled ruins of the old, with the floor at a cor-respondingly higher level. It is this process which largely explains the great height and bulk of a Near Eastern TELL.

Müller, Sophus succeeded WORSAAE as Director of the National Museum of Denmark in 1865. He was rather over-shadowed by his contemporary MON-TELIUS, but withstands comparison in two aspects of his work. In the field he improved considerably the techniques of excavation, particularly in recognizing the significance of superposed burials under BARROWS, STRATIGRAPHY in other words. And in interpretation he had a clearer understand-ing of the patchwork of prehistoric cultures, as opposed to Montelius's concept of continent-wide chronological periods.

multivallate Having more than one rampart.

mummy The body of a man or animal embalmed according to the rites practised in ancient Egypt. After removal of the organs to separate CANOPIC JARS, the body was treated with natron to dry it out thoroughly. It was then wrapped tightly in linen bandages, accompanied by jewellery, religious texts and unguents of various kinds. Human mummies were then generally enclosed in cartonage, wooden, stone, or gold cases of human form, before being placed in the tomb [125]. All stages of the procedure were accompanied by elaborate rituals, culminating in the ceremony of the 'opening of the mouth',

Fig. 125. The soul revisits the mummy on its bier, from a papyrus

which symbolically restored to the completed mummy the faculties of life. The practice probably arose from the accidental preservation of bodies by desiccation in the desert sand, giving rise to the idea that such preservation was necessary to the survival of the dead man's soul. It continued until the end of pharaonic times.

By extension, the name is applied to crouched bodies wrapped in textiles and naturally preserved by desiccation in the desert regions of Peru and in certain Andean caves.

Mundigak A TELL near Kandahar in Afghanistan in which Casal in the 1950s found the following stratigraphy: PISÉ building with plain coarse pottery; Chalcolithic levels with mudbrick, black-on-buff painted pottery (cf QUETTA Ware) and a radiocarbon date of 2625 ± 300 BC; a curious pilastered building, perhaps a temple, its pottery showing parallels with KULLI and the INDUS CIVILIZATION; a later version of the same, now with deep purple-on-red painted pottery; nomadic occupation with dark pottery; mudbrick granaries with plain grey or red ware and

some iron. The whole occupation probably spans from the late 4th to early 1st millennia BC. The poorly understood monumental buildings hint at Mesopotamian influence.

Munsell Soil Color Charts Accurate colour description is extremely difficult, being so subjective. An objective scheme already much used for describing soils (in itself of interest to archaeology) and increasingly employed for pottery, is that devised by A. Munsell. In this, three factors are assessed: hue (the spectrum divided into ten colours, each subdivided into ten), value (the darkness or lightness of the colour, rated 0–10) and chroma (the greyness or purity of the colour, again rated 0–10). A colour can be matched in the charts and recorded as, for example, 5YR 6/3, so that anyone else with a set of charts can immediately find out the original colour without the ambiguity implicit in some such description as 'light brown'.

Münsingen-am-Rain (near Berne, Switzerland) An Iron Age cemetery with more than 200 graves of the early and middle LA TÈNE periods. The graves are scattered along a ridge, and the cemetery has a HORIZONTAL STRATIGRAPHY with the oldest tombs at the north and the more recent ones at the southern end. This, together with the opportunities for studying the TYPOLOGY of objects from 'closed' grave groups, has made Münsingen the key site for establishing the dating and subdivision of the La Tène period in central Europe.

murex A Mediterranean sea-shell which provided the purple dye for which the PHOENICIANS were famous. It figures also on the painted pottery of the MINOANS.

murus gallicus ◊ TIMBER LACING

Mycenae The chief city of the MYCENAEANS of Bronze Age Greece, it overlooked the Plain of Argos in the eastern Peloponnese. It was surrounded by massive walls of CYCLOPEAN MASONRY, and entered by the monumental Lion Gate [126]. Little remains of the palace on the crest of the hill, though houses lower on the slope have in part survived. More still was learnt from

Fig. 126. The Lion Gate, Mycenae

others in the lower town, outside the walls. An underground cistern supplied the defenders with water. Just inside the gate was the Shaft Grave Circle A, discovered by SCHLIEMANN in 1874. The six tombs yielded a great treasure of metalwork of high quality and artistic skill – weapons, drinking vessels, jewellery, face masks – and pottery dating to C16 BC. STELAE, carved with CHARIOTS, hunting scenes and spirals in relief, stood over the graves. In 1951 a second shaft grave circle was found outside the city, slightly earlier in date and less rich. Later members of the royal family were buried in the great THOLOS tombs, wrongly attributed to individuals in the Homeric legends, Atreus, Clytemnestra, etc. The city escaped the disasters of C13 better than others on the mainland, but fell C1100 BC, to survive only in ruin and legend.

Mycenaeans Strictly, the inhabitants of MYCENAE, but generally used to cover the Late Bronze Age peoples of eastern and southern Greece and related areas who shared the same culture and language. Their name for themselves was ACHAE-ANS, and their achievements were remem-bered in legendary form by the classical

Greeks. Their forebears probably arrived in Greece soon after 2000 BC, bringing MINYAN WARE and an INDO-EUROPEAN language with them. Mycenaean civiliza-tion arose in C16 by the sudden influx of many features of material culture from the MINOANS. Later traditions speak of the arrival of new rulers also, adventurers from the east. By C1450 the Mycenaeans were powerful enough to take over both KNOS-SOS and the profitable trade across the East Mediterranean, especially in Cypriote copper (◊ GELIDONYA). Trade was ex-tended also to the central Mediterranean and continental Europe, where Baltic AMBER was one of the commodities sought. The peak of their power lasted a scant

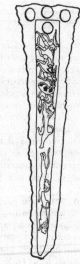

Fig. 127. Mycenaean warriors hunting lions, an inlaid dagger from Shaft Grave V

century and a half until a succession of upheavals on the mainland destroyed it. The reasons for decline are obscure. The Trojan War at the end of C13 points to unrest east of the Aegean. There is evidence of increasing depopulation of southern

Greece about the same time, paving the way for invasion by the DORIANS and for the Greek migrations overseas.

At home, the Mycenaeans dwelt in strongly walled citadels containing palaces of the MEGARON type, exemplified at Mycenae, TIRYNS and PYLOS. To these were added the more Minoan features – frescoes, painted pottery, skilfully carved seals, artistic metalwork, clay tablets, etc [127]. Their writing, LINEAR B, well illustrates the relationships of the two. It was an adaptation of the Minoan script, presumably first made by the mainlanders who had occupied Knossos, for the writing of their own, Greek, language. It subsequently appears on many of the mainland sites yielding, incidentally, a wealth of new information on a people who a few years ago, before it was deciphered, were still strictly prehistoric. Outside their towns are their tombs. At Mycenae itself the famous and enormously rich shaft grave circles, with the tombs marked by fine carved STELAE, belong to the beginning of the Mycenaean period. More typical are the rock-cut chamber tomb and above all the THOLOS.

Abroad, though Mycenaean power was short-lived, its influence was far ranging, from AMARNA in Egypt to TROY, west to Sicily and Sardinia, and north to the Baltic and Britain. Indeed, the legacy of the Mycenaeans to the economy and technology of Late Bronze Age Europe, and to the population of the east Mediterranean coasts after the Egyptian defeat of the PEOPLES OF THE SEA, are as important as their legacy to the language and literature of their descendants in Greece itself.

Mykerinus, Mycerinus, Men-kau-re The pharaoh of the Egyptian 4th dynasty who erected the third PYRAMID of the GIZA group. He reigned c2510 BC.

N

Nagyrév A habitation site near Szolnok, central Hungary, which gives its name to the earliest stage of the Bronze Age in Hungary and Slovakia. Its first phase shows connexions with the BEAKER and VUČE-DOL cultures, while the later phase is contemporary with early ÚNĚTICE. ⟨⟩ TÓSZEG

Náhuatl The language spoken by the AZTECS and many other Mexican tribes. Related languages, belonging to the Uto-Aztecan family, are distributed sporadically from the northwestern USA to Panama.

Nal The Sohr Damb (Red Mound) of Nal is a TELL in central BALUCHISTAN containing Chalcolithic material, flat axes and chisels of copper, and pottery similar to that from the ZHOB valley. It is better known for the cemetery cut into its occupation levels after the settlement had been destroyed by fire. The rite employed was fractional BURIAL, the graves containing fragmentary skeletons together with quantities of distinctive pottery. Nal ware is related to that of Nundara and AMRI, a fine buff ware forming bowls and distinctive angular canisters [128]. It was

Fig. 128. Nal canister

painted in black before firing, with multi-outlined steps or circles, omegas and fish or animals. Red, yellow, blue and green paint was often added after the firing. Some traits in the pottery, a glazed steatite seal and many FAIENCE beads point to contact with the INDUS CIVILIZATION.

Nannar The Sumerian moon god = the Semitic Sin. With his consort Nin-gal, he

was the patron deity of UR, where his temple and ZIGGURAT were excavated by Woolley.

Naqada or **Nagada** A large predynastic cemetery in Upper Egypt which yielded some 2,000 burials of the AMRATIAN and GERZEAN periods.

Narmer One of the first pharaohs of Egypt, perhaps to be equated with MENES who founded the 1st dynasty c 3200 BC. The most important record of him, indeed one of the first from Egypt, is a slate PALETTE [129] on which he is shown in the

Fig. 129. Reverse of the Narmer Palette

White Crown of Lower Egypt conquering his enemies on one side, and in the Red Crown of Upper Egypt reconstructing the land on the other.

Nasbeh, Tell en- (perhaps the biblical Mizpah) A site near Jerusalem, occupied throughout the Iron Age. Noteworthy were its massive rubble walls, 13 ft thick, with projecting towers and a very strong gateway formed by overlapping the wall for 45 ft.

Nasca The culture which developed out of PARACAS on the south coast of Peru. The earliest pottery, of roughly C2 BC, still shows Paracas influence in the iconography and the use of many colours, but the paint was now put on before firing. Typical Nasca pottery with designs of fish, birds, severed heads, human figures and demons, shows a long internal development [130].

Fig. 130. Nasca spout and bridge pot

The final Nasca sub-style incorporates patterns taken from the art of HUARI, and this contact was soon followed by invasion. With the expansion of the Huari empire to the coast around C7 AD, Nasca culture came to an end and was replaced by a local version of Huari.

Natufian A Late MESOLITHIC culture of the Levant, with its type site at Wādi an-Natūf in Palestine. Hunting and gathering were still the basis of subsistence, but some Natufian communities had adopted a settled mode of life with permanent villages like the one at Eynan, which had about 50 circular houses. A fine series of burials was excavated at MOUNT CARMEL. The shrine at the base of the TELL at JERICHO was built during the Early Natufian phase, and the descendants of the Natufians built the earliest Neolithic town at the site. Diagnostic implements include MICROLITHS, sickles, pestles, mortars, fishing gear and ornaments of bone and shell.

Naukratis A town on the western branch of the Nile Delta which became the centre for Greek trade with Egypt, a sort of treaty port, from C7 BC.

Navdatoli A Chalcolithic site excavated by Sankalia on the Narbada river of central India. Its rectangular houses were of timber and bamboo, with lime-coated clay or dung floors. Simple copper and microlithic stone industries were employed, the latter mainly of chalcedony and agate. The gracefully shaped pottery, the MALWA ware, was yellow, painted in black with geometric designs or friezes of stylized men or animals. Only wheat was recorded from the lowest level, but from period II (carbon dated to 1660 ± 130 BC) rice was also known, an early occurrence. The site was abandoned in the 1st millennium when Maheshwar, on the opposite bank, became an outpost of the rising civilization on the Ganges.

naveta A type of MEGALITHIC CHAMBER TOMB [131] peculiar to the island of Minorca and dating to the earlier part of the Bronze Age (c1800–1200 BC). As the name suggests, the shape resembles an upturned boat, with an elongated U-shaped plan, a vault roofed by CORBELLING and a flat or slightly concave façade. The gallery-shaped burial chamber is approached by a corridor through the thickness of the wall, and there is occasionally a PORTHOLE SLAB.

Nazca ♢ NASCA

Neanderthal man (*Homo neanderthalensis*, *Homo sapiens neanderthalensis*) An extinct form of man. Neanderthal skeletons have been found in a broad belt of territory from Uzbekistan, through the Near East, North Africa and most of unglaciated Europe. Related forms are known from the Far East and from Africa south of the Sahara (♢ BROKEN HILL, FAURESMITH). Neanderthal man was normally chinless, had prominent brow ridges and a receding forehead, but his brain was as large as modern man's [87d]. His flintwork, which in North Africa and Eurasia was of Middle PALAEOLITHIC (MOUSTERIAN) type,

Fig. 131. Naveta Es Tudons

was technically more advanced than anything which had gone before, and the careful burial of dead Neanderthalers with funerary offerings provides the oldest surviving evidence for religious beliefs (◊ LA FERRASSIE, SHANIDAR).

The oldest skeletal remains belong to the RISS-WÜRM interglacial period, but Neanderthal man persisted through the earlier stage of the succeeding Würm glaciation until he was replaced by modern man. This replacement probably took place between 40,000 and 35,000 BC, but the scarcity of skeletal evidence from the period makes it impossible to give a more precise date. The manner of this replacement is also in doubt (◊ HOMO SAPIENS, MOUNT CARMEL). Neanderthal man is sometimes classified as a distinct species of the genus HOMO, but has also been considered as falling within the same species as Homo sapiens, whose ancestor he may have been.

Nea Nikomedia An Early Neolithic settlement in northern Greece, dug by Rodden in 1961 and 1963. It yielded the remains of rectangular mud houses, a larger building, perhaps a shrine, and a number of crouched burials. Finds included plain and painted pottery, terra-cotta female figurines and others of frogs carved from greenstone, and many ground stone axes. A radiocarbon date of c6200 BC was obtained.

Nebuchadnezzar, Nebuchadrezzar (anc **Nabu-kudurri-usur**; 605–562 BC). The most famous of the kings of BABYLON, the second of that name. His father, Nabopolassar, ejected the Assyrians to restore Babylon's independence and to found CHALDAEA or the Neo-Babylonian kingdom in 626. Nebuchadnezzar extended these conquests to the Mediterranean, capturing Jerusalem twice, and on the second occasion, 586, sacking it and deporting its people to exile 'by the waters of Babylon'. It was under his rule and that of a successor, Nabonidus (556–539), that the civilization of Babylon reached its highest level.

necropolis A cemetery or burial place, often near a town.

negative painting A technique of pottery decoration employed in many parts of the Americas. The design is painted on to the surface of the vessel with a resist material such as wax or clay, and the pot is then either smoked or dipped into a black wash. The dark coating is unable to reach those areas of the surface protected by the resist, and when the wax or clay is removed the pattern stands out in the original colour against the black background. A similar method of resist dyeing, with wax as the agent, can be used on cloth.

Nene Valley Ware A pottery ware being produced by an organized industry on either bank of the River Nene west of Peterborough, centred on the Roman town of Water Newton (anc Durobrivae), from C2–C4 AD. It was formerly known as Castor Ware. The commonest shapes are drinking vessels, made of a light clay with a dark slip, sometimes described as colour-coated. Decoration is by applied scales, rouletting, or on more ambitious pieces BARBOTINE. The best known are the Hunt Cups, showing dogs pursuing deer or hares, but human scenes also occur and slip-trailed scroll vegetation, often in white on the black surface, is commoner than either.

neo- Literally 'new', as in Neolithic. As hyphenated prefix it is used to describe the reappearance of a culture after a period of decline, eg neo-Babylonian, neo-Hittite.

Neolithic A neo-Grecism invented by Lubbock (Lord AVEBURY) in 1865 to describe that section of the human past, as classified by the THREE AGE SYSTEM, in which man was producing his own food by CULTIVATION of crops and DOMESTICA-TION of animals, but was still relying solely on stone as the material for his tools and weapons. These criteria become progressively more difficult to apply as we learn that both food production and metal-working took a long time to develop. In Britain the period has other more specific characteristics: the use of pottery and of ground stone (beside the long-employed flaked stone), and the appearance of construction works like the long BARROW, CAUSEWAYED CAMP and MEGALITHIC TOMB. Elsewhere, however, some MESO-LITHIC cultures made use of pottery, in Japan for example; and certain so-called pre-pottery Neolithic groups had none, as

at JERICHO. If the term Neolithic is to be retained at all, it must be based on the appearance of food production, sometimes called the Neolithic revolution, commencing in southwest Asia 9000–6000 BC. This might be considered the most important single advance ever made by man, since it allowed him to settle permanently in one spot. This in turn encouraged the accumulation of material possessions, stimulated trade, and by giving a storable surplus of food allowed a larger population and craft specialization. All these were prerequisite to further human progress.

nephrite ⟡ GREENSTONE

net sinker A term applied loosely to any perforated stone or terracotta object which cannot immediately be identified as anything else. On waterside sites this interpretation may well be correct.

New Forest Ware One of the pottery wares (cf NENE VALLEY WARE) current in southern Roman Britain in the late C3–C4 AD, produced by small-scale craftsmen in the New Forest area. Decoration is scarce, consisting of white slipped scrolls or rosette stamps on the red surface. Vessel shapes are, however, very varied.

Newgrange One of the finest decorated PASSAGE GRAVES in Ireland [132], New-

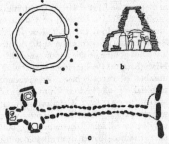

Fig. 132. Newgrange: (a) overall plan; (b) section; (c) ground plan of tomb

grange forms part of the cemetery on the bank of the river BOYNE 25 miles north of Dublin. The burial chamber is roofed by

CORBELLING and has three subsidiary cells. Many stones of both chamber and passage carry PECKED designs including an unusual triple spiral. Excavation has shown that the upper surfaces of the CAPSTONES had drainage channels, as well as art (✧ CUP MARK) which would have been invisible once the overlying cairn had been built. The cairn itself was carefully made of alternate layers of stones and turf, and was surrounded by a KERB of decorated slabs. On either side of the entrance the green kerbstones were topped by a retaining wall of white quartz. Some distance from the original base of the mound is a surrounding circle of free-standing stones. Traces of cremation burials were found in the cells of the chamber, and soil scraped up from a habitation site had been used to pack the interstices of the passage roof. This material may have come from a settlement discovered close to the tomb. There are two radiocarbon dates around 2500 BC from charcoal included in the soil. The site was re-occupied (after the tomb-builders had left it and the cairn had begun to slump) by a group which used Late Neolithic and BEAKER pottery. ✧ KNOWTH

Newstead (anc **Trimontium**) A Roman fort on the Tweed near Melrose, it was first built by Agricola c AD 81. Rebuildings in c 86, 145 and 158 enlarged and strengthened it to hold a garrison of a thousand men. It remained the main base for the Roman army of occupation in the Scottish lowlands as long as this region was held.

Niah (Sarawak) A limestone massif with a number of caves which have produced material of all periods from PALAEOLITHIC to c AD 1300. The most important site, the Great Cave, has deposits which may be of Middle Palaeolithic age, but a later stratum (dated around 38,000 BC) yielded a HOMO SAPIENS skull which is probably the oldest yet known.

Nimrud (anc **Kalhu,** bibl **Calah**) The third capital city, with ASSUR and NINEVEH, of ASSYRIA. The site was discovered by LAYARD near Mosul and excavated 1845–51. The statues and inscriptions he sent back, together with his book on his discoveries *Nineveh and its Remains* (only later was the site correctly identified as Calah), was one of the first archaeological discoveries to stir the public imagination, in the way TROY, TUTANKHAMEN and UR did later. More recent work by Mallowan and Oates, 1949–63, has filled in many missing details.

The city was first founded by SHALMANESER I (1274–45), fell into decay, and was refounded on a larger scale by ASHURNASIRPAL II (883–859). Its wall was some 5 miles in circuit, enclosing at one corner a citadel which contained a ZIGGURAT, temples and palaces. It is these last which have yielded the richest finds, enormous stone winged bulls, reliefs, and on a quite different scale the exquisite carved ivories which once adorned the royal furniture [133]. Another rich collec-

Fig. 133. Openwork ivory plaque from Fort Shalmaneser, Nimrud

tion of ivories was found in the arsenal of Shalmaneser III in the outer town. Some of the ivories show traces of the fire which accompanied the overthrow of the city by the MEDES in 612 BC.

Nin An Iron Age cremation and inhumation cemetery in Dalmatia. There was much trade with Italy in c8 to c5 BC.

Nineveh (mod **Kuyunjik**) across the Tigris from Mosul. The site was identified by Rich as early as 1820, though confirmation came only when the CUNEIFORM tablets could be read. Excavations by many hands from 1842 (BOTTA) to the present day have assembled the information on the site. The most important finds were probably the two libraries of clay tablets found in the palaces of SENNACHERIB and ASHURBANIPAL by LAYARD and Rassam in the 1850s. It should be noted that the Nineveh of Layard's books is not this site but NIMRUD.

The site was occupied from the earliest times, with pottery from the HASSUNA phase on. Ninevite, or Nineveh V (the level in which it was found), Ware represents the comparatively backward culture of the north contemporary with the Early Dynastic of SUMER. Little of importance is then recorded of the site until it became a joint capital of ASSYRIA, with ASSUR and Nimrud, in the early 1st millennium. To this period belong the site's spectacular monuments, the palaces with their elaborate architecture, carved reliefs and cuneiform inscriptions.

Nippur A city state and more importantly a religious centre at the heart of SUMER in Mesopotamia. The excavation of the TELL was begun by the Americans 1890–1900 and resumed in 1945. Its fame rests primarily on the discovery of CUNEIFORM tablets of the sacerdotal library, which have yielded more of the literary tradition of the Sumerians (as opposed to the far commoner business documents) than any other Mesopotamian site.

Nitra ◊ ÚNĚTICE

nome An administrative unit or province of ancient Egypt. Each consisted of a town or group of villages with its own guardian deity and symbol or standard.

Northern Black Polished (NBP) Ware A fine metallic ware with a glossy black surface characteristic of the Iron Age civilization of northern and central India. Its dates are approximately 500–200 BC.

Northumbria The Anglo-Saxon kingdom of northeast England resulting from the union of Deira, with its capital at York, and Bernicia, based on Bamburgh, under Edwin in 622 AD. In the later C7 and C8, despite political decline, it was the scene of a cultural renaissance, attested by the history of Bede, the illuminated manuscripts of LINDISFARNE, etc. In these, the fruitful fusion of immigrant and native cultural influences can be detected. Archaeologically its most important site is YEAVERING, a series of palaces built by Edwin and his successors in northern Northumberland.

Nubia That area south of ancient Egypt proper which extends up the Nile from the neighbourhood of Aswan and the first cataract into what is now the Sudan.

nuraghe A type of tower built of CYCLOPEAN MASONRY [134] and peculiar to

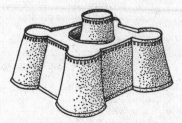

Fig. 134. Reconstruction of the central element of the Barumini nuraghe

Sardinia from the mid 2nd millennium BC until the Roman conquest of the island. The walls of the tower slope inwards towards the top, and there are commonly two or more storeys. Each floor consists of a single round room roofed by CORBELLING and sometimes provided with lateral cells. The more complex examples consist of several towers, courtyards and curtain walls, and many nuraghi (eg BARUMINI) are surrounded by houses. The Corsican TORRE and the Balearic TALAYOTS share many architectural features with the nuraghi.

Nydam A bog in Schleswig, southern Jutland, which yielded a rich VOTIVE DEPOSIT of the Roman Iron Age. The main finds were more than 100 iron swords (some with damascened blades, others stamped with the maker's name), and a wooden BOAT some 70 ft long. The boat was clinker-built, had no mast or sail and was provided with 15 rowlocks on each side. The bow and sternpost were upturned, and the vessel was steered by an oar.

O

Obanian culture A MESOLITHIC culture named from Oban in Argyll. The sites are ROCK-SHELTERS, and also shell middens on post-glacial raised beaches. The way of life was adapted to coastal conditions. Flintwork is scarce, but diagnostic tools include barbed spears and stone limpet-picks.

obelisk A stone pillar of tapering square section with a pyramidal top, erected for religious or monumental purposes by the ancient Egyptians. Obelisks frequently bear carved inscriptions in hieroglyphs. Old Kingdom examples were squat and closely related to the PYRAMIDS, both being solar symbols. Later ones, such as Cleopatra's Needle, one of a pair erected by Thothmes III at Heliopolis, were much more slender. They have been imitated frequently in more recent times.

obsidian A natural GLASS found in restricted volcanic areas. It is usually grey to black and semi-transparent. It was very popular as a superior form of flint for flaking into tools or for grinding into vessels or statuary. It was very widely traded from the anciently exploited sources in Hungary, Sardinia, LIPARI off Sicily, MELOS in the Aegean, central and eastern Turkey, Mexico, etc. SPECTROGRAPHIC ANALYSIS of their trace elements now allows most of the sources to be distinguished, so that the pattern of trade spreading out from each can be traced.

obsidian dating When a fresh surface of OBSIDIAN is exposed by flaking, a physical change begins to take place at a very slow constant rate as water is taken into the material's structure. This rate varies with temperature but apparently not with the quantity of water available. It can be calculated from samples of known date in the same or a climatically similar region. The thickness of the hydration layer on an artifact, measured optically in a prepared thin section, can then be converted readily into age in years.

ochre Yellow or red oxides of iron. They occur naturally and were much used for colouring matter, as in CAVE ART, pottery painting and probably, though unprovably, for decorating the person. Red ochre was certainly used ceremonially to give an impression of life to the corpse during funerary rites. There are many records from the Upper Palaeolithic onwards of ochre staining of skeletons.

Ochre-coloured Pottery A thick and usually badly preserved red ware with an ochre wash found on sites in the upper Ganges valley in India. Its importance lies in the fact that it serves to bridge the gap in the later 2nd millennium between late Harappan material of the INDUS CIVILIZATION and the BLACK-AND-RED and PAINTED GREY WARES of the Iron Age. It has been found associated with the GANGETIC HOARDS.

Ocucaje ◊ PARACAS

oculus A decorative motif consisting of paired circles or spirals [135], as on the

Fig. 135. Oculus on one of the Folkton Drums

Spanish SYMBOLKERAMIK. In some examples eyes are certainly intended, and its use may, but need not, symbolize a god's (or goddess's, ◊ DOLMEN DEITY) protective watch over his (or her) worshippers. The design was widespread in western Europe in the 3rd millennium.

ogam or **ogham** A script of which the letters are represented by groups of parallel lines meeting or crossing a straight base line, often formed by the angle of a stone slab. It is better suited for carving on stone (or possibly wood) than for writing in ink. It is believed to have originated in Ireland or south Wales as a secret script around C3 AD, whence it spread throughout the Celtic areas for use on memorial stones. It is also found associated with the symbols and carvings of the PICTS, among whom it remained in use down to C9. [148]

Old Bering Sea An ESKIMO culture, best known for its ivory objects. It flourished in northern Alaska and northeast Siberia during the first five centuries AD.

Old Copper Culture A culture of hunters and fishermen in the Great Lakes region of Canada and the United States. Pottery and agriculture were lacking, but these people mined native copper around Lake Superior and used it to make tools. Smelting and casting techniques were unknown, and the metal was worked by hot- and cold-hammering and by annealing. The culture came to an end C1500 BC, but the date for its beginning is not well established. There is a radiocarbon date of 5556 ± 600 BC (which some scholars consider too early) and another of 3646 ± 600.

Old Cordilleran culture A cultural tradition based on the hunting of small game and the collection of wild foods in the mountain and plateau region of western North America (in particular the states of Oregon and Washington) between C9000 and 5000 BC or later. The diagnostic tool is the leaf-shaped Cascade point, which was usually accompanied by scraping tools and occasionally by milling stones.

Older, Oldest Dryas ♢ LATE GLACIAL PERIOD and ZONES, VEGETATIONAL

Oldowan Adjective formed from OLDU-VAI, and applied to the PEBBLE TOOL industries of south and east Africa.

Olduvai (northern Tanzania) One of the most important sites for the understanding of both human evolution and the development of the earliest tools. The stratified deposits exposed in the sides of Olduvai gorge cover the whole of the Lower PALAEOLITHIC period. POTASSIUM-ARGON DATING suggests that the basal deposit (Bed I) began to accumulate around 1.9 million years ago. Within Bed I were living-floors and camp sites with PEBBLE TOOLS [140], CHOPPERS and a few artifacts made on FLAKES. The same bed yielded the bones of two primitive forms of hominid (ZINJANTHROPUS and HOMO HABILIS) belonging to the genus AUSTRALOPITHECUS. The Zinjanthropus level has a date of 1.75 million years ago. Pebble tools were still predominant at the base of Bed 2, but crude HANDAXES (cf ABBE-VILLIAN, CHELLEAN) first occurred in the upper part of this bed. Bed 2, dated C1.2–0.5 million years ago, contained several hominid fossils of which some from the upper part are clearly HOMO ERECTUS. Beds 3 and 4 show the further development of the handaxe tradition, and from Bed 4 (with ACHEULIAN tools) came human remains reminiscent of NEANDERTHAL MAN, or of the skull from BROKEN HILL. Bed 5 contained a Kenya Capsian industry.

olive A staple oil-producing fruit grown around the Mediterranean. There is a wild species there, but the cultivated one is thought to derive from another, native to Afghanistan. It spread early, being recorded from El GARCEL in Spain in the Neolithic.

Olmec The Olmecs were the people who lived in historic times in the hot and humid plain of the Mexican Gulf Coast, but by extension the name has come to be used for the PRE-CLASSIC civilization which grew up in southern Veracruz and the neighbouring parts of Tabasco by about 1200 BC (for Olmec origins ♢ SAN LOREN-ZO TENOCHTITLAN). The Olmecs were great stone-carvers whose products ranged from basalt heads almost 10 ft high to small jade figurines in which the attributes of a baby-faced human being merge and blend with those of a jaguar to form a composite monster [136]. This creature is probably

Fig. 136. Olmec stone figurine

the ancestor of the IZAPA long-lipped god and of the Rain God known to the MAYA and other Mexican peoples (◊ TLALOC). Carvings in this distinctive style have been discovered over much of Mexico and as far south as El Salvador and Costa Rica. Olmec figurines and pottery have been found at various sites in central Mexico (eg TLATILCO), and contacts were strong with the cultures of Oaxaca before the construction of MONTE ALBÁN.

Olmec civilization was one of the great formative influences on Mesoamerican culture. On the Gulf Coast a farming population built and supported great CEREMONIAL CENTRES (◊ LA VENTA), importing tons of serpentine and basalt from outside the region. Olmec HIERO-GLYPHS cannot yet be read, but they may perhaps be ancestral to those of the Maya. The Olmecs may also have invented the LONG COUNT system of calculating dates, for Stela C at Tres Zapotes bears on one side a Long Count date equivalent to 31 BC and on the reverse a jaguar mask derived from Olmec art, though showing certain later (IZAPAN) influence. This stela, however, came from a later, post-Olmec, occupation of the site.

The Olmec golden age was the early part of the 1st millennium BC, and Olmec civilization came to an end sometime between 600 and 400 when the main centres were destroyed or abandoned.

Omari, El A site near Helwan, on the east of the Nile Delta, showing primitive Neolithic material closely comparable to that from MERIMDE.

Onion Portage A site (125 miles up the Kobuk river in northwest Alaska) with one of the longest stratigraphies in the Americas. The oldest industries, called Akmak and Kobuk, are thought to span the period 13,000–6000 BC, and include chipped tools which are closer to Siberian types than to those of temperate America. After a break in occupation, the Palisades II industry (4000–2600) seems to show links with the ARCHAIC cultures of the forest zone to the southeast, as does the succeeding Portage complex (2600–2200). Next came tools of the DENBIGH FLINT COMPLEX, followed by Chloris (1500–500 BC) with the oldest pottery in the Arctic, and then in succession by a local version of IPIUTAK, by a forest-adapted Indian culture (AD 500–1000), and finally by Arctic Woodland Eskimo. The sequence compares with that of CAPE KRUSENSTERN on the coast.

oppidum The ROMAN oppidum was a town which served as administrative centre for its surrounding area, or, in the provinces, was a community of Roman citizens, either Italian immigrants or enfranchised natives. Caesar applied the term to the major settlements of the CELTS in Gaul, and it is now used for comparable sites in Celtic territory, from Spain and Britain to the Carpathians. Celtic oppida of C2 and C1 BC were large permanent settlements, usually of HILLFORT type, and often complex enough to be classed as true towns, the first in Europe north of the Alps. Caesar records that each Gaulish tribe had several oppida, though not all were of equal importance.

oracle bones Animal bones, particularly ox shoulder-blades and tortoise shells, were employed by the ancient Chinese for divination purposes. A groove was cut in the bone, after which a hot point was applied nearby, and the shape of the resulting cracks determined the answer. These first appear in deposits of the LUNG SHAN culture, but became far more common during the succeeding SHANG dynasty. Their importance is enormously increased by the fact that they were often inscribed with the question being asked and occasionally even with the answer received. These inscriptions preserve the earliest known Chinese writing and sometimes, by naming kings and ancestors, confirm the historical basis of early legends.

Oranian (or **Ibero-Maurusian**) A North African culture of late Upper PALAEOLITHIC type, with many backed BLADES and some MICROLITHS. A few inland sites are known, but most are concentrated along the Mediterranean littoral from Cyrenaica (the HAUA FTEAH) to Morocco. The time range is c12,000–8000 BC.

Ordos The desert region in the northward loop of the Yellow River in northern China. An Upper Palaeolithic site at Sjara Osso Gol yielded a microlithic industry and fauna showing much less desiccated conditions than those of the present day. In the last few centuries BC the region was important for its metal industry, passing decorative motifs from the STEPPES to China and vice versa.

Ornament Horizon The period marked by the occurrence in Middle Bronze Age HOARDS of southwest Britain of tools and bronze ornaments which owe their inspiration to types current in north Germany from c1100 BC. These 'foreign' objects include TORCS, coiled finger rings, ribbed bracelets, knobbed sickles and square-mouthed socketed axes. In Devon, Somerset and Sussex, hoards of the Ornament Horizon also contain native spearheads, PALSTAVES and quoit-headed pins.

orthostat A large stone or slab, set vertically. Orthostats often formed part of the walls of MEGALITHIC CHAMBER TOMBS.

Osiris The ancient Egyptian god of death, represented as a MUMMY. He was linked with his wife ISIS and son HORUS in the vegetation cycle myth. Slain by SET in the autumn, his dismembered and scattered remains were collected by Isis, reassembled, and came to life as Horus with the new vegetation in the spring. The pharaohs, later the common people also, once the appropriate rituals had been performed, became assimilated with Osiris at death. His chief sanctuary was at ABYDOS.

ossuary A container for the burial of human bones, usually in an unburnt state. It may be either a small portable article for a single interment (◊ LARNAX, PITHOS, URN) or a cave or built structure to take a number of burials (CHAMBER TOMB, THOLOS).

ostrakon or **ostracon** (pl ostraca) A sherd of pottery, or more rarely a flake of stone, bearing an inscription in ink or paint. In Greece they were employed for voting; in Egypt for memoranda, business accounts, writing exercises and the like.

Otomani A Middle to Late Bronze Age culture of eastern Hungary and northwestern Romania, the type site just within the latter. It dates to the period 1600–1300 BC, and shows connexions with ÚNĚTICE.

Otzaki A Neolithic settlement forming a small TELL or *magoula* at Larisa, Thessaly. Early Neolithic pre-SESKLO occupation was succeeded by a deposit nearly 4 metres thick containing Middle Neolithic Sesklo ware. Houses were of mudbrick and rectangular, some having stone footings and internal buttresses. The MEGARON type appears later in the period.

oven A closed structure, in contrast to a HEARTH, resembling a KILN but designed for cooking food. Sometimes the fire was lit within the chamber and removed before the food could be put in. More elaborate versions have the firebox and cooking chamber separate.

Overton Hill Sanctuary ◊ AVEBURY

Ozieri culture The Copper Age culture of Sardinia, known from open villages, caves and rock-cut tombs (◊ ANGHELU RUJU). The pottery shows links with Malta in the TARXIEN phase, and sometime during the lifespan of the Ozieri culture BEAKER pottery reached Sardinia from France.

P

Painted Grey ware A fine ware with simple designs of circles and pothooks characterizing the Ganges civilization of northern India before 500 BC. ⟡ HASTI-NAPURA

palaeobotany The study of ancient plant remains. Much of man's material equipment came, and comes, from vegetable matter – food, fuel, fibres, constructional material for tools, houses, vehicles, etc. Because of its poor survival value compared with bone or inorganic materials, the botanical evidence was until recently little studied. But it is occasionally preserved by desiccation, waterlogging or charring, or its imprint survives in baked clay. From these sources various useful results have been obtained, notably in ascertaining the early history of cultivated crops. ⟡ CHARCOAL IDENTIFICATION, GRAIN IMPRESSION and POLLEN ANALYSIS, and for a more specialized application, DENDROCHRONOLOGY

Palaeolithic Beginning with the emergence of man and the manufacture of the most ancient tools some 2½ to 3 million years ago, the Palaeolithic period lasted through most of the PLEISTOCENE Ice Age until the final retreat of the ice sheets in about 8300 BC. It is generally subdivided into: Lower Palaeolithic, with the earliest forms of man (AUSTRALOPITHECUS and HOMO ERECTUS), and the predominance of CORE tools of PEBBLE TOOL, HANDAXE and CHOPPER type; Middle Palaeolithic, the era of NEANDERTHAL MAN and the predominance of FLAKE-tool industries (eg MOUSTERIAN) over most of Eurasia; Upper Palaeolithic (starting perhaps as early as 38,000 BC), with HOMO SAPIENS, BLADE-and-BURIN industries and the CAVE ART of western Europe. During this stage man colonized the New World and Australia. [137] ⟡ THREE AGE SYSTEM

palaeontology The study of the fossil remains of animals. Human palaeontology is the study of the origins of man himself.

palaeopathology Some of man's ills – fractures, malnutrition, dental decay and some diseases – leave their mark on his bones. Where his bones survive, evidence can be recovered which may reveal much about the conditions in which he lived, and died. Though evidence of war wounds and CANNIBALISM have long been looked for, this wider application is of recent growth and has already yielded significant results.

palaeoserology The use of blood groups in the study of living human populations is well known, even if its interpretation is sometimes difficult. It has been discovered that some human remains preserved by either cold or desiccation can also be made

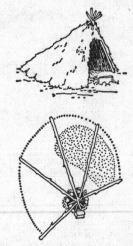

Fig. 137. Palaeolithic hut of the Magdalenian period

to give positive results. Further results have come from testing the spongy bone tissue of skeletons. The method is still of restricted value until it can be shown that the different antigens have an equal survival rate, and until enough tests have been carried out to give statistically reliable samples.

palafitta (pl palafitte) The local name for villages of PILE DWELLINGS in northern Italy. Most of these lakeside villages belong to the Neolithic period and earlier part of the Bronze Age. ◊ LAGOZZA, POLADA

Palenque A MAYA centre in Chiapas where the buildings have fine relief decoration modelled in stucco or carved on limestone panels [114]. A richly furnished tomb of the CLASSIC period was found underneath the pyramid of the Temple of the Inscriptions.

Palermo Stone A slab of black basalt bearing a record of the first five Egyptian dynasties, compiled in the 5th dynasty, c2400 BC. Only five small fragments survive, the largest of them now in the Palermo Museum.

palette A small slab of stone for grinding and mixing substances like paint or cosmetics. A series from early Egypt, such as that of NARMER [129], is particularly important, since their relief decoration provides valuable evidence on the art and history of the country at the very beginning of dynastic times, c3000 BC.

Palmella A cemetery of Copper Age rock-cut tombs near Lisbon in Portugal. In the four excavated examples a kidney-shaped chamber is entered by a long passage or through a hole in the roof. They form the type site of a culture flourishing in central Portugal c3000–2500 BC. A variety of amuletic objects in stone includes decorated plano-convex or cylindrical stylized human figurines, crescents, model hoes or adzes and, oddest of all, a pair of sandals (from Alapraia). Stonework follows Neolithic traditions, but adds deeply concave-based arrowheads. Pottery, too, follows on from the ALMERIA culture, though foreign elements have been connected with the dark-slipped URFIRNIS

ware of Greece. BEAKERS appear commonly with subsequent burials in these tombs. Copper was used for flat axes and daggers, and a distinctive type of ARROW-HEAD with near-circular blade and long tang, the Palmella point. The settlements are best illustrated by the site of VILA NOVA DE SÃO PEDRO.

palstave A form of AXE with side flanges, STOP-RIDGE, and sometimes one or (rarely) two loops attached. It was current during the middle part of the Bronze Age over much of Europe. [20h]

palynology ◊ POLLEN ANALYSIS

Pan Shan A branch of the YANG SHAO culture of Neolithic China. Extensive cemeteries in the hills of the upper Yellow River basin in Kansu province were excavated by Andersson in the 1920s to yield great quantities of distinctive pottery with inhumation burials. Commonest were large globular urns painted with bold spiral or other curvilinear designs in red and black [138]. The 'death pattern' con-

Fig. 138. Pan Shan jar

sists of a red band between two black ones internally fringed. Striking parallels in Turkestan, the Caucasus and the Ukraine have not been satisfactorily explained.

Pantalica A naturally fortified Late Bronze to Early Iron Age town site inland from Syracuse in Sicily. A single large house was excavated by Orsi in 1895–7 in the settlement. The 5,000 rock-cut tombs which honeycomb the hillside around have yielded great quantities of material. The characteristic pottery is wheel-made, red-slipped and burnished. Four phases run from Late MYCENAEAN c1200 BC to well after the planting of the first Greek colonies in c8.

papyrus A reed growing in Mediterranean lands, particularly Egypt. Its flower spray was very popular as a decorative motif. [139]

Fig. 139. Papyrus motif

By splitting and opening out its stems, and pasting them together in two layers at right angles to each other, a cheap writing material was obtained. Examples preserved by the dry climate of Egypt and neighbouring regions, in tombs, caves, or simply among domestic rubbish, have yielded invaluable evidence on the ancient history of the area. 'Papyrus' is the Latin form, from which our word 'paper' derives. Its stems were also bound together in bundles to make light boats.

Paracas A peninsula near the mouth of the Pisco valley on the south coast of Peru where desert conditions have preserved all kinds of organic materials, including sumptuous textiles, in a series of rich burials. Pottery of the Paracas style (called Ocucaje in the nearby Ica valley) shows influence from the contemporary culture of CHAVÍN DE HUÁNTAR but is a highly individual polychrome ware with designs executed in resinous paint applied after the pot was fired. The best known graves belong to the closing stages of the culture and are of two types: deep shafts leading into underground chambers with several mummy bundles (Paracas Cavernas), and pits or abandoned houses filled with sand and containing more than 400 mummy bundles (the Necropolis site dug by TELLO in 1929). Much of the material from the Necropolis belongs to the earliest stage of the NASCA culture, which developed out of Paracas in about C2 BC.

Paranthropus (*Australopithecus robustus*) A large and heavy species belonging to the genus AUSTRALOPITHECUS, which includes the oldest and most primitive forms of man. Found on South African sites of the early Middle PLEISTOCENE at Swartkrans and Kromdraai.

Parthians A steppe people who entered northeastern Iran about 250 BC and set up a kingdom at the expense of the Seleucid empire and Bactria. Between 160 and 140 Mithridates I extended the Parthian state into an empire, which survived 350 years of almost constant conflict with the Seleucids and later the Romans until its overthrow by the SASSANIANS.

passage grave One of the main categories of MEGALITHIC or CHAMBER TOMB. The diagnostic features are a round mound covering a burial chamber (often roofed by CORBELLING) approached by a narrower entrance passage (◊ THOLOS). The distinction between passage and funerary chamber proper is very marked (cf GALLERY GRAVE). Features occurring in some, though by no means all, tombs include PERISTALITHS around the BARROW, subsidiary niches opening from the grave chamber, and forecourt entrances. In Brittany (eg GAVRINIS), Ireland (NEWGRANGE [132] and other BOYNE tombs) and Anglesey, the ORTHOSTATS or kerbstones may bear abstract designs pecked into the rock. (For local variants of the basic plan ◊ ENTRANCE GRAVE, HUNEBED.) The distribution of passage graves is western, usually close to the sea, and often grouped in cemeteries. Although the architectural similarities suggest that passage graves are all related and may therefore have spread from a single centre of origin, the funerary offerings are always of local native type. This implies the spread of a religious cult without any accompanying changes in population.

In Iberia passage graves belong to the COPPER AGE (◊ MILLARES, LOS), but further north (in Atlantic France, west and north Britain, the Low Countries, Denmark and Sweden) where metal-working was still unknown, these tombs fall within the Neolithic period. The origin of the passage grave is anything but clear, and the radiocarbon dates range from before 3000 BC to the mid 2nd millennium.

Pasteurs des Plateaux The general name for the Late Neolithic and Copper Age peoples who lived on the uplands of Languedoc during the centuries around 2000 BC, and who made pottery of the FERRIÈRES and FONTBOUÏSSE styles.

Pazyryk or **Pazirik** A group of some 40 tombs in the High Altai of central Asia, of which six of the largest have been excavated. They consisted of pits some 20 ft square covered with low cairns. The construction and altitude have combined to keep their contents frozen, and thus remarkably well preserved, since their deposition in c5 to c3 BC.

A rich collection of clothing and felt hangings was freely decorated with the animal art of the STEPPES, here showing influences from both China and ACHAEMENID Iran. Dismantled four-wheeled wagons were included, one of much lighter construction of Chinese type with a felt hood. Despite violation of the tombs, three bodies also survived: a Mongoloid man and his wife in tomb 2, and a man in tomb 5. These last two were both of European physical type. The men had been extensively tattooed and all the bodies were embalmed. Many horses, with bridles, saddles and saddlecloths, had been buried in neighbouring chambers. Some had elaborate reindeer headdresses of felt. The burials clearly belong to the rulers of a nomadic people of the eastern steppes related to the SCYTHIANS.

pebble tool The earliest and most primitive type of recognizable artifact. The oldest examples, made perhaps 2·6 million

years ago, are from Koobi Fora, Kenya (◊ AUSTRALOPITHECUS, OLDUVAI) [140]

Fig. 140. Pebble tool from Olduvai

and were manufactured by striking a few flakes from the edge of a pebble or nodule to produce an irregular working edge. By a process of refinement these pebble tools developed into the HANDAXES of Africa, Europe and southwest Asia, and into the CHOPPING TOOLS of the Far East. ◊ CHOPPER

Pécel culture ◊ BADEN

Pecica or **Pécska** ◊ PERJÁMOS

pecking A technique of shaping, or producing a design on, stone by hammering. The surface is crushed, usually with a stone hammer, and the dusty fragments swept aside.

pectoral An ornament of jewellery worn on the breast.

pedology ◊ SOIL ANALYSIS

Pekin Man (*Sinanthropus*) The old name, now outmoded, for the variety of HOMO ERECTUS found at CHOUKOUTIEN.

penannular In the form of a ring, but with a break at one point. Used particularly for forms of BROOCH [36b] and TORC.

Pendlebury, J. D. S. His career began in Egypt, notably on the site of Tell el-AMARNA, in the 1920s. His interest then moved to the Aegean, attracted by the ancient Egyptian imports to that region, which are vitally important for CROSS-DATING. His most famous book, *The Archaeology of Crete*, was published in 1939, the year before his death in the German invasion of the island.

Pengelly, William A geologist who became interested in cave excavation. One of his first jobs was the re-excavation of KENT'S CAVERN, where he was able to confirm the conclusions of MACENERY that flint tools were associated with the bones of extinct animals. In 1858 he turned his attention to a cave near Brixham, in Devon, under the auspices of a committee of the Royal and Geological Societies. Again he found implements and extinct fauna in the same stratum. This time he had powerful academic support, and in 1859 John EVANS with several of Britain's leading geologists joined him in an onslaught on the Biblical chronology which put the creation of man in 4004 BC. The work of BOUCHER DE PERTHES supplied further confirmation.

Peoples of the Sea, Sea Peoples or **Peoples of the Islands in the Midst of the Sea** A group of peoples of mixed origin who attempted to overthrow and settle in Egypt in C13–C12 BC. They were defeated by the pharaoh Merneptah in 1219 and finally driven off by RAMSES III c1170. Identifications of the people mentioned have been made, some more, some less, convincing: Pulesati = PHILISTINES [145], Luka = Lycians, Akawasha = Ahhiyawa = ACHAEANS, Danuna = Danaoi, Sherdana = Sardinians, Shekelesh = Sicels = Sicilians, Tursha = Tyrsi = ETRUSCANS. These were all peoples of the MYCENAEAN world, at this date crumbling towards collapse, and were resident in the Aegeo-Anatolian area. After their defeat some of the survivors settled the Palestinian coast, others returned home, and some it is suggested went off to colonize lands in the west. It is these last which are most hotly debated.

Periam or **Periamus** ◊ PERJÁMOS
periglacial ◊ GLACIATION

Périgordian French terminology for a series of Upper PALAEOLITHIC flint industries which are thought to represent a continuing technological tradition. The sequence begins with the CHÂTELPERRONIAN (or Early Périgordian) from

which, according to certain French scholars, develops the first of the 'Upper Périgordian' industries (GRAVETTIAN, or Périgordian IV). The later stages are represented by industries with Font Robert points [75b] and Noailles BURINS, and finally by the Proto-Magdalenian. The Périgordian tradition comes to an end in western Europe with the intrusion of a new SOLUTREAN style of flintwork. The term 'Upper Périgordian' usefully describes a group of related industries, but the idea of continuity from the Châtelperronian to the Gravettian depends on TYPOLOGY alone, and lacks the support of STRATIGRAPHY. No known site has a complete and unbroken 'Périgordian' sequence, and in many caves the Lower and Upper 'Périgordian' levels are separated by strata of the intrusive AURIGNACIAN industry, which must represent a break of several thousand years. The French scheme requires the Périgordian and Aurignacian people to have lived side by side with each other for millennia without any apparent contact between them.

peristalith A ring or kerb of stones surrounding a CAIRN or BARROW.

Perjámos, Periam or **Periamus** A village site on a tributary of the River Mureş, near Arad in western Romania. The material belongs to the first stage of the Pecica culture, which is named after another settlement near Arad, and which lasted from C20 to C15 BC. Both sites yielded metal objects of Early Bronze Age type.

Persepolis Founded by DARIUS shortly after 518 BC to serve as the capital of the ACHAEMENID empire. It was destroyed by Alexander the Great in 331. It is the showpiece of Achaemenid art, consisting of a series of great palaces and columned reception halls (*apadana*) built on a terrace erected against a mountainside. Monumental stairways are flanked by lines of reliefs showing Median and Persian nobles [141], tribute bearers from all quarters of the empire, servants preparing banquets, as well as the enthroned rulers themselves. The records and stylistic details attest the employment of Medes, Syrians, Urartians

Fig. 141. Persian and Median noblemen, from the great staircase, Persepolis

and Ionian Greeks among others. Elements from all these regions were fused into a single effective and distinctive style.

Persians An INDO-EUROPEAN people who moved into northwest IRAN from Turkestan during the 2nd millennium BC and finally settled in the province of Parsa, now Fars [141]. They twice built great empires through the Middle East, under the ACHAEMENID family (558–331 BC) and under the SASSANIANS (AD 224–651).

Peschiera A town at the southern end of Lake Garda in north Italy. A lake village here gave very rich material of the Bronze Age, showing close connexions with the TERRAMARA culture. In particular, a knife or dagger with a forked end to its flanged hilt is called after the site, as is sometimes the violin-bow FIBULA [63a].

Peterborough Ware An elaborately decorated pottery [142] of the British Late Neolithic (◊ WINDMILL HILL CULTURE). The ornament consists of pits, bone and stick impressions and 'maggot' patterns made by impressing a bit of whipped cord into the soft clay. The earliest (or Ebbsfleet) substyle is contemporary with the decorated Windmill Hill pottery and consists of round-based vessels with fairly restrained ornament. The later variants have more complicated decoration and show the influence of BEAKER pottery: the second (Mortlake) substyle still occurs on round-based vessels, but in the final (Fengate) substyle the pots are flat-bottomed and have many features which lead on to the collared URNS of the Bronze Age. ◊ WINDMILL HILL, AVEBURY, WEST KENNET

Petrie, Sir Flinders (1853–1942) A leading figure in the development of archaeology. Independently of PITT-RIVERS, he argued the same principles of the importance of the commonplace and the necessity of full and objective publication, and applied them in the usually much more difficult conditions of the Near East. His work, summarized in *Seventy Years in Archaeology*, 1931, began with a meticulous survey of STONEHENGE, and continued from 1881 in Egypt and Palestine. At Gurob and Kahun in 1889 he discovered

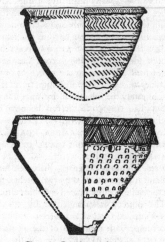

Fig. 142. Peterborough pottery

and recognized Aegean pottery, although it had not yet been identified in its homeland, and realized its significance for

CROSS-DATING. At Tell el-HESI in 1890 the importance of STRATIGRAPHY in the excavation of a TELL site was for the first time fully appreciated. At NAQADA in 1894 his discovery of the predynastic cemetery led him to devise the technique of SEQUENCE-DATING. Throughout, his careful study of the artifacts found, from scarabs to pyramids, their materials and method of manufacture, was far ahead of its time.

petroglyph A rock painting or engraving.

petrological identification By identifying the nature of the so-called bluestones at STONEHENGE, and locating their source in Pembrokeshire, H. H. Thomas in 1923 demonstrated a new source of archaeological information. Since then many British polished stone axes have been 'sliced' – a sliver of stone between two saw cuts is detached, ground down, and its mineral content identified under the microscope. Many distinctive groups have been recognized. Most can be pinned to a limited source, the only accessible outcrop where their content can be closely matched. At a few of these the AXE FACTORY has been located. Varying success has been obtained with tracing the source of other stones traded widely in antiquity. FLINT can rarely be identified by appearance, but, like OBSIDIAN, it can be now by SPECTROGRAPHIC ANALYSIS rather than by petrology. ⟡ AMBER, CALLAÏS, JADEITE, JET, LAPIS LAZULI, CERAMIC ANALYSIS

Peu Richard (Thénac, Charente-Maritime) A camp enclosed by two ditches, the type site of a French Late Neolithic culture. The pottery is ornamented by CHANNELLED decoration or narrow appliqué cordons, with some use of the TUNNEL HANDLE. Peu Richard ware, of the late 3rd millennium BC, has been found over most of west central France, and occurs in MEGALITHIC tombs of DOLMEN and PASSAGE GRAVE types.

PF beaker Abbreviation of PROTRUDING FOOT BEAKER.

Phaestos or **Phaistos** A palace of the MINOANS in south central Crete excavated by the Italians over the years since 1900. The hilltop was levelled for the palace in Middle Minoan IB/II, c 1900 BC, and most of the Neolithic and Early Minoan deposits cut away. Its plan follows closely the pattern of other Minoan palaces – a large central court with large reception rooms, domestic quarters and extensive magazines grouped round it. A narrow western entrance was enlarged in Middle Minoan III into a second court, with stepped sides, perhaps for the bull sports. In the Late Minoan period, though occupation continued, power and wealth passed to HAGIA TRIADA, 2 miles to the west. The palace stood above a town which has as yet received little attention. Phaestos apparently had few frescoes. Its best known finds are a magnificent series of Middle Minoan KAMARES Ware vases and the intriguing Phaestos Disc. This is a unique clay disc 6 ins in diameter with stamped inscriptions in a spiral on each face [143].

Fig. 143. The Phaestos Disc

The symbols hint at an Anatolian origin, but no convincing translation has yet been produced.

pharaoh The title of the rulers of ancient Egypt, who combined the roles of king and god. The latter aspect helps explain the enormous expense of labour and treasure involved in their funeral rites, exemplified above all by the PYRAMIDS and the tomb of TUTANKHAMEN. Each line of kings formed a DYNASTY, of which there were 31 in all, the peaks of power and development being known as the Old, Middle and New KINGDOMS. Pharaoh was represented with the crook and scourge, the URAEUS, and other symbols of authority. Three types of crown were worn. The White Crown of Upper Egypt, the *hedjet*, was a bulbous object of starched linen [144]. The Red Crown of Lower

Fig. 144. The White (a), Red (b), and Blue (c) crowns of Egypt

Egypt, the *deshret*, was of copper or bronze. To them under the New Kingdom was added the Blue Crown or *khepresh*, the royal war helmet.

Philae A barren island in the Nile at ELEPHANTINE, the site of one of the finest surviving temples of the Ptolemaic period. Inscriptions in Greek and HIERO-GLYPHS on a commemorative OBELISK here supplemented the evidence of the ROSETTA STONE to give CHAMPOLLION the key to the ancient Egyptian writings.

Philistines (Egyptian **Pulesati**) One of the PEOPLES OF THE SEA who, repulsed from Egypt c1200 BC [145], drove the CANAANITES from the coastal plain of Palestine (which still preserves their name) and settled in their stead. ASKELON is the only important Philistine city to have been excavated at all, and that but little. Cultural material of the Philistines, illustrating their strong Aegean and Cypriote con-

nexions, has, however, turned up on many neighbouring sites. They were eventually absorbed by the ISRAELITES under David c1000 BC.

Phoenicians Descendants of the CANA-ANITES who occupied the narrow coastal plain of the Lebanon and Syria through the early 1st millennium BC. Their chief cities were TYRE, SIDON and BYBLOS. Even after their incorporation into the Babylonian empire in 574 BC they continued to influence world politics, in the Near East through their fleets, in the west through their powerful colony of CARTHAGE. Culturally their role as merchants and middlemen was uninterrupted until they were absorbed into the Hellenistic and Roman world. They traded raw materials and manufactured goods from TARTESSOS to the Tigris, setting up trading stations or colonies all along the sea routes. Their name is thought to derive from the purple dye they extracted from MUREX shells. They were the great seafarers of the time, even exploring out into the Atlantic for commercial opportunities, though whether they visited the British Isles has not been substantiated. In the other direction they are reputed to have circumnavigated Africa. To assist their commercial activities they developed and diffused the ALPHA-BET, their biggest original contribution to world culture.

Despite this they remain a poorly understood and unsympathetic people.

Fig. 145. Philistine warrior from an Egyptian relief

Their records are too scanty to counteract the accounts of the Greeks and Romans, who heartily detested them. Their art was a hotch-potch of Egyptian and Assyrian elements with very little originality, its highest achievement being perhaps the NIMRUD ivories. One is left with the impression of a mercenary and materialistic people, an impression strengthened rather than dispelled by their religion, with its evidence of infant sacrifice.

phosphate analysis Decay of animal organic matter leaves a residue of phosphates which is only slowly washed out of the deposit by percolating water. Careful chemical analysis can therefore reveal the former presence of such matter. It has been employed particularly in the study of cave deposits (to show human or animal occupation), settlement sites (to identify the uses to which different areas were put) and burials (to show the former existence of bodies completely decayed away).

Phrygians (anc **Muski**) A people who moved from Thrace into west central Turkey after the downfall of the HITTITES. They set up a short-lived state c750–

Fig. 146. 'Tomb of Midas'

680 BC under Midas, with his capital at GORDIUM. After this was destroyed by the CIMMERIANS its culture continued under

the rule of Lydia. Noteworthy are elaborate monuments carved in rock faces [146], once considered tombs but now interpreted as religious centres. Burials were in fact placed under great tumuli, though poorer flat cemeteries are also common. The richly painted pottery is related to that of the contemporary Greeks.

Phylakopi ⟡ MELOS

Pianello A site near Ancona, close to the Italian Adriatic coast. A large URNFIELD cemetery of c1000 BC is taken as the type site of a group scattered through much of Italy. The ashes, sometimes accompanied by an arc FIBULA or quadrangular razor, were buried in a small biconical urn covered by a bowl lid [147]. By one theory,

Fig. 147. Cremation urn with bowl lid, Pianello

this material shows hybridization between the TERRAMARA and APENNINE CULTURES; by another, it represents a new band of invaders. There is similar controversy as to whether the Pianello folk developed into, or were ousted by, the Italian Iron Age peoples like the VILLANOVANS and PICENES.

Picene An Iron Age culture of the Marche on the Italian Adriatic coast, named after the Piceni recorded here by Latin writers. Rich inhumation cemeteries of c9–c6 BC show close trade contacts with central Europe (AMBER was very popular), and with Yugoslavia (notably the spectacle FIBULA [631]).

Picts The name of Pictae, or Painted People, was first used by the Romans in

AD 297 and applied collectively to all the peoples who lived to the north of the ANTONINE WALL. Their name for themselves was Cruithni. They were the principal enemies of Rome in north Britain and their kingdom retained its independence until taken over by Kenneth MacAlpin of DÁLRIADA in C9, thus forming the kingdom of Scotland.

There is little archaeological material which can be confidently attributed to the Picts except for the symbol stones. These are upright slabs incised or carved in relief with various symbols [148], animal and

Fig. 148. Pictish stone with symbols and ogams at Brandsbutt, Aberdeen

human figures, and later with ornamented crosses. Some bear OGAM inscriptions from which it has recently been shown that three languages were in use, two CELTIC and one pre-INDO-EUROPEAN.

Piette, Edouard One of the group of archaeologists working on the PALAEO-LITHIC cave deposits of southwest France in the late C19. His excavations included Mas d'Azil (1887), where he discovered the AZILIAN culture overlying a MAG-DALENIAN stratum, and the cave of Brassempouy, with its famous VENUS FIGURINE. Piette was also one of the first scholars to come out in favour of the authenticity of the CAVE ART at ALTA-MIRA, which he attributed to the Magda-

lenian culture on stylistic grounds. He was the author of various classificatory schemes for prehistory, but none of these found general favour.

pig The wild boar, *Sus scrofa scrofa*, occurs over virtually the whole of continental Europe and southern Asia, and was the ancestor of all early pigs in this area. The first records are from the BELT CAVE in Iran and JARMO in Iraq, in the 7th millennium BC, but not certainly of domesticated animals. Modern pigs derive from *S. s. vittatus*, native to southeastern Asia and bred in China since the Neolithic. They reached Europe only in C18 AD.

pile dwelling In 1853–4 a drop in the level of Lake Zürich revealed the stumps of wooden piles driven into the mud. From the same place came quantities of Neolithic material, much of it finely preserved because of the waterlogged conditions. For a long time it was believed that this site, and the other 'lake villages' discovered soon afterwards, were built on platforms raised on posts above open water, but it has since been proved that lake levels have changed and that the settlements were on damp ground at the water's edge. Similar villages were built in most regions with a lake-and-mountain topography. The most ancient are the work of 3rd millennium Neolithic farmers in southwest Germany, the Jura (CHASSEY culture), Switzerland (COR-TAILLOD culture) and north Italy (LAGOZ-ZA). Other sites (eg those of the POLADA culture) belong to the Early Bronze Age, still others to the Late Bronze Age URN-FIELD tribes and to Iron Age peoples. ⇨ CRANNOG

Piltdown A site near Lewes in Sussex from the gravels of which were recovered a number of human and animal remains from 1908–15. Skull fragments of modern type were apparently associated with a remarkably ape-like jaw, and those accepting the association claimed it to be a true 'missing link'. However, doubts steadily increased until in 1953 searching analysis by the FLUORINE TEST and other methods showed that the skull was indeed of *Homo sapiens*, the jaw that of a modern orang-utang, the animal remains of widely scattered origins, the relics extensively tampered with to make them appear contemporary, and the whole affair nothing but an ingenious and cleverly perpetrated hoax.

pin One of the simplest of artifacts, consisting of a narrow shaft with a point at one end and usually some sort of decorative head at the other. Most commonly its function was to secure garments (in this it was ancestral to the FIBULA), more rarely the hair. Metal and bone are the usual materials for manufacture of pins. Their archaeological importance resides largely in their decorative head, a highly variable, non-functional, and so culturally significant feature. A selection of the types more frequently met with is illustrated [149].

Fig. 149. A few distinctive pin types: (a) knot-headed; (b) wheel-headed; (c) sunflower; (d) hammer-headed; (e) crutch-headed; (f) globe-headed; (g) bulb-headed; (h) poppy-headed; (i) vase-headed; (j) swan-neck; (k) ring-headed; (l) roll-headed; (m) spiral-headed

pintadera A small object usually of terracotta consisting basically of a decorative stamp with a knob at the back for holding. It has been suggested that they served to apply pigments to the human skin in repeat patterns. They are found in the Late Neolithic of central Europe and Italy, and pintaderas of both stamp and roller types occur in many American cultures.

pisé (in full **terre pisé**) A building material consisting of clay or mud laid directly in position instead of being moulded into separate bricks. It was much used in the ancient Near East.

pit The pits found on archaeological sites are of many kinds. Some were storage pits or silos; others were rubbish dumps or 'borrow pits' from which clay and building daub were extracted. Still others are the remains of pit dwellings – houses whose lower parts were excavated into the ground to provide stable and draught-free walls. In the early days of archaeology, when excavators rarely distinguished POST HOLES or traces of timber buildings, storage and rubbish pits containing domestic refuse were often misinterpreted as pit dwellings.

Pit-comb Ware A coarse pottery with deep round-based bowls decorated with pits and comb impressions. It was current throughout the Neolithic to the north and east of the Baltic. Its makers were apparently hunters and fishers, making little use of the techniques of food production, although adopting such Neolithic traits as pot-making and axe-grinding. ◊ CIRCUMPOLAR CULTURES

Pithecanthropus (*Pithecanthropus erectus*) ◊ HOMO ERECTUS

pithos (pl pithoi) A large pottery jar for the storage of oil or grain. They were used on occasion for JAR-BURIAL.

Pitt Rivers, General Augustus Lane-Fox (1827–1900) His contribution to archaeology was twofold. Firstly, from his study of firearms he realized that something analogous to evolution can be traced in artifacts as well as in living organisms, with the same gradual developments and occasional degenerations. He assembled an ethnographical collection arranged by use rather than by provenance, and emphasizing the importance of the ordinary as opposed to the rare, a practical example of TYPOLOGY. In 1880 he inherited a large estate in Cranborne Chase and in the next ten years applied to excavations there the experience gained in his military career and

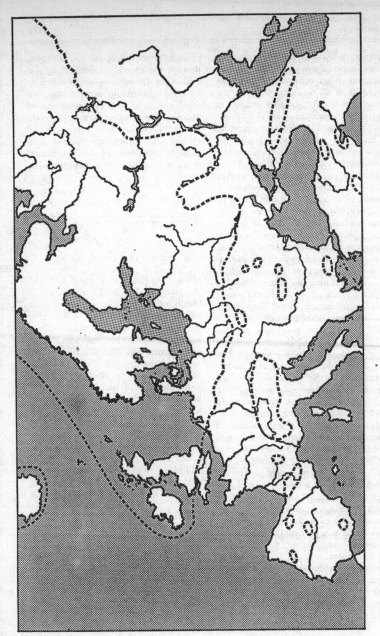

Fig. 150. Distribution of Pleistocene ice-sheets in Europe

museum collections. The result was to advance excavation to a scientific technique, characterized by precise work, meticulous recording of all detail, emphasis on the apparently trivial, complete study (in contrast to the usual sampling of his time), and full and rapid publication. In these, his example was hardly equalled until the 1920s, and is rarely improved upon today.

Pleistocene The geological period corresponding with the last or Great Ice Age [150]. The onset of the Pleistocene is marked by an increasingly cold climate (◊ GLACIATION), by the appearance of Calabrian mollusca and Villafranchian fauna with elephant, ox, and horse species, and by changes in foraminifera. The oldest form of man had evolved by the Early Pleistocene (◊ AUSTRALOPITHECUS), and in archaeological terms the cultures classed as PALAEOLITHIC all fall within this period. The date for the start of the Pleistocene is not yet well established, and estimates based on POTASSIUM–ARGON DATING and other geochronological methods vary from 3.5 to 1.3 million years ago. The period ends with the final but gradual retreat of the ice sheets, which reached their present positions around 8300 BC. The dating of the glaciations which make up the Pleistocene (◊ GÜNZ, MINDEL, RISS, WÜRM, WISCONSIN) is still a matter of controversy. The RADIOCARBON method of dating is ineffective for stages older than the last glaciation, and potassium–argon dating covers only the early part of the Pleistocene. The dates given on p 183 are approximations based on the Milankovitch curve for changes in solar radiation. Other geochronological studies based on different phenomena have produced alternative, and sometimes contradictory, time scales for the Pleistocene.

Pločnik A settlement site on the Morava river in Serbia. Its name is coupled with that of VINČA to describe the Late Neolithic culture of Serbia, Yugoslavia, c2700–2200 BC.

plough A tool designed to be drawn through the ground to break it up for cultivation. The motive power was usually provided by a yoke (or more) of oxen, but other animals or men were employed on occasion. The ploughman controls it from behind. There are two basic types of plough. The earlier, developed directly from the HOE, is the ard or scratch plough [151], which stirs the soil without turning it.

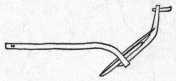

Fig. 151. The Donneruplund ard

Cross-ploughing, the result of a second ploughing at right angles to the first, is usually necessary. This type was of Near Eastern origin, where representations of it go back to the 4th millennium. There and throughout the Mediterranean it is still used on thin soils. Plough scratches have recently been recognized under monuments as early as the Neolithic in northwest Europe. The later plough, heavier, wheeled, and provided with a mould board to turn the furrow, did not appear until the early centuries AD. It is more suited to the heavier soils of Europe. Prehistoric America, lacking suitable draught animals, lacked also the plough.

Plumbate Ware A fine pottery [152] made on the Pacific coast of America, near the Mexico–Guatemala border, in

Fig. 152. A Plumbate vessel

GENERAL	N. AMERICA	N. EUROPE	BRITAIN	ALPS	APPROXIMATE DATES (YEARS BEFORE PRESENT)
POSTGLACIAL	POSTGLACIAL	POSTGLACIAL	POSTGLACIAL	POSTGLACIAL	10,250
LAST GLACIATION	WISCONSIN	WEICHSEL	LAST	WÜRM	70,000
LAST INTERGLACIAL	SANGAMON	EEMIAN	IPSWICHIAN	RISS–WÜRM	187,000
PENULTIMATE GLACIATION	ILLINOIAN	WARTHE / SAALE	GIPPING	RISS	230,000
PENULTIMATE (OR GREAT) INTERGLACIAL	YARMOUTH	HOLSTEIN	HOXNIAN	MINDEL–RISS	435,000
ANTEPENULTIMATE GLACIATION	KANSAN	ELSTER	LOWESTOFT	MINDEL	476,000
ANTEPENULTIMATE INTERGLACIAL	AFTONIAN	—	CROMERIAN	GÜNZ–MINDEL	550,000
EARLY GLACIATION	NEBRASKAN	—	—	GÜNZ	590,000

The Pleistocene glaciations of Europe and North America

early POST-CLASSIC times. It was traded over a wide area, from Nayarit in north-west Mexico to Nicaragua in the south, and was present in all but the lowest levels in the TOLTEC centre at TULA. The glazed appearance of the surface of Plumbate Ware is due to the unusual composition of the clay from which it is made.

pluvial In lowland and subtropical regions which were never covered by PLEISTO-CENE ice sheets, alterations in climate were expressed as changes in rainfall. Prolonged periods of high rainfall are called pluvials, and are marked by changes in lake levels and in flora and fauna. Attempts have been made to correlate the series of African plu-vials with the main GLACIATIONS of colder regions, but the results are ambiguous.

Poidebard, Father A. ◊ AIR PHOTO-GRAPHY

Polada A lake village site near the southern end of Lake Garda in north Italy. It has been made the type site of an Early Bronze Age culture, characterized by a coarse undecorated ware forming deep carinated cups and various simple jars. The strap handles were often surmounted by knobs. Bronze was in use for flat and slightly flanged axes. Antler was much employed, and objects and vessels of wood survive on waterlogged sites.

Poliochni A settlement on the island of Lemnos in the northern Aegean. Its seven successive phases span the Early and Middle Bronze Age, parallel to the first six cities of TROY.

pollen analysis or **palynology** Pollen grains are produced in vast quantities by all plants, especially the wind-pollinated tree species. The outer skin of these grains is remarkably resistant to decay, and on wet ground or on a buried surface it will be preserved, locked in the humus content. Moreover, pollen varies appreciably in shape and can in most cases be readily identified as to genus, occasionally even to species. Fern spores are similarly preserved. The pollen analyst's task is to extract the pollen from significant samples, to ex-amine it under the microscope, to identify and count a representative sample (usually taken as 200 grains), and to interpret the results.

Since the last Ice Age the vegetation of temperate zones such as northwest Europe has gradually progressed from being non-existent, through a stage of dense forest, to its present form. The intermediate stages, shown by the spread of trees requiring progressively greater warmth, have been worked out in considerable detail (◊ vegetational ZONES). Any sample, pre-ferably a series of samples, can now be matched against this scale [pp 186–7]. RADIOCARBON dating has been used to convert the sequence to an absolute chron-ology. Corresponding changes during the PLEISTOCENE are beginning to be docu-mented. The sample will also show the composition of the vegetation in the immediate neighbourhood. As a result, the technique is invaluable for disclosing the environment of early man's sites and can even, over a series of samples, reveal man's influence on his environment by, for ex-ample, FOREST CLEARANCE. These two results may prove contradictory, one showing the vegetational make-up over a larger area, the other being concerned only with the immediate surroundings. Inter-pretation is correspondingly difficult, but a wet site, like a lake clay or peat bog, will be likely to reflect the former more closely, and a dry site, such as a turf line buried beneath a barrow, the latter.

polypod bowl A bowl standing on several little feet. Four of these are usual, but three and two have been recorded. The form was popular amongst the southwestern groups of the BEAKER folk, in VUČEDOL and related central European wares, and recurs elsewhere. Tripod vessels are com-mon in Middle American archaeology.

pond barrow ◊ BARROW

population estimation One of the fac-tors for which the archaeologist would most like figures is the size of ancient populations. Such figures are very difficult to obtain. Estimates can be made of the number of inhabitants of settlements, on the basis of the number of houses or of population density. Both, of course, involve assumptions about the contemporaneity of all houses, the size of the household, etc. For a country, similar guesses have to be made about the number of settlements, discovered or undiscovered, occupied at any one time. A cemetery is little more help. How long was it in use? Did everyone qualify for a grave, including infants? How many died at sea, in battle, or otherwise away from home? Such guesses may be worth attempting, as when the population in Palaeolithic Britain was estimated (on the basis of the population density of a modern people in north Australia in a similar environment and with a similar technology) at only 250 people.

Porchester (anc **Portus Adurni**) A fort of the SAXON SHORE built at the head of Portsmouth harbour as part of the Roman coastal defences. The wall remains, with a Norman castle built into one corner of it.

portal dolmen A form of MEGALITHIC CHAMBER TOMB found mainly in Ireland [153], but with outliers in Wales and Corn-

Fig. 153. Portal dolmen at Haroldstown

wall. The rectangular burial chamber usually becomes narrower and lower towards the rear, and is approached through two tall portal slabs which form a miniature porch or forecourt. The entrance to the chamber is often blocked by a slab which may reach right up to the CAPSTONE. The scarce grave goods are similar to those from the COURT CAIRNS, and both types of tomb are early within the Neolithic period, with dates close to 3000 BC. Architecturally the portal dolmens are related to the court cairns, but whether the dolmens are ancestral or degenerate versions of the court cairn is still uncertain.

port-hole slab A stone slab with a circular hole, often, though not exclusively, forming the entrance to a CHAMBER TOMB. Sometimes the hole is square, or the entrance is made from two slabs set side by side with notches cut from their adjoining edges.

Post-Classic period Term used for those stages of Mexican civilization which came between the collapse of the CLASSIC cultures in C10 AD and the Spanish conquest in C16. ◊ TOLTEC, AZTEC, MAYA

Postglacial period The period from the end of the PLEISTOCENE Ice Age (c8300 BC) to the present. It includes pollen zones IV–IX in the north European scheme [pp 186–7]. The sub-stages in northern Europe are: *Pre-Boreal* (c8300–7700 BC), *Boreal* (7700–5550), *Atlantic* (5550–3000), *Sub-Boreal* (3000–500), and *Sub-Atlantic* (500 BC to present). ◊ POLLEN ANALYSIS, LATE GLACIAL PERIOD and ZONES, VEGETATIONAL

post hole A socket which at one time held an upright post. Even when the wood has decayed and the hole silted up, the existence of a post hole can be recognized by differences between the colour and texture of its fill and those of the earth into which it was dug.

potassium-argon (K-A) dating The earth's crust contains potassium, of which the isotope K^{40} decays to argon A^{40} at a known rate, its half-life being 1,300 million years. In certain volcanic minerals any argon (a gas) within them must have escaped when they were last molten. The argon produced since then will have been

Period	Economy	Tree Cover	Fauna	Vegetation	Pollen Zone	Climate	
IRON / BRONZE	Settled agriculture pastoralism hunting and fishing	FOREST		Pine beech; Spread of grasses and heather	IX	SUB-ATLANTIC Deterioration, wetter, colder	500 BC
BRONZE / NEOLITHIC	Shifting agriculture pastoralism hunting and fishing — Forest clearance	FOREST	Tame horse, Red & roe deer, wild pigs, etc, domesticated ox, pig, sheep, dog	Oak forest; Introduction of cereals and weeds of cultivation	VIII	SUB-BOREAL Drier, more continental	3000
MESOLITHIC	Hunting, gathering, fowling, fishing, strand-looping	FOREST	Aurochs, red and roe deer, wild pig, etc, dog	Mixed oak forest (oak, elm, lime, alder)	VII	ATLANTIC Maximum warmth, moist, oceanic	
		FOREST	Aurochs, elk, red and roe deer, wild pig, beaver, bear, dog	Pine/hazel; start of mixed oak forest	VI	BOREAL Rising temperature, continental	5500
		FOREST	Aurochs, elk	Pine/birch forest	V		7700
	Hunting, gathering,	FOREST	Reindeer, bison, wild horse	Birch forest	IV	PRE-BOREAL Slow rise in temperature	8300

POST-GLACIAL

fowling, fishing

OPEN VEGETATION

Date (BC)	Period		Vegetation	Fauna
	YOUNGER DRYAS Sub-arctic	III	Tundra / Park tundra	Reindeer, bison, alpine hare
8850				
	ALLERØD OSC. Warmer	II	Park tundra / Birch forest	Giant Irish deer, elk, beaver, bear
9850				
	OLDER DRYAS Sub-arctic	Ic	Tundra	Reindeer
10050				
	BØLLING OSC. Warmer	Ib	Park Tundra	
10450				
	OLDEST DRYAS Arctic	Ia	Tundra	Reindeer
13000 BC				

LATE GLACIAL

The Late Glacial and Postglacial subdivisions of northern Europe trapped in their crystal lattice. Determination by careful analysis of the ratio K^{40}/A^{40} can be turned into a date before present in the same manner as RADIOCARBON dating. Because of the long half-life, the amount of argon produced in samples less than about a million years old is too small to measure accurately, but useful, if controversial, results have been obtained on Early Pleistocene material, notably in the OLDUVAI Gorge. Here lava flows interbedded with the deposits containing archaeological material have been dated.

potato Botanical evidence shows that the plant must have been brought into cultivation in the Andes of southern Peru and north Bolivia (the area between Cuzco and Lake Titicaca), and documentary accounts show that at the time of the Spanish conquest potatoes were grown all over the highlands from Colombia to Chile. The date at which cultivation began is still uncertain, and the archaeological record does not go back beyond the 2nd millennium BC.

potter's wheel A wheel rotating in the horizontal plane to assist a potter in shaping the clay into vessels. Actual examples do not survive, so that it is not possible to document the different varieties of wheel, the kick-wheel, the treadle-operated, the power-driven, etc. The evidence of the pottery itself is usually conclusive. Some sort of turntable, known as a tournette or slow wheel, was first used to true up a handmade pot, particularly its lip. By the URUK phase in Mesopotamia, c3400 BC, the fast wheel was already in use. It spread slowly, reaching Europe with the MINOANS c2400 BC, and Britain with the BELGAE in CI BC. Its presence can be taken to imply an organized pottery industry, often using also an advanced type of KILN. Its use was never discovered in America.

pottery Clay when dried loses much of its water, but regains it when wetted again. When clay is baked, further water begins to be lost from the molecules at c400°C,

and cannot be replaced – the clay is turned to pottery. Somewhere above 1000°C the particles begin to fuse, but such temperatures were beyond the control of most early potters. Pottery has many advantages for making containers (the term is usually reserved for the material of vessels, TERRACOTTA being the term for baked clay used in other ways). Its raw material is common, shaping and baking it are simple, and it can be given an infinite variety of forms and decorations. The disadvantage that it is fragile proves to the archaeologist to be yet another advantage, since in sherd form it is almost indestructible.

These factors give it enormous value in archaeology. It is one of the commonest finds on any site at which it was used, it is one of the clearest indicators of cultural differences, relationships and developments, and its techniques of manufacture can be comparatively easily recovered by CERAMIC ANALYSIS. It can be shown whether it was modelled, coil-built or wheel-made. The nature of its fabric, ware or body can be identified, as can any surface treatment such as SLIP, paint or BURNISH. The wide range of methods of decoration can also be studied. Ease of decoration made it the medium which many early peoples first turned to for outlets for their artistic creativity, and so it can often tell us much which we cannot learn elsewhere.

pre-Aurignacian ◊ AMUDIAN

Pre-Boreal period ◊ POSTGLACIAL PERIOD

Pre-Classic (or Formative) period Used in American archaeology for the period in which agriculture, or any other subsistence economy of comparable effectiveness, formed the basis of settled village life. Normally it is also marked by the introduction of pottery. Strictly speaking, only those cultures which had in them the seeds of development into CLASSIC should be labelled Formative. In some places both pottery and agriculture are known by

2000 BC, but the Pre-Classic period in Mexico is usually considered to begin C1500 BC (◊ OLMEC, MAYA, MONTE ALBÁN, TLATILCO). A similar level was attained in Peru at about the same time (eg CHAVÍN). In many other areas this potential was never fulfilled, and life remained on a Formative level until the Spanish conquest. In the chronological sense, however, the Pre-Classic period is usually taken to have ended c300 AD, whatever the cultural status of the later centuries.

predynastic The period before recorded history in Egypt, covering the 5th and 4th millennia BC. Its main phases are described under FAYUM, BADARIAN, AMRATIAN and GERZEAN.

prehistory In the strict sense, 'history' is an account of the past recovered from written records, but such an account can be prepared from other sources, notably archaeology. The term 'prehistory' was coined (by Daniel Wilson in 1851 though in France Tournal had used '*préhistorique*' as early as 1833) to cover the story of man's development before the appearance of writing. It is succeeded by PROTO-HISTORY, the period for which we have some records but must still rely largely on archaeological evidence to give us a co-herent account.

Prehistory differs from history in many other ways. It deals with the activities of a society or CULTURE, not of the individual; it is restricted to the material evidence, and only such of that as has survived; and it is in the strictest sense anonymous, since without records we cannot know the names of people, peoples or places, and are forced to invent arbitrary labels to serve instead.

pressure flaking A technique for shaping stone tools, in which thin FLAKES are removed by pressure applied by means of an implement of bone, stone or wood. Pressure flaking is commonly found on thin flat artifacts such as daggers, arrow-and spear-heads.

primary or **rapid silt** The silt deposited at the bottom of a ditch by the rapid weathering of the sides and upper parts within a few years after the ditch was cut. Thereafter the weathering processes act much more slowly, and the accumulation of secondary silt is more gradual. Nor-mally an object found in the rapid silt will be roughly contemporary with the digging of the ditch, with the proviso that a more ancient artifact which was lying on the ground surface close to the lip of the ditch may tumble into the fill when the edges of the trench crumble and collapse.

Primary Neolithic ◊ WINDMILL HILL CULTURE

probe A metal rod pushed into unexca-vated deposits to locate as yet unexposed hard features such as walls, floors or bed rock. ◊◊ AUGER

promontory fort A defended area on the tip of a hill, spur or cliff, with the defence works barring the line of easiest approach along the neck of the peninsula. The other sides rely chiefly on their natural defensi-bility.

proto- An early developmental stage of the main root word, eg prototype, proto-Villanovan.

protohistory The period in any area following PREHISTORY and preceding the appearance of coherent history derived from written records. The first mention of Britain is in C6 BC, but no one could claim that our history goes back earlier than Julius Caesar (56 BC), Claudius (AD 43) or even the later Anglo-Saxons of C7 or C8 AD.

proton magnetometer ◊ MAGNETO-METER

protruding foot beaker The typical vessel of the Late Neolithic in the Nether-lands. The basic form has a splayed neck, S-shaped profile and flat everted base[154]. It bears CORD ORNAMENT, dentate spatula impressions or herringbone incisions. The vessel defines a culture, distinguished also by burial of a single corpse in either a flat grave or a pit under a BARROW, and by the use of the BATTLEAXE. These traits show that the culture represents the Dutch branch of the widespread Corded Ware-Battleaxe complex, or SINGLE-GRAVE

Fig. 154. Protruding foot beaker

CULTURES, which may in turn derive from the KURGAN cultures of south Russia. In Holland there is some hybridization between the Protruding Foot Beaker culture and the one represented by the bell BEAKER. Radiocarbon dates range from C2500–1900 BC.

provenance or **provenience** The findspot, the place where an object was recovered in modern times.

Ptah The god of MEMPHIS in ancient Egypt. He was patron of crafts, represented as a MUMMY.

Pucara A large urban site near the Peruvian shore of Lake Titicaca. The important buildings included a walled sanctuary, but the city is best known for its carved stone statues and its polychrome pottery with designs including the divided eye motif found later at TIAHUANACO. Radiocarbon dates cluster in C1 and C2 BC, and the entire occupation probably falls within the period 200 BC to C1 AD.

pueblo An agglomeration of rectangular living rooms, built close together and often arranged in several storeys or terraces. These great apartment houses are characteristic of the later ANASAZI peoples of the southwest United States. ◊ HOHOKAM, MOGOLLON and KIVA.

Puerto Hormiga A shell midden on the Caribbean coast of Colombia. Fibre-tempered pottery from the site has a radiocarbon date of 2925 ± 170 BC which makes it one of the oldest wares in the Americas, rivalled only by the VALDIVIA pottery of Ecuador.

Punic ◊ CARTHAGE

Punt A district bordering the mouth of the Red Sea, probably Somaliland, from which Egyptian naval expeditions brought myrrh trees, gold, ivory, etc. The most famous of these expeditions is recorded at DEIR EL-BAHRI in the funerary temple of Queen Hatshepsut of the 18th dynasty, C1478 BC.

pygmy vessel ◊ INCENSE CUP

pylon A monumental gateway to Egyptian temples or palaces built in stone and usually decorated with relief figures and hieroglyphs.

Pylos A palace and town of the MYCENAEANS, traditionally ruled by Nestor, and overlooking Navarino Bay on the west coast of the Peloponnese in Greece. It is perhaps the best preserved of all mainland palaces. A MEGARON with frescoed walls and painted floor opened on to a courtyard [116]. Around this are the domestic quarters, storerooms, guard chamber and (most important of all to us) the archives room. The 1200 tablets from this, baked by the fire which destroyed the palace in C13 BC, have been of enormous value in deciphering the LINEAR B script. Of particular interest is the opportunity the site gives of comparing the contemporary records, the archaeological remains and the traditions of this very building preserved in the *Odyssey*.

pyramid A monumental tomb in the shape of a pentahedron built by the ancient Egyptians to cover or contain the burial chamber of a PHARAOH. Its origin lay in the mudbrick MASTABA of the Archaic Period, which in the Old Kingdom rapidly became more elaborate with the use of stone, regularity of shape, and above all increase of size. Stages in this development are marked by the Step Pyramid at SAKKARA, the Bent Pyramid at Dahshur and the Pyramid of Meidum. The largest and most famous, the GIZA group, belonged to pharaohs Cheops, Chephren and Mykerinus of the 4th dynasty. The Great Pyramid of Cheops measured 756 ft a side with an original height of 481 ft. It

Fig. 155. Pyramid with associated buildings, Abu Sir

was laid out with remarkable accuracy, its sides of the same length to within 8 ins and aligned on the cardinal points to within $\frac{1}{10}$ of a degree. Many devices to prevent violation were incorporated but to no effect. The elaborateness of the funerary ritual, witnessed by the mortuary temples attached to all pyramids [155], had the same purpose, of guaranteeing the eternal well-being of the deceased. The construction of the pyramids as early as C26 BC was an extraordinary achievement of engineering and architecture, illustrating the lengths their builders would go to in securing immortality for their deified rulers.

pyxis A cylindrical canister-like vessel with a flat shoulder and lid, used by the Greeks to hold trinkets. The name is more loosely applied to other pots approximating to this shape. [128]

Q

quadrant method A layout of trenches for the EXCAVATION of a circular feature such as a BARROW, pit or circular hut. The removal of two alternate quarters exposes a complete transverse SECTION along each major axis, and allows a better interpretation of the STRATIGRAPHY of the site.

Quaternary era The geological era which includes both the PLEISTOCENE and HOLOCENE periods.

quern A stone for grinding corn. A rough but hard stone was necessary, to avoid grit in the flour. Lava was widely traded for the purpose. The primitive form was the saddle quern, the corn being ground on its concave surface by means of a hand-operated rubbing stone. This type continued little altered from the later food-gatherers of the Mesolithic to the Romans, since when the rotary quern has been the standard form. In this, one stone is rotated on another by hand, or in larger examples by a capstan or water power.

Quetta A city of north BALUCHISTAN with many TELL sites in its neighbourhood. The most important were dug by Fairservis in the 1950s. Kili Gul Mohammad started with an apparently pre-pottery occupation with domestic animals (radio-carbon date 3700 BC) and continued with creamy handmade and basket-marked pottery, later joined by red and black painted ware. Mudbrick was general, stone blades were used, but copper appeared only at the very end. Damb Sadaat succeeded this site, and ran through the rest of the 3rd millennium. Its material is fully Chalcolithic, with close links at MUNDIGAK and RANA GHUNDAI. It is characterized by geometric designs painted in solid black with stepped or curved outlines on a buff or greenish fine wheel-turned ware, the Quetta Ware.

Quetzalcóatl The NÁHUATL name for the AZTEC god usually depicted as a plumed serpent [156]. He was the god of self-sacrifice, patron of arts and crafts, inventor of agriculture and the calendar. In another form he was also the wind god and

Fig. 156. Statue of Quetzalcóatl

god of the morning star. His cult can be recognized in the CLASSIC period at TEOTIHUACÁN and subsequently at many Mexican sites. He was an important figure in the early TOLTEC pantheon (becoming identified with a local ruler), and his effigy appears in the MAYA territory after the Toltec invasion of CHICHÉN ITZÁ. According to legend, Quetzalcóatl was driven away from Mexico, but before leaving he gave a promise to return. For a while the Aztecs believed that the invading Spaniards were the god and his followers returning to fulfil this prophecy.

Quimbaya The name given to fine pottery and goldwork from tombs in the middle Cauca valley and Central Cordillera of Colombia. All the material comes from unscientific excavations and several phases seem to be represented. The dating is uncertain but probably falls within the millennium before the Spanish conquest. The historical Quimbaya were latecomers into the region, and were responsible for only part of the material which bears their name.

quipu A device used by the INCA for keeping accounts and records. It consisted of a number of cords of various thicknesses and colours, on which numbers and other data were indicated by knots of different sizes and positions on the strings.

Qumran ⟡ DEAD SEA SCROLLS

R

Ra or **Re** The supreme god of ancient Egypt before his displacement by AMEN. He was god of the sun and of the city of HELIOPOLIS.

rabotage The technique of careful horizontal scraping of a surface to disclose features in it distinguished by colour differences. It is particularly useful in sandy soils and gravels, in which organic matter is often completely destroyed. It can reveal surprising detail, not only pits and postholes but on occasion the outline of a long since decomposed body beneath a barrow.

racloir ⟡ SCRAPER. The racloir is one of the most characteristic MOUSTERIAN implements [124], and may have served as both knife and scraper.

radiate Describes those imperial Roman coins on which the emperor is shown wearing a radiate or solar crown [157], the usual practice in C3 AD, though occurring

Fig. 157. Coin of Postumus wearing the radiate crown

earlier and later. The barbarous radiates are later and inferior, usually unofficial, examples of the same type.

radiocarbon Carbon14 is a radioactive isotope of C^{12} produced from nitrogen14 in the atmosphere by cosmic radiation. Thereafter it acts exactly like C^{12}, being taken into the organic compounds of all living matter. The proportions of radioactive and inert carbon are identical throughout the atmosphere and biosphere (the vegetable and animal kingdoms). When organic matter dies it ceases to exchange its carbon, as carbon dioxide, with the atmosphere, so its C^{14} dwindles by decay and is not replenished. Determination of the radioactivity of carbon from a sample will reveal the proportion of C^{14} to C^{12}, and this will in turn, through the known rate of decay of C^{14}, give the age of, or more accurately the time elapsed since the death of, the sample.

Since the method was first suggested by W. F. Libby in 1946 a vast amount of invaluable evidence has been obtained on man's past. The method gave the first universal means of absolute DATING quite independent of subjective archaeological methods. Many of the results surprised archaeologists, but the fact that the dates are so consistent with each other has overruled the early reluctance to accept inconvenient ones. Certainly many faulty dates have appeared, due to contamination of the sample, poor association between sample and archaeological context, and the like, but the more samples tested, the fuller and securer the chronological framework becomes.

Three flaws in the method have to be allowed for. Firstly, the 'date' given is never exact. The ± figure, which should always be quoted, is a statistical one, meaning that there is a 2 to 1 chance that the correct date lies within that bracket. Secondly, the rate of decay of C^{14} is based in all published examples on a half-life of 5568 ± 30 years (after 5568 years, one half of the C^{14} will have disintegrated, after another 5568 years one half of the remainder, and so on), and it is becoming clear that the figure is too small. 5730 has been suggested but it has been agreed not to change the figure until a new one can be internationally accepted. More seriously, the assumption that the rate of production of C^{14} has been uniform throughout past time is now challenged. The agreement between C^{14} dates and historical ones or ones based on DENDROCHRONOLOGY for the past 2000 years or so has been very close. With the extension of dendrochronology on the Californian bristle-cone pine over some 6500 years, serious discrepancies have been found, suggesting that there was then much more C^{14} occurring naturally, so that true solar-year dates of samples are substantially earlier than the radiocarbon dates. The method, however, still has many advantages over others, even if the dates given are in radiocarbon years rather than solar ones.

radiometric assay A method of determining the quantity of uranium in a specimen by measuring its radioactivity. The significance is very like that of the FLUORINE TEST. Like fluorine, uranium is cumulatively absorbed by bone from percolating ground-water, and can give relative dates to material from a single deposit. It varies greatly from site to site and showed, for example, that an elephant tooth from PILTDOWN almost certainly came from Tunisia.

raised beach An ancient shore line dating from a period when sea level was higher than at present (◊ EUSTASY, ISOSTASY). Changes in relative heights of land and sea can often be correlated with fluctuations in the PLEISTOCENE climate.

Ramses, Ramesses, etc The name of two pharaohs of Egypt of the 19th dynasty and nine of the 20th. Ramses II's victory at KADESH, however doubtful, at least stabilized his frontier with the HITTITES for many years. He also carried out much temple building within Egypt and NUBIA, as at ABU SIMBEL. Ramses III saved the country by defeating invasions of the PEOPLES OF THE SEA and the Libyans CII70 BC.

Rana Ghundai A TELL in the Loralai valley of north BALUCHISTAN important for the stratigraphy observed in it by Ross. The 40 ft of deposit showed a plain handmade ware preceding, and coarse painted and plain relief patterned wares overlying,

the levels with fine black-on-red ZHOB wares.

rapier An offensive weapon of bronze distinguished from the SWORD by the slenderness of its blade and the simple butt for rivet hafting [158], both of which would limit its usefulness to a thrusting, rather

Fig. 158. Rapier: (a) rivets; (b) butt; (c) midrib; (d) flutes

than a slashing blow. It developed in the Middle Bronze Age by lengthening of the DAGGER, and was replaced by the slashing sword in the Late Bronze Age of central and northwest Europe.

Ras Shamra ◊ UGARIT

rath The Irish term for a small ring-fort, rarely more than 200 ft in diameter, and enclosed by a bank with an outer ditch. Sometimes there is more than one rampart, and the enclosed area normally contains hut foundations or occupation debris. Usage is not consistent, but the word *rath* is generally used to describe a fort with earthen banks, while a stone-built fort is described as a *cashel*. The oldest forts belong to the Late Bronze Age, but they continue beyond CII AD.

Rawlinson, Lt Col. Henry Creswicke ◊ CUNEIFORM

razor A bronze blade, often double edged, for shaving. Some distinctive types are shown [159]. Recognizable examples in iron rarely survive.

Re ◊ RA

Recuay A pottery style from the north highlands of Peru. The vessels, found in underground galleries and box-shaped tombs, are decorated with black NEGATIVE PAINTING over a red and white ground, and shapes include elaborately modelled scenes. The Recuay style belongs in the early centuries AD and shows contacts with the GALLINAZO and MOCHICA styles of the coast.

recumbent stone circle ⟡ STONE CIRCLE

Red Hills The local name for the mounds of burned clay, ash and coarse pottery which dot the coasts of eastern England.

particularly gold and bronze, produced by hammering up projections from the back. A mould of appropriate shape held against the outer face during the process would have ensured regularity of shape. Circular bosses are by far the commonest form.

resistivity survey A technique for in-

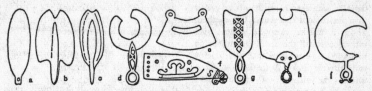

Fig. 159. Some razor forms – British: (a) Class I; (b) bifid (Class II). Continental: (c) tumulus; (d) horse-shoe; (e) Hallstatt; (f) Scandinavian. Italian: (g) Terramara; (h) quadrangular; (i) crescentic (Villanovan)

They mark the sites at which salt was obtained by artificial evaporation of sea water during the later Iron Age and the Romano–British period.

Regional Development period The term used in Ecuadorian archaeology for the period 500 BC–AD 500, when local adaptation led to the proliferation of regional cultures. Some of the coastal variants produced fine pottery, elaborate figurines and many small art objects. There are hints of Asiatic influence in the cultures of BAHÍA and Jama-Coaque, which occupied the coastland from La Plata island to Cape Francisco.

remanent magnetism ⟡ ARCHAEO-MAGNETISM

Remedello (Brescia) A village in the Po valley of north Italy which in 1885–6 yielded a famous cemetery of 117 tombs, the type site of a Copper Age culture. Skeletons were crouched in trench graves, accompanied by flat axes, triangular daggers and HALBERDS in copper, and barbed-and-tanged flint arrowheads. Pottery was scarce and variable. Sherds of BEAKERS have been found associated with this material, and a date c2000 BC is likely.

repoussé Decoration of sheet metalwork,

vestigating the nature of underlying deposits without, or in advance of, digging. It relies on the principle that different deposits offer different resistance to the passage of an electric current, depending largely on the amount of water present. A damp pit or ditch fill will offer less resistance, stone wall foundations more, than the surrounding soil. The instrument consists of a source of electricity (a handle-operated dynamo in the megger earth tester, batteries in the tellohm, a transistor oscillator in the Martin-Clark meter) and a meter to record the results. All systems employ four steel probes connected by cable to the meter, two to carry the activating current, two to pick up the current passing through the ground. The work can be speeded up by the use of a fifth probe, this being moved up ready to become the first in the next reading while the previous reading is being taken. Different spacing between the probes is employed in different conditions. Where the probes are spaced equally, as in the Wenner configuration, features up to a depth equal to the probe-separation can be detected. Interpretation of the results is often difficult, but as with the MAGNETO-

METER, any anomalous reading may be significant.

revetment A wall or fence built to prevent the slipping of a steep or vertical face of a bank, less commonly of a ditch.

Rhodesian man ◊ BROKEN HILL

Rhône culture The Swiss and east French counterpart of the Early Bronze Age cultures of central Europe (◊ ÚNĚTICE). The metalwork and pottery are closest to those of the Straubing group in Bavaria.

rhyton A deep vessel with a single handle [160] intended for the pouring of libations or liquid offerings to gods, spirits of the dead, etc. Some examples are provided

Fig. 160. Minoan rhyton of CI 500 BC

with a hole at the lowest point, to be covered by a finger of the hand until the appropriate moment in the ceremony. Rhytons were often made of precious materials and of elaborate form. They are typical of the MINOANS, MYCENAEANS and classical Greeks, and of the ACHAE-MENID Persians.

ricasso The blunting of the cutting edges of a SWORD just below the hilt so that its owner can grip it firmly without damage to his fingers. [186.7]

rice (*Oryza sativa*) Native to, and for a long period now the staple cereal of,

southeast Asia. The earliest datable record is from Chirard in the Ganges valley, before 4500 BC. By the third millennium it was widely grown in south China. Its original centre of cultivation could lie anywhere between the two.

Richborough (anc **Rutupiae**) A Roman port of some importance on the estuary then separating the island of Thanet from the rest of Kent. Its remains summarize clearly the Roman occupation of Britain. A camp was built in AD 43 to house Claudius's army of invasion, and a commemorative monument was added c85. It was refortified as a lookout post c250 when the threat of raids by ANGLO-SAXONS was increasing, and enlarged into a stone-walled fort of the SAXON SHORE in the following century.

ridgeway An ancient and traditional communication route following the line of an upland ridge. Often there is no artificially constructed roadway, but some routes became Roman roads or medieval drove-ways. The number of finds clustering along the ridgeways suggests use well back in prehistoric times, continuing to beyond the Middle Ages. Important British ridge-ways are the Jurassic Way along the lime-stone ridge from Dorset to Lincolnshire, the Icknield Way in the Chilterns and the Pilgrims' Way along the North Downs.

Rigveda The earliest and most important of the Vedas, the religious writings of the ARYANS at the time of their conquest of northwest India. It contains over a thousand poems of great variety of content, written in SANSKRIT. It can be dated only loosely, to the second half of the 2nd millennium BC. It probably assumed its present form CI000 BC, and was transmitted orally, with great accuracy, for many centuries.

Rinaldone A cemetery of trench graves southeast of Lake Bolsena, in Italy. They have been taken as the type site of a Copper Age culture lying between those of REME-DELLO and GAUDO, showing some connexions with both. Elsewhere in Tuscany and Latium rock-cut SHAFT-AND-CHAMBER TOMBS have yielded identical material – crouched skeletons, pottery including the necked flask, flat copper axes and daggers (or magnificent copies in flint), stone battle-axes and numerous barbed-and-tanged arrowheads.

Rinyo-Clacton A Late Neolithic pottery style of Britain [161]. The name indicates the distribution, with finds concentrated in

of curious projections from the top. There are connexions with DANILO across the Adriatic. Notable among the flintwork are tanged and single-barbed arrowheads.

rippled decoration A form of pottery burnish in which the whole surface is worked into ripples, in extreme examples approaching FLUTING.

Riss glaciation The third major GLACIATION of the PLEISTOCENE in Alpine Europe [p 183].

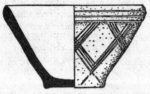
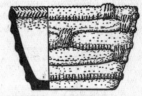

Fig. 161. Rinyo-Clacton pottery

Scotland (at Rinyo, SKARA BRAE and in several MEGALITHIC CHAMBER TOMBS), and in southern England (at settlements round the east coast near Clacton, and further west at such sites as AVEBURY, STONEHENGE, WEST KENNET, WINDMILL HILL and WOODHENGE). The characteristic vessel is a flat-based pot with straight flaring sides. In Scotland the usual decoration consists of appliqué cordons, but in England the patterns are more often executed by grooving. For its place in the Neolithic sequence, ◊ WINDMILL HILL CULTURE.

Ripoli A village of Middle to Late Neolithic hut foundations (*fondi di capanna*) and some crouched burials, situated in the Vibrata valley on the Adriatic coast of Italy. It yielded a painted ware named after the site, and also LAGOZZA-like material. Ripoli Ware has a buff fabric painted with geometric designs in black, separated from areas painted red by a pair of lines enclosing a row of dots. The usual shape is a round-based cup with straight vertical wall and single handle, this sometimes with a pair

ritual Connected with some magic or religious practice. With the near-impossibility of understanding beliefs from archaeological evidence alone, the term is sometimes used simply to mean that no functional explanation can be found for the site or object so described. This usage is to be deprecated: honesty is the best policy.

river terraces These are the result of alternating periods of erosion and aggradation (silting) within a river valley, brought about by oscillations of sea level relative to land (◊ EUSTASY). When sea level is low (eg during the climax of a GLACIATION) the gradient of the river is increased, the water flows more quickly, and cuts away the river bed. During a period of high sea level the gradient is less, the river flows sluggishly, and gravel is deposited on the valley floor. A second period of erosion will carry away most of this gravel, except at the edge of the valley where a residual platform, or terrace, may remain. It is often possible to correlate cycles of erosion and aggradation with the fluctuations of PLEIS-

TOCENE climate, and thus to work out the relative dating of artifacts incorporated in the gravels of the terraces. [162]

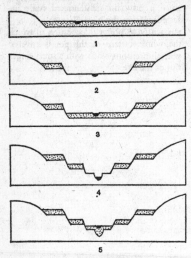

Fig. 162. Stages in the formation of river terraces

rivet A small metal rod used to attach a metal blade to its haft or to fasten two sheets of metal together. Each end of the rivet is burred over (spread and flattened) by hammering after it has been passed through the two elements to be joined.

robber trench ◊ GHOST WALL

rock-cut tomb A CHAMBER TOMB cut into solid rock.

rocker pattern A pottery decoration in which a straight or curved edge is moved

Fig. 163. Rocker pattern

across the soft clay by pivoting on alternate corners. The result is a zigzag of curved lines [163]. The technique was discovered and employed in a number of different

times and places – the Neolithic IMPRESSED WARE of the central Mediterranean, the Iron Age of the Sudan and of Manchuria, in North America (HOPEWELL), and widely in PRE-CLASSIC cultures of Middle and South America.

rock shelter A naturally formed hollow or shelter in a more or less vertical rock face. The overhang may protect a large area, but a shelter is not deep enough to be classed as a cave.

Roquepertuse (Velaux, Bouches-du-Rhône, France) A Celto–Ligurian OPPI-DUM with a sanctuary famous for its stone sculptures. These included large human figures seated in a cross-legged position, and a portal with niches for the display of severed human heads. Many carvings bear traces of their original paint. ◊ ENTRE-MONT

Rosetta Stone A basalt slab discovered at Rosetta, at the western mouth of the Nile, during Napoleon's occupation of Egypt. It is now in the British Museum. An honorific decree of Ptolemy V (196 BC) was carved on it in Greek, DEMOTIC and hieroglyphic. This provided Champollion with the key to the decipherment of the ancient Egyptian HIEROGLYPHS, illegible for fifteen centuries, thus paving the way to modern Egyptology.

Rössen A cemetery near Merseburg in central Germany, and the type site for a Late DANUBIAN CULTURE of north Bohemia, Saxo–Thuringia, Bavaria and parts of the Rhineland, Switzerland and east France. Radiocarbon dates cluster around 3500 BC.

roulette A cogged wheel rotated over the soft clay of a pot to leave a series of impressed dashes at right angles to the line of progress. The technique recurs in widely scattered places.

round barrow ◊ BARROW

runes An angular script for carving on wood or stone developed by Germanic peoples through contact with Mediterranean alphabets [164]. It is first recorded in

C3 AD in Denmark and Schleswig, and spread widely across northern Europe. The voyages of the Vikings later carried it as far as Russia and Iceland, where it remained in use into the Middle Ages. With the discrediting of the KENSINGTON STONE, there is now no substantiated runic inscription from the New World.

Fig. 164. Runic inscription from the Franks Casket

rusticated A pottery decoration in which the whole surface of the pot is covered with impressions made with a stick, finger tips or the like.

S

St Ninian's Isle An islet on the west coast of Shetland bearing the ruins of a chapel dedicated to St Ninian of Whithorn in C12. When excavated by Professor O'Dell in 1955–8, a treasure consisting of seven bowls, a spoon and a possible fork, a sword pommel, two possible chapes, three thimble-shaped objects and 12 penannular brooches came to light, all of silver and many elaborately decorated. It had been buried, together with a porpoise jawbone, in a larchwood box beneath the floor of an earlier chapel on the site, probably to save it from a Viking raid in the early C9 AD. It is now in the National Museum of Scotland in Edinburgh.

Saite The 26th dynasty of Egypt (664–525) is known as the Saite period as its pharaohs took Sais in the Delta as their capital. It was characterized by a notable revival in Egyptian art in, however, a consciously ARCHAISTIC style. The Saites were overthrown by the Persian invasion under Cambyses.

Sakçe Gözü or **Sakjegeuzu** A TELL close to the Amanus mountains in southern Turkey, excavated by Garstang 1907–11. There were two periods of occupation, an Early Neolithic settlement comparable to that at MERSIN and a palace of the Syro-HITTITES of the early 1st millennium. The latter has produced quantities of important reliefs and inscriptions.

Sakkara or **Saqqara** A cemetery area west of the Nile behind MEMPHIS, near Cairo. The most famous tomb here is the Step PYRAMID erected by Imhotep for Djoser, pharaoh of the 3rd dynasty, c2630 BC. The MASTABA tombs of the nobility making up most of the cemetery have yielded the greater part of our evidence on the Archaic Period and Old Kingdom of Egypt, the first six dynasties and particularly the 4th dynasty. Also buried here, at the Serapeum, were the sacred APIS bulls.

Saladero (Venezuela) A site near the Orinoco delta where pottery-making farmers were established just after 1000 BC. At the type site, Saladero pottery was soon replaced by wares of the BARRANCAS style. Along the middle Orinoco and on the coast this Barrancas incursion had little effect, and pottery in the Saladero TRADITION (the Saladoid SERIES) continued to be made until c AD 1000. Some Saladoid groups migrated to Trinidad and the Antilles during the first three centuries AD, and this movement may represent the ARAWAK colonization of the West Indies.

Saladoid series ◊ SALADERO

Sălcuţa A Late Neolithic culture of western Romania c2700–2000 BC. It derives from the VINČA culture, with further influence from the Aegean. By its end, copper was coming into use.

Saldanha skull ◊ FAURESMITH

Saliagos A Neolithic village on an islet once joining Paros and Antiparos in the Cyclades, excavated by Evans and Renfrew 1965. The community relied largely on fishing for its sustenance, though farming and trading were also practised.

Salinar The pottery style which follows CUPISNIQUE in the Chicama and Virú valleys of north Peru. It is distinguished by modelled vessels, pots with STIRRUP SPOUTS and whistling jars. Some vessels have simple white patterns over a red slip. Salinar begins during the final centuries BC, and gives way to the GALLINAZO style.

Samaria A site near Nablus in central Palestine excavated by Reisner 1908–10 and Crowfoot 1931–5. The archaeological evidence can here be tied very closely to the historical. The city was founded by Omri, king of Israel, in 880 BC, and to him and his son Ahab are to be attributed the earliest, and very fine, buildings and planning. Influence of the PHOENICIANS is visible in this, and in a collection of carved ivories comparable to those of NIMRUD. To c800 belong a group of OSTRACA, tax receipts, throwing light on political conditions and the development of the Hebrew script. The site continued to be occupied after its destruction by the Assyrians c722, though in an impoverished style. It regained importance through the Hellenistic, Roman and Byzantine periods.

Samarra A painted pottery ware of the 6th millennium discovered immediately beneath the capital of the Abbasid caliphs in northern Iraq. It replaced HASSUNA ware, on which it marked a considerable advance. Birds, fish, animals, human beings, etc, were represented very effectively, if somewhat conventionally, within geometric borders. Open bowls were particularly elaborately decorated. The ware may have connexions with Iran, but is found only in upper Mesopotamia, where it was absorbed by the MALAF tradition c5000 BC.

sambaquí The term used for shell middens along the Brazilian coast. The oldest debris was left by non-agricultural peoples who used no pottery and who made artifacts of chipped and polished stone. The middens are of widely differing ages, from the 6th millennium BC until the centuries before the European conquest.

Samian Ware or **Terra Sigillata** A distinctive pottery ware produced mainly in south and central Gaul and the Moselle valley in the first three centuries AD. It was copied from Italian ARRETINE WARE and was itself widely imitated. It is a red ware with a bright glossy surface, plain or elaborately decorated by means of moulds. Its second name derives from the stamp with which the potter frequently added his name to his products. The shapes clearly betray metal prototypes, for which they were indeed merely cheap substitutes. Its archaeological value arises from its commonness on sites of this period, and its closely studied variability. For dating purposes it is often superior to coins.

San Agustín A locality in the south Colombian Andes where tombs, anthropomorphic statues and stone-built temples are unusually numerous. Several stages of development are represented. The oldest remains go back to c6 BC and the most recent are of late pre-conquest date.

Sandia Cave (New Mexico, USA) The type site for a kind of tanged and unfluted projectile point with a shoulder on one edge only [47c]. Sandia points were stratified below FOLSOM points, but the radiocarbon dates of pre-20,000 BC are usually discounted, and the true date probably falls somewhere in the range 12–8000 BC, overlapping with CLOVIS. Associated fauna included bison, mammoth and mastodon.

Sangoan A central African PALAEOLITHIC industry which may have developed from a late ACHEULIAN basis, and which was roughly contemporary with the MOUSTERIAN of Europe. New kinds of implement include picks and a variety of wood-working tools. ◊ KALAMBO FALLS

San Lorenzo Tenochtitlan A complex of three CEREMONIAL CENTRES in southern Veracruz, Mexico, where excavations in 1966–8 revealed a long PRE-CLASSIC sequence providing much new data on OLMEC origins. According to preliminary reports, the first phase of occupation (Ojochi, c1500–1350 BC) left no architectural traces, but during the next period (Bajío, 1350–1250) a start was made on the artificial plateau with lateral ridges which forms the basis of most subsequent structures. The Chicharras phase (1250–1150) foreshadows true Olmec in its pottery, figurines, and perhaps also in stonecarving. The San Lorenzo phase (1150–900) marks the Olmec climax at the site, whose layout now resembles that of LA VENTA. Around 900 the stone monuments were mutilated and buried, possibly by newcomers responsible for the Nacaste phase (900–750). After a short hiatus the site was reoccupied by a group whose culture still shows late Olmec affinities (Palangana phase, 600–400 BC), but was again abandoned until AD 900 when it was settled by early POST-CLASSIC (Villa Alta) people who used PLUMBATE and FINE ORANGE pottery.

Sanskrit The language of the ARYANS of India, still in use for religious purposes. It is an INDO-EUROPEAN tongue related to Greek and Latin, as was recognized by Sir William Jones in 1786.

Santa Isabel Iztapan (Valley of Mexico) In the 1950s two sites were discovered where early hunters had killed and butchered mammoths. With one skeleton were found scrapers, knives and blades of flint and obsidian, as well as a stemmed projectile point of flint. A radiocarbon date on the sediment in which this material lay gave the figure 7050 ± 250 BC. The second mammoth site yielded a chert knife, a leaf-shaped point of flint and a lanceolate point with a flat base. Similar kill sites were found at San Bartolo Atepehuacan, on the outskirts of Mexico City, with a date of 7710 ± 400 BC, and at TEPEXPAN. All these sites were within the Upper Becerra formation which is geologically dated c9000–7000 BC.

Santa Lucia or **Sv. Lucia** An inhumation and cremation cemetery near Ljubljana in Yugoslavia. More than 6,000 graves were studied, dating to C9–C2 BC. Their contents showed extensive trade with north Italy and central Europe.

Santa María A culture which developed in northwest Argentina in the centuries after AD 1000. Characteristic are burial urns with polychrome geometric patterns incorporating stylized faces with the brows modelled in relief.

Saqqara ◇ SAKKARA

sarcophagus A container of stone or terracotta for a human corpse.

Sargon Sharru-kin rose from a humble position to found the empire of AKKAD in Mesopotamia c2370 BC. History and legend are difficult to separate, but his conquests seem to have extended from

western Persia to the Mediterranean and the Taurus Mountains.

The name reappears in the king-lists of ASSYRIA, Sargon I in C19, Sargon II 721–705. The latter spent his active career suppressing the revolts which at remarkably-frequent intervals threatened the stability of the Assyrian empire. It was he who founded the city at KHORSABAD, with his palace within it.

sarsens Sandstone blocks found on the chalk downs of Wiltshire. The sarsens are the remnants of a cap of Tertiary sandstone which once covered the area. They were employed by the builders of STONE-HENGE, AVEBURY and several MEGA-LITHIC CHAMBER TOMBS.

Sassanians The Persian dynasty which overthrew the PARTHIAN empire in AD 224 and ruled in its stead until conquered by Islam in 651.

sati or **suttee** The rite recorded from India of a widow taking her own life in order to accompany her deceased husband into the afterlife. The practice is often suggested when a male and female skeleton are found in the same grave, but even when re-opening of the tomb for a later burial can be excluded, many other explanations of the circumstances are possible.

satrapy One of the administrative units of the ACHAEMENID empire, eg Ionia, Media, Bactria.

Sauveterrian An Early MESOLITHIC culture of France and neighbouring parts of Europe. It is characterized by the lack of wood-working tools and by an abundance of geometric MICROLITHS. ◇TARDENOI-SIAN

Saxons One of the Germanic peoples known collectively as ANGLO-SAXONS who took part in the settlement of England in C5 AD after the breakdown of Roman rule. Their original home was on the North Sea coast north of the Elbe. The present Saxony in central Germany was called after an offshoot of the same people. In England their name has survived in

Wessex, Sussex, Middlesex and Essex. Essex soon absorbed Middlesex before itself passing under the control of Mercia. Sussex too disappeared early. WESSEX had a more distinguished history, culminating in the unification of England under its royal house C AD 900.

Saxon Shore A system for defending the coasts of southeast England against raiding ANGLO-SAXONS was begun by Carausius and Allectus AD 287-96 and was later constituted a separate command under the Count of the Saxon Shore. It consisted of a series of forts at strategic sites from the Wash to the Solent, usually at the mouth of estuaries which served as harbours for attached naval units. Burgh Castle near Yarmouth, RICHBOROUGH in Kent and PORCHESTER near Portsmouth are the best preserved of these forts.

scarab The dung beetle, held sacred by the ancient Egyptians as a symbol of the motive power of the sun, which was equated with the beetle's ball of dung. It figured frequently in jewellery and other art forms but is best known as the standard form of Egyptian stamp seals from the Middle Kingdom on [165]. These are made of stone or FAIENCE in the shape of a beetle

Fig. 165. Scarab

resting on a flat base, the underside of which is carved with a distinguishing inscription in HIEROGLYPHS. Scarabs were perforated lengthwise and were worn round the neck or as a finger ring, serving as amulet as well as seal. They have been extensively forged for the antique market.

Scarlet Ware A pottery ware found in the Early Dynastic period of Mesopotamia, more especially in the Diyala valley and southwest Iran, c2900-2370 BC. It was derived from JEMDET NASR Ware. Geometrical designs in black on buff, separated by large areas of red paint [166], became progressively more elaborate, in later stages including animal and human figures in red outlined in black. There are hints

Fig. 166. Scarlet Ware jar

of connexions with the wares of BALU-CHISTAN, especially in the elongated bulls.

sceatta A silver coin struck when the Anglo-Saxons reintroduced currency into England in C7. The earliest identifiable ones are of Eorpwald of East Anglia (625-7) and Penda of Mercia (625-54). Our penny may owe its name to the latter. With this change of name it remained the standard coin from the reforms of Offa of Mercia (757-96) until C12.

Schliemann, Heinrich (1822-90) At the age of 41, Schliemann retired from commerce, which had brought him from poverty to wealth, in order to devote his efforts to an ambition he had long held, to identify Homer's TROY. In four campaigns, 1871-3, 1879, 1882-3, and 1889-90, the last two with Dörpfeld as assistant, he did far more than this – he discovered on the site overlooking the Dardanelles nine superimposed cities covering a long and unsuspected prehistoric development and containing a startling wealth of material. He was the first to recognize STRATI-GRAPHY in a Near Eastern TELL, he aroused world-wide interest in the capabilities of the archaeological method, and he set standards of careful observation, record and rapid publication which are not always followed today. His barely controlled enthusiasm and acceptance of the literal truth of the classical writers, which led him to some serious errors of interpretation, do not seriously undermine his reputation for brilliant work when compared with other archaeologists of his time.

As if Troy were not enough, in 1874–6 he dug at MYCENAE, where his discovery of the shaft graves and their implications was as important as his work at Troy. They revealed the wealth and civilization of the Aegean Bronze Age, and gave added support to the reliability of the classical legends. More details were added at Orchomenos in Boeotia in 1880 and TIRYNS 1884–5. He postulated an antecedent culture to explain Mycenaean Greece and would have revealed this too by digging at KNOSSOS if the landowner's price had not been too high for his business training to accept.

Scilly-Tramore tomb ◇ ENTRANCE GRAVE

Scoglio del Tonno ◇ TARANTO

scramasax The single-edged knife often accompanying male Anglo-Saxon burials. It apparently served as general purpose knife or dagger as need arose.

scraper An artifact of chipped stone or

Fig. 167. End scraper on blade

flint, with a convex or concave working edge. Most scrapers were probably used in wood-working or for scraping hides. An end scraper or grattoir [167] is normally made on the tip of a BLADE, whereas a side scraper or RACLOIR [124] is usually on the longest edge of a FLAKE.

scratched decoration A pottery decoration in which lines are drawn with a hard point, probably of flint, on a burnished surface after the pot has been baked. A thin but characteristically ragged line results, due to spalls of brittle pot surface flying off. This was doubtless considered an advantage as it provided an excellent key for the inlay of ochre or plaster which is usually found in these lines. The technique recurs widely, notably in the Neolithic of Italy (MATERA and LAGOZZA) and France (CHASSEY).

Scyths or **Scythians** The nomadic peoples who displaced the CIMMERIANS from the Eurasian steppes in C8 BC, more strictly those living west of the Volga and north of the Black Sea. These, the Royal Scyths,

Fig. 168. The Kostromskaya stag

came in close contact with the Greeks through the latter's colonies on the Black Sea coast. Rich trade sprang up, grain from the areas under Scythian control being exchanged for luxury goods, which turn up in the barrows of the chiefs. Herodotus, who visited the area c450 BC, has left us much useful information on their customs. Their greatest contribution was their art, the bold and rhythmic animal style of the STEPPES [168]. Its influence may be seen in the developing CELTIC ART of Europe and that of LURISTAN and neighbouring areas of Iran. Contact was not necessarily peaceful since both these areas suffered Scythian raids. The western branch of the Scyths was absorbed by the Sarmatians and finally disappeared under the Gothic invasions of C3 AD.

In central Asia the influence of Greece was replaced by that of ACHAEMENID Persia, further east still by that of China. Our knowledge of this area is particularly detailed because of the preservation of the contents of the PAZYRYK tombs. Here already the process of displacement of the Caucasoid by the Mongoloid physical type had begun, which was to close the story of the Scyths in this area.

seal A small object, made of any hard substance, bearing a device in INTAGLIO which can be transferred to soft clay or wax. The usual purposes were to mark ownership or authenticity. Their social significance is therefore great, quite apart from any artistic, iconographic or inscriptional evidence their designs may give [169]. There are two main types, the stamp

Sea Peoples ⬦ **Peoples of the Sea**
Secondary Neolithic ⬦ WINDMILL HILL CULTURE

secondary retouch or **secondary flaking** The trimming which gives a chipped stone tool its final shape after the primary flaking has produced a blank (BLADE, FLAKE or CORE) of roughly the required form.

Secondary Series ⬦ CALENDAR

section A vertical exposure of archaeological deposits to reveal their STRATIGRAPHY. Also a drawing of such a face.

segmented cist A CIST or burial chamber divided into compartments by jambs projecting from the walls, or by sill stones (SEPTAL SLABS) set transversely on edge across the floor.

Seine-Oise-Marne (SOM) culture The final Neolithic–Copper Age culture of the Paris basin (c 2400–1600 BC) best known for its MEGALITHIC tombs of GALLERY GRAVE type with a PORT-HOLE SLAB separating the entrance chamber from the funerary area. In the chalk country of the Marne rock-cut tombs were made to a similar plan, and some examples have

Fig. 169. Types of cylinder and stamp seals: (a) Sumerian cylinder seal and impression; (b) Egyptian scarab and impression (other animal forms are called theriomorphic seals); (c) Indus seal; (d) compartmented; (e) button seal; (f) bead seal; (g) prismatic; (h) signet type; (i) amygdaloid; (j) ring seal; (k) lentoid (i-k are Mycenaean examples)

seal and the cylinder seal. The first can have a very wide range of shapes, and gives single impressions. The second, characteristic of ancient Mesopotamia, is rolled across the surface to yield a frieze of repeat designs. Some more important forms of seal are illustrated.

hafted axes or schematized 'goddess' figures carved on their walls [55]. Native artifacts include transverse arrows, ANTLER SLEEVES and rough, plain flat-based pots of cylinder and bucket shapes. Trade brought copper, CALLAÏS and GRAND PRESSIGNY flint to the region. The culture seems to have a composite origin, and certain elements of the assemblage occur in other – perhaps unrelated – cultures outside the SOM area proper. The SOM type of megalithic tomb is found from Brittany to Belgium, Westphalia and Sweden, while similar crude pottery occurs in Brittany, west France (by 2600 BC) Switzerland (HORGEN) and Denmark.

Semites Like INDO-EUROPEANS, a name to be applied solely to the speakers of a group of related languages. They cannot be distinguished racially from, for example, the early Mediterranean stock, who were also short, dark and long-headed. Semitic languages are characterized by the importance of the consonants, usually three forming the root of each word. Indeed the vowels are omitted altogether in a number of the scripts.

The Semites are first recorded on the steppe margins of the Arabian desert, encroaching upon the Sumerians to form the kingdom of AKKAD c2400 BC. The AMORITES appear c2000 in the same area and in Syria–Palestine, where they settled to become the CANAANITES. The KHABIRU (Hebrews) appear in the same context. In C12 the Amorites were followed by the ARAMAEANS, particularly in inland Syria. The PHOENICIANS from C9 BC on carried their Semitic language over much of the Mediterranean, an area conquered in C7–C8 AD by the Arabs. Arabic and Hebrew are the most important surviving Semitic languages.

Sennacherib King of ASSYRIA 704–681. His military successes served only to hold together what had already been won. Pestilence prevented his attack on Egypt, which remained free until the reign of his son Esarhaddon. In 689 he conquered and devastated BABYLON. On the constructive side, he greatly enlarged NINEVEH, where he had a new palace built.

septal slab A stone slab set up on edge across a burial chamber to divide it into compartments (eg in a COURT CAIRN).

sequence dating A technique for relative dating devised by PETRIE for dealing with Egyptian PREDYNASTIC cemeteries. By study of TYPOLOGY the changing forms of certain artifacts, such as the degeneration of the wavy-ledge handles, could be set into sequence. Correlation of several such typologies gave a sequence of burials to which Petrie assigned numbers from 30 to 100 (1 to 30 were wisely left to allow for subsequent discovery of earlier phases). Any tomb group could then be typologically equated with a numbered one, and so fixed in the sequence relative to all others. The system was little applied elsewhere because it required rather special conditions, with many closed ASSOCIATIONS containing specimens from several typological sequences.

seriation Once the variations in a particular object have been classified by TYPOLOGY, it can often be shown that they fall into a developmental series, sometimes in a single line, sometimes in branching lines more as in a family tree. Outside evidence, such as dating of two or more stages in the development, may be needed to determine which is the first and which the last member of the series.

series In American terminology, this is a broad unit of classification embracing a number of related CULTURES or pottery styles. A series has both duration in time, when one culture or style develops into another (◊ TRADITION), and extent in space (the area occupied by the various cultures or styles making up the series).

Serra d'Alto A hill 2 miles north of MATERA in southern Italy. On it Rellini in 1919 found Neolithic hut villages yielding a distinctive painted pottery now called after this site. Geometric designs making much use of diagonal meanders and solid triangles are painted in black or purple-brown on a buff surface [170]. A frequent motif, particularly in a later phase, is a zig-zag line between parallels, the *linea a tremolo marginata*. Jars and handled cups are the standard forms. The handles are note-worthy too. They are horizontal, tubular, either with more or less zoomorphic additions on the top, or with remarkable

Fig. 170. Serra d'Alto cup

convolutions of the clay, a trick found also in vertically pierced lug handles. In the later phase a thin and markedly splayed trumpet lug was adopted from the Diana Ware of LIPARI.

sese (pl sesi) The name given to the Bronze Age tombs on the Mediterranean island of Pantelleria, between Sicily and Tunisia. The sesi are stone cairns containing from one to 11 burial chambers, each of which consists of a cell roofed by CORBELLING and approached by an entrance passage.

Sesklo A Neolithic settlement site near Volos in Thessaly. It has given its name to a pottery ware known over much of continental Greece in the Middle Neo-lithic, 5th millennium BC. Its most dis-tinctive feature is a fine white slip painted in red with geometric designs, often giving zigzag patterns. The pre-Sesklo which it succeeds is a local branch of the widespread STARČEVO culture.

Set With his consort Sekhet, the ancient Egyptian god of evil, opposed to the trinity of OSIRIS, ISIS and HORUS. He was represented as an animal-headed man.

Seti or **Sethos** Pharaoh of Egypt at the beginning of the 19th dynasty, 1304–1291 BC. He strengthened Egypt's defences by successful campaigns in Palestine and Syria.

Severn-Cotswold tomb A kind of MEGALITHIC CHAMBER TOMB found in southern Britain on either side of the

Bristol Channel. These monuments fall within the GALLERY GRAVE tradition, and consist of long trapeze-shaped mounds, one end of which has a cusp-shaped fore-court from which opens a rectangular burial chamber. In the finest tombs the funerary area is a long gallery with up to three pairs of side chambers opening from it. In other examples the courtyard leads only to a false entrance while the burial chambers open laterally onto the side of the mound. The Severn-Cotswold tombs were built early in the NEOLITHIC period, and there is a radiocarbon date of 2820 ± 130 BC from Waylands Smithy, Berkshire. The WEST KENNET tomb (2570 ± 150) [209] was constructed at much the same time as the nearby CAUSEWAYED CAMP at WINDMILL HILL. Many of the Severn-Cotswold tombs remained open through-out the whole of the Neolithic. In plan, these graves show a general similarity to the French TRANSEPTED GALLERY GRAVES around the mouth of the river Loire.

shadow mark ◊ AIR PHOTOGRAPHY

shaft-and-chamber tomb A tomb in which the burials are laid in a side chamber opening from the bottom of a pit.

shaft grave A tomb in which the burials are made at the bottom of a deep narrow pit. Shaft graves occur in various parts of the world and are not all of the same date. The most famous examples are the richly furnished tombs at MYCENAE.

shaft-hole The perforation running through an implement or weapon to take the haft [20.3]. Contrast a SOCKET, which is open at one end only.

Shahi Tump A small TELL in western BALUCHISTAN where Sir Aurel STEIN found a small inhumation cemetery cut into a settlement of the KULLI culture. Its rich contents included fine grey ware bowls with swastika motifs in soft black paint, and rich copper work. A shaft-hole axe and five compartmented stamp seals [169d] were noteworthy. It probably represents the invaders from the northwest who afflicted this area in the early 2nd millennium BC.

Shalmaneser Five kings of ASSYRIA bore this name. The first (1274–45) extended Assyrian power over URARTU and the HURRI as far as Carchemish. The second, fourth and fifth were comparatively unimportant figures. Shalmaneser III (858–24), son of ASHURNASIRPAL II, spent most of his reign in military campaigns as far as Palestine, the Persian Gulf, Urartu and Cilicia, but these were raids rather than permanent conquests. They are graphically recorded on the Black Obelisk found by LAYARD at NIMRUD (where the royal arsenal, 'Fort Shalmaneser', has recently been excavated) and on the bronze gates discovered at Balawat, another of Shalmaneser's palaces, by Layard's successor Rassam.

Shang or **Yin** The first Chinese dynasty of which we have archaeological confirmation. It replaced the HSIA in c1500 BC and was overthrown by the CHOU in 1027 BC. Though the equipment of the common people had changed hardly at all from the

Fig. 171. Bronze hu with t'ao t'ieh mask

Neolithic, particularly of the LUNG SHAN culture, the Shang dynasty belongs technically to the advanced Bronze Age. That metal was used for tools (socketed axes,

knives, etc), weapons (halberds, spears and arrowheads) and most notably for a brilliant series of highly ornamented and artistic ritual vessels [171]. These are magnificently decorated with a wide range of motifs, such as the T'AO T'IEH mask, k'uei DRAGON, cicada, and a running meander pattern. Similar designs appear on the carved jade and marble and, more rarely, on a fine white pottery. Coarser grey wares, now wheel-made and occasionally glazed, clearly derive from the preceding Neolithic pottery and several of the bronze vessel shapes have a similar ancestry, notably the LI and TING tripods.

The period's claim to rank as a civilization is supported by the size and complexity of its cities and its use of writing. Two of its capitals have been identified, at CHENG CHOU and ANYANG, both in Honan province near the middle Yellow River. It is to a large extent from these, and even more from their rich cemeteries, that our evidence comes. Building was mainly in timber on rammed earth foundations. City walls were also of rammed earth. Burial was by inhumation in pit graves with the skeletons extended, some face down. The royal tombs at Anyang were particularly rich. Human and animal sacrifices accompanied both important buildings and burials. The pictographic writing appears as occasional inscriptions on the bronzes, much more commonly on the ORACLE BONES recovered in enormous numbers. These provide many useful correlations with the historical traditions. The Shang dynasty is in a very real sense the beginning of Chinese history and civilization. If it owes anything to formative influences from outside, these must have been slight and rapidly absorbed.

Shanidar A cave in the Zagros mountains of Iraq with a long cultural sequence. At the base was a MOUSTERIAN deposit with several NEANDERTHAL burials, including that of an arthritic and one-armed cripple some forty years old. The Mousterian was followed by a BLADE industry of Upper PALAEOLITHIC type (the Baradostian), then, after a hiatus, by the ZARZIAN, a Late Palaeolithic industry with many small tools and some true MICROLITHS. The microlithic element became more marked in the upper levels, and by the 9th millennium BC there is evidence for a shift away from hunting and towards the gathering of wild plant foods. The nearby, and contemporary, settlement of ZAWI CHEMI SHANIDAR yielded bones of domesticated sheep, together with flint sickles and with grain-rubbers for processing seeds, and from this stage it was only a short step to a fully NEOLITHIC way of life.

shawabti A statuette buried with the dead in ancient Egypt in order that it might perform any duties required of the deceased in the hereafter. Made in wood, stone, terracotta or faience, such statuettes were placed in the tombs often in large numbers. The name is thought to come from the *shawab* or Persea tree. Later it altered to **ushabti**, 'answerer', from the purpose they were to serve. They have been extensively forged for the antique market.

Shechem (mod **Balatah**) A site just outside modern Nablus in central Palestine dug by the Germans between 1913 and 1934, and currently by the Americans. Its most important period of occupation was in the Middle Bronze Age CC17 BC, when it was given a great insloping wall of CYCLOPEAN MASONRY 6 ft thick and still standing over 30 ft high. To the same period belongs a stone plaque bearing one of the earliest known alphabetic inscriptions. The site was replaced by Nablus (Neapolis) 2 miles away in AD 67.

sheep Three wild species enter into the ancestry of the modern sheep. The mouflon (*Ovis orientalis*) of Syria, Turkey and Iraq, was the first food animal to be tamed. The age distribution of the bones from ZAWI CHEMI SHANIDAR shows that the stock

was under domestication there C9000 BC. The urial (*O. vignei*) lived further east, between the Caspian and Tibet. Its bones have been identified at ANAU C4000 BC, and it was introduced into Europe in the Neolithic. Most modern breeds descend from it. The argali (*O. ammon*) of central Asia has been of little importance except in its homeland. In practice, the bones of sheep and GOATS from archaeological sites have to be lumped together as only a few of them, notably the horn cores, are firmly diagnostic.

shell Many varieties of shell were employed in antiquity, quite apart from the use of their contents as food (◊ KITCHEN MIDDEN). Heavy ones of the oyster type (*Tridacna*) and conch could be used for tools where suitable stone was unobtainable. From large shells like the SPONDYLUS and mother-of-pearl were cut bangles, beads and plates for decorative inlays. In a rather different category is the shell of the ostrich egg, much used for beads. Smaller sea-shells, both bivalve and spiral-shelled, have been perforated and strung for necklaces since at least the Upper Palaeolithic. Fossil shell was also employed, especially *Dentalium*, which is found in long bead-shaped pieces. Shell was traded widely to areas where it was not locally available. ◊ MOLLUSCS

sherd or **shard** A broken fragment of pottery.

shield A piece of armour carried in the hand or on the arm, usually the left, to ward off offensive weapons. Examples in bronze are the best known, a particularly fine series of the Bronze and Iron Age coming from bogs and rivers of northwest Europe, but these were probably more in the nature of parade pieces. Leather shields, surviving much less commonly, are functionally more efficient, and wooden ones are also known, notably in Mexico, where they were decorated with feather mosaic.

shoe-last adze or **celt** A long thin stone adze employed by the DANUBIAN farmers of the Early Neolithic, possibly as a hoe for cultivating their fields.

Shubad (a name now read as **Puabi**) A queen of UR c2600 BC whose tomb was discovered by WOOLLEY in the Royal Cemetery 1927-8. She lay on a wooden bier within a stone-built chamber beside that of Abargi, probably her husband. She was wearing a cloak of beads of gold, silver and precious stones, an elaborate head-dress of gold ribbons with gold and LAPIS LAZULI pendants, and large lunate gold earrings. There was also a great wealth of bowls and other vessels of gold, silver and copper, as well as pottery. In the shaft of the tomb were a wooden sledge with mosaic decoration and two oxen to draw it, an inlaid gaming board, a magnificent harp also inlaid with shell, red and blue stone, and more precious vessels. A score of other skeletons accompanied that of the queen, two women attendants beside her bier, a harpist with the harp [172], two

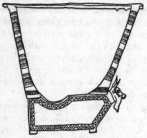

Fig. 172. Inlaid harp from Queen Shubad's tomb

grooms beside the sledge, ten ladies of the court in full finery and five guardian soldiers at the entrance, despatched to attend her into the afterlife.

Sialk, Tepe An important TELL near Kashan at the western edge of the plateau of Iran, excavated by Ghirshman 1933-4 and 1937-8. Its phases can be summarized briefly: I, dating to the 6th-5th millennia BC, a simple village of recently settled farmers who used pottery painted with basketry designs and copper only in the form of hammered ornaments; II, a village of mudbrick architecture with very fine pottery elaborately painted with stylized animals; III, the wheel and the kiln assisted the potter and much fuller use was made of copper; IV, around 3000 the site fell under the influence of SUSA and Mesopotamia, the painted ware was replaced by monochrome grey or red, a great advance is shown by the wealth of jewellery, and proto-Elamite writing was introduced. After a hiatus, cemetery A represents new people from the northeast (connexions have been traced with HISSAR) perhaps Indo-European speaking; the people of cemetery B certainly were. This contained richly painted figured pottery, bronze, iron, jewellery, etc, of the early 1st millennium.

sickle A knife for reaping corn. Flint blades mounted in a wooden or bone haft (Samson's jaw-bone of an ass was probably one such) were the earliest form, as in the NATUFIAN of Palestine. Later sickles of bronze [173], exceptionally of terracotta in

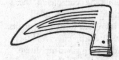

Fig. 173. British bronze socketed sickle

Sumer, are more crescentic in shape. Since the introduction of iron, the balanced sickle has become the standard form. This has a deeply curved blade bent back from the handle.

sickle gloss A distinctive shine produced on flint tools which have been used to reap cereal grasses. The polish comes from the abrasive action of silica present in the stems of both wild and cultivated cereals, and the occurrence of reaping tools with sickle gloss need not by itself imply agriculture.

Sidon (mod **Saida**) A city of the PHOENI-

CIANS on the coast of Lebanon south of Beirut. It shared the supremacy with TYRE for most of its life, but outstripped the latter in importance under the ACHAE-MENID (Persian) empire, C6–C4 BC. Little archaeological work has been done on the site as it has been continuously occupied since.

Sigillata ◊ SAMIAN WARE

Silbury Hill (5½ miles west of Marlborough, Wiltshire) The largest prehistoric man-made mound in Europe. Tunnelling has revealed that the 'hill' was built in three stages, either as one continuous operation or with only a very short interval between each phase of construction. Stage I was a round BARROW consisting of a gravel core capped by a turf layer which was revetted by a circle of stakes or hurdles interspersed with SARSEN boulders. This core was covered in turn by layers of soil and chalk rubble. Stage I has a radiocarbon date of 2145 ± 95 BC from organic material incorporated in the turf. During Stage II, the primary mound was enlarged by a thick capping of chalk taken from a ring ditch, but before this stage could be completed the plan was abandoned, the ditch filled in, and the mound increased to its present size. Today it is 130 ft high, covers 5¼ acres, and is surrounded by a silted-up ditch.

Silchester (anc **Calleva Atrebatum**) A Roman town 8 miles southwest of Reading, extensively excavated at the turn of the century. All that stands now is the impressive wall, of CI AD, enclosing about 100 acres. Within it were traced the FORUM, an inn, a church, four temples, two baths, the grid street plan, and a sprinkle of shops and houses. An amphitheatre stood outside the wall. Building was scattered and the population may have been as small as 2,500, although the town served as a cantonal capital of the Atrebates. It failed to survive the breakdown of Roman rule.

silver A metal too soft for functional use but prized for its decorative value. It is found nearly as early as COPPER and GOLD, in the form of beads, trinkets and display vessels.

Sinai The peninsula between the Gulfs of Suez and Akaba at the head of the Red Sea. From very early times it was an important source of malachite, turquoise and copper. Certain inscriptions found by Sir Flinders PETRIE associated with the copper mines are believed to be among the earliest examples of the ALPHABET. They date to the early C16 BC.

Sinanthropus (Pekin man) The name once given to the variety of HOMO ERECTUS found at CHOUKOUTIEN.

Single-Grave cultures The general name for the new intrusive cultures which appeared in north Germany and Scandinavia during the later part of the Neolithic period, c2500–2000 BC (◊ TRB CULTURE). The burial rite was inhumation of a single corpse under or within a BARROW, and sometimes laid in a pit grave or a MORTUARY HOUSE. This rite, together with use of the stone BATTLEAXE and pottery decorated with CORD ORNAMENT, links the Single-Grave cultures with the great Corded Ware-Battleaxe complex which may itself be derived from the south Russian KURGAN cultures. ◊▷ PROTRUDING FOOT BEAKER

Sinjerli A site at the foot of the Amanus mountains in southern Turkey excavated by the Germans 1888–92. It had grown slowly to importance under the HITTITES, flourishing after their downfall as the independent state of Sam'al until annexed by the Assyrians in C7 BC and then abandoned. Its fortified citadel contained two palaces, each including the architectural unit known as a HILANI. The town had a wall exactly circular in plan. The palaces and gateways were freely decorated with the reliefs and hieroglyphic inscriptions of the Syro-Hittites.

situla A bucket-shaped vessel of pottery or sheet bronze [174]. Examples of the latter from the north Italian Iron Age were particularly elaborately decorated.

Fig. 174. The Certosa situla, Bologna, c5 BC

Siwa An oasis in the Libyan desert 300 miles west of the Nile which had a renowned sanctuary and oracle of the Egyptian god AMEN.

Siyalk, Tepe ♢ SIALK

Skara Brae (Orkney) A Neolithic village excavated by CHILDE in 1928–30. Because of the lack of timber on the island, the houses and their internal furnishings were built of stone and are unusually well preserved. In its latest phase the village consisted of six or seven houses and a workshop hut, all clustered together and linked by paved alleyways. These alleys were roofed over, and the entire village became buried under a layer of refuse to make a snug, if insanitary, home. The associated pottery was of RINYO–CLACTON type.

skeletal analysis Where human bones survive they may give much information not otherwise obtainable. The physical anthropologist can to some extent determine the racial affinities of their former owner, a matter of great importance with earlier forms of man (PALAEONTOLOGY). Occasionally even the blood group (PALAEO-SEROLOGY) may be identifiable. The skeleton's sex will be shown clearly by the pelvis, with less certainty by the skull. The age at death will appear from the state of fusion of the long bone epiphyses and skull sutures, and the eruption and wear of the teeth (LONGEVITY). The bones may show signs of injury or disease (PALAEO-PATHOLOGY). All this information will be of greater value when many associated skeletons can be studied as a population rather than as individuals.

skeuomorph An object which in its shape or decoration copies the form it had when made from another material or by another technique. For example, pellets at the base of a pottery handle suggest the rivets in a metal prototype. The semicircular mark on the back of a teaspoon represents the broadening of the handle where it was soldered to the bowl when it used to be made in two pieces.

slag Partially vitrified waste material, a by-product of several industrial processes (glass-making, smelting, occasionally pottery-making), any, in fact, in which high temperatures are obtained.

slash and burn A primitive and widespread form of agriculture. FOREST CLEARANCE was carried out by chopping down all scrub and small trees, ring barking the larger ones to kill them, and firing the lot after allowing them to dry. Seed would be planted in holes poked through the ashes with a DIGGING STICK. In temperate regions it is a wasteful method since soil fertility and crop yields, though initially high, decline rapidly, after which a new stretch of forest must be cleared. Alternative terms are *Brandwirtschaft* (German), *roza* (Spanish American) and *swidden* (North American).

sleeper beam In early timber-framed buildings, Roman, Saxon and medieval, the framing was often erected not on a wall foundation but directly on a horizontal beam resting on or slightly recessed into the ground. From its recumbent position this is known as a sleeper beam. Though very rarely surviving, its wood will often leave a dark stain in the ground detectable by careful excavation.

sling A weapon consisting of two thongs attached to a pouch. By whirling this, then releasing one of the thongs, a slinger can hurl a stone from the pouch with considerable velocity and, with practice, accuracy. Except in desert areas, such as the Peruvian coast, the sling itself does not survive, and representations of it are rare. Sling-bolts or shot, of stone, terracotta or lead, often prove its presence. It is rarely found in the same cultural contexts as the bow and arrow.

slip A thin layer of fine clay over pottery. It is applied before firing by dipping the pot in a thick liquid mixture of clay and water. The object is twofold: to decorate the pot by coating the coarser body fabric with a fine clay, which is often selected to bake to a good colour, red, yellow, or black; to make it more watertight by clogging the pores of the earthenware.

slow wheel ◊ POTTER'S WHEEL

Smithfield A Late Stone Age hunting and gathering culture of southern Africa, on much the same level as that of the MESOLITHIC people of Europe or the modern Kalahari bushmen (who are probably the cultural and biological descendants of peoples of Smithfield/WILTON type). The Smithfield culture came to an end with the introduction of farming and iron-working in the early centuries AD.

snailshells ◊ MOLLUSCS

Soan A PEBBLETOOL and CHOPPER industry of the Punjab and northwest India. After a pre-Soan phase, the Soan proper begins during the second Himalayan interglacial, and its final stage, with an increase in flake tools (including some made by the LEVALLOIS TECHNIQUE) is probably contemporary with the early part of the WÜRM GLACIATION of Alpine Europe.

socket A hole made in an object to take a haft [20.7]. It is usually closed at one end, in contrast to a SHAFT-HOLE which is open at both.

soil analysis or **pedology** Given the nature of the subsoil, climate, vegetation cover and human disturbance, a predictable soil type will develop. Conversely, where

a soil is buried beneath some earthwork, the expert pedologist can describe the environmental conditions at the moment of burial. POLLEN ANALYSIS will often give useful confirmation. The soil analyst can give the archaeologist further help in interpreting particular deposits, such as the nature of a pit fill. His tools are primarily mechanical grading of particle size and certain chemical tests like PHOSPHATE ANALYSIS.

soil mark ◊ AIR PHOTOGRAPHY

solifluxion During a GLACIATION, the subsoil of the land around the margin of an ice sheet is more or less permanently frozen. In spring the top layer thaws, but the water cannot drain away because the underlying strata remain frozen. This water combines with the fragments of disintegrated rock produced by frost action, and the resultant sludge tends to flow downhill and to accumulate in the valley bottoms. This process is called solifluxion, and when it can be recognized geologically it is a valuable indicator of glacial conditions in areas which remained free of ice.

Solutrean An Upper PALAEOLITHIC industry (named after the site of Solutré, near Macon, Saône-et-Loire) which precedes the MAGDALENIAN in parts of France and Spain. After a proto-Solutrean phase, dis-

Fig. 175. Solutrean flintwork

tinguished by unifacially chipped leaf-shaped points, the Early Solutrean shows the gradual development of bifacial working. At LAUGERIE-HAUTE this stage has radiocarbon dates of 19,000–18,000 BC. The Middle phase is characterized by fine large bifacial points and by the introduction of PRESSURE FLAKING. In the Late Solutrean this technique was used to produce slim leaf-shaped projectiles and small single-shouldered points. In southeast Spain this final stage also has barbed and tanged arrowheads. [175]

SOM culture ◊ SEINE-OISE-MARNE CULTURE

sondage A deep trench, often of restricted area, to investigate the STRATIGRAPHY of a site. It may later be enlarged into an area excavation to give more evidence on the cultural levels or building phases disclosed.

Sothic cycle The ancient Egyptians noted that the heliacal rising of the Dog-star Sirius, or Sothis (ie its appearance just before the light of the sun at dawn obscured it) immediately preceded the Nile flood. It was therefore a useful check on their civil calendar which, based on a year of exactly 365 days rather than the correct 365.2422 days, lagged steadily further behind the true solar year. The cycle is strictly not of Sothis, which did not vary, but of the civil calendar. The length of this cycle was 1,460 years, to the time when the two calendars were again exactly in step, as happened according to a record of Theon of Alexandria in AD 139.

souterrain A stone-built gallery with a slab roof below ground level, usually, perhaps in its earliest stages always, associated with a settlement. Such galleries are widespread in Ireland and the highland zone of Britain, and seem, like the BROCH culture with which they are also associated, to reflect an immigration up the Atlantic seaways from western Gaul in the last centuries BC. In Cornwall they are called 'fogous' and considered locally to be refuges; in eastern Scotland they are mis-leadingly known as Pictish houses; in general they are more likely to have been storage cellars.

Southern Cult A religious cult, represented by a complex of ceremonial objects, which made its appearance throughout the southeastern United States in C14 AD. The material includes ear-spools, ceremonial axes, and discs made of shell or copper and engraved with mythological designs which recall those of the Huastec region of northeast Mexico.

spacer plate A flat bead with several perforations in the same plane intended to hold apart in regular order the threads of a multiple strand necklace [176]. Some-

Fig. 176. Multi-perforated spacer plates of amber from Greece, Germany and Wiltshire

times, as in the amber multi-perforated spacer plates of the central European and British Bronze Age, the perforations themselves are used decoratively. ◊ WESSEX CULTURE

spatula A tool, usually of bone, consisting of a broad but thin blade. Its uses are so general that they can rarely be specified in any one case, but they probably included burnishing pottery, working pelts, spooning flour, etc.

spearhead A thrusting blade mounted on a long shaft as a weapon for war or hunting. Early examples in flint were usually leaf-shaped, and hafted simply in a cleft in the spear shaft. In the Early Bronze Age, bronze dagger blades were similarly mounted, and ferrules were soon added [177]. When these came to be cast in one piece with the blade, the socketed spearhead had made its appearance. This became the standard form, with comparatively minor variations, for the rest of prehistory.

spear-thrower A device which increases the power with which a spear can be hurled [178]. The implement consists of a stick or narrow board, usually 1 to 2 ft long, with finger grips at one end. At the

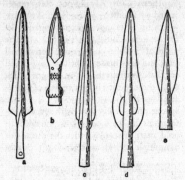

Fig. 177. British Bronze Age spearheads: (a) tanged; (b) looped; (c) basal loops; (d) lunate openings; (e) standard Late Bronze Age type

other is a hook, knob or pouch which engages with the butt of the spear. The device thus becomes an artificial extension of the thrower's arm, giving him increased leverage and range.

Fig. 178. Spearthrower in use

specchia (pl specchie) A type of Iron Age burial monument found in Apulia, southern Italy. It is normally a stone cairn containing a single crouched skeleton in a slab-built CIST with traces of an entrance passage, but the name is also given to larger cairns of uncertain function. These large specchie contain neither burials nor offerings, but traces of circular walls have been found within their cairns, and some have external staircases.

spectrographic analysis A very accurate method for quantitive analysis of small samples of various compounds. It depends on the fact that light emitted by any element on volatilization shows a characteristic pattern when split by a prism into its spectrum, as sunlight is split in a rainbow. In a compound or mixture, the elements present can be identified by the lines in the resulting spectrum, and measured by the intensity of the lines in comparison with control spectra of known composition produced under the same conditions. The small sample needed, less than 10 milligrams, makes the method particularly suitable for unexpendable archaeological material. The sample is volatilized with graphite by an electrical discharge, and the resulting light refracted onto a viewing screen or photographic plate, where its information can be recorded. The method has been used especially for metal analysis, giving useful information on technology and sources of the raw materials. Other applications are in the analysis of glass, FAIENCE, pottery, OBSIDIAN, etc.

spelt A primitive variety of WHEAT.

sphinx A statue of a lion with a man's, or more rarely a ram's, head. Originally considered by the Egyptians to represent the guardian of the Gates of Sunset, the statues were usually erected to guard tombs or temples from intruders. The ram was the sun god RA, the man the deceased PHARAOH, assimilated to the sun. The largest and most famous of the sphinxes is that of GIZA, carved from a knoll left by the quarrying of stone for the Great PYRAMID. Its features are those of the pharaoh Chephren of the 4th dynasty, C26 BC. It is 240 ft long and 66 ft high.

Human headed lions, usually female, were also portrayed by the Hittites and Greeks.

spindle whorl A circular object with a central perforation intended to act as a fly wheel on a spindle, giving momentum to its rotation. They may be of bone (rarely), stone or pottery, vary from flat discs to spherical or pyriform, and range from about 1 in to 4 ins in diameter. They provide valuable evidence for the spinning of thread, which itself rarely survives in archaeological deposits.

spinning A technical process by which fibres are twisted together to make continuous threads. Occasionally the threads, or cloth woven from them, are found in archaeological .contexts, preserved by desiccation, water-logging or metal corrosion products. Far more commonly, proof comes from the discovery of a SPINDLE WHORL or LOOM weight, though these are not essential to simple spinning and weaving. Closely related techniques are employed in making rope-work.

spiral A widely popular artistic motif, consisting of a curve of constantly increasing diameter. A double spiral is one in which two spirals are conjoined at the centre. A running spiral is a series of regularly interconnected spirals.

Spondylus gaederopus A Mediterranean sea-shell from which shell bangles were cut. It was traded for this purpose into central Europe in the Early Neolithic.

spout and bridge pot A closed vessel with two spouts connected by a strap handle [130]. One of the spouts may be replaced by a head or a figure (sometimes containing a whistle). Common on the Peruvian coast, especially in the south, and occasionally found in other parts of America.

square-mouthed pot A vessel in which the circular mouth has been pinched into a form approaching a square while the clay was still soft. It is characteristic of the north Italian Middle Neolithic, especially at ARENE CANDIDE, and has been held to demonstrate influence from the DANU-

BIAN culture of central Europe. There are scattered examples from as far afield as Crete, Sicily and Spain.

stadial There were climatic fluctuations within each GLACIATION, and the phases when temperature was lowest and ice sheets most extensive are called stadials (or stadia). They are separated by warmer INTERSTADIAL periods.

stamped decoration Ornamentation of the soft clay of a pot by repeatedly impressing a simple design previously carved on a bone or wooden tool. Sometimes a natural object, such as a bird bone, was used for this purpose.

standing stone ◊ ALIGNMENT, HENGE, MENHIR, STONE CIRCLE

Stanwick The largest earthwork fortification in Britain. The site is 6 miles north of Richmond, Yorkshire, and was excavated by Wheeler in 1951–2. It encloses about 850 acres, and had three construction phases: Phase I was a 17 acre HILLFORT of the early CI AD. This was partly demolished in Phase II (c AD 50–60) when a larger enclosure was added at the north, then (Phase III, c AD 72) a further 600 acres were enclosed on the south side. Stanwick was probably a centre of the Brigantes, an Iron Age tribe which always had a strong anti-Roman faction and was in rebellion around AD 70. In 1845 a hoard of Celtic metal objects, mainly CHARIOT gear of CI AD, was found close to the earthworks.

Star Carr An important Early (or proto-) MAGLEMOSIAN site 5 miles south of Scarborough, Yorkshire. Excavation revealed a small seasonal habitation site of which the main feature was a brushwood platform beside a lake. Because of the fine preservation, Star Carr has produced the best collection of flint, bone and wooden objects yet recovered from a British MESOLITHIC site [83]. There is a radiocarbon date of 7538 ± 350 BC.

Starčevo A Neolithic settlement site on the north bank of the Danube opposite Belgrade in Yugoslavia. It has given its name to a widespread pottery style and associated culture covering Serbia and closely related to KÖRÖS in Hungary, Maritza in Bulgaria, Criş of Romania and the pre-SESKLO in Greece. It seems to represent the earliest farming occupation of the area, although hunting and food-gathering remained important. The pottery is often coarse and rusticated, but finer fluted and channelled wares and simple painted ones are also found in later levels. A bone spatula, perhaps for scooping flour, is a distinctive type for the culture. It dates to the 6th–4th millennium, and was succeeded in Serbia by VINČA wares.

statue menhir A slab or pillar on which are carved, often very schematically, the attributes of a human figure, sometimes including details of clothing or weapons [179]. Europe has a number of local groups

Fig. 179. Statue menhir from s.w. France

which may be independent of each other and, although difficult to date, most seem to belong to the Late Neolithic period and early metal age. The main concentrations

are in south and west France, Corsica (✧ FILITOSA) and Italy where there are groups in Apulia, the extreme northwest of Tuscany, and near the Swiss and Austrian borders. North Italy also has a more recent group of statue menhirs set up by Ligurian peoples during the Iron Age.

steatite or **soapstone** A greyish or greenish stone which could be cut easily to make figurines, vessels, seals and the like. Its resistance to high temperatures made it particularly suitable for MOULD making. In the Indus Civilization seals of this material were whitened by heating with lime, a process misleadingly called glazing.

Stein, Sir Aurel A great traveller in central Asia in the 1920s and 30s, who recorded an extraordinary amount of archaeological material from Iran, BALU-CHISTAN, and areas further north. It was he, for example, who discovered the TOKHARIAN inscriptions.

Steinheim (near Stuttgart, Germany) A locality at which a human skull was discovered in gravels of MINDEL-RISS, or second INTERGLACIAL, age. No artifacts were found, but the Steinheim skull is older than any Neanderthal or HOMO SAPIENS skeleton, and is closer to the SWANSCOMBE skull than to any other specimen. Many features recall *Homo sapiens*, but the massive brow-ridges seem to presage NEANDERTHAL MAN. The Steinheim and Swanscombe skulls may belong to a distinct subspecies of *Homo*, but have also been classified as early Neanderthaloids.

stele, stela (pl stelae) A stone column or upright slab, often decorated with carvings or inscriptions.

Stentinello A Neolithic ditched village near Syracuse in Sicily. It is the type site of the Sicilian version of IMPRESSED WARE, which survives later here than elsewhere. In this, round-based dishes and necked jars bear impressed and, more distinctively, complex stamped designs and multiple excised chevrons filled with white inlay [180]. On some vessels a pair of stamped lozenges are combined with an applied knob near the lip to suggest a

Fig. 180. Impressed Ware bowl from Stentinello

human face. The time span of this ware was probably c4000–3500 BC.

Stephens, John Lloyd An American traveller and amateur archaeologist who visited the abandoned MAYA centres during the years 1839–42. His books became best-sellers and did much to arouse popular interest in what was then an almost unknown civilization, while the drawings by his colleague, Frederick Catherwood, set a new standard of scientific accuracy.

steppes The open grassland region running from eastern Europe to the heart of Asia. It is bounded on the north by forest, on the south by the Black Sea, the Caspian and the mountains of central Asia. For most of its history and prehistory it supported a population of nomadic pastoralists who from time to time spread into the settled lands around, and came to exert a profound effect on ancient history. The INDO-EUROPEANS, the SCYTHIANS, the Huns and the Mongols were four such peoples. Their nomadic movements across the steppes served also to spread cultural traits widely, from the Caucasus across the Ukraine into Europe, and from Iran through Turkestan to China. Since the nomads had no permanent settlements, they are particularly difficult to study. The rich burials from PAZYRYK for example

illustrate the wealth of material culture which has not survived elsewhere.

Stichbandkeramik ◊ STROKE-ORNA-MENTED WARE

stirrup jar A jar of medium size having in place of the central mouth a flat knob connected to the shoulder by two handles. A separate spout was added elsewhere on the shoulder. It was much used by the MY-CENAEANS for storing perfumed oil, etc.

stirrup spout A semicircular tube set vertically, like a croquet hoop, on top of a closed vessel [121]. The lower ends open into the body of the pot, and from the apex of the curve rises a single vertical spout. In side view the appearance is rather like a stirrup. Common in parts of the New World, especially in north Peru.

Stone Age The earliest technological period of human culture, when metals were unknown and tools were made of stone, wood, bone or antler (◊ PALAEO-LITHIC, MESOLITHIC, NEOLITHIC). The dates for the Stone Age vary considerably from one region to another, and some communities were still living a Stone Age life until very recent times. ◊ THREE AGE SYSTEM

stone circle In prehistoric Europe this form of ritual monument is confined to the British Isles, with two atypical examples in Brittany. The standing stones which make up the circle are widely spaced, but in many examples are incorporated into a ring-bank of smaller piled stones which is continuous except for a single entrance. Many ring-banks lacking upright stones seem to be poor relations of the more elaborate forms. A local variant is the recumbent stone circle of Aberdeenshire in which the entrance is marked by a large horizontal stone flanked by tall portal stones. A recumbent stone is also a feature of circles in southwest Ireland, but here the two tallest stones are placed diametrically opposite the horizontal stone and not on either side of it. Two of the Scottish recumbent stone circles have yielded BEAKER pottery, while URN burials in various 'standard' circles were of Bronze Age type. Circles are frequently associated with CAIRNS, MENHIRS and ALIGNMENTS.

Stonehenge (nr Amesbury, Wiltshire) This, the finest of the British HENGE monuments, is architecturally unique [181]. It stands at the centre of Salisbury Plain, surrounded by a whole complex of BAR-

Fig. 181. Central feature of Stonehenge

ROW cemeteries and ritual sites, and the many phases of reconstruction prove its continuing importance. Apart from a CURSUS, the oldest structure was a circular earthwork about 380 ft in diameter, consisting of a ditch with an inner bank broken by a single entrance. Just inside the bank was a ring of 56 pits (the AUBREY Holes), some of which contained cremations. There were further cremations in the ditch and on the inner plateau. The presence of RINYO-CLACTON pottery, together with radiocarbon dates of 1848 ± 275 BC from a cremation in one of the Aubrey Holes and 2180 ± 105 BC from near the bottom of the ditch, suggest that Stonehenge I belongs to the end of the Neolithic.

Stonehenge II no longer exists, but excavation showed that in c1700–1600 two concentric rings of sockets were dug at the centre of the site for the erection of 82 bluestones imported from the Prescelly mountains, in Pembrokeshire. To this period belongs the Avenue, two parallel banks and ditches which run from the entrance to the river Avon 2 miles away. Stonehenge II probably corresponds with the BEAKER pottery found in the ring ditch, and there is a radiocarbon date of 1620 ± 110 from the very end of this phase.

Stonehenge III: the bluestones of the previous phase were removed, and SARSEN stones, some weighing over 50 tons, were brought from the Downs 24 miles away to the north. These blocks, unlike those of any other henge or MEGALITHIC tomb, were dressed to shape before erection, and were then set up as a circle of uprights with a continuous curving lintel, enclosing a U-shaped arrangement of five TRILITHONS. An antler pick found in the erection ramp of one of the sarsens has been dated 1720 ± 150 BC. This work was carried out by the bearers of the WESSEX CULTURE, which had trading contacts with MYCENAE, and certain scholars see Mycenaean influence on the architecture of Stonehenge. The plan and overall concept are, however, purely native, and no comparable stone monuments are known anywhere outside Britain. The dagger carved on one of the sarsen uprights is no longer thought to be of Mycenaean type, and the axeheads which appear on many of the stones are certainly of local form. At a later stage the bluestones were re-erected in their present positions, duplicating the sarsen structure. There is a radiocarbon date of 1240 ± 105 BC for the early part of this final stage, and the whole of Stonehenge III probably falls within the Early Bronze Age [181].

The function of the monument is usually held to be religious, though – in spite of popular misconceptions – it had no connexion with the DRUIDS. The northeast–southwest axis may suggest some form of sun cult, while a recent study has claimed that the stone settings were used for astronomical observations in connection with the

CALENDAR, and the Aubrey holes for calculating the occurrence of eclipses.

stop-ridge A flat AXE mounted in a right-angled cleft haft is in use likely to split the haft. Transverse ridges were added to the faces of the axe to transfer some of the impact from the base of the cleft to the tips, thus obviating the danger [20.6]. Axes with stop-ridges form an intermediate step in development between the flanged axe and the PALSTAVE.

posits, burrowing by animals, etc). The law, too, gives only the order of deposition of layers; some of their contents may be of much earlier date, and accidentally incorporated from another deposit, but they cannot be later. (This point is further explained under TERMINUS ANTE QUEM.) The law still holds if one deposit cuts through, rather than overlies absolutely, the other [182]. The words 'deposit', 'layer' or 'level' must all be used in the

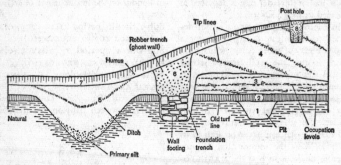

Fig. 182. Diagrammatic section of wall, with some terms illustrated. Deposits are numbered in chronological order

Strathclyde The British kingdom occupying southwest Scotland in the post-Roman period. Its capital was Dumbarton Rock on the Clyde. Its people were in frequent conflict with the Anglo-Saxons of NORTH-UMBRIA and later the Scots of DÁLRIADA. They were converted to Christianity by St Ninian and his successors from the monastery of WHITHORN.

stratigraphy One of the major tools of archaeological interpretation. The law of superposition states that, where one deposit overlies another, the upper must have accumulated later in time than the lower, which could not have been inserted beneath a layer already there. The principle was adopted from geology. In archaeology a number of provisos must be added, notably that there must have been no subsequent disturbance (slipping of de-

widest sense, to cover any solid feature in the ground. A posthole or a wall is as much a deposit as a floor or the rubbish accumulated on it – it is later than any deposit it cuts through or overlies, and it is earlier than any deposits which cover it or are banked against it.

Except on a site such as an individual grave, representing a single moment in time, stratigraphy is vital to the interpretation of an EXCAVATION. An excavator has to master the skill to recognize it – to distinguish one deposit from another by its colour, texture or contents; to understand it – to explain how each layer came to be added, whether by natural accumulation, deliberate fill or collapse of higher-standing buildings; and to record it in measured drawings of the SECTION so that other workers can follow his arguments and conclusions. In the illustrated section, the deposits are numbered in order, the oldest first, this being the order in which they were laid down.

Straubing ◊ ÚNĚTICE

striking platform The area on a CORE of flint or stone on which a blow is struck to detach a FLAKE [65] or BLADE. Part of the original platform is removed with the detached flake. The platform itself is prepared by the removal of one or more flakes, and in the latter case is described as a faceted striking platform.

strip method An excavation layout designed to investigate a large area for a modest outlay of effort. After the first long trench is dug, the spoil from a second parallel and immediately adjacent one is dumped straight back into it, and so with subsequent trenches. It has the disadvantage that no longitudinal SECTION is ever available for study, only transverse ones, and that the site can never be seen in its entirety. With the introduction of prospecting methods such as the MAGNETO-METER and RESISTIVITY SURVEY it is now little used.

Stroke-ornamented Ware Pottery with zigzag patterns made by a series of distinct jabs rather than continuous lines [183]. It

Fig. 183. Stroke-ornamented vessel

was current during the centuries after 4000 BC in Bohemia, west Poland, Bavaria and central Germany.

studded Pottery decorated by the addition of pellets of clay to its surface.

Stukeley, William (1687-1765) On the one hand, he was a distinguished antiquarian and field archaeologist, describing accurately relics of Britain's distant past. His records of STONEHENGE (1740) and AVEBURY (1743) are particularly valuable. On the other hand, his excesses of interpretation, attributing everything uncritically to the DRUIDS, give him a place of honour on the lunatic fringe of archaeology.

Sub-Atlantic period ◊ POSTGLACIAL PERIOD and ZONES, VEGETATIONAL

Sub-Boreal period ◊ POSTGLACIAL PERIOD and ZONES, VEGETATIONAL

submarine archaeology ◊ UNDER-WATER ARCHAEOLOGY

Sumer (adj Sumerian) Lower Mesopotamia, between Babylon and the head

Fig. 184. Gudea of Lagash

of the Persian Gulf. The world's first civilization arose here c 3400 BC. The main stimulus to development was probably supplied by the organization needed for a farming people to cope with the floods and droughts of the Tigris-Euphrates valley. The results included the appearance of cities (such as ERIDU, LAGASH, URUK and above all UR) with all the advantages of craft specialization they allow: administrative organization, great advances in architecture and sculpture [184], the accumulation of wealth, and above all the invention of writing, the importance of which can hardly be over-emphasized. How far these innovations were passed on to other areas like ELAM, EGYPT and the INDUS CIVILIZATION, and how far they were independently developed there, is still uncertain.

But the achievements of these people, even if confined to their immediate homeland, were enormous. The political unit was the city state, in which the patron deity, through the priesthood and temple organization, was the major power in all matters. Secular rulers were required in time of war but had little power otherwise. The various city states were united by a common culture and religion, the patron deities such as ENKI, ENLIL, NANNAR and the rest being members of a single Sumerian pantheon. Political unification, however, came only through conquest by the SEMITES of AKKAD under SARGON c2370 BC. But Sumerian culture survived this and later foreign conquests with surprisingly little change.

sun disc A decorative disc believed, unprovably, to symbolize the sun. It occurs quite frequently throughout the European Bronze Age in bronze, gold or both.

Susa A TELL on the bank of the Karkeh river in southwest Iran under excavation by the French since 1897. Its first four phases parallel more or less closely those of Mesopotamia: UBAID, URUK, JEMDET NASR and Early Dynastic. As the capital of ELAM it had a distinguished history through the 2nd millennium, and again in the first as a capital of the ACHAEMENID empire. It continued under the name of Seleucia on the Eulaeus under the Greeks, until it passed to the PARTHIANS and SASSANIANS.

Sutkagen Dor A site near the Makran coast of BALUCHISTAN representing an outlying trading post of the INDUS CIVILIZATION. It was defended by a massive stone wall enclosing an area 125 by 170 yds.

Sutton Hoo 'The richest treasure ever dug from British soil', the funeral deposit of a C7 East Anglian king, and now in the British Museum. The Sutton Hoo estate lies beside the River Deben in Suffolk, opposite the town of Woodbridge. The largest of its group of burial mounds was excavated under the direction of C. W. Phillips in 1939. It was found to cover a Saxon boat, its form preserved only by the impression left in the sand by its vanished timbers, with their iron bolts still in their original positions. The boat had been propelled by 38 oars; there was no provision for a mast. Reinvestigation of the site began in 1965.

The grave goods had been placed beneath some sort of chamber amidships. They included an iron standard and a ceremonial whetstone, both probably symbols of royalty, a gilt bronze helmet of Swedish type, a decorated shield, a sword with elaborate gold embellishments inset with garnets, a magnificent purse lid [185],

Fig. 185. Decorative devices from the purse mount, Sutton Hoo

a jewelled gold buckle and wrist-clasps, together with lesser buckles, strap ends, scabbard bosses, etc. The purse contained 37 Merovingian gold coins. Of silver were a great dish of Byzantine work, a fluted dish, a nest of nine simpler bowls, and two baptismal spoons, the only Christian elements in a very pagan context. There were many other objects of bronze, iron and wood, in varying states of preservation.

No body was apparently ever laid in

the ship; it was a cenotaph rather than a grave. The coins place it within 25 years of AD 650, though any closer dating is a matter of controversy. The memorial is most likely to have been erected in honour of either Redwald or Aethelhere. Redwald (599–625) was much the most important East Anglian king and known to have been a half-hearted Christian, but the coins are held by some to rule him out. Aethelhere (654–5) was probably pagan and died in battle in Northumbria. Whoever the treasure belonged to, it demonstrates a far higher cultural level and much wider commercial contacts than had previously been imagined for the early Saxon period in England, and parallels remarkably closely the record of ship burials preserved in the literature.

Swanscombe (Kent) A locality on the 100 ft terrace of the lower Thames valley with a succession of artifact-bearing strata of the MINDEL–RISS INTERGLACIAL period. The earliest tools, from the Lower Gravel and the Lower Loam immediately above it, are of CLACTONIAN type. The overlying strata (the Lower and Upper Middle Gravels) contained Middle ACHEULIAN HANDAXES, and the next level (the Upper Loam) also yielded Middle Acheulian tools, but of a more evolved form. The most recent stratum (the Upper Gravels) showed evidence of SOLIFLUXION. Parts of a human skull were found with the handaxes of the Upper Middle

Gravel and were for a time thought to be of HOMO SAPIENS type. Scholars who accepted this interpretation were forced to believe that *Homo sapiens* had evolved before the appearance of NEANDERTHAL man, but more recent opinion holds that the skull is non-sapiens and, like the similar and contemporary one from STEINHEIM, has closer affinities with those of Neanderthal type.

swastika A cross in which the arms are bent at a right angle in the same relative direction. It has been widely used as a decorative motif, sometimes with a symbolic value (it is supposedly a solar symbol), probably more often without.

sword A weapon of war and prestige, made of bronze or iron, characterized by a blade for slashing, thrusting or more generally both. It is distinguished from a DAGGER by its length, and from a RAPIER by its broader blade and flanged hilt. Single-edged swords are rare, and better described as sabres or falchions. The blade varies in shape somewhat, but most classifications are based on the form of the hilt and shoulders [186]. It was developed probably in Hungary and spread rapidly to the Aegean (where it is found in the shaft graves at MYCENAE c1650 BC) and the rest of Europe and western Asia. From then until the development of firearms it remained one of the main weapons of war.

syllabary A system of writing in which

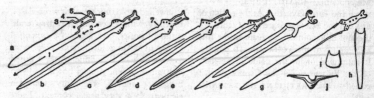

Fig. 186. Sword types: (a) Mycenaean; (b) Boiu; (c) U-type leaf-shaped; (d) V-type leaf-shaped; (e) carp's tongue; (f) antenna; (g) Hallstatt
Chapes: (h) tongue-shaped (associated with c-d); (i) purse-shaped (with e); (j) winged (with g)
Sword terms: (1) blade; (2) hilt; (3) shoulder; (4) flange; (5) rivet hole or slot for attaching hilt-plates; (6) pommel; (7) ricasso

each symbol represents a syllable, consonant + vowel. The Bronze Age Aegean LINEAR A AND B scripts were of this form, as is modern Japanese. Most languages would require about 80 symbols to cover all syllables in use.

Symbolkeramik A pottery ware current in the Spanish Copper/Early Bronze Age, as at LOS MILLARES, decorated with stylized designs, particularly the OCULUS, which would seem to have had particular significance to its makers.

T

Tairona The people living in the Sierra Nevada de Santa Marta, Colombia, when the Spaniards arrived. Their largest villages contained several hundred houses, but although Tairona culture was more advanced than that of neighbouring tribes it never achieved CLASSIC status.

talayot Found only in the islands of Majorca and Minorca, the talayot gives its name to the local Bronze and Iron Age culture which flourished C1000–300 BC. In its oldest and most simple form, a talayot is a round tower built of large stone blocks. It may be solid, or enclose a single cell roofed by CORBELLING. Sometimes there are subsidiary niches in the thickness of the wall. In other examples the roof is of flat slabs supported by a central pillar. From C850 BC square talayots were also built, and some of these have a second chamber above the one on the ground floor. Talayots are found in villages enclosed by walls of CYCLOPEAN MASONRY (◊ TAULA), and the architecture shows resemblances to contemporary structures in Sardinia and Corsica (◊ NURAGHE, TORRE).

talud-tablero The architectural principle [187] used in the construction of certain

Fig. 187. Pyramid with talud-tablero on subsidiary platform at Teotihuacán

stepped pyramids in Mexico. Each terrace consists of a vertical panel with a recessed inset, and a sloping BATTER which leads to the foot of the tier above. The technique was used primarily at TEOTIHUACÁN, and in a modified form elsewhere.

Tammuz or **Dumuzi** The consort of the Sumerian goddess ISHTAR. He figured prominently in the fertility rituals of the Sacred Marriage and on death became a god of the underworld. Recent work has cast doubt on the old view that he was a god of vegetation, being resurrected each spring with the new crop.

tang A narrow projection from the base of a tool or weapon blade to secure it to its haft (eg [177a]).

tanged point cultures A group of cultures of the POSTGLACIAL PERIOD whose tool kits include small tanged or shouldered points (◊ AHRENSBURGIAN, HAMBURGIAN). Since tanged points occur in industries both earlier and later than these, the general term is best abandoned.

Tanit The aspect of the PHOENICIANS' goddess ASTARTE under which she was worshipped at CARTHAGE. Of particular note was a precinct or *topheth* in which were buried jars containing the cremated ashes of infants sacrificed to her.

t'ao t'ieh A monster mask [188] figuring frequently in the decoration of Chinese

Fig. 188. T'ao t'ieh mask

bronzework of the SHANG and CHOU dynasties.

Tara The site is in Co. Meath, 21 miles northwest of Dublin, and was the original residence of the high kings of Ireland. The oldest monument is a decorated PASSAGE GRAVE with radiocarbon dates ranging from 2300–1920 BC, but most of the RATHS, burial mounds and enclosures are of the early historic period. There was a settlement on the site as early as C1 AD, but the development of Tara as a political capital began only in the time of Cormac Mac Airt during C3. The site was a royal capital when St Patrick visited it in c5, and was still a residence and assembly place in c6.

Tara torc A TORC made from a twisted gold bar and having everted solid terminals. Found in hoards of DOWRIS type.

Taranto A city at the head of the Ionian Sea in southern Italy. A rocky headland north of the town, the Scoglio or Punta del Tonno, was excavated in 1899 before being destroyed by an enlargement of the port. It was first occupied by a Neolithic village with SERRA D'ALTO ware. This was succeeded after an interval by one of the APENNINE CULTURE, to which c1250 BC was apparently added a colony of MYCENAEANS, who were using the fine harbour for their trade with the west. The local and foreign material of this period is exceptionally rich. Trade up the Adriatic continued after the fall of Mycenaean Greece in c12, distributing TERRAMARA bronzework from north Italy. Contact was maintained with Greece down to 706 BC, when the Greek colony of Taras replaced the native site.

Tardenoisian The MESOLITHIC culture which in southwest France succeeded the SAUVETERRIAN. Typical artifacts include trapeze-shaped chisel-ended arrowheads and small BLADES. Tardenoisian and similar industries are found from Iberia to central Europe, and span the period from the early 6th millennium BC until the arrival of the first NEOLITHIC farmers.

Tartaria A Neolithic site in Transylvania, the TORDOS level of which has produced three controversial clay tablets. They bear incised signs which some hold to be derived from the pictographic script of URUK in Mesopotamia despite the geographical and chronological difficulties.

Tartessos (bibl **Tarshish**) A semi-mythical city of the far west referred to by ancient writers, now confidently located near the mouth of the Guadalquivir valley in southwest Spain, although its physical remains have yet to be discovered. Certainly there is strong circumstantial evidence, notably the HUELVA hoard, for a people in this area trading with Sardinia, Sicily, Cyprus and the PHOENICIANS on the one hand, and with France, Brittany and Ireland on the other c700–500 BC. Their influence in Spain, on the civilized IBERIANS of the east coast and the less advanced peoples of the centre and north, was considerable.

Tarxien A site in eastern MALTA excavated by Zammit 1915–17. It proved to be a complex of four temples of the Maltese prehistoric type, now known to date c2800–1900 BC. The most notable find was the lower half of a giant statue of the corpulent goddess of these temples, some 9 ft high when complete. Into the ruins Bronze Age invaders had dug a rich cremation cemetery, dating 1900–1400 BC.

Tasian A culture named after the site of Deir Tasa in Upper Egypt, a settlement of primitive farmers. It is now regarded as at best a local variant of the BADARIAN culture.

taula A T-shaped stone structure found on the island of Minorca in villages of the TALAYOT culture. A taula may attain 12 ft in height, and consists of a horizontal block supported either by a monolithic pillar or a column made of several stones. It is often surrounded by a U-shaped enclosure wall.

Taxila Successive settlements, the Bhir Mound and Sirkap, were cities of the ACHAEMENID empire (c5–c2 BC) and of the Indo-Greeks (c1 BC–c1 AD). The irregular plan of the first contrasts with the neat grid layout of the second. They stand near Rawalpindi in northern Pakistan and were excavated by Sir John MARSHALL and, briefly, Sir Mortimer Wheeler.

Tayacian Term applied indiscriminately to a series of rather formless Lower and Middle PALAEOLITHIC FLAKE industries which lack HANDAXES and carefully retouched implements. Originally the term was coined for the industries from the lower levels at La Micoque (commune of

Tayac, near Les Eyzies, in the Dordogne), but it has subsequently been applied to industries over a wide geographical and chronological range, many of which are probably unrelated to each other. ⟡ FONTÉCHEVADE, MOUNT CARMEL

Tehuacan valley (Puebla, Mexico) A desert valley where the good preservation of plant material and other organic remains has yielded a wealth of data on all aspects of life from c9000 BC until the Spanish conquest. The earliest inhabitants were nomadic food-gatherers and hunters, but by 7000 a small part of their diet came from cultivated peppers and squashes. MAIZE was grown by c5000, pottery was first made around 2300, and settled village life may go back to the 3rd millennium, though it is not well attested before 1500 BC. From the PRE-CLASSIC PERIOD onwards the culture of the valley was overshadowed by those of the richer and more fertile areas of Mexico, but in the centuries before the conquest Tehuacan was a thriving centre of MIXTECA-PUEBLA CULTURE.

tell A mound resulting from the accumulation of debris on a long-lived settlement. Tells are normally found only in regions where buildings were of mudbrick, a material of limited life and too plentiful to be worth salvaging when it collapses. This, coupled with the accumulation of domestic refuse, can build up vast mounds a hundred or more feet high. The tells of the Middle East figure largely in archaeological writings because of the valuable stratigraphic evidence they enclose and the long periods of time they represent. The name comes from the Arabic, alternative forms being tepe (Persian) and hüyük (Turkish).

Tello, Julio César (1880–1947) was, with UHLE and KROEBER, one of the founders of Peruvian archaeology. His main contributions were the excavation of the PARACAS cemeteries and the study of CHAVÍN, but he also dug at Pachacamac,

Cajamarquilla and the burial ground of Ancon. He held at one time or another all the important administrative posts in Peruvian archaeology, and the organization of the Museums service owes much to his influence. Unfortunately Tello disliked the routine work of publication, and his writings give only an inadequate idea of his abilities.

Telloh ⟡ LAGASH

Tenochtitlán The AZTEC capital. It was built on islands and on reclaimed land in a lake which formerly occupied the centre of the Valley of Mexico. The city was destroyed by the Spaniards who built their own capital on the site, but a few remains survive underneath the present-day Mexico City.

Teotihuacán A great urban centre 25 miles north of Mexico City, it was one of the most important sites in Mexican prehistory.

The oldest pottery goes back to C1 or C2 BC, but the first important ceremonial buildings (the pyramids of the Sun and Moon, the shrines along the 'Avenue of the Dead', the 'Citadel' and the temple of QUETZALCÓATL) were built during the 2nd century of our era [187].

During the CLASSIC climax at the site (c300–650) Teotihuacán was a great city, covering about 8 square miles and laid out in a regular grid pattern of temples, squares, compounds and houses, some of them decorated with polychrome frescoes. At the height of their power, in about 600, the people of Teotihuacán controlled the central highlands of Mexico and were in contact with the principal centres of civilization in Oaxaca (MONTE ALBÁN) and the MAYA zone (eg TIKAL). KAMINAL-JUYÚ, in the Guatemalan mountains, seems to have been a Teotihuacán colony. Round about AD 650 the parent city entered a period of cultural decline which lasted until c750, when Teotihuacán was sacked and burned.

tepe Persian for TELL. For particular sites,

look up the second element, eg Tepe
HISSAR.

Tepexpan A site in the Valley of Mexico
where the burial of a woman was found in
1949. There were no grave goods and
there is some doubt about the stratigraphy,
but the skeleton was probably contemporary with fossil elephant bones in the
Upper Becerra formation. This can be
correlated with the VALDERS ADVANCE
(9000–8/7000 BC). ⟡ SANTA ISABEL
IZTAPAN

**terminus ante quem, terminus post
quem** Archaeological dating is rarely
exact, but will frequently show that something cannot be later than, or earlier than,
something else. Datable material accumulated in use on a floor by the law of
STRATIGRAPHY gives a *terminus ante quem*
for that floor, which cannot have been
inserted beneath the material after it was
deposited. Material sealed beneath a floor
gives a *terminus post quem* for that floor,
since it cannot have got there after the
floor was laid.

terp (pl terpen) Artificial mounds built by
the FRISIANS and other Germanic peoples
on the coastal plains of northern Holland
and Germany to raise their settlements
above the level of sea flooding. The earliest
go back to C3 BC; many remained in use
until the Middle Ages. Careful excavation
of sites such as Ezinge has revealed not only
the durable pottery and metalwork but
also remains of organic materials like wood
and leather, giving an exceptionally full
picture of the way of life of their inhabitants.

terracotta Literally 'cooked earth', more
accurately 'baked clay'. POTTERY for
vessels is much the most important form,
but the term is normally restricted to other
uses of the material. Terracotta was most
appropriate, and commonly used, for
small and solid functional objects like
spindle whorls, loom weights and net
sinkers. Inscribed clay tablets were often
baked to give them greater durability.

More fragile objects like figurines were
frequently made of it since they were kept
in safe places or were required to serve
only on a single brief occasion, as offerings.
Even for children's toys, the easy replace-
ability of terracotta apparently outweighed
its disadvantages. It is also found as a
structural material in hearths and kilns,
where the clay of which they were built
has been baked in use. A special variety of
it, DAUB, was produced only by accidental
burning.

terramara (pl terremare) The local name
for a mound of rich dark earth which
marks the site of a class of Bronze Age
village found between Bologna and Parma,
in the Po valley of north Italy. The deposit
represents the accumulation of rubbish
from a permanent settlement occupied for
a long period. Some sites have enclosing
banks and piles, suggesting defences
against flooding, but the elaborate recon-
structions of the early excavators are no
longer credited. The bearers of the Terramara culture migrated to Italy from the
Danubian region during the Middle
Bronze Age (mid 2nd millennium BC),
and introduced the rite of URNFIELD
burial into Italy. They were excellent
bronzeworkers whose products, including
the winged AXE [20j], violin bow FIBULA
[63a] and two-edged razor [159g], were
traded over much of Italy. The distinctive
pottery is a dark burnished ware, with concentric groove decoration, bosses and
curious horned handles. The Terramara
culture strongly influenced the APENNINE
culture in its last phase, and, according to
one theory, the two were both ancestral
to the PIANELLO urnfields of the peninsula
(c1000 BC), and through them to the
Italian Iron Age cultures.

terret A metal ring through which passed
the reins of a CHARIOT or other horse-
drawn vehicle.

tessera (adj tesselated) A small square-
sectioned block of tile, stone or glass set in
cement to form part of a MOSAIC, or

tessellated, floor. A plain tiled floor might have tesserae an inch square. Black and white stone tesserae $\frac{1}{4}$ to $\frac{1}{2}$ inch square were often used for simple patterns. More elaborate ones were produced with variously coloured glass tesserae of much smaller size for floors, walls or even ceilings, by Roman and later craftsmen.

Teutons The Germanic-speaking peoples who moved into north central Europe behind the CELTS in C2 and C1 BC. The frontier of the Roman empire for long roughly separated the two peoples, but a good deal of admixture had already taken place, as with the BELGAE, before the frontier collapsed. Archaeologically the distinction is slight; it depends more on the classical records of linguistic and social differences.

textiles Fabrics produced by spinning and weaving fibres, whether of animal or vegetable origin. Fragments may be preserved by waterlogging and tanning (EGTVED), by desiccation (in Egypt and Peru) or by corrosion of copper or bronze lying alongside. More commonly their former existence is shown by objects connected with their manufacture, such as SPINDLE WHORLS and LOOM WEIGHTS.

Thapsos A promontory, once an island, near Syracuse in Sicily. Virtually nothing remains of the Bronze Age trading village which stood on it, but the cemetery of rock-cut tombs with DROMOS entrances was excavated by Orsi in 1894. The local ware named from this site has large cups and vases, often on high tubular pedestals, some with high handles, in a grey ware bearing grooved chevrons and relief cordons, comparable to Milazzese on LIPARI. There were also numbers of imported pots, painted wheel-made jars from the MYCENAEANS of Greece and red-slipped pedestal bowls from MALTA. Bronze weapons show Mycenaean affinities too. This material is dated c1400–1200 BC.

theatre An important adjunct of most Greek and Roman towns. Its form is basically D-shaped, the stage forming the straight side, and the tiers of seats, either carved from a hillside or built up artificially, the curved one. The name amphitheatre should be used only of a circular or oval structure in which the seating completely surrounds the stage, as in the Colosseum. Most examples in Roman Britain (Caerleon, Dorchester, etc) are of the latter form, though the former is well represented at VERULAMIUM.

Thebes The city on the east bank of the Nile which was the capital of Upper Egypt and, during much of the Middle and New Kingdoms, of the whole country. Its main importance lay in its being the seat of AMEN, in those periods the chief deity. Surviving remains include the temples at Karnak and Luxor and, even more impressive, the tombs and temples of the cemeteries on the west bank, including the VALLEY OF THE KINGS and DEIR EL-BAHRI. This region has always been known as one of the richest hunting grounds for antiquities to fill the museums of the world.

There is a second city of the same name in Boeotia, central Greece. It was founded by the MYCENAEANS in the Late Bronze Age, and has remained in occupation down to today.

Thermi A village site on the Aegean island of Lesbos, the five Early Bronze Age phases of which parallel TROY I and II on the Turkish mainland nearby. It was dug by Miss Lamb in the 1930s.

thermoluminescence A technique for dating, still in the experimental stage. Flaws in the lattice of any crystal will trap α particles, produced by radiation, which on heating will be released in the form of light. The quantity of light emitted will depend on three factors – the number of flaws in the crystal, the strength of the radioactivity to which it has been exposed, and the duration of exposure. The second can be measured directly from the sample, and the first by retesting the sample after exposure to a radioactive source of known strength. These will allow the all-important third factor, the time since the crystal was last heated, to be calculated.

The mineral crystals in the clay and tempering material of pottery will have been absorbing α particles since the pottery was fired, and so are very suitable for testing. As the analysis is done on the pottery itself, there can be no danger of faulty association. Once the method is perfected, it will give a valuable check on RADIOCARBON dating for all periods of the past when pottery was in use.

Thin Orange Pottery A thin-walled orange ware [189] with a distinctive mica schist temper and a decoration of incised and dotted patterns. It was widely traded

Fig. 189. Thin Orange Pottery

in Mesoamerica during the CLASSIC period and has been found from Colima and Jalisco in northwest Mexico to KAMINALJUYÚ in Guatemala and the MAYA site of Copán in Honduras. It was present at MONTE ALBÁN (Period IIIA) and TEOTIHUACÁN (Periods II and III). Some Teotihuacán shapes were made in Thin Orange Ware, but one centre of manufacture was probably in southern Puebla.

tholos (pl tholoi) A beehive-shaped

chamber built of stone and roofed by CORBELLING. In Aegean archaeology the term was used for tombs in this form (eg the 'Treasury of Atreus' at MYCENAE), and more generally for the burial chambers of certain PASSAGE GRAVES of similar plan and construction. ⟡ NURAGHE, SESE, TALAYOT

Thomsen, Christian (1788–1865) First curator of the National Museum of Denmark, a post he held from 1816 to his death. His main contribution to prehistory was the THREE AGE SYSTEM, first devised as a method of classifying the museum collections, but soon recognized as a tool of enormous value in interpreting the prehistoric past.

Thoth The ibis-headed god of ancient Egypt, patron of scribes and learning.

Thothmes, Tutmose or **Tuthmosis** The name, in various forms, of four pharaohs of the 18th dynasty of Egypt, of whom Thothmes III was the most important. In 20 years from c1489 BC he secured Egypt's Asiatic possessions in Palestine and Syria by constant campaigning against the MITANNI.

Thrako-Cimmerians ⟡ CIMMERIANS

Three Age System The scheme for dividing PREHISTORY into a STONE AGE, BRONZE AGE and IRON AGE. It was first formulated by C. THOMSEN 1816–19 as a means of classifying the collections in the National Museum of Denmark. The ages, he argued, must have followed each other in that order as stone would not have been used if bronze were available for tools and weapons, nor bronze after the introduction of iron. The scheme became progressively elaborated by dividing the Stone Age into Old and New, the PALAEOLITHIC and NEOLITHIC. A Middle Stone Age or MESOLITHIC was later added. The further subdivisions Early, Middle and Late (of the Palaeolithic Lower, Middle and Upper) were introduced, and a COPPER AGE was inserted between New Stone and Bronze.

As a system it was vastly superior to the

undifferentiated prehistory which had gone before. The subdivisions gave progressively greater refinement; all other cultural traits could be brought into the scheme by ASSOCIATION with the major tools and weapons; STRATIGRAPHY soon gave welcome confirmation that the system was a valid one. But its drawbacks became apparent as well as its advantages. It was soon realized that the Ages were only developmental stages and gave no dates – the Old Stone Age still survived in Australia, the Neolithic in South America. Further, some areas had skipped one or more of the stages. Africa south of the Sahara had moved directly from Stone to Iron. And in any one area, as study was intensified, the difficulty of separating adjacent ages increased. The earliest copper trinkets may precede a full metal technology by centuries; and tools of flint continued to be used long after metal was introduced. The system has consequently largely outgrown its usefulness, and will doubtless be replaced as soon as some better one can be found and we can break the ingrained habit of glibly using the Three Age terminology.

Thule An ESKIMO culture distributed throughout the northern Arctic from Siberia to Greenland, and ancestral to most of the historic Eskimo cultures of that area. Radiocarbon dates suggest that the culture had already taken shape in Alaska between 500 and 1000 AD, and its latest phase in that region dates to c1300. Sometime around 900, however, some Thule groups moved eastwards to Canada and Greenland where they replaced the DORSET people. ◊ CAPE KRUSENSTERN, ONION PORTAGE

Tiahuanaco A large urban and ceremonial site high in the Bolivian Andes near Lake Titicaca. It may first have been occupied by c200 BC, but it was only during the Early Tiahuanaco, or Qeya, stage of the early centuries AD that the pattern of future development began to

emerge, with stone buildings and characteristic pottery designs [190]. To this period belong most of the temple-platforms. During the succeeding Classic Tiahuanaco

Fig. 190. Tiahuanaco pot

period a huge gateway was set up, cut from a single block of lava and decorated with the carved figure of a god wearing a halo of puma heads and geometric appendages, and holding two staves with eagle head terminals. Similar felines and birds appear on the pottery, including the KERO beakers which first come into use at this time.

Objects in Classic Tiahuanaco style occur as far south as the Atacama desert in Chile, and around AD 600 designs taken from Tiahuanaco mythology make their appearance on pottery at Chakipampa in the central highlands. Shortly afterwards the same influence can be recognized at HUARI in a style modified to suit local tastes. With the expansion of the Huari empire, this derivative Huari (formerly 'Coast Tiahuanaco') style is carried to the

Pacific where it replaces those of NASCA and MOCHICA.

Tievebulliagh ◊ AXE FACTORY

Tiglathpileser Three kings of ASSYRIA bore this name. The first (1115–1077) brought about a brief but brilliant revival of Assyrian power by conquests in Syria, URARTU and BABYLON. The second (966–935) was unimportant. Tiglathpileser III (744–727) was the real founder of the later Assyrian empire, setting up the administration needed to give some permanency to the military conquests, from Palestine to Urartu and the Persian Gulf. He also annexed Babylon outright instead of trying to control it as a puppet state.

Tikal (Petén, Guatemala) One of the most important sites in the MAYA lowlands. Beginning as a simple farming village in about 600 BC it had grown by CI AD into a CEREMONIAL CENTRE with monumental buildings and rich tombs roofed by CORBELLING. Tikal continued to develop throughout the Early CLASSIC period (C2 to C6), and before the close of this stage there is evidence for contact with the civilization of TEOTIHUACÁN. Late Classic Tikal (600–900) was the largest of all Maya sites, and is famous for its carved wooden lintels. Like the other lowland Maya centres, it was all but abandoned at the close of the Late Classic.

timber lacing A technique for strengthening a stone or earthen rampart by means of a timber framework [191]. Timber lacing was used in the second city at TROY, and

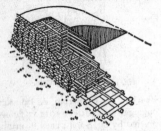

Fig. 191. Timber-laced rampart (*murus Gallicus*)

for various MINOAN and MYCENAEAN buildings. In temperate Europe its use in defence works goes back to the URNFIELD cultures of C9 and C8 BC, and it was employed at many of the great Iron Age sites of HILLFORT type in the HALLSTATT and LA TÈNE periods. One specialized form of timber-laced rampart, the *murus gallicus* or Gaulish wall, was encountered by Caesar during his campaigns against the Celtic tribes, and has its main distribution in Trans-Alpine Gaul with outliers as far away as Bavaria. The *murus gallicus* is unique in having no vertical timbers; instead it employs a series of horizontal frames made of transverse and longitudinal beams fastened with iron nails at the intersections. Each level of timbers is separated from the one above by a layer of stones or earth, and the core of the wall is normally of rubble faced with drystone masonry through which the ends of the transverse beams protrude. The destruction of a timber-laced rampart by fire can produce a VITRIFIED FORT.

tin A comparatively scarce metal of great importance as a constituent (normally about 10 per cent) of BRONZE. In the Old World ancient sources are known in Cornwall, northwest Spain and Bohemia. There were probably others in central Italy and eastern Turkey, and there may well have been lesser ones, unlocated or completely worked out before modern times. From these the metal was widely traded. Though the New World had no BRONZE AGE, some tin was used in Mexico for vessels and ornaments, and it was alloyed with copper in both Middle America and the Andean countries.

ting A tripod bowl common in pottery and bronze in early China.

tip line When rubbish, or rubble used in mound-building, is tipped out, the loose material will slip until it becomes stable by reaching its natural angle of rest [182]. The STRATIGRAPHY of such a deposit will show a number of sloping levels, or tip lines, and by studying the direction and disposition of these it is often possible to see how the deposit accumulated.

Tiryns A fortified citadel of the MY-CENAEANS 10 miles south of MYCENAE itself. It was first dug by SCHLIEMANN in 1884-5, and later by other German expeditions. The palace of its rulers, a MEGARON opening onto a porticoed court, was decorated with frescoes after the style of the MINOANS. They include, for example, one of the best surviving representations of the bull-leaping rite. Also famous is the fresco of a court lady carrying an ornamental casket. More impressive even than the palace are the walls, of CYCLOPEAN MASONRY containing CORBELLED galleries, whose construction was attributed by the ancients to the Cyclopes from Lycia. These defences were not sufficient to save the city from the destruction which overtook the Mycenaeans in the later C13 BC.

Tisza A late DANUBIAN CULTURE centred on the middle Danube region east of the river Tisza, and belonging to the early-middle 4th millennium BC. Characteristic are anthropomorphic vessels and pottery with incised basketry designs or with painting applied after firing. Copper objects make their first appearance in the area at this time. The term Tisza is extended by some writers to include the LENGYEL cultures to the north and west.

Tiszapolgár The oldest stage of the Hungarian Copper Age (3300-3100 BC). It takes its name from Tiszapolgár-Basatanya, a cemetery in the plain of eastern Hungary with 156 graves containing single inhumations accompanied by pottery and a few copper objects. The oldest graves belong to the Tiszapolgár phase, while the more recent ones are of the BODROG-KERESZTUR culture. ⟡ BADEN, TÓSZEG

Tlaloc The AZTEC Rain God [192]. He is usually depicted wearing a fringed mouth-mask or a spectacle-shaped frame round his eyes, and in this form can be recognized in the art of the people of TEOTIHUACÁN.

His roots may stretch deeper into the past, for the baby-faced monsters of the OLMEC period gradually transform themselves into classical Tlalocs. Another line of development leads from these Olmec carvings to the long-lipped god of IZAPA and eventually to the MAYA rain god, Chac, with his trunk-like appendage. Under various names (eg ZAPOTEC 'Cocijo') Tlaloc was worshipped by many of the Mexican tribes.

Tlapacoya A site in central Mexico, on the edge of the ancient Lake Chalco, with the oldest undisputed date for man in the Americas. Implements, including a SCRAPER and an obsidian BLADE, were found in strata with radiocarbon dates of about 22-20,000 BC.

Tlatilco An early-to-middle PRE-CLASSIC village on the edge of the present day Mexico City. In its earlier stages, which must reach back to 1000 BC or beyond, Tlatilco was a farming village on much the same cultural level as its neighbours in the area. Soon, however, it came under OLMEC influence. Offerings from the cemetery of more than 300 graves included both indigenous artifacts and Olmec figurines. Olmec connexions can also be recognized in the stonework. The site was abandoned around 300 BC.

Fig. 192. Sculpture of Tlaloc

Tokharian or **Tocharian** A language belonging to the INDO-EUROPEAN family discovered by Sir Aurel STEIN in manuscripts he found in Turkestan. The inscriptions date to the early centuries AD, after which the language became extinct. It may be connected with the European physical type of some of the people buried in the tombs at PAZYRYK.

Tollund A peat bog in central Jutland, Denmark, which yielded a finely preserved corpse of the pre-Roman Iron Age. Tollund Man had been hanged with a leather rope, and his body, dressed only in cap, belt and cloak, cast into the bog. Even his stomach contents were sufficiently preserved for analysis.

Toltec A people of composite origin – apparently a mixture of CHICHIMEC tribes and more advanced groups from Puebla and the Gulf Coast – which held sway over most of central Mexico from the CIO until CI2 AD. The Chichimec element seems to have entered the Valley of Mexico in about 900, and the second Toltec ruler, Topíltzin (born c935 and later identified with the god QUETZALCÓATL), founded the capital at TULA.

As the result of religious conflict, Topíltzin-Quetzalcóatl was driven from Tula and fled with his followers to the Gulf Coast. There, according to legend, he sailed away, promising to return to his people at some future time. This version of the story is probably responsible for the belief that the AZTEC ruler, Montezuma II, some six centuries later, that the Spanish invaders were the followers of Quetzalcóatl returning to Mexico.

It is possible however that the refugees moved on to Yucatan where MAYA records describe an invasion in 987 by foreigners led by Kukulcán (a translation of Quetzalcóatl into the Yucatec Mayan language). Archaeological evidence shows that at about this time a Toltec dynasty established itself at the Maya city of CHICHÉN ITZÁ and controlled the whole of Yucatan for over two centuries.

Meanwhile the central Toltecs flourished; but after a period during which their state was weakened by internal dissension

Tula was destroyed (probably by barbarian CHICHIMECS) in 1168, and Toltec refugees were dispersed all over Mexico. Archaeologically the Toltec period is marked by the introduction of metallurgy into Mexico, by the use of MAZAPAN and imported PLUMBATE wares, and by architectural innovations (discussed under TULA).

torc or **torque** A penannular neck-ring, so called (from the Latin *torquere*, to twist) because many, though by no means all, examples are made of spirally twisted gold or bronze. The type appeared in the Early Bronze Age of central Europe and continued to the Roman occupation, being particularly popular among the CELTS. [42]

Tordos or **Turdaş** A site on the Mureş river in Transylvania. Its name is coupled with that of VINČA to describe a Middle Neolithic culture covering parts of Yugoslavia, Romania and Hungary.

Torralba A Lower ACHEULIAN site some 60 miles northeast of Madrid, in the Spanish province of Soria. Torralba and the nearby site of Ambrona were places where animals (mainly elephant) had been killed and cut up. Recent excavations have uncovered a fine and representative selection of Acheulian tools, including CLEAVERS and many FLAKE tools as well as HANDAXES, and have given much information about butchering processes in the Palaeolithic. Both sites belong to the later stages of the MINDEL GLACIATION.

torre The local name for the tower-like structures built in Corsica during the Middle and Late Bronze Ages (◊ FILITOSA). The typical torre is built of CYCLOPEAN MASONRY and has a single room, sometimes with subsidiary niches or passages, but this basic plan is often modified to incorporate natural rock formations or to include extra corridors. The oldest examples belong to the late 2nd millennium BC, but the date at which they ceased to be used is still uncertain. Some show Roman reoccupation. Related monuments are found in Sardinia (◊ NURAGHE) and the Balearic islands (◊ TALAYOT).

torsade A decorative band in which two ribbons twine regularly around a row of circles. In the double torsade, three ribbons twine round two rows of circles.

tortoise core ◊ LEVALLOIS TECHNIQUE

Tószeg A TELL near Szolnok, close to the river Tisza in eastern Hungary. The succession begins with the Neolithic TISZA culture, followed by the Copper Age TISZAPOLGÁR culture, then by the Bronze Age cultures of NAGYRÉV (Tószeg A), HATVAN (Tószeg B) and FÜZESABONY (Tószeg C and D).

tournette ◊ POTTER'S WHEEL

trace elements Elements occurring naturally but in very small proportions in mineral compounds. They are often distinctive of particular deposits, and therefore allow the source of some COPPER, OBSIDIAN and FAIENCE to be identified.

trackway A communication route which is unsurfaced and does not merit the status of road (◊ HOLLOW WAY, RIDGEWAY). An exception is the group of timber trackways discovered in boggy areas of the Netherlands and southwest England. In both these areas the oldest trackways belong to the Neolithic (3rd millennium BC), but many other examples are of Bronze Age date.

tradition (American terminology) A sequence of cultures or pottery styles which develop out of each other and form a continuum in time.

trait Any element of human CULTURE, material (an object) or non-material (a practice).

tranchet A chisel-ended artifact with a sharp straight working edge produced by the removal of a flake at right angles to the main axis of the tool. The technique was used during the MESOLITHIC period for the manufacture of axes and adzes [112c], and allowed a blunted tool to be resharpened by removing another flake from across the

edge. Transverse arrowheads were used during both Mesolithic and NEOLITHIC periods in various regions. [13b]

transepted gallery grave A variant of the MEGALITHIC GALLERY GRAVE in which side chambers, or transepts, open from the main burial chamber. These tombs are found only in three areas: near the mouth of the river Loire in France, in the Bristol Channel region (◊ SEVERN-COTSWOLD TOMB, WEST KENNET) and in northwest Ireland (◊ COURT CAIRN). The three groups of tombs are in some way interrelated, and all lie on the western seaways linking Atlantic France with the British Isles.

Traprain Law A rocky hill 20 miles east of Edinburgh which was a tribal stronghold of Iron Age peoples before and after the brief Roman occupation of this area. In it was found in 1919 a silver treasure representing loot from the disintegrating Roman provinces, probably Gaul, in C4–C5 AD.

TRB culture The first Neolithic culture of northern Europe, established by 3000 BC in south Scandinavia and the north European plain. The characteristic vessel is the FUNNEL BEAKER [193]. Many regional sub-

Fig. 193. TRB pottery

groups can be recognized, and each to some extent follows its own line of development. In Denmark monuments of DYSS type were built at the end of the Early Neolithic (TRB 'C'), and at the same time a few imported copper objects show contact with the more advanced cultures of central Europe. This trade increases during the next phase, which is marked by the introduction of PASSAGE GRAVE architecture and by contact with the SINGLE-GRAVE CULTURES. In the Netherlands the HUNEBED is the local equivalent of the passage grave, while in Poland this is the period of the KUJAVISH GRAVE. The Danish Neolithic comes to an end with the development of a local metal industry around 1800–1600 BC. In the Netherlands the regional version of the Single-Grave culture (◊ PROTRUDING FOOT BEAKER) was established by c2400 and marks the end of pure TRB culture, though hybrid cultures persisted until about 1900 BC. ◊ ANLO, BARKAER

treasure trove In Britain antiquities are the property of the owner of the land on which they are found unless, in the present state of the law (reform is being urged), they have been declared treasure trove by a coroner's inquest. To be so, they must be of gold or silver, must have been lost or hidden with the intention of recovery, and by someone who is no longer traceable. In these circumstances the Crown takes possession, rewarding the finder with the market value or with the object itself if it is not required for the national collections. By way of examples, a hoard of loot (TRAPRAIN) or personal possessions containing precious metal would be treasure trove, a votive HOARD or GRAVE GOODS (SUTTON HOO) would not.

Trebenište A cemetery near Skoplje in Yugoslav Macedonia. Rich Iron Age graves contained datable Greek imports of c6 and c5 BC.

tree ring dating ◊ DENDROCHRONO-LOGY

trepanning or **trephining** The cutting of a disc of bone from the skull of a living person. There are many prehistoric records of the practice, particularly in Neolithic France and pre-Columbian Peru. The usual purpose was probably to relieve skull fractures or tumours, as today, but it survives among some primitive peoples as a drastic cure for insanity or even headache. The idea here is apparently to release a devil imprisoned inside. Healing of the bone shows that the patient frequently, though by no means always, survived the operation, but it cannot tell us if his cure was complete. It appears that in some cases it was not, since skulls have been found with as many as seven healed trepanations.

Tres Zapotes ◊ OLMEC

trilithon A structure consisting of two upright stones with a third placed like a lintel across the space between them, as at STONEHENGE. [181]

Tripolye The type site, near Kiev, of a Neolithic–Copper Age culture which formed in the western Ukraine and east Romania (◊ CUCUTENI CULTURE) in the centuries before 3000 BC. It is best known for its villages of up to 100 timber long-houses, and for fine polychrome vessels painted with curvilinear and geometric designs [194]. A few copper and gold

Fig. 194. Tripolye pot

objects were in use from the beginning. Tripolye culture came to an end with the expansion westwards of steppe cultures of KURGAN or SINGLE-GRAVE type (◊ USATOVO).

Troy The mound of Hissarlik, also known to the Greeks as Ilion, overlooks the Dardanelles in Turkey. One of the most famous sites of classical legend, it was brilliantly identified by SCHLIEMANN in 1871, who thus gave an enormous boost to interest in archaeology. In three further campaigns before his death in 1890 he showed that nine successive cities had stood on the site, of which he considered the second to be that described in Homer's *Iliad*. Dörpfeld, who continued his work 1893–4 and established a chronology for the cities, preferred the sixth. Blegen, who dug on the site 1932–8 for the University of Cincinnati, argued for the earlier part of the seventh. The choice between these two has recently been reopened.

Troy I (c3000 BC) was a small fortified citadel of about 1¼ acres. Troy II was little larger, but the MEGARON palaces and treasures of goldwork [195] found within it show that its rulers were accumulating

Fig. 195. Gold head dress from 'Priam's Treasure', Troy

wealth and power from their control of trade through and across the straits. After Troy II was sacked, the next three cities, of the full Bronze Age, showed little advance. Troy VI (1800–1300) extended to 5 acres, with elaborate walls and gates. The megaron houses were replaced by other types, and innovations include a cremation cemetery, grey MINYAN ware made on the wheel, and the horse; traits so fundamental that they point to the arrival of new people. Trade was extensive, as shown for example by the presence of imported MYCENAEAN pottery. After a serious earthquake, Troy VII continued the same tradition in poorer style. The first of its three sub-phases was sacked, perhaps by the Achaeans seeking Helen, c1260 BC, and the last fell in the upheavals which heralded the Iron Age c1100 BC. The site lay waste until it was resettled by the Greeks in 700 (Troy VIII) and on into Hellenistic and Roman times (IX), after which it was finally abandoned.

trunnion One of a pair of laterally projecting knobs on a stone or metal blade (axe, chisel, etc) to assist in its hafting. [20.10]

Tula or **Tollan** The name given in native Mexican records to the principal centre of the TOLTECS. In the older archaeological literature the site is wrongly equated with the ruins of TEOTIHUACÁN, but more recent work has identified the Toltec capital as the Tula in the state of Hidalgo. The architecture and sculpture of Tula show many new and specifically Toltec features. The buildings included colonnaded halls and a stepped pyramid on which stood a temple whose roof had been supported by stone columns carved in the shape of warriors and plumed serpents. The feathered serpent (a manifestation of the god QUETZALCÓATL) occurs again, together with eagles and jaguars, in bas reliefs on the face of the pyramid. In sculpture, the most diagnostic figures are the Chac Mools, reclining human figures holding offering dishes. The Toltec city at Tula was founded in C10, and was violently destroyed in AD 1168.

Tule Springs (Nevada, USA) A site near Las Vegas where hearths and artifacts were reported from strata containing bones of extinct PLEISTOCENE mammals. Charcoal, thought to be of human origin, gave a radiocarbon date of pre-23,000 BC and was quoted as the oldest evidence for man's colonization of the New World. Large-scale excavations carried out in 1962–3 did not confirm these conclusions. The earliest traces of human occupation at Tule Springs were dated 11,000–9,000 BC, and it was shown that the tools found by the previous excavators could be no more than 9,000 years old.

tumbaga An alloy of gold and copper much used in pre-Columbian Middle and South America.

tumulus A mound covering a burial. ◊ BARROW, CAIRN

Tumulus Bronze Age ◊ TUMULUS CULTURE

Tumulus culture A group of Middle Bronze Age cultures in most of central and east Europe, where they date from c1500–1200 BC. They are defined mainly on the basis of burial customs (inhumation, or sometimes cremation, in a CIST below a round mound), and a series of bronze types shared by most of the regional sub-cultures. Bronze objects, found in both tombs and HOARDS, are numerous and varied. Tools include PALSTAVES, tanged and winged axes, swords with flanged hilts or with grips of solid metal, daggers, spears and sickles. Typical ornaments are long pins of many forms, embossed plaques, bracelets and pendants of bronze, and rare SPACER PLATES of AMBER. The heartland of the Tumulus culture was Bavaria, Württemberg and the area previously occupied by the ÚNĚTICE culture, but distribution extended into north Germany and west as far as Alsace. The spread of KOSZIDER bronzes southeastwards carried elements of the Tumulus culture to Hungary, Romania and Yugoslavia. Cremation, originally a minority rite, became increasingly important until it predominated during the final stages, and with the introduction of URNFIELD burial the Tumulus culture and the Middle Bronze Age came to an end.

tunnel handle or **subcutaneous handle** A handle flush with the surface of the pot. It is usually produced by piercing two adjacent holes in the wall of the vessel before firing, and adding a pouch of clay inside to prevent the contents escaping.

turf line A dark stain in the earth indicating a stratum of buried turf. A turf line may be the remains of a buried land surface or of some kind of artificial structure, usually either the capping of a mound or a layer of sods put down during construction to consolidate a BARROW or rampart.

Turin Papyrus A PAPYRUS document compiled about the 19th dynasty, 1250 BC, giving a list of the pharaohs of Egypt from before the unification of the country down to the New KINGDOM. It is in a poor state of preservation. The name comes from the museum in which it is kept.

Tutankhamen A pharaoh of the late 18th dynasty of Egypt who, though little known in antiquity, came into great prominence when his tomb in the VALLEY OF THE KINGS at THEBES was found unrifled by CARTER and Lord Carnarvon in 1922. A son of Amenhotep III, he succeeded the Heretic Pharaoh AKHENATEN c1352 BC, with the name of Tutankhaten. During an undistinguished reign of 9 years he began the restoration of the worship of AMEN, changing his name accordingly. His more orthodox successors attempted to obliterate him from memory because of the taint of ATEN worship which he apparently never entirely threw off.

The tomb, though probably far poorer than those of greater pharaohs, yielded a remarkable treasure and fuller detail of the ritual of Egyptian royal burials than had ever before been discovered. The pharaoh's MUMMY, with a magnificent inlaid gold mask over the head [196], lay inside three

Fig. 196. Gold mask of Tutankhamen

cases, the innermost of pure gold weighing over a ton, the outer two of gilded wood. These were enclosed in a stone sarcophagus within successive shrines also of gilded wood, nearly filling the burial chamber. Three other rooms held chariots, furniture, statues and other possessions of the dead king. So wealthy was the tomb that it took three years to clear and preserve the contents.

The discovery deeply stirred the public imagination throughout the world, and can be said to have opened the period of public participation in archaeology.

tutulus Two meanings attach to this word. (1) A circular bronze ornament worn at the waist by women of the Danish Bronze Age, eg EGTVED. (2) A short length of ditch dug to bar the direct line of approach to the entrance of a Roman camp.

twining A technique of textile or basket weaving in which the wefts are inserted in pairs, and twine round one another as they embrace each successive warp [197]. A pair of wefts is seldom long enough to pass

Fig. 197. Twining

more than once, or at most twice, across the width of a piece of cloth (unlike the single long weft wound on a spool which is normally used in simple loom weaving). The twisting together of the paired wefts makes it impossible for a twined textile to be woven on a loom.

Two Creeks Interval An INTERSTADIAL period during the final (WISCONSIN) GLACIATION of the North American Ice Age. It lasted c10,000–9000 BC (or according to some specialists 10,300–9800) and was contemporary with the ALLERØD OSCILLATION of Europe. It came to an end with the return of the ice at the start of the VALDERS ADVANCE.

type fossil An ARTIFACT with a wide distribution in space but a restricted one in time. Its value is for correlating cultural sequences over large areas, as in CROSS-DATING. In geology, where the concept originated, the lengths of time involved are

so large that it works well. In archaeology the time taken for a type to spread by DIFFUSION must be allowed for, and if possible calculated from outside evidence.

typology The study of the shape of artifacts. It has two main purposes: firstly, classification. All examples of a given class of object, be they flint knives, axes, pottery jars or anything else, can be grouped according to their form. Such a grouping is called a type series and, once this is prepared, further examples can be described simply by reference to types already recognized. The DISTRIBUTIONS of the types in space and time can often be studied with greater advantage than can that of the whole class, the sum of the types. No fault can be found with this use of the technique except perhaps that it is necessarily subjective. Attempts to produce purely objective classifications have met so far with comparatively little success.

Secondly, comparison of different types will often show which are more closely, which more distantly, related, in exactly the same way that taxonomy classifies and relates the species, genera, etc, of the animal and vegetable kingdoms. Taking this further, the relationships between similar types can sometimes be shown not merely to classify, but also to explain, their development. This process is known as SERIATION. It may show increasing complexity or functional improvement (the development of the bronze AXE), simplification and functional or artistic decline (late Mycenaean pottery), or change for neither better nor worse (the FIBULA) subject solely to fashion. The direction of change may be shown by loss of function or different technique of manufacture (◊ SKEUOMORPH) but will usually need to be determined by other evidence: STRATIGRAPHY or independent dating of two or more members of the series. This would be essential for fixing the rate of change. This use of typology comes in for more criticism, and rightly so, whenever it is used

without corroboration from other sources.
Tyre (mod **Sur**) The chief city of the
PHOENICIANS on the coast of Lebanon
south of Beirut. It occupied a small island
off the coast, with two harbours giving
sheltered anchorage whatever the wind. It
was the parent city of CARTHAGE and
flourished until its destruction by Nebuchadnezzar in 574 BC after a long siege.
Even more famous was its siege by
Alexander the Great in 332, when it was
reduced only after a causeway had been
built out to it. Excavation has found only
the Roman and Byzantine levels.

U

Uaxactún (Guatemala) A CEREMONIAL CENTRE which has yielded a stratified and dated sequence of MAYA pottery styles, beginning with Mamom wares of the PRE-CLASSIC PERIOD. There were no buildings from this stage, but to the following one (with Chicanel pottery) belongs one of the oldest Maya structures, a stepped temple platform decorated with stucco masks reminiscent of OLMEC art. Most of the surviving structures belong to the CLASSIC Maya period (C3–C10 AD).

Ubaid The site of Al 'Ubaid is a small TELL 4 miles from UR excavated by Hall 1919 and WOOLLEY 1923–4. The mound was built up by a prehistoric settlement which has given its name to a culture current before 4000 BC through most of southern Mesopotamia, where it underlies practically every city of SUMER. Later it spread to the north, displacing the HALAF culture and so becoming the first to cover the whole of Mesopotamia. It is distinguished by a well-made buff pottery, frequently overfired to a greenish colour, and painted simply and effectively in dark brown or black [198]. In the south stone

Fig. 198. Ubaid pottery

was scarce, but terracotta models of pounders, sickles, hoes and axes demonstrate its use. In the north stone was more readily available and more generally used. The architecture of the two areas shows similar differences. Temples were built in both, as at ERIDU and GAWRA, ancestral in structure and siting to those of Sumerian times.

Above this at Al 'Ubaid were the remains of a temple with copper statues and reliefs, and mosaic friezes contemporary with the 1st dynasty of Ur c2600 BC. Bulls, cows, stags and a great lion-headed eagle were portrayed.

Ugarit (mod **Ras Shamra**) An important site just north of Latakia on the Syrian coast excavated by Schaeffer 1929–39. It had a long history from the Early Neolithic (◊ MERSIN) through the Chalcolithic (◊ HALAF) and Bronze Age, down to its destruction by the PEOPLES OF THE SEA c1200 BC. In its last three centuries it was in commercial contact with EGYPT, the HITTITES and the MYCENAEANS. The influence of the last is most clearly seen in a relief of the fertility goddess ASTARTE-ASHERAH [199]. Temples to BAAL and

Fig. 199. Mycenaean ivory relief from Ugarit

Dagon have been excavated, together with an elaborate palace containing several groups of archives on clay tablets.

These consisted of commercial and administrative documents and religious texts, all of extreme importance to our understanding of the CANAANITES since elsewhere records seem to have been kept on perishable materials and so have not survived. The script is CUNEIFORM, but adapted into an ALPHABET for the writing of the local language, related to Phoenician and Hebrew. It is the earliest alphabet of

which a full record survives, dating to
C15–C14 BC.

Uhle, Max (1856–1944) One of the greatest figures in South American archaeology.
When he made his first field trip to the
New World in 1892 several local pottery
styles had already been defined, but there
was still no chronological framework for
Andean archaeology and little idea of the
antiquity of Peruvian culture. Uhle was
the first to apply the principles of STRATI-
GRAPHY and SERIATION to Andean
material, and he carried out more field-
work in western South America than any
other scholar before or since. He visited
TIAHUANACO, dug at Pachacamac and at
several MOCHICA sites, excavated an early
CHIMÚ cemetery, worked in the valleys of
CHINCHA and Ica (where he discovered
the source of NASCA pottery, previously
known only from museum specimens), and
identified a very early pottery style
(CHAVÍN horizon in modern terminology)
in a shell-mound near Ancon. Uhle later
worked elsewhere on the coast, in the
highlands near CUZCO, and finally in
Chile and Ecuador. His publications lagged
behind his field research, but the documented material he sent back to the
University of California formed the basis
of important studies by KROEBER and by
more recent scholars who have further
refined Uhle's scheme of periods and
ceramic styles in Peru.

Ujjain One of India's sacred cities, near
Indore on the main route from the Ganges
plain to the Bombay coast. It was founded
about 500 BC, as shown by sherds of
BLACK-AND-RED and PAINTED GREY
WARES, as an outpost of the Ganges
civilization. It was a mile in diameter,
defended by a mud rampart 250 ft thick
and 40 high, inside a fosse 150 ft wide and
20 deep. Only limited excavation has been
carried out.

underwater archaeology Archaeological
material lost beneath fresh or sea water is
naturally much more difficult to recover

than material that has been buried. Until
recently few attempts were made (the
diving for Maya relics in the CENOTE at
CHICHÉN ITZÁ is a rare example), though
much material was recovered sporadically
by dredging. Since the advent of the
aqualung, allowing free movement on the
sea bed, the possibilities have been more
fully appreciated and techniques for over-
coming the difficulties are being devised.
Most work has been done on classical
shipwrecks in the Mediterranean, yielding
new evidence on sea trade, shipping and
the like. Already one prehistoric wreck, a
Mycenaean vessel off Cape GELIDONYA in
Turkey, has been investigated and work
on others may be expected. The results are
already proving to be of the highest
interest.

Únětice In the strict sense, Únětice is
the name of the Early Bronze Age culture
centred on Bohemia and Moravia, but
cultures sharing a similar metal technology,
first of copper and later of bronze, are
distributed in a bloc from Hungary to
north Germany, and through northern
Austria as far as Bavaria and Switzerland.
Characteristic metal objects [200] include
INGOT TORCS, LOCK RINGS, various pins,
flanged axes, riveted daggers and (in some
areas) the HALBERD. To the earliest phase,
c1900–1800 BC, belong the following
regional groups: Nitra (western Slovakia),
Adlerberg (mid-Rhine), Straubing (Bavaria), Marschwitz (the Oder basin) and
Unterwölbling (Austria). In the classical
Únětice, 1800–1600, bronze was in common use. Distribution extended northwards along the rivers Elbe, Saale and
Warthe where the north German variant
has great hoards of metalwork and rich
burials in MORTUARY HOUSES under
BARROWS. In late Únětice times, c1600–
1500, there is evidence of commercial
contact with the WESSEX CULTURE of
Britain and, via the AMBER route, with
southeast Europe and the civilization of the
MYCENAEANS. The Věteřov culture of

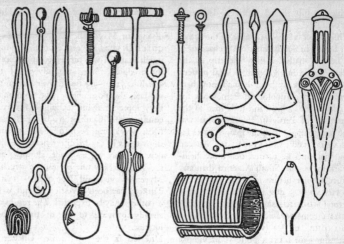

Fig. 200. Únětice bronzes

Moravia and the Maďarovče culture of Slovakia, which had links with the Mycenaean world, are sometimes considered to be sub-groups within the final Únětice tradition.

univallate Having only a single rampart.

Unterwölbling ◊ ÚNĚTICE

'Uqair, Tell A TELL 30 miles south of Baghdad excavated by the Iraqis 1940–41. In it was found a temple of the URUK phase with unexpectedly fine wall paintings.

Ur Tell Mukayyar, south of the Euphrates and 100 miles west of Basra, was discovered and identified by Taylor 1854–5. The great work on the site was done by WOOLLEY for the British Museum and the University Museum of Pennsylvania 1922–9. The earliest occupation was of the UBAID phase c4300 BC, sealed by 8 ft of river silt, claimed originally to have been deposited by Noah's FLOOD. Much more spectacular were the finds in the Royal Cemetery (◊ SHUBAD) c2800, showing a remarkably early use of the arch and dome in the building of the tombs. The wealth of precious metal and stones in them, the artistry of the animal figures, the shell, LAPIS LAZULI and carnelian mosaic inlays [201], the gold and lapis jewellery, and the gruesome evidence for the sacrifice of human attendants by the score to accompany their dead royal master or

Fig. 201. Detail from the 'Standard' of Ur

mistress, combined to bring the site fame second only to that of TUTANKHAMEN'S tomb.

Ur had another period of greatness under its 3rd dynasty, founded by Ur-Nammu c2100 BC, which saw the peak of development of SUMER of which it was at that time the capital. Ur-Nammu built the great ZIGGURAT to the moon god NANNAR, the most prominent feature of the site. After its destruction by ELAM and the

AMORITES the city recovered at least prosperity, and we have full evidence on the spacious town houses of the early 2nd millennium, one of which may have been the home of Abraham before he left Ur of the Chaldees for the west. Thereafter it declined, apart from a brief recovery in c6, to its final desertion in c4.

uraeus The royal cobra of ancient Egypt. It was worn by the PHARAOH on his brow, usually combined with one or other of the royal crowns, as a symbol of his supreme authority.

Urartu A state which flourished C9–C7 BC in the mountains of eastern Turkey. Its

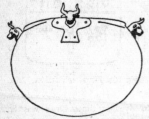

Fig. 202. Bronze cauldron from Altintepe

people, relatives of the HURRI, established themselves around Lake Van during the 2nd millennium. Their capital was at Van itself, its citadel to be entered only by a rock-cut passage. On the rock faces below were carved CUNEIFORM inscriptions which supplement the records we have from the ASSYRIANS, with whom they were usually at war. A promontory nearby, Toprakkale, held a temple which yielded most of the archaeological material.

Urartu is famous for its metalwork, particularly the great bronze cauldrons on tripod stands [202] which were traded as far afield as Etruscan Italy.

Urfirnis A characteristic ware of the Early HELLADIC II period of Greece. It has a buff fabric decorated partly or all over with a dark lustrous SLIP, often loosely called a glaze. The sauce-boat and the ASKOS are the most notable shapes.

urial A species of sheep, *Ovis vignei*, found wild in Iran, Turkestan and the Himalayas. Though apparently not domesticated until later than the MOUFLON – the first record is from ANAU c4000 BC – it replaced that species to become the ancestor of nearly all modern sheep.

urn A loose term for any pottery vessel of medium to large size and of fairly deep proportions, usually without handles. It probably served for simple storage purposes, but is most often found as a container for the ashes of a CREMATION burial, the so-called cinerary urn. [203] ⇩ JAR BURIAL

urnfield A cemetery of individual cremation graves with the ashes of the dead placed in pottery vessels, or funerary urns. Sometimes unurned cremations may also be present.

The term **urnfield cultures** is used in a special sense for a group of related European Bronze Age cultures in which the above rite was practised. The idea of urnfield burial is an ancient one in central Europe where cremation cemeteries of the early 2nd millennium BC are known in the KISAPOSTAG culture of Hungary and the

Fig. 203. British urn forms: (a) and (b) collared, (b) formerly 'overhanging' rim; (c) biconical; (d) encrusted; (e) bucket

Cîrna culture of Romania. By C13 urnfields were common in east central Europe, and from there the new rite spread north and west. It was introduced into north Italy by the TERRAMARA people in the mid-2nd millennium, and from there spread southwards through the peninsula as far as Sicily and the Lipari islands during CII to C9. From central Europe urnfield burial, with its distinctive pottery and associated bronze tools, spread westwards across the Rhine in CII. By c750 it had reached southern France, and shortly after that date urnfields appear in Catalonia, where evidence from place names suggests that the newcomers were CELTS. Over most of the region north of the Alps, urnfield cultures came to an end with the start of the HALLSTATT Iron Age in C7, while the Mediterranean lands were incorporated into the Classical world of the Greeks and Etruscans.

Uruk (bibl **Erech,** mod **Warka**) One of the greatest city-states of Sumer, 35 miles northwest of UR. It was excavated by a number of German expeditions from 1912 on.

The prehistoric culture discovered in its lower levels represents the appearance of the civilization of SUMER. There are several innovations when compared with the preceding UBAID phase. The pottery is unpainted and for the first time made on a wheel. Shapes are more developed, with spouts and handles, and often betray the influence of metal vessels. Buildings are progressively larger and more elaborate also, making much use of cone mosaic, in which terracotta cones with painted heads were pressed into the mud plaster. The best example is the White Temple, which replaced six successive earlier ones. It measured 60 ft by 70 on a 45 ft high platform. Finely carved seals, implying personal ownership, became common, the stamp

form giving place to the cylinder SEAL. Most important of all, the invention of writing, the first anywhere and perhaps ancestral to all others, shows that civilization is very close. Simplified pictures represented objects (eg a foot), associated ideas (to walk), or other words pronounced in the same way. These were drawn on soft clay tablets which were then baked [204]. They later developed into the impressed CUNEIFORM signs.

Fig. 204. Pictographic tablet, Uruk

In dynastic times Uruk was both a political power (GILGAMESH was its fifth king) and religious centre (from the supremacy of its god ANU). The archaeological remains of the temple E-anna, its archives and ZIGGURAT, are of prime importance. The city fell to the second rank after the rise of the 3rd dynasty of Ur c2100, but remained in occupation down to the PARTHIAN period (there is a fine palace of this date), a life of some 4,000 years.

Usatovo A settlement and group of KURGAN graves near Odessa, in the Ukraine. It is the type site of a copper-using culture combining elements, such as painted pottery, taken from the final TRIPOLYE culture immediately to the west, with kurgan burial appropriate to the steppe zone. The site of Mayaka has a radiocarbon date of 2390 ± 65 BC.

ushabti ◊ SHAWABTI

V

Vače A Late Bronze to Early Iron Age URNFIELD in Slovenia, Yugoslavia, in use from C9 to C4 BC. There are many imports from the VILLANOVANS and ETRUSCANS of Italy.

Valders Advance The final ice advance (or STADIUM) of the WISCONSIN GLACIATION of North America. It began c9000 BC or a little earlier, and ended 8/7000.

Valdivia A culture which flourished along the central coast of Ecuador, beginning sometime in the period 3000–2700 BC and persisting until about 1400 BC. Its pottery is one of the oldest in the New World (◊ PUERTO HORMIGA), and its resemblance to the Jōmon ware of Japan has led some scholars to believe that it was introduced into Ecuador as the result of trans-Pacific contacts.

Valley of the Kings A rocky valley cut into the western desert opposite THEBES, on the Nile in Upper Egypt. It was chosen as the royal cemetery during the New Kingdom, from 1580 BC, the tombs of the pharaohs being cut in the limestone of its walls. Each tomb had a corresponding temple on the bank of the river for the performance of the rituals necessary for the well-being of the dead king. The discovery of the undespoiled tomb of TUTANKHAMEN in 1922 revealed for the first time just how lavishly these tombs were equipped.

Vapheio cup A shape of cup first occurring in Crete in the Middle Minoan period and becoming popular among the early MYCENAEANS of Late Helladic I and II in Greece. It has straight or slightly splayed walls widening to the rim, and a single handle. It is named after the site near Sparta which produced two magnificent examples in gold, decorated with scenes of bulls.

varve dating In arctic conditions the spring thaw produces a spate in all rivers, which carry along quantities of coarse material that are later dropped in the still water of lakes or estuaries. Later in the summer the water flow decreases to that of the normal rainfall, so that only finer silt is carried and deposited. Even this ceases with the autumn freeze-up. These bands of sediment are called varves and, in any one deposit, can easily be counted to give the time span of the deposit, one varve per year. But as with tree rings (◊ DENDROCHRONOLOGY) the varves will vary from year to year, depending on the rapidity of the thaw, quantity of summer rain, winter snow, etc, the variations showing some correlation with the sun-spot cycle. By comparing the varves in different deposits, similar patterns can be found where those deposits overlapped in time. Baron de Geer in 1910 published the results for Scandinavia, giving an absolute time scale for geological events in the area going back to 10,000 BC. Its use for archaeological dating is rather limited in that sites have to be related to the geological changes (the ice-sheet moraines or changing Baltic sea-levels) before their dates can be read off.

vase support Where pottery vessels were made with round bases, the need for some support was occasionally felt. This usually took the form of a terracotta ring or a separate pedestal.

Vedas ◊ RIGVEDA

Ventana Cave (Arizona) A rock-shelter with a long STRATIGRAPHY, beginning with remains left by hunters of extinct species of horse, bison and ground sloth. After a break, the cave was reoccupied by people of DESERT CULTURE type and then by HOHOKAM folk.

Ventris, Michael An architect by profession, but trained by war service in code-breaking, he startled the archaeologists and classicists in 1952 by deciphering the

LINEAR B texts of Minoan and Mycenaean Greece and showing them to be an early form of Greek. After his death in a road accident in 1955 his work was continued by John Chadwick and others.

Venus figurines Small statuettes [205], sculptured in the round, of naked and often obese women. The figures, usually very

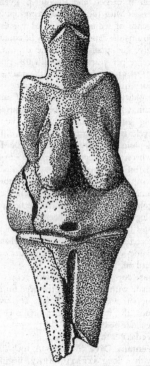

Fig. 205. Venus figurine from Dolní Věstonice

much stylized, were made of clay, stone or mammoth ivory, and have been found on Eastern GRAVETTIAN and Upper PÉRI-GORDIAN sites from the Pyrenees to east Russia.

Vértesszöllös A quarry site, thirty miles northwest of Budapest in Hungary, where hominid remains have been found in the lowest of three strata containing undisturbed occupation debris. The skull fragment was originally classified as HOMO ERECTUS, but some scholars have since considered it a primitive form of HOMO SAPIENS which they have named *Homo sapiens palaeohungaricus*. The faunal and geological evidence indicate a date during the middle-late MINDEL GLACIATION. The implements included small CHOPPERS made from pebbles, together with various FLAKE tools. HANDAXES and CLEAVERS were absent. The pebble and flake tools resemble those of Bed II at OLDUVAI and, in Europe, those of the CLACTONIAN industry belonging to the succeeding interglacial period.

Verulamium (mod **St Albans**) It was founded immediately after the Roman conquest to succeed a native settlement, was destroyed by Boudicca, and rebuilt to a larger size (200 acres), with FORUM, theatre, grid plan, and walls with monumental gates. Its periods of greatest prosperity were during C2 and C4, but it was still of some importance when it was visited by St Germanus in 429. Thereafter it faded out, to be replaced by St Albans nearby. The excavations, by Wheeler before and Frere after the Second World War, have given us fuller information on town life in Roman Britain than we have from any other site.

Veselinovo A TELL in Bulgaria which has given its name to a Middle Neolithic group in the southern Balkans. The culture marks a sharp break from the preceding STAR-ČEVO, but develops on into one of Bronze Age type. The pottery is undecorated apart from occasional cordons. It may represent an incursion from Anatolia.

Větěrov ◊ ÚNĚTICE

Vikings The 'people of the inlets', the inhabitants of Scandinavia between roughly AD 700 and 1100, when their raids terrorized the coastlands of western Europe. Their greatest achievements were in the fields of boat-building and navigation. Boats buried with their royal owners on the shores of Oslo Fjord – Tune, Gokstad and Oseberg – show that the principle of the keel was understood and exploited. Both mast and oars were provided. The efficiency of these craft is illustrated by the voyages undertaken.

Eastwards the Vikings of Sweden penetrated the rivers of Eastern Europe as traders, crossing from the Niemen to the Dniepr and so down to the Black Sea and Byzantium. Westwards the Norwegians began their raids with an attack on LIN-DISFARNE in 793, and had already begun to colonize the Scottish islands. Later, parts of the Irish coast and the Isle of Man were also occupied. Later still, at the beginning of C10, Iceland was settled, then Greenland, and even the North American coast (Vinland) was reached by Karlsefni, Leif Eriksson and others, culminating in the settlement of ANSE AU MEADOW in Newfoundland. The Danes, or Black Vikings, soon joined the Norwegians in their piratical raids, frequently based on camps established on islands like Thanet, Walcheren or Noirmoutier at the mouth of the Loire. Some raids even penetrated the Mediterranean by way of Gibraltar. In 865 raids on England for loot were succeeded by attacks for conquest and settlement, and the Great Army ultimately occupied most of eastern England from East Anglia to Northumbria, forming the Danelaw. The whole of England, though reconquered by Alfred and Edward of Wessex, finally fell to the Danes under Canute in 1016. The Normans, or Northmen, were also of Danish ancestry.

Culturally the Vikings drew on their extensive raiding and trading to produce attractive art styles based on interlaced animals. The carved woodwork of the Oseberg ship [206] and its contents provide the finest examples of this. In metalwork, as one might expect, weapons and war gear figured largely. Their literature, the

sagas, like their art, illustrates a barbaric and heroic age and people.

Vila Nova de São Pedro A fortified village site near the Tagus in Portugal. A settlement antedating the defences belongs to the PALMELLA culture, beginning c3000 BC. It included a large potter's kiln. Over this was built the 'citadel' of a township, a mere 80 ft across internally, surrounded by a 25 ft thick wall with bastions. A second and perhaps a third wall, also with semicircular bastions, ran further out, enclosing hut foundations. The defences and material contents link this settlement with Los MILLARES and a date c2500 BC. There was a still later reoccupation, at a period when BEAKERS were in general use.

villa A difficult term to define, even before the estate agents got hold of it. In Britain it describes the central buildings of a Roman country estate, usually but by no means always of some pretension, with wall plaster, HYPOCAUST heating, sometimes MOSAIC floors. It is the economic aspect which is the most important since it was primarily a working establishment. Abroad, eg Pompeii, the name is used also for any wealthy town house.

Villafranchian ◊ PLEISTOCENE

Villanovans An Iron Age people of upper Italy. They emerge as a distinct cultural group in C9 BC, occupying roughly the

Fig. 206. Prow of the Oseberg ship

modern Tuscany. Soon after, they spread through the mountains to establish an important centre at Bologna. (Villanova itself is a hamlet outside that city.) They were replaced culturally by the ETRUS-CANS in the south in C8, in the north in C6. There are problems about both their appearance and disappearance. Evidence for a foreign origin, particularly for their rich metalwork, is evenly balanced against the evidence for continuity from the local PIANELLO urnfield culture. Similarly, good cases can be made both for their being conquered by invaders, the Etrus-cans, and for them themselves becoming the Etruscans under the stimulus of foreign trade.

Little is known of their settlements, but models of huts and the distribution of the cemeteries tell us a good deal. Villages

Fig. 207. Villanovan urn and helmet lid, Tar-quinia

were large but hardly of town size. How-ever they were already industrial centres, as the $1\frac{1}{2}$ ton hoard of bronze found in Bologna shows. The craftsmen played a major part in the development of the FIBULA and the technique of sheet metal-work, especially the SITULA. The ceme-teries were urnfields, the ashes usually being contained in a storeyed urn covered with a bowl, bronze helmet or pottery copy of one [207]. Subsidiary vessels, fibulae and other ornaments, crescentic

razors [159i], etc, frequently accompanied the ashes. The pottery was handmade, dark burnished, decorated with meanders of grooved bands.

Vinča A large TELL just outside Belgrade in Yugoslavia. Its lowest level consisted of STARČEVO material. The next two, of the Middle and Late Neolithic, are called after this site but distinguished by hyphenating with others, Vinča-TORDOS and Vinča-PLOČNIK, dated by radiocarbon to c4500–4000 and 4000–3700 BC. The pottery throughout is typically dark burnished, with fluting and simple incised decoration. The site represents a settled farming com-munity but its position and contents demonstrate the importance of trade also.

Virú valley A valley on the north coast of Peru with the remains of many suc-cessive cultures. The term Virú, or Gal-linazo, is reserved for a style of pottery with black designs done in NEGATIVE PAINTING over a red background. It came into use just before the start of the Chris-tian era, and in the Chicama valley was soon superseded by MOCHICA ware. In the Virú valley it persisted longer, over-lapping in time with the early Mochica substyles elsewhere.

vitrified fort A variety of fort in which the stone rubble walls have been subjected to such heat that they have fused into a slaggy or even glassy mass. The effect was produced by the burning of their TIMBER LACING. In windy conditions great heat would be generated, leading to vitrifica-tion, a fact attackers would probably have been aware of. These forts are found par-ticularly in eastern Scotland, in the territory of the PICTS, and rather less frequently in the southwest. The scanty dating points to the early centuries AD. The Roman legions under Agricola in AD 83 may have been responsible for the destruction of many of them.

Vix (Châtillon-sur-Seine, Côte-d'Or, France) A rich Celtic burial of the Early Iron Age (HALLSTATT D period). In a

MORTUARY HOUSE under a BARROW was the body of a woman accompanied by a dismantled four-wheeled cart with bronze fittings, and by rich offerings which included a gold diadem, bronze and silver bowls, brooches, and a Greek Black Figure cup dated c520 BC. The most precious offering was a bronze crater (mixing bowl) of Greek manufacture, standing 5 ft high and with a capacity of 1,250 litres. The woman may have belonged to the ruling family of the nearby OPPIDUM of Mont Lassois, where other c6 Greek pottery has been found.

votive deposit An object or group of objects left in a sacred place, often a natural site like a cave, river, lake or peatbog. A votive deposit was an offering to the gods and, unlike other types of HOARD, was not intended to be recovered later.

V-perforation One in which two converging holes are drilled to meet below the surface. The technique was common in Europe in the Copper and Early Bronze Age, and used especially among the BEAKER folk for making buttons.

Vučedol The type site of a Slavonian culture of the Late Neolithic, lying beside the river Drave in Croatia, Yugoslavia. It is characterized above all by its pottery, excised and filled with white paste. The material is related to that from the LJUBLJANSKO BLAT and the Eastern Alps generally. Some copper was already being worked.

W

Waldalgesheim (Kreis Kreuznach) A CHARIOT burial of the LA TÈNE Iron Age in the German Rhineland. Funerary offerings included gold ornaments, a bronze flagon, an imported Italiote bronze bucket of the late C4 BC and bronze plaques with repoussé human figures. Some of the native pieces carried a curvilinear style of ornament based on tendril patterns derived ultimately from the Classical world. After c350 BC metalwork decorated in this Waldalgesheim style made its appearance all over Celtic Europe from Britain [41] to Romania and Bulgaria. ◊ CELTIC ART

Wari ◊ HUARI

Warka ◊ URUK

waster A pot or sherd discarded by the potter immediately after firing because of cracking, distortion or discolouration. Its presence implies a nearby KILN.

wattle Interlaced twigs or thin split timbers forming a sort of hurdle-work to serve as a basis for clay DAUB in building construction. Though the wattle does not normally survive, its imprint is frequently preserved on the daub.

weaving ◊ LOOM

wedge-shaped gallery grave An Irish form of MEGALITHIC CHAMBER TOMB [208]. The burial chamber is in the form of a gallery which narrows slightly at the inner end, and is often approached through a portal. The division between antechamber and burial area is marked by a sill slab or by stone jambs. Some tombs have outer walling parallel to the sides of the gallery, and at the front of the grave these walls meet a façade of stones running at right angles to the axis of the chamber. The cairn may be roundish, oval or D-shaped, and often has a retaining wall. The earliest grave goods are bucket-shaped pots of the Late Neolithic period, but BEAKER pottery is predominant. Some

tombs were still being used in the Middle–Late Bronze Age.

Wessex The kingdom of the West Saxons was founded by Cerdic in the upper Thames valley early in C6 AD. At first it extended its influence mainly to the south and west, at the expense of the British peoples. After various vicissitudes at the hands of MERCIA and the Danes, Wessex under Alfred (871–99) took the lead among the ANGLO-SAXONS to become the nucleus of a unified England.

Fig. 208. Plan of an Irish wedge-shaped gallery grave

Wessex culture The Early Bronze Age culture of southern England. No settlements have yet been discovered, and the material comes from about 100 rich graves under BARROWS of bowl, bell, disc and saucer types. In the Wessex I stage (c1650–1550 BC) burial was usually by inhumation, sometimes in tree-trunk coffins, but in Wessex II (1550–1400) cremation was predominant. Metal tools were becoming more common, and were at first made of pure copper, or of experimental alloys made by mixing copper with arsenic or with a low percentage of tin. BRONZE was normal in Wessex II, and contained up to 17 per cent tin. The wealth of the Wessex chieftains may have come from trade, for the objects in their graves show connexions with communities all over Europe. The Wessex people imported Baltic AMBER, halberd-shaped pendants from Saxo-Thuringia, pins from the ÚNĚTICE culture of central Europe and FAIENCE beads of Aegean inspiration. They had contacts – probably by way of intermediaries along the amber route through central Europe – with the civilized peoples of MYCENAE and Crete, as shown by the occurrence in both areas of amber SPACER PLATES and gold-bound amber discs. The zigzag bone mounts on the shaft of the Bush Barrow sceptre also have parallels at Mycenae. The native British element is best represented in the burial rite and the pottery, with INCENSE CUPS and the first collared URNS. Of the society which created this wealth we can say little, but the construction of STONEHENGE III suggests a strong centralized organization.

Western Neolithic One of the main divisions of the European Early–Middle Neolithic, it includes the cultures of CHAS-SEY, CORTAILLOD, LAGOZZA, WIND-MILL HILL and the Neolithic of ALMERIA in Iberia. These local cultures differ a good deal among themselves, but have more in common with each other than with cultures of the other major traditions (◊ DANUBIAN CULTURE, TRB CULTURE). This can be seen most clearly in the pottery, which shares simple round-based shapes, a liking for string-hole lugs rather than handles, and absence of painted decoration or spiral designs.

West Kennet A SEVERN-COTSWOLD TOMB situated 5 miles west of Marlborough, Wiltshire. Set in one of the longest barrows in Britain, the tomb has two pairs of transepts and a terminal chamber. The entrance opens from a crescent-shaped forecourt blocked by a straight façade of SARSEN slabs. The material of the mound was dug from flanking quarry ditches resembling those of an earthen LONG BARROW [209]. The burial deposit (with a carbon date of 2570

Fig. 209. The West Kennet tomb

± 150 BC) consisted of some 40 disarticulated and jumbled inhumations from which several of the skulls and long bones were missing. Funerary offerings included objects similar to those from the bottom of the ditches at the CAUSEWAYED CAMP of WINDMILL HILL, only 3 miles away. After the final burial the chambers were filled up in a single deposition with a mixture of soil, charcoal and sherds of PETER-BOROUGH ware (all substyles), and also RINYO-CLACTON and BEAKER fragments. This debris spans the whole of the Late Neolithic and Copper Ages (c2000–1600 BC), and the excavators suggest that the rubbish in the chambers had been collected up from a mortuary temple in which offerings were made for centuries after burials had ceased.

wheat Three groups of wheat are distinguished by their genetic makeup. **Einkorn**, *Triticum monococcum*, is thought to derive from *T. boeoticum* (= *aegilopoides*), a species native to the Balkans, Anatolia and neighbouring parts of southwest Asia. It is found occasionally at early sites throughout this area, and commonly among Neolithic DANUBIANS of central Europe. **Emmer**, *T. dicoccon*, is the cultivated form of *T. dicoccoides*, known only from Palestine and Syria. It was the standard wheat through most of prehistory, and in parts of Europe was still grown into the Christian era. The third group arose under cultivation through genetic changes in the second: there are no wild ancestors. It includes **spelt** (*T. sphaerococcum*, found largely in the Middle East, as at JEMDET NASR and HARAPPA, and *T. spelta* in the European Bronze Age), **club wheat** (*T. compactum*, sporadically from the Neolithic onwards in the west, increasing to replace emmer in the Iron Age) and **bread wheat** (*T. aestivum*, not appearing before the Iron Age, and the basis of all modern wheats). Of these some emmers, club wheat and bread wheat are naked forms, with the grain and chaff separating easily, while the others are hulled varieties. ⟡ BARLEY

wheel One of the simplest but most important of man's inventions. It is first recorded from Mesopotamia, where it is represented in URUK pictographs c3400 BC. (The specialized form, the POTTER'S WHEEL, appeared about the same time and place.) It is well illustrated too on the Royal Standard of UR rather later. These wheels were of the solid type and very unwieldy, being made of a single piece of wood, or more commonly three pieces dowelled together. There are surprisingly early terracotta models of wagons and actual wooden carts in KURGAN burials, from the Caucasus and Hungary, and it is far from clear whether one or more sources are needed to explain its spread. Egypt, having easy communications by water, did not adopt it until it was introduced by the HYKSOS in the more developed spoked form. This was invented, probably in Syria, in the early 2nd millennium. It made possible the light war CHARIOT, which was widely and rapidly adopted. The wheel was not used in pre-Columbian America, except in Mexico, where small pull-along toys in the form of animals were made in terracotta.

wheelhouse A stone-built house, circular in plan, with partition walls projecting inwards like the spokes of a wheel. The form is widespread in western and northern Scotland, where it characterizes the later Iron Age culture. Appearing in the last centuries BC, wheelhouses survived well into the Roman period as dwellings and farmhouses alongside or succeeding the defensive BROCHS.

Whithorn The monastery founded by St Ninian in C4 AD on the north shore of the Solway Firth, the territory of STRATHCLYDE. From this base southern Scotland was converted to Christianity. Inscribed grave slabs from its cemetery throw a little faint but welcome light on the very obscure period after the end of Roman Britain.

Wilburton A village 10 miles north of Cambridge, and the findspot of a hoard which has given its name to the first industry of Late Bronze Age type in south-east Britain. The Wilburton phase (c900 or 850–750 BC) is distinguished by the replacement of tin bronze by a copper-lead-tin alloy, by the increased use of metal (shown by large founders' hoards containing broken tools and scrap), and by new tools such as the leaf-shaped sword with slotted hilt [186d]. The corresponding Roscommon industry, which preceded the DOWRIS phase in Ireland, also used leaded bronze, but in northern England the contemporary Wallington industry still employed the older tin bronze.

Wilton A MICROLITH-using culture of parts of eastern and southern Africa. It is an African equivalent of the MESOLITHIC cultures of Europe, though of later date, and in its final stage shows contact with the Iron Age farmers of the 1st millennium AD. ⟡ KALAMBO FALLS, SMITHFIELD

Winckelmann, J. J. (1717–68) One of the founders of archaeology, he showed that the classical writings were not the only source of information on their period. His work on the art being recovered from Herculaneum and Pompeii was a move towards a study of artifacts as historical documents.

Windmill Hill A CAUSEWAYED CAMP [210] 1 mile north of AVEBURY, Wiltshire, which was for a time the type site of the British Neolithic (◊ WINDMILL HILL CULTURE). The oldest occupation on the sites of Abingdon and Mildenhall), closely followed by the oldest (Ebbsfleet) variant of PETERBOROUGH ware. Stylistically these sherds belong to a middle phase of the Neolithic, with which the carbon date of 2570 ± 150 is quite consistent. Continued visits to the camp are shown by the

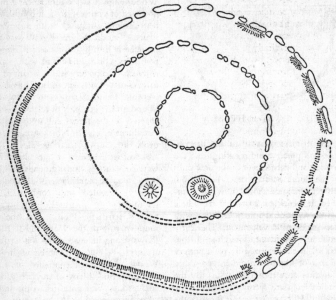

Fig. 210. Plan of Windmill Hill camp

hill pre-dates the earthworks, and consists of a series of pits dug by a farming community which made plain, undecorated pottery of a kind already known at HEMBURY before 3000 BC. At Windmill Hill this phase has a radiocarbon date of 2950 ± 150 BC. The crown of the hill was later enclosed by three discontinuous ditches (the outer of them with a diameter of 1200 ft) to create the largest causewayed camp in Britain. From the base of the ditch came sherds of Windmill Hill ware *sensu stricto* (a pottery decorated with grooves and pits of a kind found at the

occurrence higher up in the ditch of the more recent (Mortlake and Fengate) Peterborough styles, RINYO-CLACTON ware and BEAKER sherds. Besides the camp, the area has an earthen LONG BARROW (with a carbon date of 3240 ± 150) and a cemetery of Bronze Age round barrows.

Windmill Hill culture Until recently this was taken to comprise all the British 'Primary Neolithic', or 'Neolithic A', and equated with the material of the colonists who introduced the knowledge of agriculture, stock-breeding and pottery-making into Britain. New traits included CAUSEWAYED CAMPS, earthen LONG BARROWS, leaf-shaped arrowheads [13a], polished flint axes and plain or lightly decorated round-based pottery [211]. Windmill Hill culture was contrasted with the 'Secondary Neolithic', marked by

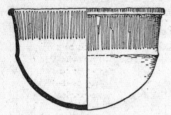

Fig. 211. Windmill Hill pottery

the use of PETERBOROUGH and RINYO-CLACTON pottery, and resulting from the adoption and debasement of the new skills by the local MESOLITHIC population. This terminology should now be abandoned. It seems best to regard the whole English Neolithic as a single tradition with three stages of development. The Early Neolithic, beginning sometime before 3000 BC, is characterized by plain pottery like that of HEMBURY and the pre-camp occupation at WINDMILL HILL. By the Middle Neolithic, decorated wares of the Windmill Hill style proper (as found in the ditches of the type site) have developed, and SEVERN-COTSWOLD TOMBS start to be built. To the Late Neolithic belong the highly decorated wares of Peterborough and Rinyo-Clacton styles, as well as the first BEAKERS. During the later Neolithic, therefore, several pottery styles co-existed and thus may be found together in the same deposits.

Wisconsin glaciation The final GLACIATION of the North American PLEISTOCENE. Some geologists consider it had begun by 70,000 BC with the onset of the Altonian sub-stage; other authorities use a different terminology in which the Wisconsin glaciation begins with the Farmdale ice advance around 28,000. By c8000 the ice had begun its final retreat. During the Wisconsin period enough water was locked up in the ice sheets to cause a drop in sea level and the creation of a land bridge between Siberia and Alaska.

Woodhenge A sacred monument 2 miles northeast of STONEHENGE. It consists of a HENGE-type earthwork with a wooden structure inside. A central grave was surrounded in turn by six concentric rings of post holes, a ditch, and a bank with a single entrance. The pottery was a variant of the RINYO-CLACTON style, and BEAKER sherds were also found. ◊ DURRINGTON WALLS

Woodland A complex of related cultures adapted to the forest and waterside environment of eastern North America. By c1000 BC the ARCHAIC peoples of this area had settled down to agricultural life, were constructing burial mounds, and had begun to make the characteristic Woodland pottery decorated with cord or fabric impressions (◊ ADENA, HOPEWELL, EFFIGY MOUND). From c AD 700 the southern part of the Woodland territory shows strong influence from the MIDDLE MISSISSIPPI cultures, but elsewhere the Woodland tradition continued until the historic period. Many of the late Woodland groups were ancestral to the Indian tribes encountered by the Europeans.

Woolley, Sir Leonard (1880–1960) is best remembered for his great work at UR for the British and Pennsylvania University Museums 1922–9. The skill and care with which he recovered the treasures of the Royal Cemetery mark him as one of the great excavators of this century. He was outstanding too in the field of interpretation, as his treatment of the evidence from the ZIGGURAT shows. And in addition he had the skill to publish popular accounts of his results, such as *Ur of the Chaldees*, of enormous value to the 'public relations' side of archaeology, besides his full scholarly excavation reports. Other sites he

worked at included Al 'UBAID, CAR-
CHEMISH, Tell el-AMARNA and ALALAKH.

Worsaae, J. J. A. (1821–85) A student of
C. J. THOMSEN who, particularly in his
Danmarks Oldtid (1842), laid the foundations of the study of prehistory. The basis
of his book was Thomsen's THREE AGE
SYSTEM, but it introduces such other con-
cepts as nomenclature, TYPOLOGY and
DIFFUSION, and discusses the value and
principles of prehistoric research. These
principles he applied in practice as an
enthusiastic excavator. He travelled widely,
playing a major part in the adoption of the
Three Ages throughout Europe and beginning the task of synthesizing the finds over
the continent.

wristguard or **bracer** The recoil of the
bow string can cause injury to the inside of
the archer's wrist if this is not protected.
The BEAKER bowmen took the precaution
of wearing a rectangular plate of bone or
stone, perforated at the corners, to receive
the blow. It may have been tied on directly
or pinned to a leather strap. It is sometimes
difficult to distinguish a wristguard from a
whetstone, and some may well have
served both purposes.

Wroxeter (anc **Viroconium**) The site of
a Roman town 5 miles southeast of Shrews-
bury. It was founded in the later C1 AD.
In 130 it was enlarged to 180 acres and
given a fine FORUM in honour of Hadrian.
There was also a set of baths. The grid
street plan and many of the houses have
been revealed by an excellent series of air
photographs and confirmed by excavations, which still continue. By C4 the
forum was in decay and the town too had
begun to fade out of existence.

Würm The fourth and final PLEISTO-
CENE GLACIATION in the Alps. [p 183]

X

Xerxes The last of the great rulers of the ACHAEMENID empire, 485–465 BC. He is remembered chiefly for his savage destruction of BABYLON after a revolt, and for his disastrous failure to conquer Greece at Salamis in 480.

X-ray fluorescence If a sample for chemical analysis is bombarded with X-rays, it fluoresces. The light given off will show by spectrometry what chemical elements are present and in what proportions. As only the surface, which is subject to corrosion, can be studied, optical SPECTROGRAPHIC ANALYSIS is more commonly employed.

Y

Yang Shao The most important Neolithic culture of China, distributed along the middle course of the Yellow River. Large open settlements of circular or rectangular houses slightly sunk into the ground cluster along the LOESS river terraces. Millet and pork seem to have been the staple foods. Burial was by inhumation in simple trench graves. Flaked and polished stone were in general use. Pottery was handmade, painted in black and red on a yellowish slip. At first designs were zoomorphic, later abstract, geometric or curvilinear. Coarser red and grey wares were also common. A few radiocarbon dates are now available, from 3944 ± 110 BC on. Though some influence from centres further west is not ruled out, it must now be regarded as primarily a local development.

Yayoi The Japanese Bronze-Iron Age, succeeding the JŌMON period about 250 BC. It is marked by the strengthening of mainland influences from Korea and China, as shown by the appearance of bronze and later of iron, rice-growing, the potter's wheel, cist and jar burials, etc. These were largely absorbed into the Jōmon tradition, which was only gradually replaced. Local development of the imported ideas can be recognized also, notably in the great decorated bronze bells.

It is a period of increasing cultural complexity leading directly into a protohistoric period in about C3 AD.

Yazilikaya A rock sanctuary above BOGHAZ KÖY, the capital of the HITTITES. A series of buildings and porticoes, since completely destroyed, led to a cleft in the rock 60 ft wide by 100 ft deep, with a narrower passage running deeper into the rock to one side. The rock faces are carved with over 60 relief figures, together with a number of HIEROGLYPHIC inscriptions, dating to C13 BC. These are now believed to represent the gods of the HURRI, with human worshippers and attendants. [32]

Yeavering (the 'ad Gefrin' mentioned by Bede) A seat of the kings of NORTHUMBRIA from the early years of C7 to about AD 680, in northern Northumberland. A succession of great timber halls forms the centre of the site. A structure consisting of concentric quadrants of timber pillars is identified as an assembly place. Of the smaller buildings uncovered, one is thought to have been converted from a pagan temple into a church. The site was revealed by air photography and excavated in the 1950s by Dr Hope-Taylor. It has advanced enormously our knowledge of Saxon timber architecture.

Younger Dryas ⇨ LATE GLACIAL PERIOD and ZONES, VEGETATIONAL

Z

Zagros The fringe of mountains separating the plateau of Iran from the plains of Mesopotamia. Work in the area has revealed a number of sites, such as JARMO, of the greatest importance for the origins of food production. The wild ancestors of wheat and barley, goats and sheep, all flourished here.

Zapotec The main territory of the Zapotecs was the valley of Oaxaca (Mexico) with its great centre at MONTE ALBÁN. It is still uncertain when these people first came to Oaxaca, but by c AD 300 a distinctively Zapotec culture can be recognized. In C14 the area was infiltrated by MIXTECS who came from the mountains to the north and west and occupied most of the Zapotec sites. Part of the region was never conquered by the AZTECS, and the Zapotecan language has persisted to the present day.

Zarzian An advanced PALAEOLITHIC industry which takes its name from the cave of Zarzi, near Sulaimaniyyah, in Iraqi Kurdistan. ◊ SHANIDAR

Zawi Chemi Shanidar A village site in northern Iraq in which large numbers of sheep bones are claimed to show signs of domestication at a radiocarbon date of c8900 BC. Sickles and querns testify to the gathering of vegetable products, probably still wild. Flimsy huts may have been occupied for only a part of the year, the rest being spent in caves, like that of SHANIDAR nearby.

zemi A divinity worshipped by the ARAWAKS of Puerto Rico, Hispaniola and Jamaica. Zemis are human or animal in form, and are found on a variety of objects of stone, wood and shell. CEREMONIAL CENTRES, BALL-COURTS and caves are associated with the cult, which may have reached the islands from Mesoamerica.

Zhob A valley in north BALUCHISTAN giving its name to a widespread Chalcolithic culture. RANA GHUNDAI in the nearby Loralai valley is the most important site. The pottery is painted in black, sometimes red also, over a red slip. Rows of attenuated stylized humped cattle and buck were a popular motif. Lower on the vessels, groups of vertical lines link narrow horizontal bands. Shapes include pedestalled dishes and deep goblets. Female figurines were common. Copper was known but scarce. Buildings were of mudbrick and burials by cremation. Related material was found stratified beneath that of the Indus Civilization at HARAPPA, and similarities to the painted ware of Tepe HISSAR in northern Iran would indicate a date in the 4th to 3rd millennia.

ziggurat (or better **zikkurrat**) A rectangular staged temple mound erected by the SUMERIANS and their successors in honour of their gods. It is thought to symbolize a mountain, an appropriate residence for the god of a people who, it has been suggested, had only recently moved into the flat plain of Sumer. Its structure was of mudbrick with a burnt brick casing, stairways giving access to a small shrine at its summit. The best known examples are those of UR, excavated by Woolley, and BABYLON, the fabled Tower of Babel. The best preserved is that at CHOGA ZANBIL in Elam.

Zinjanthropus (*Australopithecus boisei*) An early member of the genus AUSTRALOPITHECUS found in Bed I at OLDUVAI, and characterized by unusually massive jaws which have given him the popular nickname 'Nutcracker Man'. POTASSIUM-ARGON DATING suggests that he lived about 1.75 million years ago.

Zinjirli ◊ SINJERLI

Ziwiyeh A TELL southeast of Lake Urmia in northwest Iran. Villagers in 1947 discovered a hoard of gold, silver and ivory in a coffin. It illustrates the workmanship of the local Mannai, strongly influenced by ASSYRIA, URARTU and the SCYTHIANS. There are similarities, too, to the bronze-work of LURISTAN, and both can prob-ably be connected with the immediate ancestors of the MEDES and PERSIANS. The hoard is thought to date to the mid C7 BC.

Złota A Neolithic–Copper Age cemetery near Sandomierz in southern Poland. The dead, laid in a contracted position on stone pavements in simple graves, were accom-panied by pots whose shape and CORD-ORNAMENT suggest links with the GLOBULAR AMPHORA culture. Certain handles of ANSA LUNATA type hint at contact with the BADEN culture. Other funerary offerings included stone BATTLE-AXES, copper beads and V-perforated AMBER plaques.

zones, vegetational, pollen or **climatic** The changing composition of the wood-land of northern Europe since the last retreat of the ice has been closely studied by POLLEN ANALYSIS, and the period sub-divided on this basis. These zones, num-bered I to IX, are then named according to the climatic conditions deduced from the evidence of vegetation. Further, RADIO-CARBON dating has been employed to put absolute dates on the zones, giving an invaluable framework for the chronology of the period. [pp 186–7]

REGIONAL INDEX

Asterisks indicate a substantial entry in the text

AFRICA (except Egypt)

Stone Age:
- ATERIAN
- BROKEN HILL
- CAPSIAN*
- DABBAN*
- FAURESMITH
- HAUA FTEAH
- KALAMBO FALLS*
- MAGOSIAN
- OLDUVAI*
- ORANIAN
- SANGOAN
- SMITHFIELD
- WILTON

Later period:
- CARTHAGE*
- MEROE*

Fossil hominids:
- AUSTRALOPITHECUS*
- HOMO HABILIS*
- RHODESIAN MAN
- SALDANHA SKULL
- ZINJANTHROPUS

AMERICAS

Central America

Maya zone:
- BONAMPAK
- CHICHÉN ITZÁ*
- KAMINALJUYÚ
- MAYA*
- MAYAPAN*
- PALENQUE
- TIKAL
- UAXACTÚN

Rest of Mexico:
- AZTEC*
- CHICHIMEC
- CHOLULA
- EL TAJÍN
- IZAPA
- LA VENTA
- MITLA
- MIXTEC*
- MONTE ALBÁN*
- OLMEC*
- SAN LORENZO TENOCHTITLAN*
- SANTA ISABEL IZTAPAN
- TEHUACAN VALLEY
- TENOCHTITLÁN
- TEOTIHUACÁN*
- TEPEXPAN
- TLAPACOYA
- TLATILCO
- TOLTEC*
- TRES ZAPOTES
- TULA
- ZAPOTEC

Panama:
- CHIRIQUÍ
- COCLÉ

North America

Arctic:
- CAPE KRUSENSTERN
- DENBIGH FLINT COMPLEX
- DORSET CULTURE
- ESKIMO
- IPIUTAK
- OLD BERING SEA
- ONION PORTAGE
- THULE

Other areas:
- ADENA
- ANASAZI*
- ANSE AU MEADOW
- BASKETMAKER
- BLACKWATER DRAW
- CLOVIS*
- COCHISE
- DANGER CAVE
- FOLSOM*
- HOHOKAM
- HOPEWELL
- MIDDLE MISSISSIPPI CULTURE*
- MOGOLLON
- OLD CORDILLERAN CULTURE
- OLD COPPER CULTURE

TIEVEBULLIAGH
WESSEX CULTURE*
WEST KENNET*
WILBURTON
WINDMILL HILL*
WINDMILL HILL CULTURE*
WOODHENGE

Ireland:
BOYNE
DOWRIS
KNOWTH*
LOUGH GUR
NEWGRANGE*
TARA

Roman:
ANTONINE WALL
CASTOR
COLCHESTER (CAMULODUNUM)
FISHBOURNE
HADRIAN'S WALL
HOUSESTEADS
MILDENHALL
NEWSTEAD
PORCHESTER
RICHBOROUGH
SAXON SHORE
SILCHESTER
TRAPRAIN LAW
VERULAMIUM
WROXETER

Post-Roman:
CADBURY
DÁLRIADA
IONA
JARLSHOF
LINDISFARNE
NORTHUMBRIA
PICTS
ST NINIAN'S ISLE
SUTTON HOO
WESSEX
WHITHORN
YEAVERING

Central Europe

Palaeolithic:
DOLNÍ VĚSTONICE*

MAUER JAW
STEINHEIM*
VÉRTESSZÖLLÖS*

Later prehistoric cultures:
BADEN
DANUBIAN CULTURE*
FÜZESABONY
HATVAN
HORGEN
HÖTTING
KÖRÖS
KNOVIZ CULTURE
LENGYEL CULTURE
LUSATIAN CULTURE*
MICHELSBERG
MILAVČE
NAGYRÉV
RÖSSEN
TISZA
TUMULUS CULTURE*
ÚNĚTICE*

Austria:
HALLSTATT*
MONDSEE

Czechoslovakia:
BYLANY

Germany:
ALTHEIM
HEUNEBURG*
KLEIN ASPERGLE
KÖLN-LINDENTHAL
WALDALGESHEIM

Hungary:
BODROGKERESZTUR
KISAPOSTAG
KOSZIDER
TISZAPOLGÁR
TÓSZEG

Poland:
BISKUPIN*
JORDANOVA
ZŁOTA

Switzerland:
CORTAILLOD
LA TÈNE*
MÜNSINGEN-AM-RAIN

MAPS

Bold names indicate an individual entry in the text.

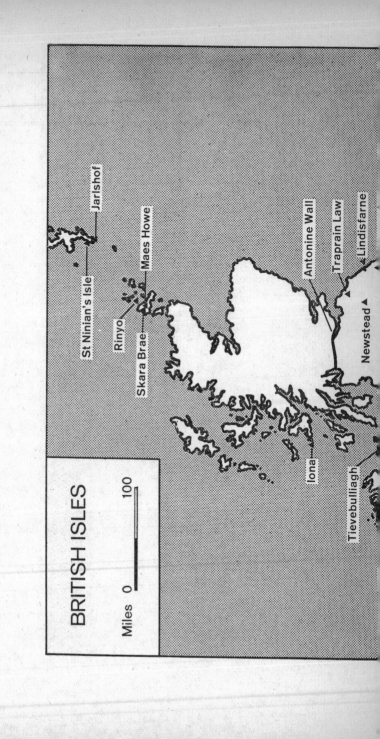

BRITISH ISLES

Miles 0   100

Jarlshof

St Ninian's Isle

Maes Howe

Rinyo

Skara Brae

Antonine Wall

Traprain Law

Lindisfarne

Newstead ▲

Iona

Tievebulliagh

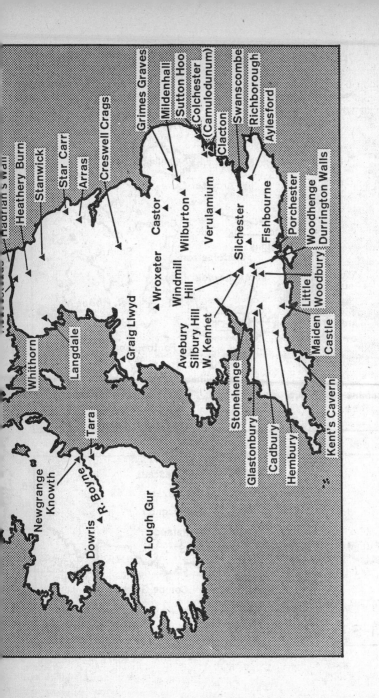

FRANCE

Miles 0 — 150

Abbeville
S.-Acheul
Chelles
R. Marne
R. Seine
Carnac
Gavrinis
Arcy-sur-Cure
Vix
Chassey
Grand Pressigny
Solutré
Châtelperron
Fontéchevade
Peu Richard
R. Rhône
(Area of Lower Map)
Grimaldi
Le Vallonet
Fontbouïsse
Ferrières
Cayla de Mailhac
Lébous
Entremont
Altamira
Aurignac
Roquepertuse

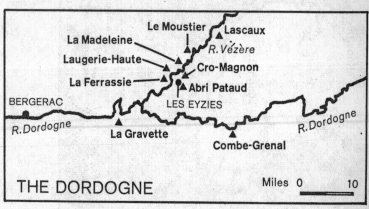

Le Moustier
Lascaux
La Madeleine
R. Vézère
Laugerie-Haute
Cro-Magnon
La Ferrassie
Abri Pataud
BERGERAC
LES EYZIES
R. Dordogne
La Gravette
R. Dordogne
Combe-Grenal

THE DORDOGNE

Miles 0 — 10

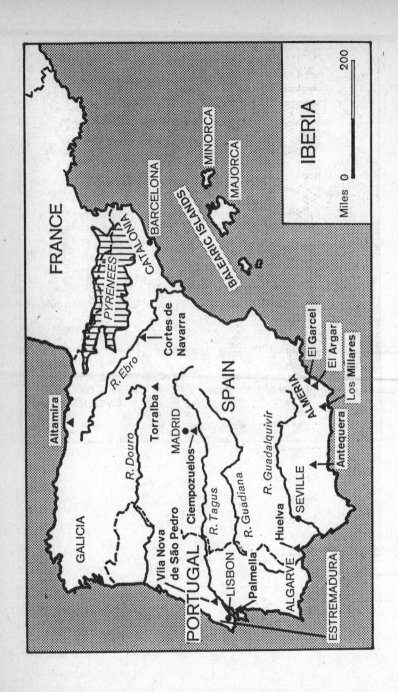

IBERIA

Miles
0 _____ 200

FRANCE

SPAIN

PORTUGAL

GALICIA

ESTREMADURA

ALGARVE

LISBON

Palmella

Vila Nova
de São Pedro

Ciempozuelos

MADRID

Torralba

Cortes de
Navarra

PYRENEES

CATALONIA

BARCELONA

BALEARIC ISLANDS

MINORCA

MAJORCA

Altamira

R. Douro

R. Ebro

R. Tagus

R. Guadiana

R. Guadalquivir

Huelva

SEVILLE

Antequera

ALMERIA

Los Millares

El Argar

El Garcel

CENTRAL MEDITERRANEAN

Miles 0 ——— 100

BALKANS AND AEGEAN

Miles 0 _____ 100

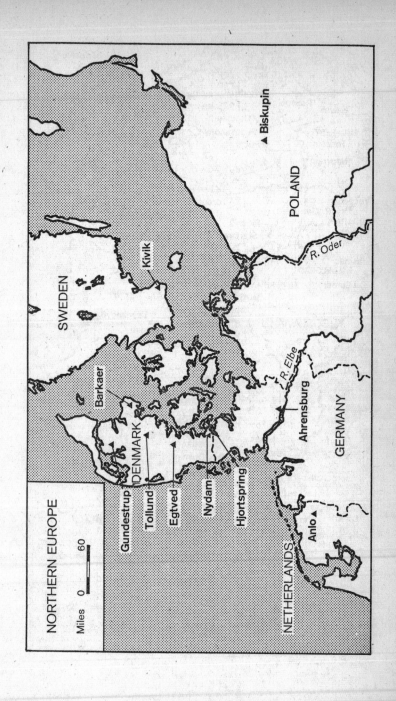

NORTHERN EUROPE

Miles
0   60

SWEDEN

POLAND

▲ Biskupin

R. Oder

R. Elbe

GERMANY

Ahrensburg

NETHERLANDS

Anlo ▲

DENMARK

Gundestrup

Tollund

Egtved

Nydam

Hjortspring

Barkaer

Kivik

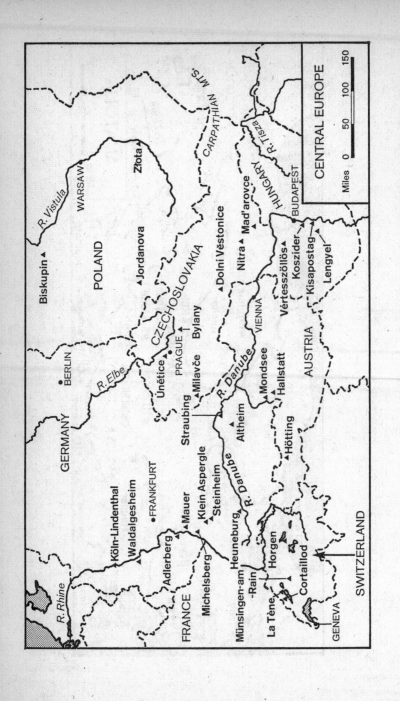

CENTRAL EUROPE

Miles 0   50   100   150

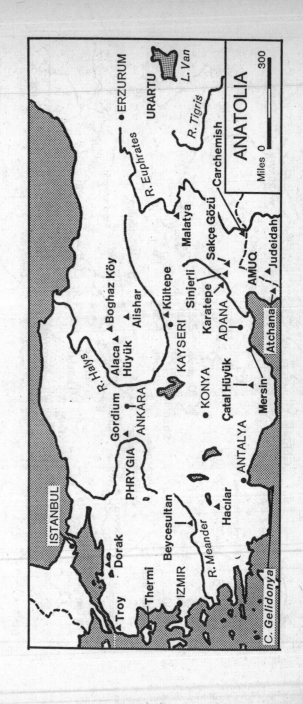

CONGO

Olduvai

TANZANIA

Kalambo
Falls

ZAMBIA

R. Zambesi

ANGOLA

Broken
Hill

RHODESIA

MOZAMBIQUE

R. Zambesi

SOUTH

WEST

BOTSWANA

AFRICA

Sterkfontein

Taungs

R. Vaal

Fauresmith

Orange R.

Smithfield

UNION OF
SOUTH AFRICA

Saldanha

Wilton

SOUTH &
EAST AFRICA

Miles 0   400

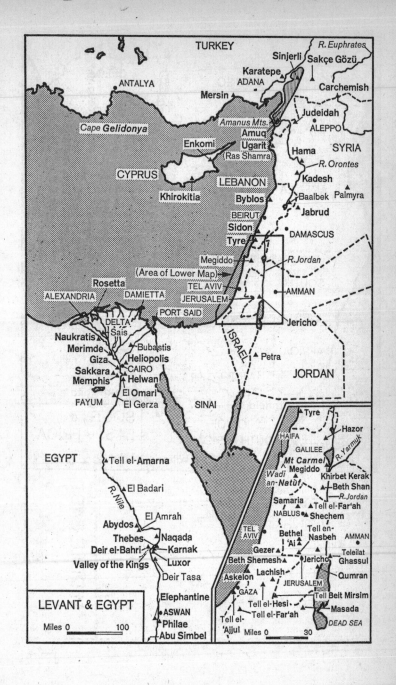

LEVANT & EGYPT

Miles 0   100

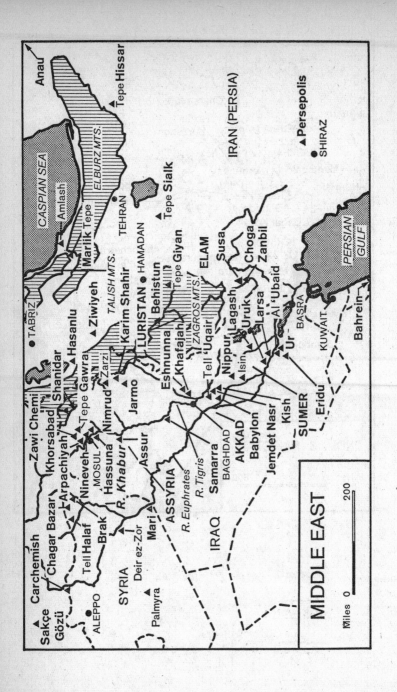

MIDDLE EAST

Miles 0   200

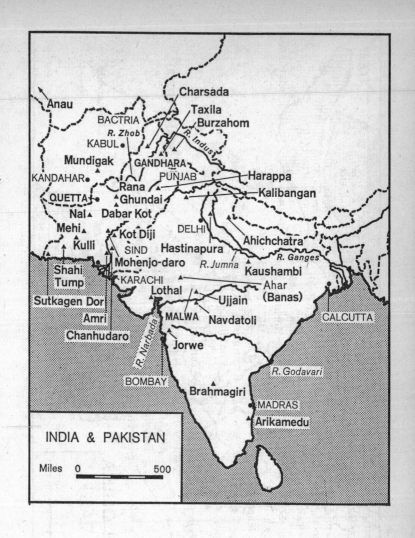

Anau
Charsada
Taxila
BACTRIA
Burzahom
R. Zhob
R. Indus
KABUL
Mundigak
GANDHARA
KANDAHAR
PUNJAB
Harappa
Rana
Kalibangan
QUETTA
Ghundai
Nal
Dabar Kot
Mehi
DELHI
Kulli
Kot Diji
Ahichchatra
SIND
Hastinapura
R. Ganges
Mohenjo-daro
R. Jumna
Kaushambi
Shahi
KARACHI
Tump
Ahar
Lothal
(Banas)
Sutkagen Dor
Ujjain
CALCUTTA
Amri
MALWA
Navdatoli
Chanhudaro
R. Narbada
Jorwe
R. Godavari
BOMBAY
Brahmagiri
MADRAS
Arikamedu

INDIA & PAKISTAN

Miles 0   500

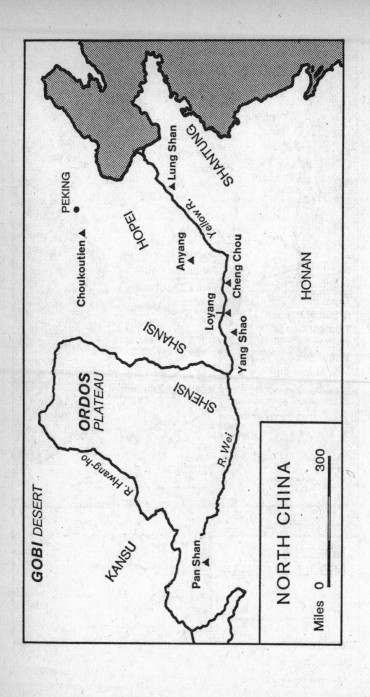

NORTH CHINA

Miles 0   300

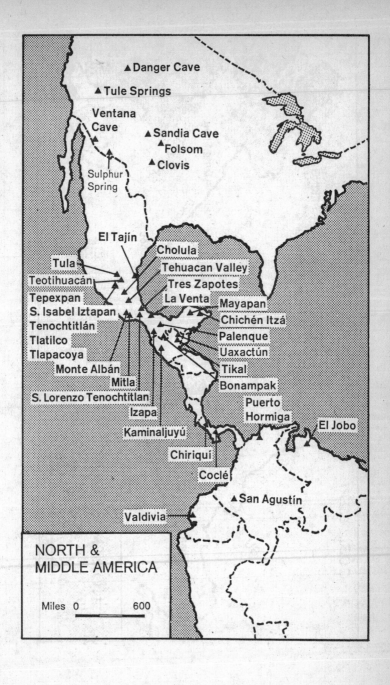

▲ Danger Cave

▲ Tule Springs

Ventana
Cave

▲ Sandia Cave
▲ Folsom
▲ Clovis

Sulphur
Spring

El Tajín

Cholula

Tula

Tehuacan Valley

Teotihuacán

Tres Zapotes

Tepexpan

La Venta

Mayapan

S. Isabel Iztapan

Chichén Itzá

Tenochtitlán

Palenque

Tlatilco

Uaxactún

Tlapacoya

Monte Albán

Tikal

Mitla

Bonampak

S. Lorenzo Tenochtitlan

Puerto
Hormiga

Izapa

El Jobo

Kaminaljuyú

Chiriquí

Coclé

▲ San Agustín

Valdivia

NORTH &
MIDDLE AMERICA

Miles 0   600

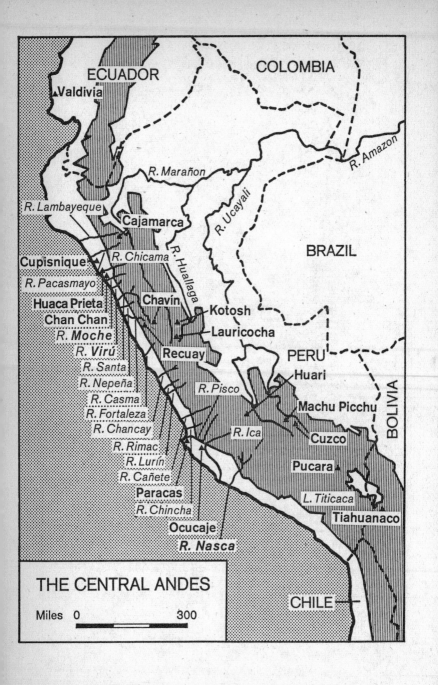

THE CENTRAL ANDES

Miles 0   300

Warwick Bray and David Trump

The Penguin Dictionary of Archaeology

From the Abbevillian handaxe and the god Baal of the Canaanites to the Wisconsin and Wurm glaciations of America and Europe, the Yang Shao culture of neolithic China, and Zinjanthropus, the 'nutcracker man' of Africa, this dictionary concisely describes, in more than 1,600 entries with copious cross-references, the sites, cultures, periods, techniques, terms and personalities of archaeology.

With its world-wide coverage and numerous maps and figures this must prove an ideal companion for the growing number of amateur enthusiasts and a very useful aid for students in fields outside their own specialities.

The range of the dictionary is from the earliest prehistory to the civilizations before the rise of classical Greece and Rome.

The cover shows a decorative detail from a silver and gilded helmet of the 4th century BC from the Agighiol Treasure, in the Bucharest Museum, Romania (photo C M Dixon, London)

UNITED KINGDOM £1.25
AUSTRALIA $3.50 (RECOMMENDED)
CANADA $2.95
U.S.A. $2.95

REFERENCE ISBN 0 14 051.045 1